PATRIOTIC LADY

By the same Author

MARY, QUEEN OF SCOTS
THE THIRD MARY STUART
THE SCANDAL OF SOPHIE DAWES
SUNDRY GREAT GENTLEMEN
WILLIAM, PRINCE OF ORANGE
PETER PORCUPINE
(A Study of William Cobbett)

ETC

In preparation

THE COCKNEY'S MIRROR
(A Study of William Hogarth)

PATRIOTIC LADY

A STUDY OF
EMMA, LADY HAMILTON,
AND THE
NEAPOLITAN REVOLUTION OF
1799

a coloured cartoon

BY
MARJORIE BOWEN

DAVID BRUCE AND WATSON
LONDON 1970

© HILARY LONG 1970
First published in 1936
This edition published in 1970 by
DAVID BRUCE AND WATSON LIMITED
277-9 Grays Inn Road
London WC1

SBN 85127 050 6

Printed in Great Britain by
Lewis Reprints Limited, Port Talbot, Glamorgan

BEAUTY IS SUCH A MARVELLOUS GIFT THAT
TALENT, GENIUS, EVEN VIRTUE ITSELF, ARE
AS NOTHING BESIDE IT ; THE TRULY BEAUTIFUL
WOMAN HAS A RIGHT TO DISDAIN EVERYTHING,
BECAUSE SHE UNITES IN HER PERSON, AS IN A
VASE FILLED WITH MYRRH, ALL THE WONDERS
THAT EVEN GENIUS CAN ONLY PRODUCE IMPER-
FECTLY AND FEEBLY AFTER FATIGUING TOIL.

ERNEST RENAN

FOREWORD

IT has been impossible to write this study of Emma, Lady Hamilton, without touching upon subjects which are extremely controversial. It is not within the scope of this book, however, to attempt to revive disputes and arguments which have long since been worn threadbare, and which concern not so much matters of fact as matters of opinion. Many writers who have dealt with the career of Emma, Lady Hamilton, have set themselves the task, not of discovering the truth, but of making out a case according to personal prejudice. The works given in the bibliography at the end of this volume cover the whole range of opinions held, and judgments given, by Italian, French, Austrian and English writers on the end of the Revolution in Naples in 1799. Any reader who doubts the accuracy or fairness of the present writer's version of this event is referred to the works of these authorities, all of which are easily procurable.

It must be added, however, that these writers differ considerably in their points of view and their knowledge, are often confused by passion, or are deliberately inaccurate through prejudice; therefore all, or nearly all, the evidence must be read, if an impartial judgment is to be formed on matters that have caused such bitter emotions and such fierce differences of opinion.

It is useless, for instance, to read *Nelson and the Neapolitan Jacobins* by H. C. Gutheridge, without reading *Lady Hamilton et la Révolution de Naples* by Joseph Turquan and Jules d'Auriac, in which the English author's points are carefully dealt with, and his arguments often refuted. Further, it is impossible to understand the situation and sentiments of the Patriots of Naples and the Italian point of view without being acquainted with the Jacobins' own statements and the opinions of Italian historians, which may be found embodied in the writings of Vincenzo Cuoco, Francesco Lomanaco, Carlo Botta, P. Colletta, and G. M. Arrighi, and in those of two modern Italian scholars of the first rank, who have made impartial and patient researches into the history of the *Novantanove*; Benedetto Croce and Pasquale Villari. The latter, in his *Nelson, Caracciolo, la Rivoluzione di Napoli*, published in *Discussioni critiche Discorsi*, gives a masterly summing up of the whole controversy and of the works of all the writers who have discussed the questions raised by the part played by the English in the Bourbon reaction.

Another cool and detached account of the affair is given by Professor Huefer in his article *La fin de la République Napolitaine*, published in Nos. 83–84 of *La Revue Historique de Paris*, and a useful book is that published under the same title as Professor Villari's essay, by F. Lemmi, Florence, 1898.

Mr. David Hannay, in his edition of Southey's *Life of Nelson*, is conspicuous for his fairness in dealing with the Neapolitan episode, while the chapter on Caracciolo, in J. Cordy Jeafferson's *Lady Hamilton and Lord Nelson*, may be cited as an example of the kind of writing that has too often misled the English reader as to the characters and events of Naples in 1799.

In conclusion, some words of personal explanation may be added. As very little is known of Emma Hamilton before 1782, this account of her life begins in that year, and references to her early youth are given as rumours or gossip only. It is most likely that there was much truth in these tales—some such life as they indicate Amy Lyon must have led—but the evidence for this part of her career is flimsy and contradictory and many of the well-known anecdotes of her early life rest on very doubtful authority.

For the same reason several often-repeated stories relating to Lady Hamilton have been omitted from the later part of the book, but there is sufficient authentic material available from which to construct a portrait of this woman, remarkable in herself and extraordinary in her life and adventures.

M. BOWEN.

16, QUEEN ANNE'S GATE,
LONDON, S.W.
July, 1935.

CONTENTS

I
HERO'S REWARD

II
RULE BRITANNIA

III
HERO'S LEGACY

xi

I

HERO'S REWARD

WHY SHOULD A MAN WHOSE BLOOD IS WARM
WITHIN
SIT LIKE HIS GRANDSIRE CARVED IN
ALABASTER ?

I

THE MAKING OF A BEAUTY

'WHEN BEAUTY PASSES NATURE IT BECOMES ART'
(LEONARDO DA VINCI)

IT has been said that Cupid writes his epistles on the leaves of a ledger; at any rate this quarrel was about money.

The great difference between the lovers was that, whereas Sir Harry could pay for at least some of his pleasures, Amy was penniless. So, when the final quarrel came, the girl, who had only her personal charms, was utterly defeated by the young man who had birth, a title, relations, friends and property.

The easy-going rake, who knew the ways of his world, certainly expected to have to pay in cash for five months of amorous felicity with the pretty creature who had such a lively tongue and such gay romping ways. But the bills were too high and came in far too frequently. Five guineas for coach hire! This was a piece of insolence not to be endured; and there were the milliners, dressmakers, haberdashers, all clamorous for their dues, and the house-keeping had reached those crazy figures which are only possible when a fashionable young bachelor entertains boon companions and ladies of the town.

Sir Harry protested sharply that he was ruined and that the fault lay with his wild, giddy mistress. She retorted insolently with the assurance of the petted toy whose impertinent follies had always been applauded.

But Sir Harry was in no mood to laugh at her flounces and grimaces; with the revulsion following infatuation he felt that the girl was not worth what she was costing him; even if he could afford so extravagant a companion, would it be worth while to empty his purse to pay the expenses of a creature whose favours he must share with all his friends?

In his opinion Amy had behaved exactly like the flower of the gutter she was, and to the gutter she might return.

3   B

He was, besides, tired of her, sick of the long debauch of which Up Park had been the scene during the autumn and winter, jaded with the drink, the gambling, the din of the disorderly women, the tipsy men, the confusion arising from bad service, the nagging visits from duns, the insolence of unpaid servants.

Amy played into his hands by losing her temper, by tossing her head and answering him in the rustic Welsh accent of which he was tired; he replied brutally, and they shouted, one at the other, amid the litter of the fashionable room in the smart mansion which occupied a hollow of the South Downs.

Bottles, decanters and glasses cumbered the sideboards, packs of fingered cards piled the small tables, wheezing lap-dogs sat on soiled lace caps and kerchiefs, flung over satin chairs; dirty clay pipes, tobacco-pouches, snuff-boxes, crowded the coquettish ornaments on the mantelshelf; there were fowling-pieces in one corner, whips in another, a basket of pups under the desk, a gross dog, smelling of the stable, before the log fire—and everywhere a confusion of unpaid bills—*un odor di femina.*

Amy, in stiff silks overtrimmed and gaudy, with stale powder clotted in her heavy hair, holes in her stockings and kicked-out shoes, with unpaid-for lace across her bosom, and a black velvet patch to show off a complexion not well cared for, held her own with coarse words, with violent gestures, maintaining her right as a young, seductive female, to spend what she pleased, to do as she pleased.

"Not at my expense," was the burden of Sir Harry's reply, as he lounged sulkily beneath pictures discreetly curtained even in that establishment, against the case of books the indecencies of which had long been staled by thumbings over.

The baronet's polished exterior had once seemed very attractive to Amy; he had all the easy airs of his class and could be elegant when with ladies, but he took a gentleman's privilege and was crude enough with females who lived—as the term went—under his protection. When Amy, in a passion at his refusal to submit to her tantrums, screamed out that she would fling out of his house—he said that she not only might, but must, go.

She could be packed off more easily than could a maidservant as she was without the written law. The right of appeal to the

4

unwritten law she had, in her lover's opinion, forfeited, when, in return for her keep and her amusements, she had not given even a brief fidelity.

With such a mood on either side the scene could have but one ending; the pretty young girl tossed out of the dishevelled mansion which had been, for nearly half a year, a slut's paradise, and her whilom lover warned her not to return. In the brutal phrase of the time, she was turned out of keeping.

Sir Harry Featherstonehaugh saw her departure with relief. She was noisy, she was common, she was expensive, she was losing her figure and he was weary of her bright, pretty face, her cheerful ignorance, and the quick insolence with which she picked up the vices and the airs that belonged properly to gentlefolk.

. . . . . .

Amy's temper soon cooled when she found herself shut out of Up Park; she was good-humoured and had meant no harm by the outburst of rage that had cost her so dear. Once the gates of that dishevelled mansion were closed on her, she realized that she had forfeited an existence perfectly agreeable to her tastes.

What could have been pleasanter than that slipshod life where dozens of wax-candles guttered over the baize cloth, where guineas glittered and cards were piled in the evening, where satin curtains kept out the daylight in the morning while a lazy girl lay cosy in cambric and down! A life where there were gentlemen to kiss, to jest with, to banter and flatter; raised pies and spiced jellies to eat, champagne and fine red wine to drink! A life where, at the cost of a few tears, a few caresses, a pout, a jest, a girl might have shawls, gauzes, feathers and frocks. Yes, a poor girl who knew all about poverty and hard work, who had been a servant on a Welsh farm, who had toiled in a London basement, might, at Up Park, enjoy all that ever gilded a kitchen-maid's dreams, just in return for being pleasant to the gentlemen. Amy began to see that she had been very wrong; she was quite ashamed of herself as she trudged to the turn in the bleak road where she must meet and stop the London coach.

It was the dead time of year, when English scenery is veiled and forbidding, when English towns are grey and chill, when a

5

poor girl wants to be cherished indoors, in a warm bed, close to a roaring fire, with good food, glasses of wine, songs and games in the evenings and milliners' boxes in the mornings.

No doubt there were other gallants besides Sir Harry, who would offer consolation to Amy Lyon, but there was a good reason why she should not engage in active adventure; for a few months at least she needed shelter and a quiet life.

She possessed only the clothes she stood up in and a few pounds, won at cards the night before, in her pocket; she thought of her mother, the comfortable widow, discreet and obliging, who was always able to earn her keep, if not much beside, with her excellent cooking; but Amy did not want to appeal to Mrs. Lyon, who had only a servant's wages to dispose of and could do nothing; besides had not the good mother given her some hints on how to handle gentlemen? How disappointed she would be to hear of her daughter's mistake! Amy was very fond of her mother and did not want her to know the failure she had made of her splendid chance at Up Park. One other resource remained to the distracted damsel, the old grandmother who, in her mud-and-wattle cottage set in the dull street of the Flintshire village, had once before proved a friend to a girl in distress.

Amy was already, at nineteen years of age, used to ups and downs, and had developed the simple philosophy of enjoying the former to the full and making the best of the latter. So she paid out her remaining stock of money for coach fare to Hawarden, where Dame Kidd looked after a dark little girl whose origin was a matter for gossip among the neighbours.

. . . .

Amy knew and detested that Welsh village; she had been born at Neston in Cheshire and when she was three years old her mother, widow of Henry Lyon, blacksmith, had come to Hawarden to share the poverty of Dame Kidd's white-washed cottage, where the continuous mists from the gaunt moorlands soaked the thatch and stained the plaster, and the frequent rains spluttered on the one fire and slashed at the dirty panes of the windows shadowed by the eaves.

To this miserable refuge the downcast girl returned because there was nowhere else to go and her grandmother knew it; they kissed and cried together; there was no need to ask for explanations, the case was obvious. Amy Lyon sat down in her draggled silks and wondered what she should do, while the dark-eyed toddling child in the red shawls eyed her curiously.

Dame Kidd regretted the fallen fortunes of her pretty grand-child who did not seem to know how to make the most of her opportunities, but she uttered no reproaches; the three women had lived together good-humouredly in the lazy squalor of a Welsh peasant's life until Mrs. Lyon had gone to London to better herself, and Amy had followed soon after, seeking the fabled glories of the capital with the high heart of ignorant youth.

And here she was, returned for the second time without a penny in her soiled pockets and with tears in her handsome eyes. What was to be done?

The old woman and the girl faced one another in some dismay in the flicker of the scanty, cherished fire.

Amy could not be considered to have made a wise investment of her charms; on her previous visit to Flintshire she had borne the swarthy child who now clung to her silk skirts and clutched at her fingers. She was evasive about the father of this uninteresting infant. Dame Kidd understood that he had been a sailor on a press-gang ship at the Tower Wharf in London, the captain, Amy had hinted—but what did it matter? He had sailed away without leaving Amy a farthing and was quite outside the present calcula-tions, which centred round the fact that in two months' time Amy would again be the mother of an unwanted child; nor was the delicate question of the paternity of the coming infant likely to be settled to the satisfaction of Amy, who, with tears, regrets, and a few outbursts against her ill luck, confessed to Dame Kidd that she had been so very wild and giddy at Up Park, had so romped and gambolled, been so anxious to please all the gentlemen that it was useless to expect any one of them to assume the responsibility for her trouble.

. . . . . .

The poor cottage, the long, narrow, village street, with the squalid inn, the forge, the tiny post office, the wide moors beyond, the scattered farms, the straggling flocks of fat-tailed, silly-faced sheep, all blurred and sodden in the wet grey winter weather, depressed Amy's spirits to a melancholy most unusual to her cheerful temperament; she felt as desperate as if she had been thrown into a lazar-house or Cold Bath Fields Prison. She wept for all she had so suddenly left, the warmth, the food, the drink, the games and caresses, the lazy ease of hours spent before a mirror, lolling on a sofa or flinging cards on the table where the *rouleaux* of guineas were piled.

Dame Kidd had no consolation to offer; she knew that Amy's plight was a common case. In the better farms hung series of cheap prints that told a story with a moral. One of these might have been Amy's story—at least in the first stages. There was a harsh title to these pictures, the first of which showed the fresh, smiling country-girl descending from the coach that had arrived in London from the provinces, looking about her on the bustle of London, all agog for fun and soft living and a fine young man to praise her and pay her bills. Even so had Amy at sixteen years of age tripped for the first time through the dubious London streets, nosing after pleasure.

Very quickly, both in Amy's case, and in that of the pictured belle, was the rich protector found—such fresh charms are easily marketed. There, in the print, she might be seen behaving as Amy had behaved at Up Park, fashionably dressed, pampered, petulant, kicking over the tea-table in a tantrum under her lover's nose.

If Amy were not very careful, she might fulfil the destiny so graphically depicted in the first episodes of this savage warning to jolly country-girls eager for town delights, she too might come to beat hemp in Bridewell, to lie in a pauper's coffin with "*anno vicesimo tertio ætatis suæ*" on the cheap lid.

The way of virtue was not only closed to her but exceedingly distasteful; she knew what it was to be a nursemaid in a Welsh farm, in the house of a fashionable London doctor, in decent establishments, where mistresses were careful of their maids' reputation; it would be quite impossible for her to return to so odious an existence—a scrubbing-brush would be no more incongruous in the hands of a nymph of Paphos than a serving-wench's cap on the well-set head of Amy Lyon.

Nor did it seem as if she would be welcomed back to the path of discretion and peace; Dame Kidd's neighbours looked askance at the returned prodigal; the girls who in homespun shawls had once herded sheep with her on the moors, sneered at the town finery that had so soon become soiled, that looked so foolish in the wattled cottage; married women who kept their own daughters respectable, wanted to know who was the teasing baby who ran after Dame Kidd and who was sometimes kissed and sometimes slapped by the despondent Amy.

Only one thing seemed possible in such a plight, an appeal to the late protector, who might surely be won round from his ill-humour by cajolery, by entreaties, as he had been won before.

Amy had learned, when in London, to read a little, to spell a little, and she sat down in despair and wrote to Sir Harry Featherstonehaugh seven letters, one after another; the gossips lounging at the village post office grinned when they read the superscription and sniggered as the days went by without a reply. In the seven unanswered letters was all her story.

.　　.　　.　　.　　.　　.

Amy Lyon had learned some other things besides how to mis-spell a love-letter; she had gathered a miscellaneous knowledge of the ways of the world from the city streets, and at Up Park she had found she had a good seat in the saddle, a quick hand with the cards, a ready tongue to answer impudent gentlemen in their cups and the insolence to order servants about as she had once been ordered. There she had learned to like champagne, dainty food, silk next to her skin and luxurious beds, to replace the slang of the kitchen by the slang of the aristocrat, the jargon of the tavern by the jargon of the stable, and the gambling-room; she had learned the intimate details of the private lives of English gentlemen taking their ease. There, too, she had learned that these same gentlemen, however spendthrift and gay they might be, however reckless with their bets, their stakes, however extravagant in self-indulgence, yet objected strangely when the bills came in and were not prepared to ruin their fortunes for the sake even of the prettiest and most charming dears.

Amy, in the gloom of the Hawarden cottage, where a farthing dip was the only light in the winter evenings, and a child and an old woman her sole company, bitterly repented of her mistake.

9

The seven letters were full of humility, of pleas for pardon, of promises for the future; never, oh! never, would she be wild and giddy again, never do anything so outrageous as run up a bill of five guineas for carriage hire. But the letters remained unanswered and Amy thought of one of the other gentlemen who had shared those pleasant parties at Up Park—one a little stiff and proud—who had never been really jolly nor roaring drunk, nor had joined in the most reckless amusements, but who had, nevertheless, shown himself susceptible to her enticements, her whims and ways.

She considered him more than a little formidable with his cold face and precise air and his hint of a sneer at the coarse frivolity of his friends, but for these very reasons she respected him—besides she knew that he had his yielding moments—if only he would deign to remember now how she had sometimes, when Sir Harry's luck was turned, known how to please him when he was a guest at Up Park. He had given her a franked envelope addressed to himself; there was hope in that. In her distress, struggling with poor scholarship, she wrote a letter, put it in the envelope addressed to the Hon. Charles Greville at Portman Square, London. It was answered with non-committal kindness and Amy wrote again in the last days of the year. She signed this frantic appeal with the romantic version of Amy which she had picked up in her adventures—Emily, the favourite name of circulating-library heroines, and Hart, a tender allusion to the warm emotions she felt and aroused.

This letter was undated, but endorsed with:

"Recd. Jan. 10, '82."

"My Dear Grevell,

"Yesterday did I receive your kind letter. It put me in some spirits; for, believe me, I am allmost distrackted. I have never hard from Sir H., and he is not at . . . now, I am sure. What shall I dow? Good God! What shall I dow? I have wrote 7 letters, and no answer. I can't come to town caus I (am) out of money. I have not a farthing to bless my self with, and I think my friends looks cooly on me. I think so. O Grevell, what shall I dow? what shall I dow? O how your letter affected me, when you wished me happiness. O G, that I was in your posesion as I was in Sr H—— what a happy girl would I have been!—girl indeed!

what else am I but a girl in distres—in reall distres? For God's sake, (Grevell) write the minet you get this, and only tell me what I am to dow. . . . I am allmos mad. O, for God's sake, tell me what is to become on me. O dear Grevell, write to me. Grevell adue, and believe (me) yours for ever—Emly Hart.

"Don't tell my mother what distress I am in, and dow aford me some comfort."

.   .   .   .   .   .

Mr. Charles Greville was gratified to receive this letter; he had not forgotten Emily Hart; he had often congratulated himself on the knowledge and cleverness that had, on so many occasions, enabled him to secure a treasure cheaply. He was used to bargaining for his pleasures, for he was a poor man of elegant tastes, a collector of *objets d'art*, a Mæcænas with a flat purse.

It had amused him to notice Sir Harry's blunder about Amy Lyon; the stupid young baronet had picked her up and turned her off, just as if she had been a mere good-for-nothing off the streets, and Mr. Greville knew that she was a great deal more than that. Sir Harry and the crew at Up Park had thought Amy merely pretty—like any other girl who could be had for the asking. And so perhaps she was in the silly finery that she did not know how to wear, with her hair stuck with pomade, rouge and white on her face, her rustic accent and loud voice; but Mr. Greville was an expert, he could detect a masterpiece even under a smear of thick disfiguring varnish, he could recognize the gem even before it was cut and polished.

He laughed in his sleeve at Sir Harry and answered the letter of the girl in distress, not, however, impetuously, nor with the least touch of impudence, nor with any disloyalty to his sex or his class. Amy had behaved badly, even though he had received some benefit from her naughtiness, and must be scolded. Sir Harry had been injured in a way he could not be expected to overlook—infidelity and extravagance, insolence and ingratitude! Amy had much to learn and Mr. Greville was quite willing to teach her; he believed she would be docile; he smiled over the sentence: "O. G. that I was in your posesion as I was in Sr. H. what a happy girl would I have been."

Well, he was willing to see what he could make of Amy Lyon,

but there must be reform, a proper bargain; he loathed establishments like those of Up Park and liked every penny of his income accounted for; he wrote to Amy in a tone of gentle reprimand; nothing must be expected from Sir Harry, least of all an acknowledgment of the unlucky child—but, if she were patient, penitent and promised good behaviour for the future, he, Charles Greville, would generously assist a naughty girl in distress.

Amy accepted the gracious offer with passionate gratitude—she would have accepted something much less inviting in order to escape from the monotony, the poverty, the hostility of Hawarden; her spirits soared at the prospect of London again; she was ready to promise anything.

Two months after her hasty retreat to Dame Kidd's cottage, Amy's second child was born without drawing breath; no one had wanted it to live, least of all the mother who found her little girl a sufficiently difficult problem; but Greville was equal to that difficulty—let the child remain with Dame Kidd, who should receive a small allowance for her keep.

.   .   .   .   .   .

Charles Greville was the second son of the Earl of Warwick; his party being in power, a small post had been found for him in the Foreign Office. It was not quite good enough for a second son of an earl, who was always on the look out for a plump sinecure—since it was a mere £500 a year; but better things might be looked for; if Mr. Greville's Government friends were not able to find him something more worthy of his merits, he had two pleasant prospects; his uncle Sir William Hamilton, a rich and childless widower, had taken him under his wing and had half promised to make him his heir. Then, whenever he chose, Mr. Greville, elegant, personable, well connected, could follow this same uncle's example and marry a woman with a comfortable income.

In the meanwhile he arranged his life with fastidious selfishness, so as to obtain the utmost satisfaction for himself out of his means and opportunities. He had remarked Amy Lyon among the disorders of Up Park and had had the curiosity to acquaint himself with her circumstances, but he did not know much of how she had spent the time since she had come to London; rumour credited her with many adventures and Mr. Greville was surprised that she could have found time for such varied experiences; she seemed so young. He wrote to her for a copy of the entry of the record of her birth, and received that of her baptism.

"Amy, daughter of Henry Lyon, blacksmith, of Neston, by Mary his wife, May 12th, 1765."

There were two crosses, one for the father, one for the mother. How old had Amy been when she was baptized? Mr. Greville did not pursue his enquiries further—it was sufficient that Amy was very young—say, nineteen years old.

Nor was he much interested in learning of her adventures; she had been a nursemaid with a Mrs. Thomas in Hawarden, a servant in the employ of the fashionable and successful Dr. Budd, of St. Bartholomew's Hospital, in the well-kept establishment his wife ran in Blackfriars—what then?

Employment in a tavern, in a shop, a brief sojourn with a lady of the half-world, adorning a shoddy *salon*, an even briefer episode as the companion of a sailor on leave, a mother at seventeen or less, an exhibit in the Temple of Hymen run by Dr. Graham in the Adelphi and Holborn.

Mr. Greville was not sure if the lovely Vestina, standing in a glass case feeding a serpent from a cup, had really been Amy Lyon; was she the fair female who had advertised the properties of the beautifying mudbath, by sitting in it up to her shoulders, her smiling face surrounded by a structure of powdered curls, braids of false pearls, rose feathers and velvet flowers?

Had the Welsh servant-girl played Hebe Vestina in this dubious temple where the virtues of the Electrical Throne and the Celestial Bed were demonstrated—in the words of the charlatan's advertisement—to the *"Amateurs des délices exquises de Vénus"*? If she had assisted at these catch-penny shows where quackery and science were impudently mingled, it was odd that she had not secured a more useful admirer than the commonplace Sussex baronet from the crowd of leering spectators.

Mr. Greville did not trouble to investigate further his charmer's past—it was her future that was to be his concern. With a deliberation that was almost solemn Amy Lyon was installed in

13

Edgeware Row, there to live under the protection of the Hon. Charles Greville—upon terms which he sternly dictated and she humbly accepted.

There was to be no more wildness and giddiness, no more tempers and whims, above all, no extravagance. Amy must forget her common ways, her coarse language, she must lower her voice, restrain her gestures, drop any vulgar acquaintances who might claim her from the past, she must be very careful, very quiet, faithful and docile.

Amy promised everything; she was anxious to put herself in the hands of this kind master; she arrived from Hawarden rosy with retrieved health and brilliant with good resolutions.

The austere country life, the pure moorland air had renewed the charms that had been slightly tarnished in the close atmosphere of Up Park; far from modish shops Amy had not been able to purchase tinsel or patches, gewgaws or pomade; the finery for which Sir Harry had paid, had been shorn of tattered trimmings and turned about into a neat, plain garment; Mr. Greville was pleased with his blooming prize when she stood modestly before him in the neat house off Paddington Green.

This was no little bounding rustic agape for crude adventure, but rather a tender dryad fresh from the woodlands; she had an air of candour that Mr. Greville found as gratifying as astonishing—with a little more training she might be made to appear positively virginal. Mr. Greville, most suave of dilettantes, looked Amy up and down through his quizzing glass.

The expert was pleased with his purchase, lucky as he was, never had he made such a good bargain.

.   .   .   .   .   .

It was decided that Amy Lyon should be forgotten and that Emma Hart should take her place—a new name for a new part and a blotting out of a past that it might not be convenient to recall. Emma, then, to Mr. Greville, and Miss Hart to whatever world there might be for the mistress of an aristocratic civil servant to move in.

Alexander Pope wrote—"out of a handmaiden we must make a Helen" and Charles Greville set himself zealously to make a

Beauty out of a pretty Welsh peasant somewhat blown upon by town airs.

First, he set his house in order; he could not afford a mistress and a housekeeper, and Amy was impossible for the latter role, so, by a stroke of careful art, Mr. Greville added Mary Lyon to the establishment, a trained manager of genteel households, an excellent cook, a duenna whose personal interest would be in guarding her charge, a factotum who would be economical and grateful.

She came eagerly, humble and thankful, dropping her curtsey, promising obedience to Mr. Greville, a strict watch over Amy, a stern eye to the pence; since there must be no connection with any little errors that might be associated with the name of Lyon, Amy's facile parent was re-named Mrs. Cadogan; two maidservants were engaged, one at nine pounds, and one at eight pounds a year, and the elegant *faux ménage* was complete.

.   .   .   .   .   .

Mr. Greville moved from Portman Square and rented a modest brick house, which stood in Paddington near the spot where the rich outlines of the baroque church showed attractively incongruous on the prim sweep of the village-green; it had a neat secluded garden, looked on trees back and front; the neighbours were quiet, genteel, and not too close, the tradesmen conveniently at hand and obsequious, as befitted those who served an Earl's son who paid cash—at least for his smaller needs.

The interior of the house was well kept and contained some treasures, the result of Mr. Greville's fine taste and careful buying. The panelled walls were dark and the furniture had a masculine severity, walnut and mahogany without cushions or fripperies, but in the parlour was a Correggio where the tones of the hyacinth and the violet, the May rose and the Italian skies melted on the canvas in voluptuous harmony. This was balanced by a modern masterpiece that Mr. Greville had obtained cheaply, a work by Sir Joshua Reynolds, the President of the Royal Academy, of which a story was told to set the gossips sniggering.

Emily Bertie had engaged the fashionable artist, whose prices had lately risen, to paint her portrait, had paid half the fee—seventy-eight guineas—in advance and given Sir Joshua several sittings when some crisis in her domestic affairs caused the lady to change her plans abruptly, and her portrait remained unfinished in the studio. Such was too often the end of the paintings of frail beauties, who lost their protectors before their features could be completely transferred to canvas. Sir Joshua, irritated by the unfinished bargain, and by hearing that Miss Bertie was sitting for George Romney, had completed the picture and sent it to the Royal Academy under the unkind title of *Thais Setting Light to the Temple of Chastity at Persepolis.* This direct allusion to Miss Bertie's profession amused the critics, but was considered a piece of unnecessary spite on the part of a rich man towards a fine girl who had paid him nearly a hundred guineas for which she had had no return.

Mr. Greville had enjoyed the scandal, admired the picture, asked Sir Joshua to retouch it here and there, according to his own ideals of beauty and had bought it cheaply.

Besides the Correggio and the Reynolds there were other treasures for Emma to admire, a cabinet of coins and medals, where the flattened, polished profiles of Kings, Queens, Popes and worthies gleamed in gold and silver from their padded drawers, a case of sparkling mineral specimens, that Mr. Greville valued very highly, some spoils from the vineyards of Tuscany in the shape of urns and vases, some curios from the sulphurous earth of Sicily and the lava of Vesuvius. Emma was not impressed when Mr. Greville tried to refine and widen her mind by showing her the lovely curve of an Etruscan vase, the delicate modelling of a royal medallion, or the manner in which Sir Joshua had handled his flesh tints, but when he told her that she herself might become a work of art, she began to be extremely interested, her vanity, hitherto that of any pretty wench, took a higher turn, and she saw herself, through Mr. Greville's eyes, as a potential beauty.

With gratifying intelligence she grasped the ideal he set before her, and what she must do to achieve it; her behaviour became exemplary, she watched Charles Greville with the pathetic keenness of the dancing-dog balancing on a pole and eyeing the master who has the sugar and the stick. All that Mr. Greville said was law to Emma; her quick docility gave him much pleasure and he was patient at his task, though he did not forgo long lectures, which Emma only half understood, on propriety, decorum, genteel

16

behaviour, good taste, what was and what was not done in polished circles and by the mistresses of well-bred men.

Emma was taught to disdain finery; no tawdry ornaments, cheap showy dresses, no fard, patches, curls stretched over pads or frames, no beads nor posies; Mr. Greville chose her dresses himself, found her a dressmaker and did not allow her a single flower for her bosom or hair. He engaged masters to teach her singing, playing on the harpsichord, deportment and dancing; he encouraged her to read refined and moral books, he taught her how a gentlewoman entered a room, how she poured out tea, how she listened to the conversation of gentlemen. There were no more rich dishes nor glasses of champagne, Emma might have one half-pint of beer daily, and that was all; she must take frequent exercise, go to bed early, rise early, she must, above all, learn to consider money with respect, to lay out every farthing to the best advantage. Mrs. Cadogan helped her there with the anxiety of a woman who knew that her livelihood depended on her zeal, neither mother nor daughter ever forgot that they might be turned off at a moment's notice; Mrs. Cadogan had only to think of the kitchen basements from which she had been rescued, and Emma of that odious cottage at Hawarden, for them to redouble their efforts to please kind Mr. Greville.

No marriage could have been quite so dull in its setting; Emma saw no one outside the house beyond the tradespeople, the milliner and the dressmaker; when she went for her dutiful walks, either her mother or her lover accompanied her, when she was at home she must read an improving book or study her music, or listen to Charles Greville's discourses on manners and refinement, or admire the treasures of *virtu* that she did not understand.

Further, she had to keep her accounts very carefully indeed; she had an allowance of £20 a year, for her mother and herself and every item of expenditure had to be noted down; she did this dutifully, "a mangle 5d., poor man ½d., cotton and needles 9d., apples 2½d."

This was all a vast change from life at Up Park, from anything that life had meant to her before; but she was not dull; she had two objects with which to fill her days, Charles Greville, the god of her little secluded universe, and the pursuit of beauty.

Her mirror assured her that she had improved under her lover's handling; her teachers assured her that she might be not only a beauty, but an accomplished beauty; she had a strong voice, sweet and powerful, she sang with an emotional stress on moods and melody that disguised the deficiency of her ear, her fingers learned to trip over the keys as quickly as they learned to move among the tea equipage of egg-shell china, beaten silver and lacquered caddy. She could strike an attitude with rather more than the usual zest and grace of the servant girl portraying a romantic heroine in a cracked mirror. Mr. Greville noticed her poses and quietly encouraged her; he bought her a plain robe, made her knot up her hair and asked her to stand in the position of one of the figurines on the orange-ochre antique vases. He was astonished at the ease and elegance with which she assumed the classic pose; he began to think that Emma Hart was even a greater bargain than he had at first supposed; surely no man had ever achieved material comfort and ecstatic delight, gratification of body and mind, at a cheaper rate. Mrs. Cadogan's exquisite little dinners were as perfect in their way as Emma's caresses—and the whole establishment including the fees of the teachers of accomplishments, cost no more than £300 a year.

.   .   .   .   .   .

Emma was touchingly happy in the charming little house, she was fonder of Charles Greville than she had been of Sir Harry, he was so much kinder, such a superior being to the sporting baronet with his low tastes; she believed her master to be vastly superior to herself, and she thought all his priggish airs and cold moralizings proofs of his wisdom and goodness. She learned from him to talk of Virtue—she did not know quite what this wonderful quality was, but she was sure that Charles Greville had it in abundance.

She had neither opportunity nor temptation to be unfaithful to her lover, but she did not wish to be; he was young, personable, flattered while he taught, caressed while he admonished, and raised her self-esteem. He had, also, with his aristocratic good looks, his charming manners, his fastidious habits captured her senses, she was as much in love with him as her nature would permit, more in love with him than his nature could understand.

.   .   .   .   .

By midsummer Mr. Greville had given his Emma, rescued from the scrap-heap, at least a superficial polish, and he wished to have his good taste and his labour applauded; he was in every thing a man of his world and he followed the fashionable course of taking his mistress to the studio of a popular painter in order that her charms might be immortalized in some modish guise.

So Emma, one blowing blue day, tripped along gaily to No. 32, Cavendish Square, where the formidable-looking mansions surrounded the plot of grass and gravel where coaches and link men waited and loungers gossiped by the pavement posts; Mr. Greville accompanied her and preceded her up the wide stair to the studio that had for long been the scene of the successful career of Francis Cotes, the charming portraitist and had for eight years been the workshop of George Romney.

Emma was carefully dressed, according to Mr. Greville's direction, in a long plain gown of white cambric, fastened under the bosom with a wide blue ribbon, with a low bodice and short sleeves; the line of the shoulders and bust was broken only by a light scarf, the girl's hair hung in ringlets round her neck and a wide Leghorn straw-hat, with a low crown shaded her face.

The painter was instantly and for ever enthralled by what nature and Charles Greville had made of Amy Lyon, who, under the pretty name of Emma Hart stood meekly in the large studio at Cavendish Square.

George Romney was a melancholy man gnawed by the bitter dissatisfaction of the artist who had given up everything for art and did not find it sufficient to fill his life. When Emma was brought into his presence by her complacent protector, the painter was forty-eight years of age, dark, stooping, with blunt features, and a manner shy to uncouthness.

His birth was little higher than that of the blacksmith's daughter; both were close to the English peasantry; they came, on the male side, from the same part of the country; George Romney's father had been a small statesman of Walton-in-Furness, Lancashire, who worked at cabinet-making and knew something of architecture; the painter's childhood had been passed in the North, his youth in severe study of his chosen art. He felt keenly that his lack of education, his limited social opportunities had handicapped him as both man and artist; he had married early in life a faithful woman who had borne him two children, and whom he had left behind in the North when he started out to seek his fortune in the city; that had been twenty years ago and it was fifteen years since he had revisited Mary Romney, who remained silent, with an odd patience, in the Cumberland farm that seemed so far from London.

George Romney had been successful; even when working in competition with the fashionable, genial and magnificent Sir Joshua Reynolds, he had earned enough by his portraits to enable him to travel in Italy, where he had studied his art with exhausting concentration.

The patronage of the Duke of Richmond and of Charles Greville's brother, the Earl of Warwick, had enabled him, on his return to London, to set up in the studio of Francis Cotes, and to become, with great rapidity, one of the most sought-after portraitists of the day. His life remained gloomy; apart from a few friends such as William Hayley, who flattered, pestered and bored him, and Richard Cumberland, who admired and encouraged him, he had no intimates, and he avoided acquaintances, diversions and distractions with a nervous dislike of his fellow-men and a gloomy mistrust of himself that were fast developing into hypochondria. He had toiled for years at the development of his art with a passionate, impatient industry that had brought about the achievement of a perfect, if limited technique.

Enraptured by the genius of Raphael and Titian, he remained for ever dissatisfied with his own efforts, and the studio, where Emma entered like a goddess, was littered by portfolios bulging with unfinished sketches, jottings for pictures never begun, while the walls were encumbered with incomplete canvases; some laid aside because a sitter had failed or a model not been procurable, some abandoned in mere impatience while the painter made another effort with equally short-lived enthusiasm.

He made more than a handsome income by his portraits, but the money brought him little pleasure; he was open-handed and had generously supported a talented wastrel of a brother until death had relieved him of that burden, and it concerned him little whether his portraits were paid for promptly or indeed paid for at all; and his prices never rose to more than half the fees demanded by

Sir Joshua Reynolds, President of the Royal Academy, from which George Romney stood nervously aloof.

When Charles Greville took Emma to the studio in Cavendish Square, he brought much happiness to the painter and conferred a very great benefit on posterity. The Grevilles had always admired and patronized Romney who, in his Italian travels, had carried about with him a letter of introduction to Sir William Hamilton, the British Minister at Naples, written by Charles Greville but never presented by the painter, who did not go so far south; the frigid dilettante had a genuine liking for the uncouth artist with his gipsy blood, his gloomy face and his incomparable talent for depicting the robust beauty of English women and children.

Greville, who always closely supervised Emma's wardrobe, had taught her to dress in the style in which Romney painted his sitters, so that everything about his patron's mistress enchanted the artist—the girl herself and the taste with which she was set off.

George Romney fell in love with Emma, with all that Emma symbolized; he had painted many fair and charming women, but so strong was his sense of an ideal beauty that he had, perhaps, unconsciously, made these sitters look much the same when he put them on canvas.

In the case of Emma there was no need of this infidelity to nature that was fidelity to an inner vision, the girl was what all painters long to find, the ideal woman in human flesh and blood.

When Emma stepped on the model's block and under the careful directions of Charles Greville assumed her classic poses, Romney knew that he had met the creature necessary for the fullest expression of his art; she excited him as had Titian's canvases which he had seen in Venice, the Raphael masterpiece he had copied in Rome; she was at once a stimulus, an inspiration, a seal of his achievement—she would take his art as far as it could go. And Emma, reading the plain, sad man's honest rapturous delight in her charms as she posed in the becoming studio light, found herself exalted, lifted out of herself, never more to be a pretty girl, a naughty girl, a girl in distress, but for ever—a beauty.

. . . . . .

Mr. Greville was well pleased with the success of his experi-

ment; the enthusiasm of George Romney confirmed his own judgment, rewarded his labour, his expense; he was gratified to find himself the possessor of a Thais in the flesh who far outshone the pictured charmer whom he had been so proud to have on his walls.

Emma was more beautiful than Emily Bertie, more beautiful than any woman in town. Romney proclaimed this truth in canvas after canvas, in hundreds of sketches and drawings.

For the first time in his sombre, lop-sided life the painter was happy, for the first time in a vagrant existence the model felt self-justification, self-respect; they combined to produce works of art that were, within definite limits, flawless.

Emma embodied Romney's faults as well as his merits; she was well within his powers of achievement; she had no charm that it was not within his perception to seize on and within his skill to reproduce. He was lucky to find a model that not only inspired but flattered his art, and she was lucky to find a painter who could celebrate her beauty with complete acquiescence in its perfection.

Emma Hart, as set out by Charles Greville and painted by George Romney, was, perhaps, as completely beautiful as any woman who has ever filled a painter's imagination, and it was a beauty for every eye. She was not the woodland lily visited by moonlight loveliness of Simonetta Vespucci, celebrated by Sandro Botticelli, that some people might have found fantastic and wan, nor the high-bred grace of the Lombard ladies with the smile of the Grecian Hermes that soothed, if it did not satisfy, the yearnings of Leonardo da Vinci.

Emma's charms neither raised nor solved any problem; she was neither wistful, tormented, nor aspiring, her fine features did not hint at any world of the spirit or at any whimsy of dreams. There was nothing of an enigma in her smooth contours, no question in her eyes, no puzzle on her lips, no subtlety in anything she did or was. Therefore she was completely within the range of George Romney, who had his yearnings after poetry and fancy, after "subject" pictures and illustrations of Shakespeare and Milton, but who never was completely successful save when dealing with the obvious graces of wholesome human nature.

Emma was the type to which he had already made some of his sitters conform; an oval face, small features in exact proportion, large dark eyes under sweeping brows, a fully curved mouth, a warm complexion richly flushed with rose, a profusion of red-brown hair, falling in heavy tresses. To these rare beauties Emma added a tall, finely shaped figure with a generously rounded bust and shoulders and swift, lovely movements.

Her defects were slight; extremely young as she was, she had more the solidity of a statue than the fragility of a flower; she was large-boned and her feet were clumsy; the face was slightly too broad, the neck slightly too long.

George Romney presented her under many names but with the fewest possible accessories, a classic robe, a muslin frock, or chemise, a sash, a Leghorn hat, a scrap of cambric to embroider, a spinning-wheel by which to sit; he painted her direct from life, taking three or four sittings of an hour or so each and finishing robes, hands and details from a professional model. He never allowed his work to be touched by pupils, and worked with great rapidity, often leaving one portrait unfinished, in his haste to begin the next. In these beloved studies his painfully acquired technique was never pushed beyond its limits; in painting Emma he was always well within the bounds of what he could do, not only easily, but almost unconsciously.

.   .   .   .   .   .

Mr. Greville was highly pleased that his mistress should be painted by so admirable and fashionable an artist, and disdained any jealousy of George Romney's open infatuation for the Emma who was partly his own creation. Her lover often accompanied her to Cavendish Square, and helped to swathe the gauze round her face, to dispose the ribbons round her waist, to tilt the broad-brimmed hat over her face; often he advised this pose or that, until Emma, under his guidance and that of the painter, could herself take a pose to admiration, simulating by the position of her limbs, the turn of her head, characters she never understood, emotions she was never to experience. When Mr. Greville was occupied with his affairs or wished for the company of his social equals, Mrs. Cadogan played the duenna and accompanied her daughter, who had suddenly become so important and so precious, from Paddington to Cavendish Square; it was all very decorous, the neat civil servant liked his Thais to have the outward gloss of an English gentlewoman; there was no touch of Sal Brazen or Moll Tawdry about Emma now.

Yet, for all that, the gossips had their say; the painter was obviously in love, the profession of the model was to be pleased with those whom she pleased—by this alone she lived, and the mother who was the servant in the establishment where her daughter was the kept woman could not be supposed to be a very vigilant guardian of female fidelity or honour.

Romney, too, passed for a morose queer fellow, with a forsaken wife, whom no one had seen, who led a secretive life, who was not a gentleman nor bound by any social conventions, and who, well out of all ordinary restrictions or obligations, might do as he pleased.

Nor need Mr. Greville, who was a gentleman and had his own code, trouble himself if Emma's old giddy wildness flared up in the presence of this new admirer, a man of her own class, of something of her own experience, yet rich and famous. Think what you will, this is what the town thought, and with no peculiar cynicism—that when Emma went from Mr. Greville's house to that of George Romney, she went from one lover to another.

Why should she be more faithful to Mr. Greville than to any of her former lovers, and why should George Romney resist the charms that had never been resisted before? There might be reasons but they were not on the surface and the question was one of little matter; what was important was that a beauty had been created and endowed with as much immortality as ever falls to the lot of mortals.

.   .   .   .   .   .

While Emma, who continued to behave herself to her master's liking, to study music and water-colour drawing, to keep her accounts, and to lead a very modest life in Edgeware Row, Romney painted her in at least thirty completed canvases. To these he gave haphazard titles; classicism was the fashion, and Emma's features were superbly classic, so Romney, with a little smattering of knowledge, named the poses *Cassandra*, *Bacchante*, *Diana*, *Euphrosyne*, *Alope* or *Ariadne*. She was *Sensibility*; she was painted as the *Spinstress* and *The Seamstress*, and knew how to imitate the modesty she had never known and the industry she detested. She was painted as a *Wood-nymph*, as *Saint Cecilia*, as

24

The Comic Muse, as *Nature*, with a dog, with a goat, with a gazelle, in the Welsh hat of her mother's country-women, and simply as *Emma*. This last is the just title of all her portraits; the fancy labels make little difference, it was always Emma, in one of her poses, whom Romney painted.

Much was made of Emma's marvellous change of expression, which her admirers so extolled, but neither Romney nor any other painter ever put on canvas Emma's features distorted or transfigured by real emotion; portrait after portrait shows the same smooth regular face undisturbed by any feeling, the eyes sometimes open wide, sometimes cast down, the lips sometimes parted, sometimes closed, now a look of gravity, now a smile, but never anything but the most superficial change on the flawless unlined countenance, which never showed either the dreadful grandeur of a Cassandra, or the lofty exaltation of a Joan of Arc, but a certain mildness, shallow loveliness that might pass for virginal candour.

Romney's technique was devoid of tricks; he made no dangerous experiments, as did Sir Joshua, his downright style was suited to the obvious beauty of his model, with clear steady sweeps of his facile brush, with an expert curve of a limited palette, he placed on his canvas the madders and umbers, the crimson lakes and siennas of his home-ground paints and reproduced with them the firm, rosy flesh tints, the lustrous blue-brown eyes, the auburn locks of Emma.

This method suited his talent, his highly finished work was inclined to be hard, lacking in atmosphere and rather like a painting on porcelain; but in these rapid studies there was breadth and freedom, and they satisfy the eye even when they are unfinished.

In common with the portraitists of his day Romney painted his sitters in a steady studio light that cast only a pale shadow on the face and with imaginary backgrounds, like drop-cloths, that had no relation to the subjects of the picture, but which were hastily roughed in to throw up the figures to advantage. In his ardent studies of Emma, Romney kept to the Titian-like colourings of which he was fond, solid, rich, a golden cream, a rosy white in the carnation, fresh crimson lips, and hair varying according to the scheme of the picture, but always warm in tone, even too hot in the shadows.

Sometimes the Emma pictures were clumsy in finish, the face

25

appearing like a mask, the arms and hands boneless, the figure
without structure, the drapery wooden, but this body of work
represented a definite achievement in art, which must be credited
to both painter and model.

Possibly the most beautiful of all these portraits of Emma is the
Ariadne, an exquisite, tender painting where the simple, downcast
girl in her plain English attire is as delicate as a rose-petal blown
on the canvas. Romney admired what he considered a natural
beauty; he disliked the great ladies of François Boucher, product of
the dressmaker and the dancing master, the grisettes and villagers
of Greuze, product of the theatre and the circulating-library novel,
and he painted his Emma without frippery or adornment.

Her loveliness was indeed natural, that of the moorland, not the
Court, the dairy, not the drawing-room, and even those who found
it lacking in breeding, subtlety or refinement had to admit that it
owed nothing to the cosmetic box, the hairdresser, the jeweller, or
the costumier; Emma's beauty shone most triumphantly in a
gown cut like that of a servant-maid with a yard of gauze for a
scarf or a milkmaid's straw for a hat.

Romney, himself a peasant, saw no defect that needed softening
in the robust and lustrous Emma, when during four years she made
his life happy by posing to him, but it is possible that Charles
Greville, looking at her with the critical eye of familiarity, and the
detached appraisal of the expert, began to perceive the coarseness
of the country-girl beneath the glow of the Hebe, the vulgarity
of the servant beneath the rich outlines of the goddess; certain it is
that after two years' possession of this treasure, he began to scheme
how he might be rid of her with full advantage to himself.

.   .   .   .   .   .

Yet Mr. Greville believed that his Emma loved him; she had so
dutifully kept the promises she had made when he had rescued her
from the squalor of Hawarden; she had never even asked for anything more than the one or two "creditable companions" he had been
induced to allow her; she had worked so hard at her music, her
poses, her pencil, she had jotted down so anxiously all her little items
of expense. When she had had a little rash on her elbows he had
sent her to the seaside with her mother, directing that her child

was to accompany her; he thought that maternal emotion might give another turn to her charms; if the child was pretty what a subject for Romney! Emma and her offspring as *Motherhood* or *Venus* and *Cupid!*

Emma went dutifully and reluctantly from Paddington to Parkgate, trying to amuse herself with little Emma as the child was named, but all the while yearning to be home again with an impatience very gratifying to her lover.

The distant coast was dull indeed after the cosy life in London; and the contrast was the sharper as a new and delightful companion had lately enlivened the neat establishment at Edgeware Row; one who amused and flattered Emma and admired her with open, if respectful, rapture. Mr. Greville's wealthy and famous uncle, Sir William Hamilton, was on leave from his post at Naples and a frequent visitor at Paddington, he had been very flattering to "the fair tea-maker" as Mr. Greville named his mistress and she had found him delightfully kind and entertaining.

Sir William Hamilton's sister had been the late Countess of Warwick, Mr. Greville's mother; Sir William was descended from two branches of the noble and ancient family whose name he bore, but had not inherited any great wealth. Pursuing fortune on the field of glory, he had served in the Foot Guards under Prince Augustus, Duke of Cumberland, until delayed promotion caused him to resign his commission in disgust. At the age of twenty-eight, it seemed prudent to him to marry an heiress, though this was, in his own words, "something against his inclination." A Miss Barlow with a Welsh estate worth £5,000 a year was secured, and in 1782 this lady put her husband under a further obligation by dying and leaving him completely free; the only child of the marriage was dead and Sir William at fifty-five (but looking, as he hoped, only forty) had nothing to consider but his own pleasure, if indeed he had ever considered anything else.

Mr. Greville, who had for some years been tacitly regarded as his uncle's heir, was disturbed by the persistent rumours that Sir William, with his tidy little fortune, his elegant sinecure at Naples, his fine manners and well-preserved charms, would soon contract a second marriage.

This growing anxiety was hidden under the cold serenity of

the young man, when he sent Emma off to cure the rash on her elbows in her native air and doubtless absorbed him so much that he was not able to answer her loving letters with the promptitude their devotion deserved, though the post was something to blame for the delays that distracted Emma.

The truth was, that, despite his removal to Paddington from Portman Square, despite Emma's care with the pence and Mrs. Cadogan's kitchen economies, Mr. Charles Greville was in money difficulties. What was £500 a year to a collector of bric-à-brac, a man of fine taste, however careful? And there was no sign that the long-promised Government sinecure was coming his way. Marriage with an heiress was the obvious solution to this difficulty, but nothing less than a fortune of £20,000 to £30,000 would do, and this was not so easily to be found.

Mr. Greville accompanied his uncle on visits to the great houses where these gentlemen were welcome guests and confided to him his situation—his inevitable debts, the inevitable crisis ahead—a state of affairs by no means his own fault since he had lived so prudently, indulging even his antiquarian tastes very cheaply.

With these same tastes Sir William had every sympathy; he was himself a most distinguished virtuoso with a taste for the more sensational aspects of science; he had ascended Vesuvius twenty-four times, visited Etna and written a book on volcanoes and in 1767 he had presented to the British Museum a collection of volcanic earths and minerals. Foster-brother of George III and an intimate of the Royal Family, Sir William Hamilton had used his influence with the Prince of Wales to obtain a pension of £100 a year for a certain Father Antonio Piaggi; this he had increased by the same amount from his own pocket and had employed the learned monk to work on the Herculaneum papyri. Taking advantage of his comfortable income, his fine taste, his position as British Minister at Naples, Sir William had enriched his country with the Porticinari collection of Greek vases, which he had purchased in 1766, added to, and sold at a handsome profit for over £8,000 to the British Museum. He was at present engaged in forming another collection of vases found in Sicilian tombs, which he hoped to dispose of for a handsome sum to the King of Prussia.

Sir William possessed, not merely an eye for a bargain, but an eye for beauty, grace and fitness, and he had added to his enthusiasm a careful knowledge; his high position among the *cognoscenti* of his day had been recognized by an appreciative Government; the Star and Ribbon of the Order of the Bath had brought him his title and the most fastidious of learned English societies had been honoured to receive him as a member; he was a Fellow of the Royal Society, of the Society of Antiquaries, and a member of the *Dilettante*; a man of the world, well-bred, tactful, amiable and used to making himself acceptable to the frivolous and the ignorant. Sir William was nothing of a pedant, and had indeed trained his monkey to quizz through a glass at a statue or a coin in mockery of the dry antiquaries who wearied with their inelegant jargon.

Beauty was Sir William's idol, that beauty which, as Leonardo da Vinci wrote, passes nature and becomes art; he received the most exquisite pleasure from painting, sculpture, music, fine scenery, poetry and all objects of *virtu*; in particular he was enamoured of the rich grace and vivid colourings of the mural designs being brought to light as the once gay city of Pompeii was excavated from the lava of centuries, and of the voluptuous shapes and precise features of the statues being discovered in distracting profusion on the sites of ancient cities and patrician villas in Italy.

Sir William, who had already resided twenty years at Naples, was Italianate to the core, and his antiquarian researches had produced in him the same kind of renaissance as the discovery of classic treasures had created in the refined minds of the fifteenth century; everything with him, in order to be tolerated, must be antique, and he was as much at home with the dancing-girls and nymphs of the Pompeian frescoes as with the tight-laced, powdered ladies of his own world.

For the rest, he was a Sybarite, with no strong feelings, who had never experienced a powerful emotion, *bon viveur*, an expert in fastidious pleasures, alive to all the tricks and tones of an idle aristocratic society, inoffensive, never meaning any harm, loyal to a gentleman's indefinable code of honour, and perfectly satisfied with the golden sinecure his embassy represented.

His modest ambitions had all been fulfilled; he was not vexed that he had been passed over when important posts were being assigned to likely diplomats, nor stung by the fact that, had his talents been brighter, or his zeal more striking, he would not have been left so long at a Court which was off the political map.

Indeed, the elegant Scotsman was only too happy to be left in his brilliant backwater; he was credited with the saying: "My country is anywhere that I am comfortable," and he had made himself comfortable, in the highest sense of the word, at Naples.

In appearance he was tall, well made, with features like those of his nephew, Charles Greville, neat and ordinary, but set off by powder, curls, ribbons and smiles, to appear quite distinguished. His manners were lively, racy with the gentlemen, arch with the ladies, and flattering to everyone. He did not deceive himself when he glanced in his mirror and thought that he appeared no more than in the prime of life. He had always tried to balance self-indulgence with prudence whenever prudence was not too galling; in his military youth, his elegant debauchery had gone with a healthy devotion to athletics; he was a good horseman, a graceful dancer, and when in Naples obtained exercise by slaughtering animals in the great *battues* in the royal parks.

In brief, Sir William Hamilton put up a very fine appearance indeed, was a vast credit to his class, his country, his family, fulfilled strictly all the obligations the world required of a fine gentleman, and was everywhere admired.

But the brilliancy, both of appearance and of attainments, was only superficial; behind that smooth façade of wit and taste, there was fast setting in a rapid decay of a feeble character; behind that air of vigour were many symptoms of encroaching ill-health. Sir William, who appeared so jocund, so youthful at fifty-five, was in reality fast approaching premature senility.

.   .   .   .   .   .

Emma had enraptured her lover's uncle; he had rather enviously congratulated Mr. Greville on the possession of a real treasure; Charles simpering a little over his good taste had declared: "She is as good as anything in nature."

But Sir William's praise went higher—"She is better than anything in nature, she is as good as anything to be found in antique art."

He gazed enthralled as this Pompeian nymph in flesh and blood posed for him in the attitudes which Mr. Greville and George

Romney had taught her—a shawl, a tambourine, a tossing of a fleece of rich curls, a downward or an upward glance, and the enraptured connoisseur gazed at one of his favourite statues come to life, with as much enthusiasm as ever Pygmalion watched his Galatea throb from alabaster into flesh.

In the studio in Cavendish Square he admired the brilliant canvases on which the gloomy painter had cast the radiance of glowing young womanhood. The ageing gentleman was in every way pleased, in his artistic taste, in his classical knowledge, in his old man's relish for a bouncing merry wench; why this was Ariadne, Cassandra, Diana, Alope, the Comic Muse!

As blind as Romney in his infatuation, he did not see that this was Emma, always and nothing but Emma, and that the famous expressions that fleeted across her smooth face disturbed it no more than a breath ruffles a placid lake.

Then her singing!

Sir William was amazed at her full ringing notes, at the drama she put into her songs, at the *bravura* with which she shook out her reckless trills. If her ear was slightly defective, that was hardly noticeable and might soon be remedied—she was worthy of the most careful training—in the opera house she would be an object of public admiration!

Emma responded gratefully to all this sincere flattery, and put Sir William second only in her affection to Mr. Greville, he was so kind—he was rich, too, and influential, he might be so useful; her lover had told her what a very important person Sir William was, and as she tried to pass the dull time at Parkgate, she thought of the wealthy uncle almost as much as she thought of the beloved nephew.

Sir William was so very civil, he never scolded or admonished as Mr. Greville did, no, he treated her just as if she were a great lady, he was courteous and respectful, as if he were always at her feet. He did not know what a romp she had been, nor anything of her past life, nor of the existence of little Emma, of the nasty plight from which Mr. Greville had so generously rescued her, nor of the squalid little cottage in Hawarden.

When she was with Sir William she was always careful to remember all that Mr. Greville had taught her—the moods and gestures she must not use, the references she must not make; a little *gaminerie*

31

suited her style of beauty, a touch of Flintshire accent was not displeasing, but Mr. Greville had always been as strict about vulgarity
as he had about economy.

The manner that Sir Harry Featherstonehaugh had approved
had to be left behind with the cards and wine-glasses, the oaths and
indecencies of Up Park. Emma, dutifully curing her marred knees
and elbows with medicine and sea bathing, was pleased to think
how well she had behaved to Sir William, what a good impression
she had made on him with her demure tea-table ways and her filial
kisses when her fresh mouth—unique, Sir William had declared,
in its classic curve—had touched so lovingly the powdered yellow-
ing cheek of the old *virtuoso*.

Despite his careful dressing, Emma had taken Sir William for
an old gentleman when she had first seen him, but Mr. Greville
had, with unusual emotion, corrected her opinion, and Emma,
always quick to take a hint, never again referred to age and Sir
William in the same breath; indeed, when she came to know him
better, she declared he was "the most juvenile gentleman she had
ever met," so coy, so arch, so lively, with such spritely ways!

He had told her to call him Pliny the elder, who was, he said,
a philosopher, and also not unknown to the slopes of Vesuvius,
though he had never, like the industrious Sir William, written a
book about the volcano. Emma, to whom one name was as good
as another, dutifully called the brilliant gentleman Pliny, while
Charles Greville was Pliny the younger; so an air of classicism was
cast over Paddington Green. If the wit ran a little thin, Emma did
not perceive it. As she moped in her hired lodging, bored with the
teasing child, loathing the seaside, missing the poses, the visits to
Cavendish Square, the music lessons, the flatteries of Sir William,
the company of her lover, she poured out her anxieties on paper.

She was worried about money; Mr. Greville had told her to be
careful, and Pliny had hinted in his kind fatherly way, that dear
Charles was really in rather a tight corner from which it would
take a good deal of skill to extricate him; then there was the anxiety
as to where Mr. Greville was and what he was doing; supposing
that, in that great world to which she had no entry, he met someone
who would induce him to forget poor Emma?

In a torment she rushed her feelings on to paper; she wrote

better now than when she had penned her seven unanswered epistles to Sir Harry, she had picked up too, from reading fashionable fiction, from listening to fashionable talk, some of the jargon of the moment, the language of melting sensibility that disguised grossness, the high-flown phrases that were such a specious form of hypocrisy. Emma's profession was to flatter gentlemen; she knew Mr. Greville's weakness for being thought a Mentor, the wise man who had made a good girl out of poor, wild, giddy Amy Lyon.

She paid him this homage readily and not entirely out of self-interest; the man was attractive and her lover. It was not an unskilful letter that Emma wrote from the boredom of Parkgate.

"Parkgate, June the 15th, 1784

"My Dear Greville,

"You see by the date where I am gott and likely to be; and yett it is not through any neglect of seeking after other places. As to Abbergely it is 40 miles, and so dear that I could not with my mother and me and the child have been there under 2 guines and a half a-week. It is grown such a fashionable place. And High Lake as 3 houses in it, and not one of them as is fit for a Christian. The best is a publick-house for the sailers of such ships as is oblidged to put in there, so you see there is no possibility of going to either of those places. Has to where I am, I find it very comfortable, considering I am from you. I am in the house of a Laidy, whoes husband is at sea. She and her grammother live to-gether, and we board with her at present, till I hear from you. The price is high, but they don't lodge anybody without boarding; and as it is comfortable, decent, and quiet, I thought it would not ruin us, till I could have your oppionon, which I hope to have freely and without restraint, as, believe me, you will give it to one, who will allways be happy to follow it, lett it be what it will. As I am sure you would not lead me wrong, and though my little temper may have been sometimes high, believe me, I have allways thought you in the right in the end, when I have come to reason. I bathe, and find the water very soult. Here is a great many ladys bathing, but I have no society with them, as it is best not. So pray, my dearest Greville, write soon and tell me what to do, as I will do just what you think proper; and tell me what to do with the child. For she is a great romp, and I can hardly master her. I don't think she is ugly, but I think her greatly improved. She is tall (has) good eyes and brows,

33

and as to lashes she will be passible; but she has over-grown all her cloaths. I am makeing and mending all as I can for her. Pray, my dear Greville, do lett me come home as soon as you can; for I am all most broken-hearted being from you. Indeed I have no pleasure nor happiness. I wish I could not think of you; but, if I was the greatest laidy in the world, I should not be happy from you. So don't lett me stay long. Tell Sir William everything you can, and tell him I am sorry our situation prevented (me) from giving him a kiss, but my heart was ready to break. But I will give it him, and entreat if he will axcept it. Ask him how I looked, and lett him say something kind to me when you write. Indeed, my dear Greville, you dont know how much I love you. And your behaviour to me, wen we parted, was so kind, Greville, I don't know what to do; but I will make you a mends by my kind behaviour to you. For I have grattitude, and I will show it you all I can. So don't think of my faults, Greville. Think of all my good, and blot out all my bad: for it is all gone and berried, never to come again. So, good-by, dear Greville. Think of nobody but me, for I have not a thought but of you. God bless you and believe me Your Truly & Affectionately

"Emma H——t."

"P.S.—Poor Emma gives her duty to you. I bathe her. The people is very civil to ous. I give a guinea and half a-week for ous all together, but you will tell me what to do. God bless you, my dear Greville. I long to see you, for endead I am not happy from you, tho' will stay if you like till a week before you go home, but I must go first. I hav had no letter from you, and you promised to write to me before I left home. It made me unhappy, but I thought you might (have no) time. God bless you once more, dear Greville. Direct for me at Mrs. Darnwood's, Parkgate near Chestter, and write directly."

In seven days she had not heard from Mr. Greville, the monotony of the bland June season became unsupportable; she wrote again and on a more emphatic note, giving Charles Greville just the stuff she thought he would like; if the incense was rather thick and luscious, well Emma knew that gentlemen liked it so, especially gentlemen like Mr. Greville who had no sense of fun and were such superior beings. She began the long epistle in the hope of having one to answer before it was finished, but no! And so the

34

letter was lengthened from the Wednesday to the Sunday morning when at last Dame Kidd forwarded a letter that had wasted a fortnight in Hawarden.

"Parkgate: June the 22nd, 1784.

"My Ever Dear Greville,

"How tedious does the time pass awhay tell I hear from you. I think it ages since I saw you—years since I heard from you. Endead I should be miserable, if I did not recollect in what happy terms we parted—parted but to meet again with tenfould happiness. Oh, Greville, when I think on your goodness, your tender kindness, my heart is so full of grattitude, that I want words to express it. But I have one happiness in vew, which I am determined to practice, and that is eveness of temper and steadiness of mind. For endead, I have thought so much of your amiable goodness, when you have been tried to the utmost, that I will, endead I will, manage myself, and try to be like Greville. Endead, I can never be like him. But I will do all I can towards it, and I am sure you will not desire more. I think, if the time would come over again, I would be different. But it does not matter. There is nothing like buying experience. I may be happier for it hereafter, and I will think of the time coming and not the time past, except to make comparrasone, to show you what alterations there is for the best. So, my dearest Greville, dont think on my past follies; think on my good—little as it has been. And I will make you amends by my kind behaviour; you shall never repent your partiality. If you had not behaved with such angel-like goodness to me at parting, it would not have had such effect on me. I have done nothing but think of you since. And, oh, Greville, did you but know, when I so think, what thoughts—what tender thoughts (I have), you would say 'Good God!' and can Emma have such feeling sensibility? No, I never could think it. But now I may hope to bring her to conviction, and she may prove a valluable and amiable whoman! True, Greville! and you shall not be disapointed. I will be everything you can wish. But mind you, Greville, your own great goodness has brought this about. You don't know what I am. Would you think it, Greville?—Emma— the wild unthinking Emma is a grave thoughtful phylosopher. Tis true, Greville, and I will convince you I am, when I see you. But how I am running on. I say nothing about this giddy wild girl of mine. What shall we do with her, Greville? She is as wild and

35   D

as thoughtless as somebody, when she was a little girl; so you may gess how that is. Whether she will like it or no, there is no telling. But one comfort is (that she is) a little afraid on me. Would you believe, on Satturday whe had a little quarel. I mean Emma and me; and I did slap her on her hands, and when she came to kiss me and make it up, I took her on my lap and cried. Now do you blame me or not? Pray tell me. Oh, Greville, you don't know how I love her. Endead I do. When she comes and looks in my face and calls me 'mother,' endead I then truly am a mother; for all the mother's feelings rise at once, and tells (me) I am and ought to be a mother. For she has a wright to my protection, and she shall have it as long as I can, and I will do all I can to prevent her falling into the error her poor once miserable mother fell into.

"But why do I say miserable? Am I not happy abbove any of my sex, at least in my situation? Does not Greville love me, or at least like me? Does not he protect me? Does not he provide for me? Is not he a father to my child? Why do I call myself miserable? No, it whas a mistake, and I will be happy, chearful and kind, and do all my poor abbility will lett me, to return the fatherly goodness and prottection he has shewn (me). Again, my dear Greville, the recollection of past scenes brings tears in my eyes. But they are tears of happiness. To think of your goodness is too much. But, once for all, Greville, I will be good to you.

"It is near bathing time, and I must lay down my pen. I wont finish till I see when the post comes, whether there is a letter. He comes in abbout one a clock. I hope to have a letter so to-day.

"I must not forgett to tell you my knees is well, as I may say. There is hardly a mark, and my elbows is much better. I eat my vittuels very well, and I am quite strong and feel hearty, and I am in hopes I shall be very well. You can't think how soult the watter is. And there is a many laidys bathing here. But, Greville, I am oblidged to give a shilling a day for the bathing horse and whoman, and twopence a day for the dress. It is a great expense, and it fretts me now I think of it. But when I think how well I am, and my elbows likely to gett well, it makes me quite happy. For at any rate it is better than paying the doctor. But wright your oppinion truly and tell me what to do. Emma is crying because I wont come and bathe. So, Greville, adue tell after I have dipt. May God bless you, my dearest Greville, and believe me faithfully, affectionately and truly yours only—Emma H.

36

"Thursday Morning.

"And no letter from my dear Greville. Why, my dearest Greville, what is the reason you don't wright? If you knew my uneasyness, you would. You promised to write before I left Howeden, and I was much disapointed you did not, but thought you might have a opportunity being at Wandower (? Wendover) Hill. I have sent 2 letters to Haverford West, and has never had no answer to them, and it is now 3 weeks since I saw you. Pray, my dearest Greville, wright to me and make me happy; for I am not so att present, though my arm is quite well.

"I think if I could but hear from you, I should be happy. So make (me) happy, do, pray. Give my dear kind love and compliments to Pliney, and tell him I put you under his care, and he must be answerable for you to me, when I see him. I hope he has (not) fell in love with any rawboned Scotchwoman, whose fortune would make up for the want of beauty, and then he may soon through her (die) in a decline—Mum! For he is fond of portraits in that whay, and then he must be fond of orriginals, and it will answer every purpose. But don't put him in mind of it, for fear—— But offer and say everything you can to him for me, and tell him I shall allways think on him with gratitude and remember him with pleasure, and allways regret laeving is (leaving his) good company. Tell him I wish him every happiness this world can afford him, that I will pray for him, and bless him as long as I live. I am wrighting, 'tis true, but I dont know when you will ever gett it. For I can't send itt, till I hear from you, and the Post wont be in tell to morro. Pray, my dear Greville, lett me go home soon. I have been 3 weeks, and if I stay a fortnight longer, that will be 5 weeks, you know; and then the expense is above 2 guineas a week, with washing and bathing whoman and everything; and I think a fortnight or three weeks longer I shall not have a spot."

"Friday morning: 12 o'clock (25th June).

"With impatienc do I sett down to wright tell I see the postman. But sure I shall have a letter to-day. Can you, my dear Greville —no, you can't—have forgot your poor Emma allready. Tho' I am but for a few weeks absent from you, my heart will not one moment leave you. I am allways thinking of you, and could almost fancy I hear you, see you; and think, Greville, what a disapointment when I find myself deceived, and ever nor never heard from you. But my heart wont lett me scold you. Endead, it thinks on

37

you with too much tenderness. So do wright, my dear Greville. Don't you remember how you promised? Dont you recollect what you said at parting?—how you should be happy to see me again? O Greville, think on me with kindness! Think how many happy days weeks and years—I hope—we may yet pass. And think out of some that is past, there (h)as been some little pleasure as well as pain; and endead, did you but know how much I love you, you would freily forgive me any passed quarels. For I now suffer for them, and one line from you would make me happy. So pray do wright, and tell me when you will be returning, as I shall be happy to see you again. For whilst Emma lives, she must be gratefully and ever affectionately Your

Emma Hart."

"P.S.—This shall not go tell I have a letter from you, which I hope to have in half an hour. Adue, my dear kind Greville."

"Sunday Morning (27th June).

"My Dear Greville, I had a letter on Friday from my Granmother, and she sent me one from you, that had been there a fortnight. I am much oblidged to you for all the kind things you say to me, and tell Sir William I am much oblidged to him for saying I looked well. I hope he will always think so; for I am proud of (his) good word, and I hope I shall never forfeit it. I will at least study to deserve it. I am in hopes (to) have a letter from you, for it is a great comfort to me to hear from you. My dear Greville, it is now going on for a month since I saw you. But I think how happy I shall be to see you again, to thank you for your kindness to my poor Emma and me. She shall thank you, Greville, she shall be gratefull, she shall be good, and make you amends for all the trouble her mother has caused you. But how am I to make you amends? God knows. I shall never have it in my power. But, Greville, you shall have no cause to complain. I will try. I will do my utmost—and I can only regrett that fortune will not put it in my power to make a return for all the kindness and goodness you have showed me. Good-by. My dearest Greville. . . . Emma is much oblidged to you for remembering her, and she hopes you will give her a oppertunity of thanking you personally for your goodness to her. I think you wont be disapointed in her; though mothers (Lord bless me, what a word for the gay wild Emma to say!) should not commend, but leave that for other people to do."

There was one more letter written from Parkgate on July 3rd; it was on the same note. Mr. Greville had suggested that little Emma should be brought to London and sent to school, and the young mother was submissively grateful—and wrote all the conventional things, hopes that Emma would become good, mild and attentive—that she would not turn out as her mother had—but then, if poor Emma the first had had the luck to have such a fine early start—"what a woman she would have been!"

Here Emma wrote not from her feelings, but from her situation; every Magdalen embarrassed by chance maternity has voiced these correct sentiments.

Leaving the subject of the child, Emma again flattered her lover; how she was longing to see him, to give him a thousand kisses—"My happiness now is Greville."

She wrote truly; she had not much in the world besides her dear Charles; but there was the rich, amiable uncle to please also. "Dear Sir William. Give my kind love to him. Tell him (that) next to you I love him above any body and that I wish I was with him to give him a kiss. . . . My mother gives her compts. to you and Sir W. Say everything that is kind and well render me dear to him."

When Emma read over this letter she was not satisfied that she had expressed all that she felt and she added a pretty postscript.

"P.S.—Good by, my dear Greville. I hope we shall meet soon, happy and well. Adue! I bathe Emma and she is very well and grows. Her hair will grow very well on her forhead, and I don't think her nose will be very snub. Her eye is blue and pretty. She don't speak through her nose but she speaks countrified. We squabble sometimes; still she is fond of me, and indead I love her. For she is sensible. So much for Beauty. I long to see you."

By August the impatient girl was back in Paddington, though Mr. Greville and his uncle were still visiting in Scotland; a slight attack of measles sent her to bed, but she soon recovered and was writing eagerly to her lover.

"Edgware Row, Tuesday, August 10th, 1784.

"I must now inform you abbout my illness. My dear Greville, I had a rash out all over me and a fevour, and I should have been

39

worse, if I had not had the rash out. But I think I am better for it now; for I look fair and seem better in health than I was before. I dare say I should have been very dangerously ill, iff it had not come out. Pray, my dearest Greville, do come to see me, as soon as ever you come to town, for I do so long to see you. You don't know how it will make me to be happy—I mean if you should come before diner. Do come (to dinner), because I know you will come at night. I have a deal to say to you when I see you. Oh, Greville, to think it is nine weeks since I saw you. I think I shall die with the pleasure of seeing you. Indeed, my dearest Greville, if you knew how much I think of you, you would love (me) for it, for I am all ways thinking on you, of your goodness. In short, Greville, I truly love you, and the thought of your coming home so soon makes me so happy, I don't know what to do.

"Good-by, my ever dearest Greville. May God preserve you and bless you, for ever prays your ever affectionately and sincerely . . . Emma.

"My kind love to Sr William; and tell him if he will come soon, I will give him a thousand kisses. For I do love him a little.

.　　.　　.　　.　　.　　.

While Emma, secured from mischief by the presence of her mother and her child, was living in such respectable fidelity at Parkgate, Sir William and his nephew were, in the intervals of their social duties, talking business.

The Knight had never been overreached in a bargain yet and Mr. Greville was shrewd and careful, so it was in an atmosphere of even-tempered prudence that they discussed their affairs, in which the uncle's appetite and the nephew's pocket were concerned, but not the heart or the sentiments of either.

The Hon. Charles civilly urged his uncle to take Emma off his hands with the same ease as an Emir might have urged a neighbouring potentate to accept a favourite odalisque.

She was, as Sir William could judge for himself, a gem of the purest lustre; her beauty, her singing, her attitudes!

To increase her value, Mr. Greville vouched for other good qualities possessed by Emma; she was nice-mannered, faithful, truthful, quick at learning, obedient and docile; she was economical, always good-humoured and lively. Then there was her mother, maid, duenna, cook in one, cheap and efficient. How much better

40

for Sir William to match his pleasant leisure with a lovely, well-trained girl like Emma, than hamper himself with a wife.

All the members of the family advised such an arrangement, the Rev. Frederick Hamilton, Sir William's sole surviving brother, declared that "to buy love ready made" was the best thing the gay widower could do.

As for himself, Mr. Greville simply could not afford such a luxury as the keeping of the rare treasure he was passing on to his dear uncle.

Was it fair to keep Emma pinching and scraping in Edgeware Row when she was fitted to adorn a Court? He could not afford the expensive tutors her talents deserved, the carriage and pair she ought to have, the fine clothes that were her right.

Besides, he had himself to think of; the Romney pictures had made Emma quite famous, and everyone knew who her protector was. It was useless for him to offer himself to an heiress until his charmer was dismissed; he had thought of Lord Middleton's daughter, who had £20,000, but how could he come forward as a suitor for the chaste Henrietta with Emma on his hands? Another point, he wanted to see Emma well established; she deserved a fair settlement, say a £100 a year from Sir William, which he, Charles Greville, would try to add to by selling a few pictures, even sacrificing the Correggio or the Thais for so laudable an end.

All this seemed very reasonable to Sir William; the complete absence of romance or sentimentality pleased him; Charles Greville had always been a man after his own heart,—but there were objections to the tempting offer. "Naples is like a village for gossip, the thing can't be hidden. Besides I don't want to be the wittol of every young rake being bear-led through Italy."

Mr. Greville was sure that Sir William's tact would be able to deal with the Neapolitan gossips—Emma would be studying music, and the mother would surely confuse, if not silence, the prudish. As for Emma's flirting with the tourists the Minister had to entertain, Mr. Greville could answer for her good behaviour—why the difficulty was that she was too faithful; Mr. Greville showed the Parkgate letters: "The girl's in love with me, and won't be got rid of so easily!" And he mentioned that she had received several fine offers from wealthy men that she had indignantly refused—

nay, Emma might even have married quite respectably had she not been so tenaciously fond of her Greville.

All this clinging fidelity might be transferred, the Hon. Charles was sure, with time and tact to Sir William, who had the leisure, the person, the means to lay siege even to the most difficult female heart.

How far from difficult of assault was Emma's heart, Mr. Greville did not mention; he glossed over the girl's past with which Sir William, a stranger to London, was not familiar and he said nothing of little Emma now comfortably boarded out with a Mrs. Blackburn and her husband at £60 a year; in short, he did the best that he could both for himself and for the poor girl in distress, to whom he had been so kind.

Sir William accepted the offer; he was to have Emma as soon as a decorous occasion for the transfer presented itself; both the girl and society had to be considered, she could not jump from one man's arms into those of another without some little delay and tact; but that she should as soon as possible pass into Sir William's possession was agreed between the two gentlemen before the Minister departed for Naples.

Something else had been agreed to also; of course, Mr. Greville could not sell his mistress, no such thing was to be thought of, but it just happened, while the delicate Emma-negotiations were going on, that Sir William was able to let his nephew know that he would be able to help him pay his debts and to assist him in obtaining a wealthy wife.

Mr. Greville owed about £6,000, not much more than a year's revenue from the Welsh estates of the late Lady Hamilton, and Sir William was so obliging as to enter into a bond whereby the creditors were satisfied by money raised on the estate to which Mr. Greville was made heir in tail. Not only by assisting him in keeping his creditors quiet did the uncle oblige the nephew, he gave him a letter written so as to be shown to a third party, wherein he declared dear Charles to be his heir—it was hoped that this epistle would help Mr. Greville in securing an heiress.

The will, leaving to Charles Greville not only the Barlow, but other estates, was duly drawn up and Charles himself left sole executor. Sir William promised to use his considerable influence at Westminster to secure his nephew some honourable and lucrative sinecure.

Of course, all these benefits were conferred on Mr. Greville out of the pure goodness of Sir William's heart and had nothing whatever to do with the secret understanding that Emma should come out to Naples as soon as possible.

.　　.　　.　　.　　.　　.

All these arrangements having been carefully made, His Britannic Majesty's Minister returned to his post at the Court of Naples, and Emma took up again her modest life at Paddington, going to and from Cavendish Square to console the moody gloom of George Romney with her bright looks, amusing Mr. Greville with her poses, her songs and her lively chatter.

By the end of 1785 there came a letter from Pliny, written within sight of Vesuvius, begging the fair Emma to come to Naples as his guest, there to perfect herself in music and painting.

As dear Charles was busily setting his affairs in order, and thought of taking a course of chemistry under Professor Black in Edinburgh, he would not be able to accompany her, but in six months' time, or sooner, he would go out to Italy and bring her home—meantime comfort and decorum would be assured by the presence of Mrs. Cadogan. Emma was a little bewildered, a little saddened; she did not want the Paddington idyll to end, she did not want to leave the lover of whom she had grown so fond—the painter who worshipped her charms.

But Mr. Greville was firm, even stern; he had a great deal of business on hand, Emma would only be in the way; it was her plain duty to go to Naples, there to learn to finish her music and painting —and also by her pretty, graceful ways to keep the wealthy, useful uncle in a good humour towards the absent Charles.

Emma consented; if she wept at the prospect of leaving Mr. Greville, there was comfort in the thought of seeing foreign lands, perhaps a foreign Court, of being admired and flattered once more by kind old Pliny.

On March 14th, 1786, Emma and Mrs. Cadogan were entrusted to the escort of Gavin Hamilton, one of Sir William's artist friends, and started for Naples, where they arrived nearly six weeks later in the full flush of the South Italian spring.

Emma, then twenty-three years old, was also in the full flush of her ripening charms. Mr. Hamilton had admitted that he "had never seen anything quite like her"—she fitted into the opulent landscape as a picture into a frame and took possession of her apartments in the Palazzo Sessa, the British Embassy in Naples, with the air of Venus returning to Paphos.

.   .   .   .   .   .

Mr. Greville remained alone, but not forlorn, in Paddington; he certainly did not intend to think of Emma again, to see her, or write to her, unless absolutely forced to do so. He had seen the last of her without regret, and proceeded to put his affairs methodically in order, selling a few treasures, paying some debts, compounding others, closing the Paddington establishment, at least for the present, while he freed himself of business annoyances and kept his shrewd eyes wide open for a rich wife.

He regarded himself as Emma's benefactor, and the harmless deception whereby he had passed her on to his uncle under the false promise of rejoining her later did not trouble him at all. There was no managing women by any other means than such tricks as these, and one day Emma, cosily installed as Sir William's *belle amie*, would be very grateful to dear Charles for so thoughtfully providing for her future.

Emma did indeed owe Mr. Greville a heavy debt; he had rescued her from squalid misery, restored her self-respect, taught her many things useful for an adventuress to know, changed her from a pert, bouncing wench into a rare beauty, brought out her talents for music, for poses, instilled into her the wisdom of keeping her temper and her accounts, and pointed out the advantages of Mrs. Cadogan's attendance. He had given her some flavour of the great world, some inkling of taste and beauty—above all, he had introduced her to Sir William Hamilton and to George Romney.

But for himself he had obtained a fair and amorous mistress very cheaply, and he had entangled his uncle in a connection likely to prevent that second marriage that he, the heir-at-law, so dreaded.

So, twice over, Emma had repaid her obligations to her friend, who had never pretended to love her, and who had certainly kept his promise to help a girl in distress.

.   .   .   .   .

Emma felt a little forlorn, frightened and homesick, when she first arrived at Naples, and she wrote by the first post to Mr. Greville, urging him to redeem his promise and come out to her as soon as possible. It was all very splendid in the Palazzo Sessa—but what could compare with the delights of love—"not fine horses, nor a fine coach, nor a pack of servants."

Sir William was much more than kind—"he loves me, Greville . . . but he can never be my lover."

She related to the absent Charles in much detail all the attentions shown her by one whom she wished to regard merely as a kind sincere friend, she ran over all the novelties of her position, she expressed herself with an emphasis learned from the theatrical attitudes, the dramatic singing, the false tone of the time, but which was touched by a sincere emotion; it was not agreeable for the healthy young woman to have exchanged the attentions of the young beau for those of the old rake. Death, poverty, hunger, would Emma face to return to her dear Charles, she would walk "bare foot to Scotland" where perhaps he was listening to Professor Black's lectures on chemistry—"if my fatal ruin depends on seeing you and I will and must (see you) in the end of the summer."

Then she scribbled on about Sir William's infatuation, his gifts, his love for dear Charles to whom he had left everything in his will, the success of her English gowns—"but the blue hat, Greville, pleases most."

Did Greville need money, well, Sir William might send some, "the tears came into his eyes and he loves us boath dearly." But her hope, her happiness was all with Greville and, after she had poured out her rigmarole, she added the postscript:

"Pray, for God's sake, wright to me and come to me, for Sir William shall not be anything to me but your friend."

.   .   .   .

This letter despatched and a few tears shed for the amorous joys of Edgeware Row, Emma began to look about her on the novel scene.

Naples was as different from Paddington as one place could be from another; Emma was lodged in a palace, waited on by servants, while His Britannic Majesty's Minister hardly disguised a boundless infatuation, within the radiance of a Court, almost in touch with a King and a Queen, with Princes and great ladies. In a flash Emma had achieved the wildest day-dreams of every poor girl who had taken her charms to market. She had pleased a rich man, a powerful man, a man who could give her everything a woman like herself admired and envied. Why, she really had to pinch herself to make sure she was awake; her mother's approving smile hinted at her luck; Sir William's adoration had that touch of senility that promised everything.

He raved, he cut capers, she could not move a limb but he loudly praised it; she was used to being admired to her face, Mr. Greville had often pointed out her charms to his friends, but with a detached enthusiasm. Mr. Romney had been deeply moved by her graces, but his homage had been awkward, shy, until it was expressed on canvas. But Sir William revealed himself in a rhapsody that would have seemed tiresome and foolish to a well-bred woman, but which Emma enjoyed very much; amusing the old fellow with good-humoured pleasantries, she kept him off while she waited for Mr. Greville and looked about her on the strange city.

．　　　．　　　．　　　．　　　．　　　．

The Kingdom of Naples spread over half the map of Italy, reaching to the frontier of the Papal States, the very gates of Rome, it also comprised the rich, fantastic Island of Sicily.

For long a Spanish province under a Viceroy, Naples had been given a King in the person of Ferdinand IV, third son of Carlos III of Spain. Ferdinand, when a child eight years old, had been installed in Naples under the tutelage of a Tuscan Minister, Bernardo Tanucci, who worked wholly under the directions of the Spanish Cabinet.

This state of affairs came to an end with the King's marriage to a daughter of Maria Theresa and Francis of Lorraine, who speedily broke off connections with her father-in-law and gathered all the business of the Kingdom into her own nervous hands; by a clause of her marriage contract she was to have a seat in the Cabinet on the birth of a Prince, and the heir had duly appeared.

To assist her in this responsibility Queen Maria Carolina had introduced a foreign favourite into her Council, an Englishman of good birth, one John Acton, who had been employed at her brother's Tuscan capital, and who fitted very cleverly into the part of adviser of the passionate Queen who ruled the foolish King. Acton had no idea in his handsome head save that of personal aggrandisement and it mattered little to him how the Kingdom was run, as long as he had money and power and Maria Carolina was pleased.

Under these three, the lazy ignorant King, touched with hereditary imbecility, the ambitious, superstitious, violent Queen and the incapable, greedy, unscrupulous favourite, Naples was as badly governed as a country could be. A system already out-of-date was eaten into by every manner of corruption and abuse; the King regarded his position as a vulgar joke, the Queen hers as a chance to enrich and advance her brood of sickly children, Acton his as a piece of luck to be exploited to the utmost.

To anyone of sense, who looked beneath the surface, it would have been obvious that South Italy was in the state of the seething pot that so nearly boils over, that bubbles already gather at the brim.

But this surface was very brilliant, and no one about the Court did look beneath it. What did obsolete laws, a crazy system of finance, an impoverished country, the discontent of the intellectuals matter, as long as the sun shone and there was money for games and festivals, for hunts and concerts?

Sir William had never looked below the glittering crust on which he had sported so long and so gaily. While he had been going into raptures over the discoveries at Pompeii he had never concerned himself with the conditions of the country where he had resided for twenty years; while he had been quizzing at his vases, or prying into the volcanic earths of Vesuvius, he had not noticed other fires as dangerous as those of the great mountain smouldering beneath the sparkling life of Naples.

The upper- and middle-class Neapolitans were proud, patriotic, intelligent and cultured; in their ranks were many brilliant men and women, philosophers, scholars, poets, writers, scientists, medical men, highly educated, lofty-minded gentlewomen, ardent, brave, ambitious youths. These people loathed the reckless, heartless tyranny under which they lived, detested the alien Bourbon rule, the meddling Austrian Queen, the sly, stupid English adventurer, and in their clubs, societies, academies, drawing-rooms and cabinets, they absorbed and discussed the highest culture of the day and ventured to dream of plans for the reform of a country beloved and oppressed.

What did Sir William Hamilton know of this? Even if he knew, why should he care? What did it matter to Emma, who had never minded anything but her own affairs; she had lived in London through the war with the American Colonies, the war with France, the trial of Warren Hastings, the rise of Pitt, but if she had been stirred to a cheer at the victories of Hood and Rodney, that was as far as her concern in the fortunes of her country had gone. All she was ever to know of Italy she knew at once; the superficial glance was always enough for Emma.

.   .   .   .   .   .

The celebrated beauty of the city of Naples lies in its situation and colouring; on a closer view, the narrow streets, the huddled houses, the featureless architecture are not of any peculiar distinction, but viewed from the magnificent bay the design is splendid, a fitting setting for a baroque fairy-tale. The flat façades of peach and cream-coloured plaster rising in terraces, the stately bulk of the royal palace to the left, the sweep out to the lighthouse on the mole to the right, the Castel dell'Ovo supposed to have been built on a magic egg provided by the wizard Vergil, to the left jutting out darkly into the bay, the majestic lines of the Castel Nuovo in the centre of the city, while on the heights behind rises the massive fort, the Castel Sant' Elmo, flanked by the long lines of the Certosa di San Martino.

And over all, when Emma first stepped into her luxurious apartments, the steady wash of sunshine, the azure sky reflected in the azure-violet waters of the huge bay, bright light gilding the crowded shipping in the harbour, flashing amid the stiff-leaved palm-trees, the black cypress-boughs, the grey twisted olives on the slopes above the town; in the drowsy gardens the dark green leaves and thick white stars of the myrtle, the vivid purity of orange blossoms, the profusion of the fragrant petals of roses, syringa and oleander, flowers Emma had never seen even in dreams.

On gilded balconies stood pots of fringed pinks, of plumy basil, of scented rosemary, while from behind the slats of green shutters came the tinkle of mandolines and guitars, the lilt of amorous voices; in the evening when the breeze blew cool from the purple sea, smart carriages with liveried lackeys rattled to the flamboyant Opera House, to luxurious balls, to concerts, or departed for delicious drives along the coast, ending in suppers beneath the soft lamps that glowed amid the tamarisk groves and citron glades of Caserta or Posilippo.

Over all the varied splendour of the surface-scene, consistent as the sunshine, as brilliant as universal, were the menace and pomp of a powerful religion sunk into gross superstitions that were shared alike by Queen and beggars, pervading every corner of life, processions and parades of monks, nuns, priests, banners, filth and ignorance. The "religious" swarmed as thick as the flies in Naples, and the focus of their gorgeous mummery was the grandiose Duomo, where, amid scenes of frantic excitement, the Archbishop showed to the hysterical mob the phial in which the blood of the patron saint of Naples, San Gennaro, changed from a solidified drop into fresh-flowing crimson liquid.

. . . . . .

On the surface the life of Naples was not only smooth but sparkling, at once elegant and informal; society had become both gay and cultured under the influence of the Austrian Queen, who, ignorant herself, liked to be a patroness of the arts, of learning and philosophy.

The fashions of Paris and Vienna enlivened the vast city; the melodies of Mozart and Haydn mingled with those of Gluck and Piccini, the nobles swung along the streets in coaches as brilliant as those which filled the court of honour at Versailles. Velvets from Genoa, laces from Venice, silks from Lyons crushed gowns from the Palais Royal, and hats designed by Marie Antoinette's milliners crowned fantastic, powdered locks that framed vivacious southern faces. Young patricians black-eyed, with dark curls heavily pomaded and coats sewn with tinsel and sequins rode their blood horses along the winding, dusty roads above the city, while their lackeys struck out of their way with canes the cringing,

49

grinning peasants. Before smooth palaces of dusty stone hung ornate coats of arms, heavy amid the masks and wreaths cut between balconies and latticed windows. Through the gilt trellis of high gates could be glimpsed court-yards where fountains flashed in marble basins and marble Tritons blew conchs of glittering metal. In the shade of arcades pots of camellias, red white and striped, stood beside statues of ancient gods, lately raised from the rich soil, or smooth blocks of lava of the surrounding *campagna*. In cool, tiled *salons* philosophy was discussed, and songs sung to harp, guitar or spinet; in the evening the fireflies danced over the moon-beam walls that shaded strolling lovers, and the lanterns of pleasure-boats glittered beyond the shipping in the bay.

Nature, too, kept up this show, this holiday, with glitter of steady sunshine for weeks together, with lavish flowers and fruit, from the first clusters of large, scentless violets to the last golden orange, the last basket of dusky grapes, with the changing waters of the bay, jade green, azure, purple, and lilac, melting to an horizon where sea and sky were one radiance blurring the island. Nature provided a luxurious background, the sloping hills where the convents and forts blazed white beneath their belfries and flags, where the pines were black in the luminous air, and beyond the vineyards and cornfields the sombre splendour of Vesuvius rising from fields of lava and ashes to cones that cast up fire and vapours.

Along the crowded quays the fisher-folk lounged, gossiped, and chaffered over their wares; their striped trousers and short jackets, their red caps and earrings were declared to be by all foreigners —"picturesque"; it was quite fashionable to leave a wax-lit *Salon* where an Italian melody had been sung by a trained singer, to loiter down to the fisher-folk's quarters to hear their nasal voices raised in "Santa Lucia" or "Stella Maris." Fireworks were a popular diversion; from the gardens, from the royal palace at Caserta, from the terraces of the noble villas at Posilippo, at Castellamare often rose the mock fires of human artifice that fell in fountains of fiery blooms before the brilliant stars, then disappeared into the purple darkness of the bay where the sea-foam curled along the indented rocks.

Naples indeed provided every device that could render life exciting and agreeable; here was for sale every possible pleasure, from the grossest to the most refined, and here, for ten months of the year, were a climate and a scene that might be likened to those of a fabled paradise. Moreover, to a casual eye the city seemed as happy as it was splendid, as gay as it was luxurious. Priests, monks, nuns, beggars alike, appeared light-hearted and indulgent towards their fellow-men and towards the saints whose worship was so easy and whose benefits were so lavish; the nobles seemed carefree with nothing to do but to spend their handsome fortunes on amusements, and the middle classes disclosed to none what was in their minds.

.   .   .   .   .   .

The British Embassy was housed in two floors of the Palazzo Sessa, which Sir William Hamilton rented in Naples; these magnificent and sumptuously handsome apartments looked out upon the glitter of the bay.

A suite of four fine rooms was given to Emma and her mother; the rooms had been newly decorated by the British Minister for his dazzling treasure; he had exhausted his taste, if not his purse, in preparing a background worthy of so beautiful an occupant; couches of Pompeian shape with gilt claw-legs and curved backs had their classic rigidity broken by tasselled cushions of brocade. The walls, exquisitely painted with light arabesques, were kept to those melting hues of cream, amber and ivory which best set off the vivid hues of Emma's carnation and the glint of her opulent tresses. Here and there was a sculptured vase that would in time come to be priceless, here and there a picture which represented the climax of some master's art. Sir William searched through the garnered hoard of a lifetime to find out the choicest pieces for the adornment of Emma's sun-bathed chambers.

She had little appreciation of all this, but she could delight in the soft canopied bed with the pale silk curtains, the carved wardrobe full of handsome clothes, the toilet-tables lavishly plenished, the rich draperies which kept off the heat, the dainty food, and the obsequious service.

She had done her best to please Charles Greville by being economical and prudent, when she had lived in Edgeware Row, but it was a relief no longer to have to count the pence, to content herself with one glass of beer, and to sigh for frocks which she could not afford. Compared to the maids at a few pounds a year who had been her sole servants at Paddington, the troop of Neapolitan attendants were as amiable and skilful as a host of genii.

Emma, like the princess in an Eastern tale, could have her every wish anticipated; she might have fine wines to drink, rich food to eat. Sir William never scolded, nor lectured, nor asked her to consider the cost. Every kind of pleasure that it was possible for her to imagine was offered her with humble delight in her acceptance. It was not possible for Emma to do otherwise than bloom with an even brighter lustre than she had worn at Paddington or in Romney's studio, to glow and smile and give out a delicious radiancy of youth and joy.

The peasant girl who had passed her childhood on the misty moors of Flintshire seemed to belong easily, as if by right, to this gorgeous background; Sir William became every day more and more infatuated, more and more excited over his good luck.

"Who was she?" Naples asked, between a smile and a shrug; and he, a man of easy tact, had his answer ready—a young *protégée* who had come to Italy to learn music and was resting awhile under his roof with her good mother.

Meanwhile, with that bad taste which infatuation will produce, even in people of high breeding, he presented Emma with some of his wife's clothes and toilet articles, a satin gown with Indian paintings on it, for which he had given twenty-five guineas, and for the hot weather loose muslin dresses something like those she had worn when sitting for Romney, with sleeves tied back with ribbons and plain knotted sashes. He told Emma that she might command anything, and she was grateful and wrote again to Charles Greville in the last week of July: why should not the fairy prince come to add the last touch of enchantment to this fairyland?

Why must she, when everything else was perfect, be content with an old lover? When she took up her pen she began to write in a facile, sentimental, emotional style, which was not wholly hypocritical:

"For God's sake send me one letter, if it be only a farewell. Think, Greville, of our former connection, and don't despise me."

If he did not come to her, she must go to him; she would be

in London at Christmas at the latest, life was insupportable without him and her heart was entirely broken. What were the language masters, the singing masters, the music masters, without Greville? Why, nothing. She would return to live with him if he would allow her but one guinea a week for everything. Then she went on with an account of all that was happening to her, full of pride and pleasure in her triumph, informing her beloved Greville that she had no more eruptions on elbows or knees, and was become so fair that the Italians declared she must use rouge and white. She had been to Pompeii and the islands and there had been a dreadful storm of thunder and lightning; she ran on with this and all the other chatter that came into her mind. She was progressing with her Italian—she would write to him in that language soon. "But Grevell, of fleas and lice, there is millions." Then at the end a flourish of good-humoured tenderness: "Pray, write to yours ever. With the truest and dearest affection. God bless you. Write me, my dear, dear Greville. Emma."

Swift and dreadful storms, alternating with hot tempests marred that resplendent summer. The heat was suffocating, and streams of lava began to pour slowly from the fearful cone of Vesuvius, while plumes of smoke hung stagnant in the heavy sky; there were rumblings of earthquake and showers of ashes. All this to Emma was but an added excitement. It was scarcely possible for her to grasp anything beside the fact of the great success of her beauty.

When she went abroad, the cheerful, insolent *lazzaroni* and the idle, jolly, picturesque crew of beggars, fishermen, small trades-people, and loungers, who formed such a large part of the population of Naples, followed her with cries of pleasure, delighting in her noble beauty, which to them was of so uncommon a type; they praised the mass of rich chestnut hair, her simple white gowns in the English or Turkish fashion, the plain straw or the famous blue hat which Greville had sent from London, and which cast such exquisite shadows over the entrancing face.

The Neapolitan aristocracy viewed, perhaps with a touch of irony, the old man's darling who had so suddenly and so dramatically appeared to take his dead wife's place in the Palazzo Sessa, but neither Sir William nor Emma perceived the hint of subtle mockery in the homage the easy Southerners paid to this fresh and uncommon charmer. The Queen was no prude; she has been described by one who knew her, as a woman "whose manners were so loose that it was possible to suspect her of every excess," and it was commonly believed that she had countered the incessant infidelity of the King with more than a few *amours* of her own, and that the handsome and elegant John Acton had been for years more to her than a friend. Whether the Queen was maligned or not, at least she showed herself generous towards the girl who appeared in such an equivocal position in the British Minister's house. Her Majesty did not herself receive Emma, but she made no objection to her courtiers' doing so.

The Italian gentlemen, in their tinsel and pomade, their pearls and their diamonds, sauntered laughing after Emma, when Sir William proudly paraded her in the trim walks of the gardens of the Villa Reale. A sparkling Viennese Prince was there; Emma could not spell his name, but he could speak her language and they got on very well together. He entitled himself her "cavaliere servente"; though the expression was new to her she soon grew to understand what it meant. The elegant admirer often dined at the Palazzo Sessa, and demanded a picture of the exquisite Emma while he smiled at her over the wine-glass; she was delighted to hear that he was a friend of the Queen:

"And he does nothing but entertain her with my beauty, accounts of it, etc."

Emma also discovered that the King had a heart and that she had made an impression on it. When, in the delicious summer evenings, after the storms had passed over, Sir William took Emma out in his boat on the waters off Posilippo, where he had a little casino or summer pleasure-house, His Majesty made a point of being there also, and put out in his own barge, which was filled with Court musicians.

Sailing close to the British Minister's party, Ferdinand gazed his fill of the English Miss, *la Signora* Hart, and ordered his musicians to play her a serenade on the French horns, sitting the while with his hat in his hand. When the concert was over His Majesty made a remark, which was translated to Emma as meaning that he regretted he could not speak English; after that he took occasion to be as often as possible in her train of admirers, when she walked in the grounds of the royal villa or when she took her seat with Sir William in the box at the Opera House, where her radiance was displayed to the lorgnettes of the boxes and the stares of the pit.

It was a curious experience for Emma. She had never seen a king before. When she had been in London, King George had been as far away from her sphere of life as an Archbishop from the village church in Cheshire where she had been baptized. The Spanish Bourbon monarch was by no means inaccessible nor fastidious; almost totally uneducated and delighting in the company of his inferiors, he was as much beloved by the lowest population of Naples as he was despised by the professional classes and the aristocracy.

When Emma caught his easily pleased eye, His Majesty was about thirty-five years old, heavily made with a rolling profile and an enormous nose, which earned him the nickname of Il Re Nasone; an athletic figure, he was careless in his dress, wearing for choice a Neapolitan fisherman's cap on his blond hair and delighting in the rough jacket, striped shirt and loose trousers of the Neapolitans who lounged on the sea-front or sauntered round the quays. For preference, he spoke the Neapolitan dialect, and indeed expressed himself with difficulty in any other language. He was good-humoured, if not thwarted, and cared nothing for what happened to anyone else as long as he was left undisturbed to those enjoyments of his appetites and that indulgence in his pleasures which were to him the beginning and end of his existence.

Ferdinand IV liked to catch fish in the bay and sell it in the market-place of Naples, haggling shrewdly over the price with the amused fishermen; he enjoyed the native dishes and especially macaroni, which he liked to eat with his fingers, and which he had been known to throw by the handful from his box in the Opera on to the crowd below.

The big, brutal man was afraid of his Queen, who could on occasions prove a screaming fury, and in order to escape from her passionate hysterics and her scathing tongue he had handed over to her every department of State, and was not in the least galled that Acton was virtually King of Naples and that everyone knew it.

Such as he was, Ferdinand Bourbon was the King, and Emma had him in her train. She had, for the first time in her life, a carriage and horses, and servants in livery, not the livery of Sir William—discretion forbade that—but still livery, and the outfit had the air of a great lady's equipage.

She threw herself with zeal into her lessons; she improved vastly in her singing; her teachers agreed that she had a superb voice. How could they do otherwise when the pupil was so beautiful and the paymaster so rich? She improved, too, with her sketching, which she found as "easy as A.B.C." In the light of Sir William's approving smile, she jotted down on paper the outline of the great mountain, which was expected to erupt at any moment. Vesuvius, dark in the brilliant light, sending forth gusts of black smoke, rising gaunt and bare from fields of lava and opulent harvests of grain and vines, was an odd subject for the fair amateur's uncertain pencil; but everything she did pleased.

Every available artist painted her portrait; a favourite pose was that of a Bacchante, and Italian admirers declared that she was exactly like those classic nymphs, attendant on the god of Wine, whose laughing faces, after the oblivion of hundreds of years, had been discovered beneath the roots of vines in the fields around the city; she was also compared to the famous Ariadne, with the firm outline, with the perfect features so voluptuously curved; a different Ariadne from that painted by George Romney.

Every Sunday Sir William took his charmer to Caserta, where among the fragrancies of orange and melon, of rose and lily, amid the sounds of mandolines and guitars, Emma was ogled and quizzed, flattered and praised; there she listened to the elegancies of the Austrian Prince who assured her that she was "a diamond of the first water and the finest creature on earth," and who, in the correct manner of a *cicisbeo* attended her to her concerts, to her bath, to her promenade.

All this excitement she wrote about in her letter of August 1st to Charles Greville. But with the cries of triumph were mingled cries of heartbreak. He had written to her at last, and not kindly, but rather with the impatience of a man bored with sentimentality and romance. He had told her bluntly that never could she be his again and that she must "oblige Sir William" and think herself fortunate for the opportunity of doing so. Emma replied in the tone of a Clarissa Harlowe.

56

Nothing could express her rage; she was all madness; he, who used to envy her smile, to advise her with cool indifference, to give herself to another man! It was too much; she suggested dreadful alternatives—if she were with him, she would murder him and slay herself; she would not have a farthing from either of the gentlemen, she would return to London and kill herself with excess of vice; her fate was a warning to young women who tried to be "good."

Greville had taught her the ways of virtue, and then cast her off again on to the path of vice. A girl that a King was sighing for to be so lightly dismissed! But she would not complain—it was enough she had the paper he had written on, the wafer that he had licked: "How I envy thee! To take the place of Emma's lips" —she would give worlds if she had had that kiss. But she could not rage long; she had a cold which made her feel very ill; besides, there was her brilliant success to write about, there was a charming present to acknowledge: "I am glad you have sent me a blue hat and gloves. My hat is universally admired through Naples."

Then a sigh of good-humoured resignation. The young love was gone—why, she must sell herself to the old man, but perhaps on her own terms. She ended her letter with the sentence: "If you affront me, I will make him marry me. God bless you for ever."

.   .   .   .   .   .

That was Emma's eighth letter and her last written to Charles Greville before she resigned herself to become the mistress of Sir William Hamilton. Her position in the society of Naples was quickly established, and she was soon acknowledged as one of the wonders of the city; Naples was always full of tourists and sight-seers, and all of these must get to see the fascinating Emma. Even discreet English ladies, careful of their reputation, contrived to gloss the thing over, when they saw they could not be received at the British Embassy on any other terms.

Useful rumours of a secret marriage were spread abroad and the Duchess of Argyle, twice a British peeress and one of the famous Misses Gunning, gave Emma her countenance when she visited Naples. Lady Elcho, too, was kind to her, and though the *salons* of many of the Neapolitan aristocracy remained closed to her, her life was as free from every social annoyance as the life of one in her odd position possibly could be. Her "attitudes" became one of the attractions of the brilliant capital.

In March 1787, a handsome young German poet, Goethe, visited Naples, and noted in the inevitable journal that every traveller to Italy felt obliged to keep: "The knight, Hamilton, who is still living here as British Ambassador, after all his dabbling in art, after all his lengthy studies in nature, has found the pinnacle of that art that nature can afford. She lives in his house, an English girl of twenty years; she is very beautiful and well-modelled. He has had a Greek robe made for her, and it suits her excellently well. When she dons it she lets down her hair, takes up a couple of shawls, and so changes her attitude, her postures and her countenance, that a man at last comes to think he is dreaming. He looks on what so many thousand artists have thought to depict in the very flesh, moving before him through many poses. She stands, she sits, she lies down, she kneels before you, now she is serious, now she is sad, now she becomes most enticing, then she withdraws, allures, approves, then gradually becomes shy. She knows how to drape the folds of her shawl to suit each pose, and how to change them again accordingly, and she makes a hundred different kinds of headgear out of the same cloth. The old knight holds the light up to her, he gives himself over heart and soul to this."

Sir William soon possessed a whole gallery of paintings of his charmer, painted by Raphael Mengs, the fashionable Neapolitan painter, by Angelica Kauffmann, by the fashionable French painter, Madame le Brun, who painted her in her favourite attitude of a Bacchante, and found her very beautiful indeed. Her face was cut on cameos and carved in stone; in every possible way her features were immortalized and her singing was almost as much admired as her beauty, and her attitudes. Sir William also gave her lessons in deportment; he tried to finish the education Charles Greville had begun; he told her how to move, how to speak, and even a little how to spell. She picked up French and Italian very quickly, and in these languages her Flintshire accent was not apparent; her youth, her vivacity, her joy in herself covered up everything that might have offended in one less lovely, or less self-assured.

It was true that the antics of the old man were a little ridiculous —*Pantaleone* in the flesh! The fine Italians laughed behind Sir William's back, the ladies smiled behind their glittering fans, the wits had their usual epigrams. The duenna, too, was most amusing; Mrs. Cadogan, to the fastidious, might rather unpleasantly fore-shadow what Emma might become, but she was, at present, a piquant contrast to Emma's rare charms.

The whole affair, to the jaded taste of Neapolitan Court society, had a delicious air of novelty. Emma's peasant manners seemed to these over-refined aristocrats to be deliciously "natural." Her simple vanity, her joyous abandon to the pleasures of the moment, her free movements, the dramatic swiftness of her poses, seemed to them to have the classic nobility associated with the antiquity then so fashionable.

To the gentlefolk, a goddess from Olympus, to the common people Emma was a saint, a madonna, an angel—to all, a wonder and a curiosity.

Emma soon reconciled herself to the loss of Greville; with a good-humoured sigh for romance she settled down to a life of com-pensation for lost illusion. She had not been in Naples a year, before she was addressing Sir William in the same tone that she had used towards her former lover. When he left her to go for a few days' hunting with the King in the park at Caserta, she wrote to him at once in the arch style she had learnt during her early adventures:

"Indeed, my dear Sir William, I am sorry. I told you one line would satisfy me. When I have no other comfort than your letters you should not so cruelly disappoint me, for I am unhappy and I don't feel right without hearing from you, and I won't forgive you —no, that I won't."

The winter was exceptionally severe for the South of Italy; snow lay in the narrow streets of Naples and frost glittered on the flat roofs of the peach-coloured houses. It was quite a different cold from the clouded damp that Emma had known in Flintshire or London, and it helped to set up her spirits, and to give a sparkle to her eyes. She went richly in satin and furs, and though those ladies of fashion who chanced to see her whispered to one another that she showed an innate vulgarity when dressed in fine clothes, and put aside her beauty with her classic robes and poses, she continued to please the gentlemen very well. Madame de Boigne and Madame le Brun might find fault with Emma, but they were in a minority.

Her theme was still herself. With unctuous delight she wrote to her protector of all her successes. She had been out to dine at one of the houses which received her and where he allowed her to go, and where there was such a profusion of food that it was impossible to describe; there were compliments, songs and sighing, and the suave Italians had brought out conventional similes of "diamond eyes" and "pearl teeth."

Purblind as he was, one there present, a certain *abbé*, had praised her— "Oh, you can't think just as if he could see me and just as if I was the most perfect beauty in the world."

Emma was pleased to tell her master also that she was praised for her "perfectly beautiful and elegantly behaved manners and conversation." She was becoming more careful too; she gave herself the air of dedicating her beauty and herself entirely to Sir William. Modestly she objected that a painting he was having done of her on a snuff-box lid was "too naked." She had her copybook phrases trippingly on the pen:

"Those beauties that only you can see shall not be exposed to the common eyes of all."

From the first few weeks of her stay in Naples she had noted his obsession, she had observed that her hold over him was very different from the hold she had had over her other lovers; she would have been a very stupid girl, if she had not remembered, and Mrs. Cadogan would have been a very remiss mother, if she had not reminded her, how very easily she had been twice left by gentlemen whom she had seemed at one time to please very much—she must not let fortune slip a third time through her fingers.

The man was old, older than he appeared under his trim exterior, and she made a grimace over that; but the defect had its advantage too; she perceived with good humour, for she was at this time without malice, that Sir William was of that age when well-bred, fastidious, and brilliant gentlemen, do very foolish things.

Indeed, she understood that she held him by the last surge of the passions, by that half-senile adoration which caused his friends to sigh, and the indifferent to snigger, and soon perceived that she might play for marriage.

The sentence over which Charles Greville had shrugged his shoulders in disdain: "If you affront me, I will make him marry me," was meant seriously.

Within a year she had become part of his life, and it was obvious to both of them that they would never separate. Even in Naples, easy as it was, she could not continue to live permanently as his mistress; already there had been some difficulties.

A Mrs. Dickinson, who had shown herself prudish on the subject of Emma, had to be, as the merry girl put it, "choked off," and even Sir William's endless tact and adroit accomplishments in all manner of petty intrigues, could not for ever maintain his false position.

Seeing Emma so admired, so successful, hearing that even the Queen was prepared to look upon her with a favourable eye, knowing very little more of her past than the easy Neapolitans knew, it did not seem to Sir William so outrageous a thing that he should marry his treasure.

Already it had been convenient to spread abroad the rumour of a secret marriage, so that the aristocratic English ladies he often had to entertain at the Embassy might feel their delicacy satisfied. Then, this success of Emma's was not the success of the ordinary kept woman who could sparkle only in doubtful circles—it was the success of a great beauty who could grace every occasion she attended; Emma did not have to play very carefully so willing a fish.

That same bitter winter when it seemed to Emma colder than it had ever been in England, she went in her favourite plain white dress with the blue sash and Leghorn hat, under, however, a pelisse of sables, to visit the Convent of Santa Romica, where the fashionable nuns led a gay and charming life, and where they received Emma, as if she had indeed been an angel from heaven, or rather an angel who had stepped from the canvas of a Correggio or Raphael. For her part Emma thought she had never seen anything quite so entrancing as the Mother Superior of this fashionable convent, who was a charming lady of twenty-nine years of age, named

61

Beatrice Acquaviva, merry and arch. Brilliants flashed on her white hands when she drew them from the depths of her fashionable muff and presented Emma with an embroidered satin pocket-book, declaring that never had she loved anyone so much; while Emma, who had seldom been so flattered by one of her own sex before, thought her "the most good and amiable woman" she had seen since she had come to Naples. Donna Beatrice was indeed very flowery in her compliments, for she not only declared that Emma looked like an angel, but she said she was a charming, kind creature, good to the poor, and noble and generous—for such a one it would be worth while to live.

To Emma's relief there was not one word of religion, but there was plenty of good things to eat: "I promise you," she wrote, "they don't starve themselves." Then with extremely bad taste, which did not however offend, she gave Sir William the nuns' opinion of his late wife, who had also visited the convent. "They did not like the looks of her—she was little, short, pinch-faced, and received coldly." How different, said the flattering nuns, from Emma, who was so tall and exactly like the marble statues they had seen when they were in the world. It was all very intoxicating and enough to turn anyone's head, and Emma found no difficulty in expressing her gratitude to "good, kind, dearest Sir William." and in writing to him as she had written to Charles Greville: "Ah, what a happy creature is your Emma. She that had no friend, no protector, nobody that I can trust [sic], and now to be the friend, the Emma of Sir William Hamilton. Oh, if I could express myself, if I have words to thank you, that I may not thus be choked with feelings for which I can find no utterance."

She was learning to play and sing Handel, and her master, of course, was delighted and declared it was the most extraordinary thing he ever knew, especially "her holding on to the notes and going from the high to the low notes so very neat," while Galucci, the musician who played the *obbligato* to her solos, seemed as if he would have gone mad with admiration. He declared that Emma would turn the heads of everyone.

Her vanity increased under this adulation, until it filled her entire world. She thought of nothing but the compliments she received and repeated them, either to Greville, with whom she renewed her correspondence, or to Sir William. She related how enchanted everybody was, not only by her beauty, but her politeness, her dramatic and musical talents—everyone who came to the Palazzo Sessa had compliments for her accomplishments, her kindness, her good Italian.

.   .   .   .   .   .

When Emma had been eighteen months in Naples, Sir William ventured to take her on a tour to some of the great country-houses, where the owners would be gracious enough to receive her. In a gorgeous villa at Sorrento Emma sang her songs and struck her attitudes to the admiration of a glittering crowd of Italian nobility. There was sea-bathing every morning and breakfast in a delicious little *gazebo* which, on a jutting rock, commanded a superb panorama of the Bay of Naples. Vesuvius was in action, its smoke darkened half the azure of the sky, and again Emma's facile pencil ran over the outlines of the rich landscape.

There was now a professor of music as well as a teacher of Latin in her train, and every evening there were singing lessons in the great painted *salon* which was lit by wax tapers and opened on to the purple night, the scene of every concert, where Emma with her heap of auburn hair, her classic robe, her rich bravura, sang to Sir William Hamilton's orchestra, arias from operas, *buffos*, some of the folk-songs of Naples; she, dressed in character, with tambourine and coloured scarf.

By then Mr. Greville had been forgiven, and she was pleased to jot down for his benefit all these triumphs, adding perhaps a little touch of exaggeration, for she wrote: "In short, I left the people of Sorrento with their heads turned, I left some dying, some crying and some in despair. Mind you, these were all nobility and proud as the Devil, but we humbled them."

The trip was in every way a success. At Ischia, an obliging Countess covered her with kisses and admired the muslin chemise with the blue sash which the English beauty had made famous. There was also a priest, who lost his wits for love of Emma, and had to be comforted with her portrait on a snuff-box. Emma, mounted on a donkey, also went some way up Vesuvius, and viewed with the complacency of one entirely self-absorbed the red-hot lava pouring down the sides of the mountain, licking up pine-trees into sheets of fire and destroying, against all precedent, a hermit's grotto in which hung several precious relics.

That same summer, while the volcano was providing an exciting background to the frivolous pleasure-makers of Naples, Emma was taken to Sir William's villa at Caserta, where he had at great expense redecorated apartments for her and provided her with a music room. Her triumphs continued and the eruption of the volcano seemed but a detail compared to the importance of Emma and Emma's beauty. She was then entertained on board a Dutch man-of-war, which came into the bay. She was given a salute of twenty cannon and a banquet, and took the seat of honour at the board where Mrs. Cadogan also found a place; the Dutchmen were overwhelmed by this vision of English beauty—the famous white muslin gown, blue sash, straw hat and auburn curls, which Emma, a little over-excited on this occasion, described "as curling round her heels" when she wrote an account of the triumph to Greville.

She had hoped to attend the Opera that night at San Carlo, when the King and Queen were to be present, but there had been so many compliments paid, so many healths drunk, and so many salvos let off that when she at last landed on the quay and got into the State coach which was to take her and the Dutch officers to Sir William's box, she found there was no time to put on the elaborate gown she had provided.

This had lately come from Paris and was a white and purple satin with spangles, and a turban with a cluster of white feathers such as the Queen of France wore. In it, Emma would have lost all distinction and looked rather like a servant-girl in her mistress's finery.

Arriving late at the Opera in the muslin and the blue sash with the flowing curls, she made, of course, a sensation.

There were other excitements to relate to Greville; "I must tell you I had great offers to be first woman in the Italian Opera at Madrid, where I was to have £6,000 for three years, but though I have not been persuaded to make a written engagement, I certainly shall sing at the Pantheon and Hanover Square except something particular happens. Sir William says he will give me leave to sing at Hanover Square. It's the most extraordinary thing that my voice is totally altered, it is the finest soprano you ever heard, and what is most extraordinary is that my shake or trill, what you call it, is so very good in every note my master says that, if he did not feel that I was a woman he would think I was an angel. Sir William is enraptured with me. He spares neither expense nor pains nor anything." It is only right, Emma added seriously, that after all this work with her singing and languages and drawing, she should have exercise, so she went out for two hours a day in Sir William's carriage.

Signora Banti, first soprano at San Carlo, had come to one of Emma's concerts and thrown herself into appropriate raptures. "Just God! What a voice! I would give a good deal for your voice!"

"In short," said Emma frankly, "I met with such applause that it almost turned my head. Banti sung after me and I assure you everyone said I sung in a finer style than her. Poor Sir William was so enraptured with me."

She had forgotten the idyll of Paddington; she was quite on good-natured terms with Charles Greville to whom, after all, she owed the introduction to Sir William. He sent her, too, charming presents, which he put down to Sir William's account. He purchased shawls, hats and gloves, for her attitudes and posing; she ended her letters with gay postscripts. "I send to you a kiss on my name. It is more than you deserve. Tell your brothers to take care of their hearts when I come back. As for you, you will be utterly undone, for Sir William already is distractedly in love, and indeed I love him tenderly. He deserves it. God bless you."

Mr. Greville was not much moved by these epistles which probably were exactly as he thought they would be. He was still, in a leisurely and patient fashion, settling his affairs. The portrait of Emma as she sat for him still stood in George Romney's studio; another connoisseur had made an offer for it; Romney asked Greville if he would care to buy it, but the Honourable Charles regretted that his purse would not run to this luxury. Circumstances, he remarked sententiously, alter and control feelings, "though it gave me some pain to part from the original of the *Seamstress*, I do not feel myself in a position to buy her picture."

65

But with unabated zest Emma continued to write to her former lover of the delicious life she was leading under the care of her new protector. In letters full of gusto and bad grammar she told him again and again of all her triumphs. When Sir William was out hunting she did the honours at the Embassy—"and they are all enchanted with me." She emphasized the point that "Sir William is really in love with me, more and more. He says he cannot live without me. In short, I am universally beloved." She sang tender arias that made everybody cry, the first tenor of the Opera accompanied her in melting, romantic duets, but when she was crossed Emma quickly reverted to the mood of Up Park. A certain Mrs. Stratford wished to come and stay at the Embassy, but Emma soon stopped that, and inspired Sir William to write that, if the lady wished to come to Naples, she might stay at an inn; then, Emma quickly made herself mistress of a letter which proved Mrs. Stratford to be by no means discreet, at which Emma was not slow in at once giving the lady a coarse name which might very well have been applied to herself by the ill-natured or the prudish.

Her self-assurance became overwhelming. "Sir William tells me I am necessary to his happiness and I am the handsomest, loveliest, cleverest, best creature in the world and no person shall come to disturb me."

In the spring of 1789 Emma accompanied the British Minister on a long excursion into Calabria, where Emma played at being a good, obliging girl, who did not mind a little hardship, and quickly acquired a reputation for good-humour by not grumbling at the mean accommodation of the Italian inns. These poor chambers were, no doubt, at least as comfortable as had been those in the cottage at Hawarden.

On her return Sir William did up her apartment for her at the cost of £4,000. He was beginning to spend money very freely. Emma cost him a good deal more than she had cost Mr. Greville; large sums went in portraits and statues to commemorate her exuberant charms; Madame Le Brun received £100 for painting Emma with a wine-cup and an enormous quantity of chestnut hair which completely covered her.

Emma's own allowance was not large, no more than £200 a year for herself and her mother, but then, everything was paid for

66

her, and hardly a day passed but that she received presents. Much as she valued these there was one splendour for which she was constantly sighing. She often coaxed and pleaded with Sir William to give her diamonds, and in 1790 he gratified her longing by an offering of these precious stones, which he had bought at a bargain price of £500 and which made Emma supremely happy for quite a long while.

The old man was now completely in her toils—he could no more escape from his Emma than the fly can escape from the jar of honey into which it falls. After nearly five years as his mistress, Emma was living as his wife and doing the honours of the Embassy, presiding at concerts, balls and entertainments; the lucky young woman had the sense to try to behave herself: "I wish to be an example of good conduct, to show the world that a pretty woman is not always a fool," she wrote to Greville. In the same letter she apprised him of an approaching visit she and Sir William were paying to London; Greville need not be afraid of her behaviour in England. She was used, she said, to fine society: "On Monday last we gave a concert and ball at our house. I had near four hundred persons, all the foreign ministers and their wives, all the first ladies of fashion, foreigners and Neapolitans. Sir William dressed me in white satin, no colour about me, but my hair and cheeks; I was without powder. As it was the first great assembly we had given publicly, all the ladies strove to outdo one another in dress and jewels. Sir William said I was the finest jewel among them." The letter ended complacently. "We shall be with you in the spring and return here in November, and the next year you may pay us a visit. We shall be glad to see you. I shall always esteem you for your relationship to Sir William, and as having been the means of me knowing him. As for Sir William, I confess to you I dote on him, nor can I ever love any person but him."

Greville was not impressed by this letter with its rather impertinent air of patronage, and its complete change of front. Since the day she had written: "All must be as God and Greville pleases," he had not understood what lay behind her excitement, what serious purpose was concealed by these flourishes of pretty vanity.

THE MAKING OF A GREAT LADY

'PATRIOTISM IS A KIND OF RELIGION—IT IS THE EGG FROM WHICH
WARS ARE HATCHED'

(G. DE MAUPASSANT)

IN June 1791, Sir William and Emma were back in London.
Greville was shocked to see them openly living together; he
thought this an outrage on propriety, which might have been
possible in Naples, but which would not be tolerated in London.
Emma laughed and Sir William smiled.

On September 6th, 1791, they were married at Marylebone
Church with the Marquis of Abercorn and a Mr. Dutens as witnesses. Emma signed the register "Amy Lyon," writing the name
for the last time; in the *Gazette* announcing the marriage she was
described as Miss Hart.

Charles Greville was greatly vexed—he felt he had been fooled;
there had been no talk of marriage in his bond, and his relations
with his wealthy uncle became as cold and stiff as he dared make
them. The letters exchanged were somewhat frigid in tone, but
what did Emma care? There were others in London who were
delighted to welcome her with tears of lively gratitude. George
Romney received her as if indeed she had been a vision from that
brighter world which was fast being clouded over for him. For
some time he had been sinking deeper into those glooms which
were soon to close for ever over his anguished mind. He had
ceased to take much pleasure in life and regarded his beloved art
as so much hack-work, and he was spending his time in sombre,
solitary reveries, when Emma stepped into the studio, radiant in a
Turkish dress, announcing her triumph, her marriage, showing
off her resplendent beauty, which had increased since Romney had
last painted her, and was now indeed in its full flower.

He at once began to sketch and paint her again, put all other work aside that he might study from this model. He named her "The Divine Lady," adding: "I cannot give her any other epithet, for I think her superior to all womankind." He was commissioned to paint two pictures of her for that expert in female beauty, the Prince of Wales. He even went so far as to abandon his usual unsocial habits and to give a party for her in his studio, where she might display her attitudes. In terms of hyperbole he wrote of this occasion to his friend Hayley: "She performed those both the serious and the comic to admiration, both in singing and acting, but her Nina surpassed anything I ever saw. The whole company were in an agony of sorrow and her acting was simple, grand, terrible, pathetic. My mind was so much heated that I was for running down to fetch you up to see her."

Soon after, the charming lady, absorbed as she was in a thousand pleasures, neglected her visits to the studio, and Romney, suspecting unjustly a studied neglect, fell into a deeper gloom, and wrote: "It is highly probable that none of the pictures will be finished, except I find her more friendly than she appeared to me the last time I saw her." The painter's terrible affliction took the form of doubt and suspicion, and he was already so unbalanced in mind as to see even in the blooming, friendly face of Emma, coldness and disdain. A few days later Emma had returned and the painter was in raptures. "Sketching the most beautiful head of her I have ever painted yet, for her mother," and noting, "I think indeed she is cordial with me as ever and she laments very much that she is to leave England without seeing you."

He painted her also as Joan of Arc, a brilliant headpiece, which was left unfinished.

Emma's poses and songs were successful everywhere; she was offered £2,000 a year and two benefits to sing at the Opera, and Sir William said complacently that "he had engaged her and for life." As a climax to all this London gaiety and excitement, the bridegroom took his Emma to see the millionaire hermit of Fonthill, William Beckford, a man much of his own type, save that he chanced to be a genius; the two men were cousins, one degree removed, and had always maintained friendly relations. Beckford was rather more than eccentric; his reputation was tarnished by scandalous rumours that were never either completely proved or disproved. No one knew whether William Beckford had with-drawn in cold disdain from a world he despised or retired in panic from the hostility of his fellows. Sir William, at least, did not care, and to Emma, Fonthill and Beckford were a kind of peep-show, to be gaped at without being understood.

Fonthill, in Wiltshire, where the author of *Vathek*, the most gifted amateur that ever graced English literature, lived in gorgeous retirement with a French *abbé* and a few obsequious companions, was a nightmare imagined by a genius. William Beckford had pulled down the handsome mansion that his father, the wealthy Lord Mayor, had raised, and had built a fantasy, only possible to a genius and a millionaire, with a monstrous top-heavy tower, which had cost £20,000, an English park circled by walls that gave an air of Eastern scenery to a domain that was like a dream of Asia, expressed in the terms of the Gothic revival.

Beckford's huge chambers and long galleries were filled by treasures that were reputed to be of fabulous value; odd proportions, fantastic objects, lofty ceilings, arched windows, gave an air of bizarre enchantment to this weird interior, to which Beckford had endeavoured to give the lurid, smoky atmosphere of the Hall of Eblis.

The huge fortune and large income (£1,000,000 in hand and £100,000 a year) that Beckford derived from his Jamaican estate, were expended in this outlandish display, in the midst of which he moved, not in the guise of a wizard or Arabian potentate, but in that of a fastidious English gentleman, delicate and slender, with a fine profile and attired in neat green and buff; he was then under forty years of age and engaged in building a vast abbey in his grounds.

Sir William viewed his cousin's statues, pictures and prints, with shrill cries of envy—but he would not, for all the nightmare of virtuosity that encumbered Fonthill, have surrendered one charm of the wifely Emma, who hung so coaxingly on his arm, and who so prettily pressed Mr. Beckford to visit the British Embassy at Naples.

. . . . .

Only an eccentric like Beckford could have condoned this crazy marriage, for the rest, London had sniggered, gossiped, and held aloof.

Sir William's relatives had done what they could to dissuade him from so ridiculous a match, but he had replied with pettish humour that he was marrying Emma "for himself alone"; in that he was mistaken.

Horace Walpole remarked that "Sir William was marrying his gallery of antique statues" and added pertinently, that he was surprised that there should be so much talk of the classic Emma's change of expression, since expression was what antiques did not possess. However, the difficult wit admitted that Lady Di, who had seen one of Emma's displays, had found that her poses were very beautiful and striking. But the new Lady Hamilton, according to her custom, avoided all society where she was not likely to be received with applause, and decided soon to quit that London where she might meet one of the gentlemen from Up Park, some-one who had seen her as a nursemaid, as a grisette, as the quiet little mistress of Charles Greville.

Thomas Lawrence painted her—finding her "very agreeable to the eye of an artist." Romney tried to hurry through as many likenesses of her as possible in the time she could give him, Sir Joshua Reynolds represented her as a laughing Bacchante. In his white mansion on the green banks of the Thames at Richmond, where weeping-willows and stately swans, floating on the grey river, found a pretty background for some of the more broad-minded of London society, the Duke of Queensberry entertained the bride—the handsome Bacchante was quite agreeable to one who had the reputation of being a satyr.

There Horace Walpole at last saw the famous poses and was ravished—Emma's singing, too, was admirable—she sung "Nina" to perfection.

There was a dark side to these triumphs; despite his friendship with the King, Sir William dared not take his lady to Court; the wife of the British Minister at Naples had to leave London without dropping a curtsy to the Queen.

Charlotte of Mecklenburg-Strelitz, with her plain, pug face, her Bible and her wool-work, her happy marriage that had not created happiness for others, was not considered of much importance in a society where virtue was associated with dullness, but she remained staunch to her ideals; she had heard something of the past of Lady Hamilton, and Emma was not received at St. James's Palace.

Paris held compensations. Emma powdered the rich fleece of hair, put in it, among her feathers, her five hundred pounds' worth of diamonds, laced herself into brocaded satins, and made her curtsy before the Queen of France, whose weak eyes were already stained with secret weeping, whose haughty face had long since hardened into a passive defiance of an implacable destiny.

The National Assembly had been sitting for nearly two years, in this September of 1791, and France was already split from side to side by the first shudderings of the incredible upheaval that was soon to come.

But on the surface—and it was always on the surface with Emma—Paris was gay enough, with the fading chestnut-trees yellow in the thick golden air, with the smart shops in the Palais Royal showing a seductive array of novelties for an Ambassador's lady's choice, with the gaily curtained windows through which less fortunate Emmas peeped to see if any rich old men were looking up, the well-filled theatres, the costly equipages that rolled over the cobbles, and only here and there a hint of change in a short-haired, dark-trousered deputy, in the tone of the free caricatures in the print-shop windows, in the tricolour stuck here and there incongruously, in the distant mutter of the ironic refrain—*liberté, égalité, fraternité.*

So, with no notion of the first whisperings of the whirlwind that was blowing so near, Sir William and his Emma rolled back to Naples across the Italian cornfields and vineyards, through the last profusion of autumn flowers and under gaudy southern skies, with the Hamilton livery on the lackeys, and maids, and quantities of baggage.

Emma's gratitude to her kind husband overflowed; by the simple standards of her class he had made an "honest woman of her," she was now honourable and innocent, a wedding-ring had dowered her with all the virtues necessary to gain feminine respect.

She had taken many poses in real life besides those she had taken in "the attitudes," and now she had assumed another, as novel as delicious, that of the married woman.

Her reception at Naples exceeded her expectations; since she

delighted in describing her own triumphs, she detailed her success
to poor George Romney in a letter that besought him to come to
Naples, a kindly thought; Sir William would pay the expenses,
and it would be delicious to have the adoring painter at her feet in
Naples.

There was honest satisfaction with her astonishing luck, mingled
with the hypocritical phrases that Emma felt to be proper to the
occasion.

"I have been received with open arms by all the Neapolitans of
both sexes, by all the foreigners of every distinction. I have been
presented to the Queen of Naples by her own desire. (She [h]as
shown me all sorts of kind and affectionate attentions. In short, I
am the happiest woman in the world. Sir William is fonder of me
every day, and I hope he will have no cause to repent of what he
[h]as done; for I feel so grateful to him, that I think I shall never
be able to make him amends for his goodness to me. But why do
I tell you this? You know me enugh. You were the first dear
friend I opened my heart to. You ought to know me, for you have
seen and discoursed with me in my poorer days. You have known
me in my poverty and prosperity, and I had no occasion to have liv'd
for years in poverty and distress, if I had not felt something of
virtue in my mind. Oh, my dear Friend! for a time I own through
distress my virtue was vanquish'd. But my sense of virtue was not
overcome. How gratefull now then do I feel to my dear, dear,
husband, that [h]as restored peace to my mind, that [h]as given me
honor, rank, and, what is more, innocence and happiness. Rejoice
with me, my dear Sir, my friend, my more than father. Believe
me, I am still that same Emma you knew me. If I could forget for
a moment what I was, I ought to suffer. Command me in anything I can do for you here. Believe me, I shall have a real pleasure. Come to Naples, and I will be your model:—anything to
induce you to come, that I may have an oppertunity to shew you
my gratitude to you. Take care of your health for all our sakes.
How does the pictures go on? Has the Prince been to you? Write
to me."

Then Emma had another kind thought; she wanted to pay a
compliment to Mr. Dutens, who had been one of the witnesses at
her marriage before the altar which had replaced that where

Hogarth's Rake had stood with his old heiress—would Romney give him the little picture of herself that he had painted?

It was a valuable present, and Emma had not paid for it; she always contrived so that others paid for everything to do with her; when Mr. Greville himself had become coldly restive about paying for little Emma, the mother had contrived to shift the bothersome child on to Sir William—a protégée of her's, whom she was looking after out of kindness—how often the word occurred in Emma's affairs!

Sir William accepted this simple tale without question and the Blackburns continued to receive little Emma's allowance but from the uncle instead of from the nephew.

The new Ambassadress's first winter at Naples was a triumph; when the Queen had received her, everyone else could do so.

"We have a many English at Naples as Ladys Malmsbury, Malden, Plymouth, Carneigee, Wright, &c. They are very kind and attentive to me. They all make it a point to be remarkably civil to me. You will be happy at this as you know what prudes our ladies are."

She was quite happy at it herself; at last she had learned all she ever need know—how to please a gentleman who was worth pleasing.

She told Romney that she was reading *The Triumphs of Temper* by his friend Hayley, and that nothing had vexed her since her marriage-day—with respectability had come peace, and Sir William should never fear that she would be out of humour.

It was not only her amiability that held her husband; he was sixty years of age, and she was the last love of this *flâneur* who had had too many loves; with the last despairing ardour of failing passions he doted upon her superb femininity, which was a little more costly than any other treasure he had ever bought, but undoubtedly more worth the price.

.   .   .   .   .

The Queen of Naples had her reasons for receiving so graciously the new Lady Hamilton; European affairs had changed in the five years since Maria Carolina had first heard of the new English lady at the Palazzo Sessa who might amuse her royal husband as transiently as so many other women had amused him; Sir William was no longer, to the Queen, a mere agreeable companion, a pleasant ornament of her idle Court, he was the representative of Great Britain, a country which, in the present combination of European politics, might prove of infinite importance to the Sicilian Bourbons.

It was obvious that his wife dominated him, and therefore obvious that the Queen must gain over the wife. Maria Carolina did not find this either difficult or distasteful; the daughter of the Cæsars and the English peasant-girl had much in common. Emma, who had dragged herself up from the mud solely by the adroit use of her charms, was no more stupid, vulgar, selfish or hysterical than the high-bred daughter of an Emperor. Indeed, in a comparison between the two women's characters Emma would have had the advantage; she was neither so vindictive, so superstitious, nor so pretentious as the Queen, who, besides, lacked all the good humour that softened the Englishwoman's monstrous vanity.

.   .   .   .

Maria Carolina had been born in Vienna on August 13th, 1752, and was therefore three years older than her sister, Marie Antoinette, Queen of France. In the spring of 1768 she had been married to Ferdinand the Fourth. Her betrothal had followed the death of two sisters, both destined to be Queens of Naples. On the birth of the Crown Prince in 1775 she had received a seat on the Council and had begun to dominate entirely Neapolitan politics; she and her favourite, Sir John Acton, an English baronet, from 1791, entirely ruled the kingdom between them—her supreme authority being only occasionally disturbed by outbursts of jealousy from the King, such as that which had set the French Chargé d'affaires gossiping in 1778. The misgovernment of the Queen and the rapacity of her minister were both an agony and a jest in Naples. Her mischief-making was incessant, her domination absolute; she regarded Naples and every person and everything in the country as her children's patrimony, to be treated as she pleased; she had no ideals higher than those of Court and intrigue, and her keenest ambition was to unite herself to Austria by intermarriages between her children and those of the other members of the House

75

of Hapsburg. It was said of her *"la vie de la reine n'est qu'une longue crise de vapeurs."* When her brother, the Emperor Joseph the second, died in 1790 and Leopold, Grand Duke of Tuscany, succeeded, the Queen contrived an alliance between Naples and the Empire, which took the form of a triple wedding—her daughter Teresa married the Emperor's eldest son, the Archduke Francis of Tuscany, Amelia married the Archduke Ferdinand; the Prince Royal, still too young to marry, was affianced to the Princess Clementine, sister of the Archdukes. This was very satisfactory to the restive Queen, who, ruling as an absolute monarch in Naples, and having her children handsomely betrothed or married, might have considered that things were going very well for her, had it not been for the horribly disagreeable news from France.

Although, like too many members of her House and like most of those of her husband's House, the Queen kept her eyes shut to everything about her, save what happened in her intimate circle, and although she had no conception of modern tendencies or of the trend of events in Europe, she could not for long remain oblivious of the French upheaval, which seemed likely to cast the thrones of her sister and brother-in-law into ruin. Maria Carolina possessed much of that passionate family affection which is largely passionate family pride. She was a good mother and her children were loved with the fierce possessiveness of the tigress for her cubs.

There could not have been much personal feeling in her anxious love for Marie Antoinette, who had left Vienna to be married in her fifteenth year. Two years afterwards Maria Carolina herself had departed for Naples, so that the sisters had known each other only as children. They were, however, sisters, and Royal sisters, and Maria Carolina could not forget that the present Queen of France was a Hapsburg. She was terrified, moreover, on her own account; her husband was a Bourbon and not superior in intelligence, courage or resource, to Louis XVI, though his very vices might make him more popular in Naples than the King of France had ever been in Paris. As the French Revolution spread, from the year 1789 to the years 1791–92, when Lady Hamilton installed herself in triumph in the Palazzo Sessa, Maria Carolina was watching with intense alarm and fury the progress of events in her sister's Kingdom.

The Liberal ideas that began to be voiced under the Gironde, and that seemed to so many ardent and sensitive people all over Europe like so many messages of hope and relief, were to the Queen of Naples incredibly vile and dangerous, but what really shocked her so deeply that she lost all the little patience and reason that she might have ever possessed was the knowledge that these same hideous doctrines were creeping into her own Kingdom.

Like all arbitrary governors, she and Sir John Acton employed an elaborate system of espionage, and through this they learned that the brilliant intellectuals of Naples, the cultured aristocracy, and the scholarly middle classes were riddled by what the Queen termed "the blackest treachery," but which was in reality an enthusiastic enquiry into all modern and liberal ideas and a grave, if necessarily secret, resolve to reform their own country.

When the Queen had first come to Naples, she had dabbled a little in philosophy, in poetry and music; she had loved to preside at meetings in elegant drawing-rooms where ladies touched the harpsichord or the guitar, where there were charming little philosophic discussions between learned priests and flattering blue-stockings, and, ignorant and stupid as she was, she had been quick to catch up a few superficial catchwords and stale witticisms, which had been sufficient to give one of Royal birth a reputation for culture and intelligence.

But when the Queen heard that these same witty ladies whom she had patronized, these same learned abbés, doctors, botanists, antiquarians and scientists, were meeting together under the excuse of freemasonry, clubs, literary societies and academies, to discuss politics, her rage and fear amounted to panic.

She and Sir John Acton at once resolved to crush all Liberal tendencies in Naples as swiftly as they would have crushed a poisonous snake, had it come winding among the luscious dishes of a picnic held on the grass of the Palace lawns.

This, however, was not to be so easily accomplished, even by a Queen with a furious passion for governing and a minister willing to obey her in every detail. The Government of the Kingdom of Naples embodied a chaotic mass that had originated in Roman,

77

Ecclesiastical and Feudal Law, on which had been superimposed the Charters of the various conquerors of the country from the Norman to the Arragonese. Such efficient laws as there were a system of complete and shameless corruption prevented from being carried into effect. Naples, on which the Queen now cast such an angry and suspicious eye, was, next to Paris, the largest city in Europe. Out of a population of 437,000, 30,000 were *lazzaroni*, vagabonds, fishermen or small tradesmen. There was a large population of idlers, who lived at the expense of the wealthy, as well as some heavily endowed convents and nunneries. Added to these two burdens on the State was the enormous number of monks and priests, of whom there was said to be one in every twenty-two of the population. Neither the Queen nor Sir John Acton, however, nor even the King himself, had any dislike to the *lazzaroni*, the monks, priests and nuns, and the idlers whom they maintained, for these were loyal to the House of Bourbon and wished for no reform whatever in a system of government under which they did so remarkably well.

What the Queen began to dread was the native aristocracy and the literary and scientific men who, under noble patronage, had founded many new Chairs in the University of Naples, Academies of Painting, Sculpture and Architecture, had endowed libraries and museums, founded a school of anatomy, a chemical laboratory, and a botanical garden.

The reports that the Royal spies brought in showed the Queen with alarming clearness that all these people, including many of the greatest families in the Kingdom, were infected with the new doctrine which seemed to have taken such appalling hold in France, and without a second's pause to consider what might be the rights or wrongs of the matter, who these people really were and what they really represented, Maria Carolina began at once to regard them as her natural enemies, as a most dangerous menace to her House and her family, to be stamped out at the first possible opportunity.

When, at the end of 1791, the Queen so warmly welcomed Lady Hamilton not only to her Court, but to her bosom, she had been for some time harassed by all these terrible problems, of which the "lady of the poses" knew nothing.

78

On the Queen's return from Vienna, where she had been to be present at the wedding of her children to their cousins, the King and Queen had heard much disturbing news of the state of Europe. They had stopped at Rome, and had there found, living under Papal protection, the two aunts of Louis XVI, the Princesses Adelaide and Victoire, who had thought it well to hasten from Paris before the tide of revolution rose any higher. These ladies had entertained Maria Carolina with heartrending accounts of the plight of the Royal Family of France, of the abominable behaviour of the revolutionaries, and of the incredible martyrdom that appeared to be waiting for the Hapsburg Princess who was Queen of France and Navarre.

Maria Carolina had returned to Naples in a state of fierce nervous tension. She resolved not to find herself in her sister's predicament, if energy or ingenuity could prevent it; she began by heavily policing the city, putting the new force under the command of a certain Luigi di Medici, on whom she believed she could rely. She also greatly extended the espionage system so that nobody, neither the professor in his laboratory, nor the poet in his cabinet, nor the lawyer studying his case, nor the peaceful family in their parlour, was free from the observation and snares of spies. Everything that was Liberal, that was cultured, that was advanced, that was free, was to be suppressed, and, if possible, persecuted. Not idle in other directions, the Queen, who possessed the extraordinary energy that shallow, passionate women so often misdirect, started on shipbuilding by day and night, filled the arsenals with cannons and munitions of all kinds, quartered troops in every village in the Kingdom, called upon the nobles to supply horses and horsemen, conscripted the peasants, and invited foreign volunteers to enrol themselves as hirelings in the Neapolitan Army.

The progress of the revolution in France justified Maria Carolina's most sombre fears; every time she opened the *Gazette* she read bad news. She shared her alarms, her misgivings, and her furies with her dear Lady Hamilton, who, thus whirled so suddenly into high politics, knew nothing about any of it, but was quite sure that a Queen in distress must be right and was perfectly prepared passionately to champion the woman who offered her this dazzling friendship. Nothing would have pleased her better than to help her agonized Majesty to the best of her power, but for the moment there did not seem anything she could do. Sir William was harassed and did not know which way the British Government would lead; he found the whole imbroglio inexpressibly boring—why did a world which held the Tuscan vases and Emma, music and soft Italian airs, also hold revolutionaries, wars, and such tiresome creatures as reformers and idealists?

It seemed as if England would allow the French to turn their country upside down unaided. In 1792 William Pitt declared that he expected fifteen years of peace; the same year saw the Empire and Prussia at grips with France.

Maria Carolina, distracted with ravaging emotions, wished above everything to help her sister and her brother-in-law, but she had not the power to move either hand or foot.

After the King and Queen of France had been taken back to Paris from their abortive flight to Varennes, the Emperor had refused to receive the French Ambassador at Vienna, and the Baron de Talleyrand had resigned his post at Naples leaving his secretary, as chargé d'affaires. Maria Carolina did what she could by withdrawing the Neapolitan Ambassador, the Marchese di Circillo, from Paris, and by permitting him to intrigue with the French émigrés at Brussels. She dared not, however, break off all diplomatic relations with France and she was obliged to accept M. de Mackau, the new Ambassador sent by the Gironde Government. He chanced to be an aristocrat, his mother had been "*gouvernante des enfants de France*." and so, he was able to make himself more or less tolerable at the Court at Naples, where he preached moderation and tried to break the Austrian alliance.

The atmosphere of Naples was tense with fear and rage, the Queen hating and dreading the French, the aristocracy and the intellectuals hating and dreading the Queen and the Court, war rumbling in the background and no one knowing which way Bellona would unloose her hounds, while the representative of Britain fussed and lamented, did not quite know what to do, and tried to forget everything in the pleasure of the concerts where Emma sang, or of the receptions where she posed in her alcove.

The Queen went as far as she dared in affronting France, and it was further than most women would have dared; but when the

Neapolitan frigate, the *Sirene*, chased two Algerian pirates into French waters, Naples had to apologize to Paris. There were some affronts, however, that the Queen could not swallow. When M. de Mackau put up the tricolour cockade before his residence, and then waited on the King on August 24th, when the news of the taking of the Tuileries had reached Naples, the Queen showed her hand and refused to receive the representative of revolutionaries and rebels. Nor could M. de Mackau obtain satisfaction though a stormy scene passed between him and Sir John Acton.

The Queen of Naples's brother, Leopold, died and was succeeded by his son Francis, who was married to Maria Carolina's daughter.

A Republic was proclaimed in France and M. de Mackau, although his papers were from Louis XVI, performed a sharp *volte-face* and remained in Naples as representative of the French people; he was watched by the Neapolitan police and Court spies to see that he was not in touch with the aristocrats and the intellectuals whom Maria Carolina termed "revolutionaries and Jacobins."

Hysterical with fear and vexation, however, the Queen had to give way on the arrival of a French Fleet in the bay and of the news of the defeat of the Austrians and Prussians at Valmy, followed by that of the French invasion of Nice and Savoy; Britain did not move, no satisfaction was to be gained from Sir William or his sympathetic lady. Naples had to play for time and recognize the French Republic, while M. de Mackau, tricolour or no, had to be received at the Court of Naples.

.   .   .   .   .   .

All these excitements Emma looked upon as the necessary, rather monotonous background of a diplomatic life—they disturbed her no more than the sullen rumblings and lurid flashes from Vesuvius did. After all, the mountain had never yet dangerously erupted during her stay in Naples, and the revolution might be equally considerate. She continued her entertainments, her trips on horseback along the enchanting coast, and her sailings in a canopied boat on the bay, nor did she cease to practise her songs and her music, to invent new attitudes to charm Sir William and his guests.

The old Minister, however, did not enjoy any diversion, not even his Emma's poses, with his former relish. The excitement of pursuing, possessing, and marrying Emma had been rather exhausting for one of his decaying physique. He began, despite his care of his health, to pay for a lifetime of persistent, if elegant, indulgence, and during the summer of 1792 was continually laid up with attacks of biliousness and dysentery, which caused Emma to think rather dubiously of the future. It caused her also to think of Charles Greville, and to play with a not altogether displeasing idea. Perhaps, after all, they might enjoy the old man's money together. In the end of the year she wrote to him very formally, the aunt to the nephew by marriage, with fitting sentiment and emotionalism:

"Dear Sir,

"I have the pleasure to inform you that Sir William is out of danger and very well considering the illness he has had to battle with. He has been fifteen days in bed with a bilious fever, and I have been almost as ill with anxiety, apprehension and fatigue. His disorder has been long gathering and was a liver complaint. I need not tell you, my dear Mr. Greville, what I have suffered. . . . I was eight days without undressing, eating or sleeping."

Emma found, however, as usual, compensation. "The English ladies and the Neapolitans have been so kind; though they were at Caserta, fifteen miles from Naples, Lady Plymouth, Lady Webster, several others, have sent twice a day, the King and Queen, morning and night, the most flattering messages."

Still, as Emma reflected, what would all this mean if Sir William were lost? "For surely no happiness is like ours. We live but for one another. Pray excuse me," added the lady of sensibility, "but you, sir, who loved Sir William, may figure to yourself my situation at that moment."

Emma had not written to the Honourable Charles wholly in an attempt to revive her charming image in his dry heart, nor to remind him how dutifully she had nursed his uncle through an unbecoming illness. She entrusted him with a little commission which did credit to her good nature.

Would he please see that her grandmother, whose address was still Mrs. Kidd, Hawarden, Flintshire, received the £20 that

Emma had undertaken to send her every Christmas? "I have two hundred a year for nonsense and it would be hard if I could not give her twenty pounds, as she has so often given me her last shilling."

The order was not to be got from Sir William, as he was too ill, and as Emma did not seem able to raise the money herself, why, would Mr. Greville pay it? Sir William would refund later. "The fourth of November last I had a dress on that cost £25. . . . Believe me, I felt unhappy all the while I had it on."

Yet Emma had not been able to save the price of these fineries to send to her old grandmother, but must have this charity put to Sir William's account.

This letter was written in December, and in the following February exciting news came to Naples. Chauvin, the Minister of the French Republic, had been asked to leave London, and war had been declared by Great Britain on France in February, 1793.

This was some balm to the woes, lamentations, and hysterical excitement, of the Queen of Naples, whom Emma had done her best to comfort and support during those anxious winter months.

.   .   .   .   .   .

Not only the Queen, but the woman, had been outraged by the terrible accounts of her sister's suffering; Maria Carolina endured almost step by step the martyrdom of Marie Antoinette, until, on the news of the arrest of Louis XVI and his family, she had sunk for a while, overwhelmed by this blow, which struck not only at her family affection, but her firmly rooted family pride, and her implacable belief in the sanctity of royalty.

Emma sympathized passionately with all this Royal fury. She was willing to believe that all Frenchmen were monsters, the Queen of France a saint. She took an eager part in the campaign, instigated by the Queen, which made the lives of every French person living in Naples, every liberal-minded person, from aristocrats to shopkeepers, insupportable; the drama in which she lived enriched her personality. When she sang her dramatic songs, her voice took on a fuller, more emphatic note; when she struck her impressive attitudes, they became those of an avenging goddess, hastening to rescue a Queen in distress. A certain womanly

83   G

affection grew up between these two vain, undisciplined creatures; Emma became really fond of Maria Carolina, who to her was indeed adorable, a gracious Queen, a devoted mother, a charming friend. Unhampered by any scruples, delicacy or reserve, the two women gossiped, lamented, condoled together, with freedom and zest, they had many vices and a few virtues in common. The Queen gave Emma carriages and horses with her livery; they wandered together in the huge gardens of Caserta or sat in the sun-washed chambers of the palace; they strolled together to the baths or loitered side by side in groves of tamarisk and myrtle, the Queen raving about the atrocious horrors of the French Revolution, the insolence of the Neapolitan aristocracy, the appalling growth of atheism and republicanism in the world, and Emma listening eagerly, and agreeing heartily, and with complete sincerity.

.　　.　　.　　.　　.　　.

Maria Carolina was not without personal attractions, and they were such as would be likely to impress Emma Hamilton; Her Majesty was then forty years of age and still possessed a certain beauty, a smooth pink and white Hapsburg complexion, the full, impressive, Hapsburg underlip, blue eyes, keen and formidable, but, like those of Marie Antoinette, weak and red-lidded. Her jaw was too powerful, her forehead too high. Though her walk was majestic, her limbs were clumsy; her arms and hands, however, were well-rounded and delicate. Some critics considered her far more beautiful than the Queen of France, some far less. Both the sisters were able to play the dignified Princess to perfection, and looked superb with towering structures of hair, knots of jewels, clusters of ribbons and feathers, gems and pearls on the corsage, like a cuirass, with embroidery and trailing brocades, and satins in yards of stiff, flounced skirts. Both these Austrian arch-duchesses were very suited to sit for a *portrait de parade*, and both could very well become a throne, both were as much in place in the grandeur of a State ball as they were disastrously out of place in the state cabinet.

Maria Carolina, however, unlike Marie Antoinette, had no passion for dress, and on ordinary occasions was as careless and as untidy as Emma herself, and, in a neglected chamber-robe, with

her hair unbound, lost her beauty and her distinction and disappointed the spectator as much as did Emma, when she descended
from the dais, put out the candles, took off her Greek robe and
slipped into an unbecoming, fashionable dress.

.   .   .   .   .   .

The menace of the French Revolution became an obsession
with the harassed Queen; she did not lack energy or courage and
would willingly have cast herself against France with every ducat
and every soldier she could raise.

But neither the King, comfortable and complacent, nor Sir
John Acton, cynical and incapable, dared to make any stand against
the arms of the Republic so oddly victorious.

A painful incident forcibly brought home to Maria Carolina
her utter helplessness.

The French Minister at Genoa, Semonville, had been writing
and publishing pamphlets in favour of Republicanism, despite the
efforts of Sir John Acton, who continued to intrigue against him at
the Porte, where he had afterwards been sent. Semonville complained to his Government and soon after the French Fleet under
the command of Admiral La Touche put into Naples and demanded satisfaction, *égal à égal* for the treatment that Semonville
had received in Constantinople. This was a day of acute humiliation
for the Neapolitan Court, and one of great satisfaction for the intellectuals of Naples.

Not only did the warships of France overawe the great city and
overwhelm the frigates in the bay, not only did the loathed tricolours flutter by the dozen in the same air as that which Maria
Carolina breathed, but a simple grenadier of the National Guard
came ashore, walked unescorted and unarmed to the imposing
entrance of the Royal Palace, and delivered a sharp ultimatum from
Admiral La Touche. The guns of the French Fleet were pointed
on Naples and King Ferdinand had one hour in which to decide
whether they should be fired or not.

While the Republican soldier waited contemptuously amid the
leering, timid, Bourbon lackeys in the gilded antechamber, Ferdinand, flabby with fright, dictated terms of abject submission in
his painted cabinet.

Naples cringed before the Convention, and the ponderous French ships moved slowly out of the bay, in the pocket of La Touche the grovelling surrender of the Sicilian Bourbon.

There were many Neapolitans who watched the departure of the tricolour with keen regret.

.   .   .   .   .   .

This incident was a horrible warning to the Queen that she was not strong enough to strike at France; she felt her position to be intolerable and resorted to foolish, treacherous, and cruel means to gain her ends. Maria Carolina was the type to whom La Rochefoucauld referred, when he wrote of those who "were rogues because they had not wit enough to be honest."

Never for one second could the passionate woman see any points of view save her own, nor even dimly realize that an honourable, tolerant policy might bring success where dishonourable fanaticism would fail.

The Queen was unleashed for mischief; in all her designs she had Sir John Acton, "endowed with every talent necessary for intrigue," at her service, and Emma, representing Great Britain, to flatter and encourage. Little did Emma know or care what might be the outcome of it all, she was the Queen's champion and reckless of everything save the moment's enjoyment.

Maria Carolina did what she dared to annoy and insult the Minister of the French Republic in Naples, but she was forced to countenance the sending of a Neapolitan Ambassador, the Prince di Castelcicala, to Paris, while she filled her arsenals, equipped her army and navy, and strengthened her secret police and her spies.

The political position of Naples was not good; the King was on bad terms with his nearest neighbour, the Pope, to whom he had refused the annual tribute of a white hackney with eight thousand ounces of gold, which had been sent to Rome by all former Kings of Naples.

M. de Mackau cunningly exploited this trouble between the two countries, and the Papal States themselves were being irritated and insulted by Mackau's secretary, the parvenu Hugo de Bassville, who, under the excuse of negotiating with His Holiness, was making himself very unpleasant in the streets of the Eternal City, call-ing the Cardinals "Purple geese of the Capitol," and referring to the two refugee Princesses, the daughters of Louis XV, as the *Demoiselles Capet*.

The haughty Romans soon put an end to this irritating foreigner; acting under Mackau's orders, Bassville spoke to Cardinal Zelada, the Papal Secretary of State, about the French Consul's still having the *fleur-de-lis* over his door. On receiving an unsatisfactory reply, Bassville so far lost his head as to endeavour to put the emblem of the Republic over the Academy of Painting in the Villa de' Medici. This insolence so infuriated the mob that they tore him to pieces in the street, before the authorities could intervene, and Mackau, furious at the murder of his secretary, endeavoured to goad Naples into war with Rome.

At this critical moment arose the extraordinary situation that was created by the execution of Louis XVI and the general European coalition against France.

The news arrived at Naples in the midst of the *Carnevale*, when Emma was taking out her diamonds for the State balls, when the San Carlo was wreathed with tinsel roses for the gala performances, when on every hand was noisy gaiety, added to the bustling prepara-tions for festival. All this was changed as suddenly as a trans-formation scene of gauze and silver tissue fades when the Demon King leaps on the stage.

The finery disappeared, the theatres were closed, the balls and concerts cancelled, upholsterers quitted the decorations of the Opera House and the Palace to fasten up crape draperies in the churches, where, amid black-veiled statues, the clergy held pompous funeral services.

The Queen went in heavy gloom, as if she had been a widow, spending hours prostrate on the floor of the Royal Chapel, weeping away the last traces of her sensual beauty.

She was indeed struck to the heart; she had never seen Louis XVI, but she regarded him as symbolic of all crowned heads, and she agonized over her sister's fate; her letters to Marchese di Gallo,

87

her envoy at Vienna, were full of heartfelt lamentations over the fate of Marie Antoinette and pious hopes that death would soon put the Queen of France out of her atrocious suffering. The execution of Louis XVI rendered M. de Mackau's position impossible; the young aristocrat had been a personal friend of the King of France, but, loyal to the Republic, he refused to wear mourning, when he was ordered to do so by Sir John Acton. This caused the final break; the French Minister withdrew from a Court where he knew he would not be received, but owing to the difficulties of travel in time of war, he remained in Naples.

.   .   .   .   .   .

Strained as the political situation was between Naples and France, it was rapidly to become worse, and the Queen's most dreadful fears were to be realized.

In the autumn of 1793, whilst the King and Queen were visiting the Hamiltons, to drink tea in the English garden, and Emma and her husband were practising their little pieces for voices and viola, news came from France, long expected but none the less terrible, that plunged Maria Carolina in an agony of sincere grief. She learnt of the execution under atrocious circumstances of her sister, and though the first paroxysms of her distress were sincere enough, they were soon disfigured by personal fear and a vindictive desire for vengeance, not only upon the murderers of Marie Antoinette, but upon everyone who bore the name of Frenchman or might be suspected of bearing the name of Jacobin. She called her children together in the Royal Chapel and made the dreadful announcement to them with every circumstance of drama and fury; she wrote across the portrait of her sister, which hung above her bureau: "Never will I sleep till vengeance is satisfied."

The poor woman wept on the bosom of Lady Hamilton and sent her a portrait of the unfortunate Dauphin, bidding her look on the features of the miserable child, "who was either slain or enduring a captivity worse than death." Emma wept too; she thought it was all horrible and violently championed her adorable and distressed Queen; she hoped that England would do something, and do it soon; besides, all this was such an interruption to her gorgeous life of praise and flattery; she saw only one side of the

question and she saw that vividly; knowing nothing whatever about
the case she delivered on it that emphatic judgment of which only
the vulgar and ignorant are capable; she cared nothing for the
Neapolitan Liberals, though there might be thousands of them and
they might be the most brilliant and cultured members of the
population.

The Queen's methods of espionage, secret imprisonment, and
tyranny which were enforced by every possible use of reckless
means, did not appal Emma; she did not consider, any more than
did Sir William, that possibly in the methods of the Queen of
Naples might be found the explanation of the incredibly brutal fate
of the Queen of France—how should she understand what was
happening around her, or know of anything save the surface of life?
It was not for Emma Hamilton to have one second's glimpse of the
minds and hearts of the brave, intelligent, patriotic people who,
hidden in the city, pursued quietly their ideals.

The continual emotional disorder of the Queen was increased
when she heard that the French Convention had published a decree
promising help "to all people wishing to be free." Soon after this
La Touche's Fleet, still cruising in the Mediterranean, was scattered by a tempest and the Admiral put into Naples in his flagship
to refit. The Neapolitan Court was forced to offer him all the
help he desired, and he had the indiscretion to come ashore with his
officers and to get into touch with the patriots and the intellectuals
who had been so long the subject of Maria Carolina's suspicion and
espionage.

The Queen held her hand until after the departure of the
French Admiral, then cast into prison all those with whom he had
been in any way in touch. In particular her vengeance fell on the
young aristocrats who had given a supper to the French officers
at the Villa Rocca Romana at Posilippo, a feast which each had
left with a red cap, the emblem of liberty, pinned in his coat lapel.
These and many more young nobles and intellectuals—Jacobins,
as the Queen called them—were arrested secretly, it appeared,
during the night. It was some while before their families discovered
that they were in the underground dungeons of Sant' Elmo,
chained to the foul, bare ground, fed on bread and water, each in a
separate *fossa* or grave. The result of this act of tyranny was the

formation of a patriotic society, which rose out of the suppressed Freemasons' Lodges.

M. de Mackau did what he could to encourage these unhappy Neapolitan patriots, but he did not go beyond the bounds of prudence, for, when the Queen committed the outrage of searching the French Embassy and of stealing the papers, she found nothing of a compromising nature. M. de Mackau soon, however, found his position impossible; he was insulted while the émigrés were caressed, and on the occasion of the birth of an Archduke openly affronted, when he arrived at the Palace to participate in the fête that was held to celebrate the event.

Maria Carolina gave herself the satisfaction of turning her back on the Frenchman, who was soon after recalled, but who still could not leave Naples, as the way by land through Rome was closed, and he had to wait till a French ship came to Leghorn. Another envoy, Maret, was sent from France to Naples. General Maudet surrendered Toulon in the name of Louis XVII to the English and as the triumphant result of the policy of the Queen, Naples and Great Britain began to approach an understanding.

All these political thunders and lightnings did not disturb Emma's cheerful mind. A year after the execution of the King of France, she wrote again to Mr. Greville, who had now taken another and larger house in Paddington, this time on the Green; her news was of the continuous gaiety of her life. The Hamiltons had been living for eight months at Caserta, going twice a week to town to give dinners, balls and concerts in the Palazzo Sessa. Emma by then was used to entertaining fifty guests to dinner and three hundred to a ball and supper, and, as she was careful to inform Mr. Greville, she dined very, very often with the Royal Family. Despite the war there were plenty of noble and fashionable travellers in Italy, and none of them failed to arrive at Naples, where the Hamiltons had to receive them, so that their house at Caserta was "like an inn." Duchesses had been plentiful. Her Grace of Devonshire, Her Grace of Lancaster; a rich sprinkling of the noble names of England. She had had her dinner with that noble, amiable lady, the Princess Royal of Sweden, and, most precious of all: "In the evenings I go to the Queen, and we are tête-à-tête two or three hours."

Emma had not neglected her music. She had learnt to sing duets with the King, who was credited with a fine voice; Emma's comment, however, was "It was but bad, and he sings like a king."

The beauty ascribed much of her astonishing success to her naturalness; she informed Mr. Greville that, however familiar she might be with the Queen in private, she always remembered to keep her distance in public, "paying her as much respect as though I had never seen her before, which pleased her very much; but she showed me great distinction that night, she told me several times how she admired my good conduct."

Once more she repeated how happy she was with dear, dear Sir William. "We are not an hour in the day separable; we live more like lovers than husband and wife." She sketched in two pretty pictures of conjugal affection for Mr. Greville's appreciation. One of her songs had been set for a viol on which Sir William accompanied her; taking much pleasure in providing a tender *obbligato* for her soaring notes. Then they had an English garden, in which the King walked every day, and where she and Sir William were learning botany: "Not to make ourselves pedantical creatures, but for our own pleasure." Politics, then so important a factor in every life, Emma hardly mentioned in her letters to Greville. She knew nothing of the noble families, the cultured middle-classes who were maintaining Liberal principles and working for Liberal ends, even while all they possessed and their very lives were under the heels of the Bourbon-Hapsburgs. While the secret meetings were held, and spies crept about, and the Neapolitan nobility encouraged the Neapolitan intellectuals in opposition to the vicious queen and imbecile king, Emma skimmed the surface of social life, gay as a May-fly on the brilliant waters of a stagnant pool; her only real trouble was her husband's health—the old man's constitution was breaking up; he was perhaps slightly harassed by the constant din in which Emma lived, a little dazzled by the frequent posing, a little deafened not only by the singing of Emma herself, but by the ringing voices of the tenors and sopranos who came to assist at her concerts.

In the autumn of 1794 she found time to write again to "dear Greville," congratulating him on having attained at last the sinecure which would have made such a difference to them in the Paddington days:

"I congratulate you with all my heart on your appointment as a Vice-Chamberlain."

She wrote with her usual good humour, never forgetting how much she owed him:

"I don't know a better, honest or more amiable and worthy man than yourself."

Unfortunately there was not good news of the uncle:

"My dear Sir William has had the disorder that we and all Naples have had since the eruption. Violent diarrhœa that reduced him to so very low an ebb that I was much alarmed for him."

But there they were in the Royal Palace at Castel del Mare "enjoying every comfort and happiness that good health, Royal favour and domestic happiness can give us."

Sir William had told her that he loved her better than ever and "never for a moment repented." Greville was still executing little commissions for her; he was to settle with Mrs. Hackwood, her dressmaker, "though the last things were spoiled and I had no right to pay for them, but I will settle it." He was also to get her "an English riding-habit, very fashionable" and put it down to Sir William's account. "Mother is the comfort of our lives."

Mrs. Cadogan had adapted herself excellently well to her daughter's life of splendour. Placid, discreet, and an excellent housekeeper, she had filled an odd position with credit to herself, and satisfaction to others, and her comfortable presence rounded off Emma's brilliant existence.

They were indeed halcyon days for the lucky young woman, on the stormy waters of a universal tempest her little nest rode high and dry on a becalmed patch of sunlight. Everyone whom she met was pleased with her, those whom she was likely to disgust kept away from the Court.

To the crowd who circled round the King, the Queen, and Sir John Acton, Emma was very acceptable with her classic beauty, her high animal spirits, her bold manners which passed for "naturalness," her expensive, free and easy parties, her perpetual good humour.

She had not enough reputation herself to permit her to be censorious, not enough wit to be critical, and the glow of her immense luck was about her like a radiance, so that she was very good company indeed for the idle, the dissipated, the bored and the extravagant medley who formed the Court of the Sicilian Bourbons. Sir William was delighted with his wife's success; it had become his sole interest in life and supported him through the vexation caused by a European war, the exhaustion produced by a constant biliousness, and the secret burden of mounting debts.

Emma was soon, and in a most effective and even dramatic manner, to come into direct touch with great affairs and a great man.

After the Allies had seized Toulon, a British ship was sent with dispatches from Lord Hood to the British Minister in Naples, asking him to raise Italian troops to garrison the French port; this ship was the *Agamemnon*, which, with a fine show of canvas and the Union flag flying, put into the bay one September evening.

The Captain, pacing the scrubbed deck that sultry night, admired the magnificent outlines of Vesuvius from whose fiery cone the lava was pouring and the smoke spreading. He wrote a letter to his wife, "at anchor off Naples," mentioning how impressed he had been by the sight of the flaming mountain. As soon as it was light, acting with his usual energetic promptitude, he landed, and early in the morning presented himself at the Palazzo Sessa, and gave his credentials to Sir William Hamilton.

The meeting was enthusiastic; the Captain of the *Agamemnon* spoke warmly of the success at Toulon, and Sir William promised the required six thousand Neapolitans; the visitor was pressed to stay at the Embassy. Emma was very willing to play the kind hostess; she put at the little sailor's disposal the room prepared for the Prince Augustus, then on his Italian travels, and for four days the Captain of the *Agamemnon*, and his stepson Josiah Nisbet, were guests in the brilliant apartments overlooking the bay.

When he sailed back to Toulon he wrote again to his wife, commenting on the kindness and goodness he had received from the Hamiltons. His beautiful hostess, however, he disposed of with a prudish comment. "She is a young woman of amiable manners and does honour to the station to which she is raised."

She had been kind to Josiah, noted the little Captain whose name was Horatio Nelson; both the Hamiltons approved of him; they thought him slightly odd, but Emma, at least, believed he had the air of a man who would go far. Besides, despite, or perhaps in consequence of, her early Tower Wharf adventure, she had a tender feeling for the British Navy.

Captain Nelson had wished to return the hospitality which had been offered him by the British Minister; on board his ship, the pig-tailed sailors with the striped shirts and flapping trousers cleaned and polished and made ready the great cabin for the reception of notable people; provisions came aboard, rowed across the bay in native boats, lemons, oranges, onions, chickens, baskets of grapes and peaches.

But the *Agamemnon* had to put out to sea hurriedly on a report that there was a chance of prize money; news had come of a French frigate's escorting a convoy into Leghorn Harbour; Captain Horatio Nelson cancelled his breakfast party at which he was to entertain the Hamiltons and most of the better-class tourists who happened to be in Naples, and put off the luncheon which he was to have offered the King.

From her window Emma, leaning on the hot sill, watched the pale sails of the splendid vessel, vivid amid the brown and amber canvases of the Italian shipping, while the English flag and the swallow-tailed scarlet Captain's pennant fluttered in the bright blue air.

This visit of the British battleship seemed to increase Emma's stature; she was now something more than the wife of His Britannic Majesty's Minister; she represented the country to whom her adored Queen was looking for succour; if the Royal Family that had been so kind to Emma were to be saved, who could save them but the British Navy?

A glow of patriotism stirred Emma's heart; this surely would be the most impressive of the attitudes—Saviour of the Queen!

It was a time when everyone had to take sides; France had declared for the "rights of man," and in the chorus of a nation's shouting denial of this startling doctrine the voice of William Pitt, representing Britain, was the loudest; Emma, impulsively embracing her Queen, who passed from tears to furies when she thought of France, promised the protection of the British Navy for Naples. She had every reason to feel self-confident; it was so long since she had met with a rebuff.

And indeed it seemed that the Sicilian Bourbons, who were about to reap the harvest of years of shameless bad government as surely as the peasants on the slopes of Vesuvius were about to pluck the red and white grapes for the Lacrima Christi wine, would soon need protection. The Liberals of Naples, fired by the news from France, were ripe for revolt and, as the Queen believed, for anarchy and murder; the city seethed with suppressed panic.

News came of the *Agamemnon*; that she had missed the convoy, then, that she was outside Toulon. When this superb naval base was attacked from the land by the Republicans, Lord Hood was forced to abandon it, amid scenes of frantic horror, which were not without a powerful effect on the nervous, bitter little Captain of the *Agamemnon*.

In his austere cabin, amid the charts and maps, on the writing-case where he had lately penned his approval of Emma Hamilton, Captain Nelson wrote to his brother, the Rev. William Nelson, to his wife, his dear Fanny, waiting for him on the Norfolk flats, to H.R.H. the Duke of Clarence, his one distinguished friend, and told them what war meant at a close view;—"the mob rose," scribbled the Captain, using those bombastic phrases which Emma also liked to employ. "Death called forth all his myrmidons, which destroyed the miserable inhabitants in the shape of swords, pistols, fire, water. Thousands are said to be lost. In this dreadful state, and to complete misery, already at its height, Lord Hood was obliged to order the French Fleet, 20 sail of the line, 20 other men-of-war, together with the Arsenal (dockyard), powder magazine, etc., to be set on fire . . . only three of the French Fleet saved: all the forts are blown up.

"I cannot write all; my mind is deeply impressed with grief. Each teller makes the scene more horrible."

Lord Hood removed his base to Corsica, which surrendered to Colonel John Moore. Captain Nelson's small squadron tried to dislodge the scattered Republican garrisons that held out along the coast. When the sudden Southern spring covered the island with pink cyclamen, dark violets and wild strawberry-flowers, the Captain of the *Agamemnon* landed near Bastia, ordered the cutting down of the Tree of Liberty, and with his own hand struck the tricolour of the French Republic, which really did seem to him a badge of the most shameless infamy.

Emma, with a palace full of painters, modellers and lapidaries, "striving to outdo the life" with her famous features, expressed a vast interest in the little Captain who seemed to have an heroic outline; he was often mentioned in Naples; this was just the kind of Paladin for whom the harassed Queen was looking; a reckless man who loathed the French.

In March came his greetings to her, when he wrote to her husband for the artillery stores which he could not obtain owing to his squabbles with Colonel John Moore—"respectful compliments" and a grateful memory of kindness to a stranger.

The valiant Captain's mood fluctuated as the fleet prepared for the siege of Bastia; to his wife he maintained a brave strain—"I am on active service, which I like, I am well, never better. I have no joy separated from you."

But there were no prizes, no rewards—"nothing but salt beef and honour—we are absolutely getting sick from fatigue. . . . I trust my name will stand on record, when the money-makers are forgot."

Lord Hood slighted him, the attacks on the Corsican heights were perilous and tedious, but he wrote spirited letters to Sir William, keeping him in touch with events. Emma was intensely interested in the news; she was sorry to hear in July of his wounded eye—a hurt received when he had landed to attack Calvi, but there was a British victory and Emma glowed in the radiance of that glory at the Bourbon Court; neither the war so near on either side, nor the revolution seething so close underfoot, had as yet impinged on her gorgeous life; these lurid cross-lights rather enhanced her attitudes.

Captain Nelson, from the *Agamemnon*, who had then returned to Leghorn, wrote bitterly: "What I have got at present is nothing. What I have lost is an eye, £300, and my health, with the satisfaction of my ship's company being absolutely ruined."

This last lament was sincere, he really loved his sailors; that year he had written to his wife: "My seamen are now what British seamen ought to be . . . almost invincible. They mind shot no more than peas."

The ambitious, worldly man was sharply disappointed that he had been once more passed over, slighted; he had not made enough even to buy a cottage in the country—and he hated cottages and the country, he wanted splendour and glory, fame and applause. "They have not done me justice; but never mind; I'll have a *Gazette* of my own."

Within a few days of the dispatch of these letters to England, Emma was writing to Charles Greville; she was still cheerful and jolly, though Sir William was shrivelled and yellow as his own monkey with casting up bile and swallowing the sovereign powders of Dr. James, and the war was harassing them both.

She wrote from the charming palace of Caserta, where the palms and tamarisks even in winter shaded the marble balustrades of the terraces, and the painted walls showed beribboned *amorini* for ever pointing at mirrors whence a dozen Emmas were reflected.

"Caserta: Decber. 18th, 1794.

"I have onely time to write you a few lines by the Neapolitan Courier, who will give you this. He comes back soon, and pray send me by him some ribbands and fourteen yards of fine muslin worked for a gound or fine Leno. Ask what Leno is, and she will tell you, and pray pay Hackwood's (bill), and put (it) down to Sir William's account with his banker. He told me I might; for I have so many occasions to spend my money, that my 2 hundred pounds will scarcely do for me, (with) a constant attendance at Court now, once and generally twice aday, and I must be well dress'd. You know how far 2 hundred will go. To-day we expect the Prince Augustus from Rome. He is to be lodged at the Pallace here, and with us in town. To-morrow we have a great dinner at Court for the Prince. The Queen invited me last night herself. No person can be so charming as the Queen. She is everything one can wish, —the best mother, wife and friend in the world. I live constantly with her, and have done intimately so for 2 years, and I never have in all that time seen anything but goodness and sincerity in her, and, if ever you hear any lyes about her, contradict them, and if

97

you should see a cursed book written by a vile french dog with her character in it, don't believe one word. She lent it me last night, and I have by reading the infamous calumny put myself quite out of humour, that so good and virtus a princess should be so infamously described.

"Lord Bristol is with us at Caserta. He passes one week at Naples, and one with us. He is very fond of me, and very kind. He is very entertaining, and dashes at everything. Nor does he mind King or Queen, when he is inclined to show his talents. I am now taking lessons from Millico, and make great progress. Nor do I slacken in any of my studys. We have been here 3 months, and remain four or five months longer. We go to Naples every now and then. I ride on horseback. The Queen has had the goodness to supply me with horses, an equerry, and her own servant in livery every day. In short, if I was her daughter, she could not be kinder to me, and I love her with my whole soul.

"My dear Sir William is very well, and as fond of me as ever; and I am, as women generally are, ten thousand times fonder of him than I was, and you would be delighted to see how happy we are,—no quarelling, nor crossness, nor laziness. All nonsense is at an end, and everybody that sees us are edified by our example of conjugal and domestick felicity. Will you ever come and see us? You shall be received with kindness by us booth, for we have booth obligations to you, for having made us acquainted with each other. Excuse the haist with which I write, for we are going to Capua to meet the Prince Augustus. Do send me a plan, how I could situate little Emma, poor thing; for I wish it.

"E. Hamilton."

The last lines came in a little oddly; Sir William was paying for the forsaken child, but only Mr. Greville knew her parentage; therefore, he must be asked "to think of a plan." This posssible scheme could not include any acknowledgment of the poor creature by her brilliant mother; Sir William might, as one of his friends wrote to Greville, show "dotage" in his fondness for his wife, but he could hardly be expected to permit this second Emma to run about the Embassy, provoking curiosity and sneers.

Nor did Emma's frustrated maternity disturb her robust good humour, she had no longing for a child, no longing for anything, her life was full of achievement; if she had not had this new interest in the navy which had provided Emma's father, perhaps she would never have remembered Emma at all. She never lacked the excitements she craved; while the British Mediterranean Fleet was cruising along the ragged Italy coasts, and the French Republic, rising fiercely to the cry "*La patrie en danger*," was building a fleet at Toulon, Emma was entertaining the eccentric Lord Bristol, whose bizarre personality fitted well into the gilded hubbub of courtly Naples.

William Beckford, travelling with nearly a hundred servants, had set out to visit his dear friends in the South, but had struck across the track of war, been held up in Lisbon, then chased by pirates, and, after hiding in a queer Spanish palace, much to his romantic taste, had returned, disgusted at the barbarities of mankind, to England and safety.

In his place Emma had an entertaining creature, the Earl Bishop, who was for ever travelling about in great pomp, diverting himself and amusing others. He became at once Emma's *cavaliere servente*, flattering her, admiring her, making her laugh with his racy stories and piquant ways.

He viewed Naples with the eyes of a tourist—as a city of pleasure where the *valets de place* hung about the modish inns *I tre Re* and *Il Capello del Cardinale*, offering in broken English to show "Milord" where vice and amusement might be found cheaply. His Grace was surprised to hear from the Hamiltons of the troubles beneath the surface—what—Jacobins in so brilliant a city!

As many as forty thousand, he was told, and the easy prelate was incredulous.

.   .   .   .   .   .

The figure was higher, beyond the most anxious computation of the Queen's spies; no anti-French movement, no setting up of a Giunta, no policing could check the Liberals from organizing themselves while awaiting their opportunity. Joseph Garat, the new French Minister, continually demanded in vain the release of the patriots who had been imprisoned for dining with La Touche's officers at the famous *Cena di Posilippo*; neither the Hapsburg nor the Bourbon knew the meaning of generosity or common sense. And Garat, who had announced the death sentence to Louis XVI, was not likely to make himself acceptable to any Court, least of all to that of Naples.

The French, bearing the cap of liberty at the point of the sword, swarmed over Italy, a ragged, starved, inconquerable horde, organized by one man of genius Lazare Carnot, led by another, General Bonaparte. A fleet sailed from Toulon to retake Corsica. Prussia and Austria, who had been beaten to their knees, made peace with the Republic, whose trees of liberty were planted on the very frontiers of the Kingdom of Naples.

A violent epidemic of typhus that broke out in the unwilling army the Queen had so ruthlessly recruited, profoundly encouraged the Neapolitan patriots, who were hardly troubled to disguise their contempt and defiance of the Court. Young Liberals wore trousers at the Opera, short hair and scarlet waistcoats in the streets.

Emma often found the Queen in a convulsion, brought on by fear and rage; Maria Carolina indeed worked with a heedless, reckless energy, the word vengeance was frequently on her lips; she had all Emma's sympathy, she too loathed this nation of which she knew nothing, save that they all were monsters.

The two women did what they could, the King and Sir William were goaded until a small fleet was sent out to help the British off Toulon, lying in wait for the new Republican Armada. This fleet was under the command of a Neapolitan Prince, who was known to be a sailor of genius and who had devoted himself to clearing from his native coasts the Corsairs who had infested them for centuries. In this task he had been very successful, and both his equals and those under his command admired him for his vigilant attention to duty, his patriotism, his honourable character, and his high personal courage. His seamanship was superb, and he was greatly beloved by the sailors of the Neapolitan Navy.

He took the blessing of the Queen and of Emma with him to Toulon, where the captain of the *Agamemnon* made his acquaintance and liked him. This was the only time Horatio Nelson favoured a foreigner, but of this gentleman, with his scanty line of ships, he wrote—"We all love Prince Caragholillo or whatever his name is."

The name that the Englishman found so difficult was Francesco Caracciolo, Duca di Bersina. He was a man of Horatio Nelson's own age, of middle height, very swarthy, serious, but not melancholy, of few words, and courteous manners; he was absorbed in two interests—his country, and ships.

.   .   .   .   .   .

The Queen had to endure what she considered extraordinary affronts from the Neapolitan aristocrats; noble ladies hardly disguised their Jacobin leanings, lodges and clubs met to discuss the questions raised by the French Revolution; despite the secret police, French newspapers and pamphlets circulated freely.

One of the most splendid of the sons of the ancient families, the handsome Ettore Carafa, Duca d'Andria, refused the scarf of the Order of San Gennaro, when the King offered it to him on his father's death; in consequence of this and his blacking out of his own arms in his family chapel the highborn young democrat joined the hundreds of political prisoners rotting mind and body, in Sant' Elmo.

The Giunta pretended to discover a conspiracy; the Queen and Sir John Acton struck with the force of fear; there were sentences of imprisonment, of exile, of torture, of death, which were passed without a pretence of legality.

Three students, aged respectively twenty-two, twenty and nineteen, of good families and characters, were chosen as victims and were hanged on a gallows erected in the Largo del Castello; they died with that courage which alone can render such scenes endurable. Mario Pagano, one of the most famous jurists in Italy, who had defended them, was cast into prison, where he remained four years.

A fellow-countryman wrote of these boys who were the first sacrifices to the ideal for which so many were to perish; "they had no fault beyond aspirations, discourses, and hopes."

The French Minister, Garat, reported that the prisons of Naples were full of the most enlightened men in the country; but the Queen was still afraid.

Emma never mentioned these things, when she wrote to her former lover about millinery and her domestic felicity.

Yet the Ambassador's lady was not without great ideas. Might not she, with her influence over a doting husband and Maria

Carolina, with her lord who meant as much as and no more than the pavilion on which his honours were emblazoned, play together a large part in Europe?

When the Queen received news from Spain that this country was likely to join France, and sent a copy with a cipher-key to Emma to give to her husband, the Ambassadress felt that she was directing high destinies and beginning to render great services to her country.

Did not Sir John Jervis, when he took over the command of the Mediterranean Fleet, name her again and again the Patroness of the Navy? She was proud of the name—did it bring back to her some early memories of a press-gang ship at the Tower Wharf, where she had joined the laughing ladies of the pavement who had swarmed down dark gangways and into foul cabins to comfort the homing sailors? Did it bring back pictures of a Wapping ale-house, when the rolling seamen had come ashore for their drink and their doxies, and her admired beauty had graced their rough leisure?

Whatever she thought or remembered, she was discreet, the friend of a Queen, representative of Great Britain in this dangerous, assailed spot, and she learned to express triumphant self-assurance in every gesture.

. . . . . .

In London, George Romney was building a vast picture-gallery out of his garnered fortune and his sinking wits; involved in the appalling gloom of incipient insanity, no thought of Emma came to cheer the doomed painter—if he could have drawn her likeness then, when he was in the frenzy of his dementia, and she in her half-crazy elevation, he might have left something more magnificent than the lovely insipid pictures he had made of her in Cavendish Square.

He had named her "the divine lady" and said that she surpassed all other women, would he still have thought her divine, could he have seen her in Naples, and glimpsed her background?

Emma, wearing English clothes selected by Charles Greville, walking by clear leaping fountains, in blue cypress shade, by carved vases of arbutus, the blonde hysteric Queen on her arm, the pale, pampered royal children by her side, Sir John Acton with his smooth adroit face, never far away, never intruding.

And the background—not only the great curve of the bay, the piled-up hills, the towering volcano, the black spreading pines, the white-washed churches and convents—but the huge prisons where the young, the noble, and the brave, lay chained in their foul graves, the barracks where the pressed soldiers died of typhus amid filth, the squares where the gallows had been set up, the chamber where the Giunta (Committee for governing Naples,) sat, the cabinets and taverns where the spies made their plans.

Emma in her gorgeous riding-habits, ahead of a cavalcade taking the coast roads set with palms, laurel, and tamarisk. Emma lifting a tazza loaded with grapes and peaches, while she stood on a terrace hung above purple rocks where azure waves broke. Emma watching the light flowerets of fireworks burst among the stars, the cresset lights of festival bloom before the sullen flames of Vesuvius. Emma singing in a bark with golden silk sails, reclining on a brick-red Pompeian couch—Emma like Cassandra indeed, with raised arm and open mouth and fillet-bound hair, prophesying the destruction of France. And, most inspiring picture of all, Emma reading the *Gazettes* that told of the triumphs of the British Navy and of Captain Horatio Nelson.

But it was not all glory to be on such a pinnacle; the British Government began to notice its Minister at Naples, who had now a delicate role to play—that of making Ferdinand Bourbon and his Kingdom useful to the Allies. All very well, and His Majesty eager enough and the Queen frantic to help, but what of the chaotic conditions of the wretched country, the revolution ready to break out, the French on the frontiers?

Sir William was past the work for which he had never been fitted; he fell ill again, half-crazed by the clatter of his wife's parties, by the *brouhaha* of women's tongues, by the incessant flatteries cast on the English, by the feverish abuse hurled at the French, by wondering what he could or should do. Even Emma had her moments of depression, when Naples was forced into keeping a humiliating peace by the stern terms that General Berthier sent from Rome; but she dashed off a letter to Greville; she had not forgotten her millinery.

"Naples, Sepbr. 21st, 1796.

"We have not time to write to you, as we have been 3 days and nights, writing to send by this courrier letters of *consequence* for our government. They ought to be grateful to Sir William and myself *in particular*, as my situation at this Court is very *extraordinary*, and what no person [h]as as yet arrived at; but one [h]as no thanks, and I am allmost sick of grandeur.

"We are tired to death with anxiety, and God knows w[h]ere we shall soon be, and what will become of us, if things go on as they do now. Sir William is very well, I am not, but hope, when the cold weather comes on and we go to Caserta, I shall be better. Our house—breakfast, dinner and supper—is like a fair; and what with attendance on my adorable Queen I have not one moment for writing, or anything comfortable. I however hope soon to get quiet, and then I will write to you fully. Pray settle Hackwood's account. We desire it. And send me by the bearer a Dunstable hat, and some ribbands, or what you think will be acceptable. Pray do you never think on me? He is *our* Courrier; so pray, do not spare him. In haist,

"Ever your sincere,

"Emma Hamilton.

"P.S.... I have now to-night an assembly of 3 hundred waiting!"

. . . .

There continued to be news of Horatio Nelson in the *Gazettes* Emma read in Naples, and he often wrote to Sir William—how could he forget the kindness that the lady of the Embassy had shown him and Josiah Nisbet, his stepson?

The captain of the *Agamemnon* began to lose the embellishments proper to a hero, his wounded eye darkened until it was useless; he had to wear a patch and began to despair of the future, he was always overlooked, he was done for, approaching forty years of age without money or fame, in poor health and in partial darkness.

Then, by a rude chance of war, came something of what he had always so desperately longed for—glory. Emma, with lustrous eyes and high cries of joy could rush to her adored Queen with news of another British victory.

On February 14th, 1799, Sir John Jervis had beaten the

top-heavy Spanish galleons, manned by pressed men, reluctant foot-soldiers and ignorant fishermen, flying the cheap canvas supplied by a monopoly, hampered by slender masts, twenty miles off Cape St. Vincent, in the South Atlantic.

Horatio Nelson had commanded *The Captain*, and had snatched the fame he so hotly pursued out of the bloody day; it was as if a goddess with a trumpet had heard his name at last and shouted it abroad. He had boarded the *San Josef* and received an armful of swords from vanquished Spanish officers; nothing could have been more dashing and romantic.

This exploit had been accomplished by disobeying orders and throwing out of action the Admiral's plan for capturing the entire Spanish flotilla; but it had been daring and showy, and had made Captain Nelson the hero of the victory; "they shouted for *me*."

Sir John Jervis did not mention Nelson in his dispatches, but the little captain knew how to look after his own fame; he sent an account of his exploits to his friend, Sir William Locker, begging him to insert it in the newspapers; he sent to the city of Norwich the sword of the captured Spanish Rear-Admiral and set all his companions talking about "Nelson's Patent Bridge for Boarding First Rates."

Unfortunately the *San Josef* had already struck her flag to the *Prince George* (Captain Sir William Parker), when Captain Nelson boarded her, so that the glory he so eagerly snatched really belonged, in part at least, to another man.

But he was made Rear-Admiral of the Blue, Knight Commander of the Bath, received a handsome share of prize money and just that kind of fame relished by Emma—his name was on the lips of hundreds of people who did not know what he had really done —a popular hero was in the making.

.   .   .   .   .   .

Affairs did not go well for the Allies, Ireland was in revolt, there were two attempts to land French troops there, the Pope was made a prisoner, the Roman Republic was proclaimed and Neapolitan patriots slipped over the frontier to serve under the French generals, mutinies broke out at the Nore and Spithead, and even in the fleet before Cadiz, where Sir Horatio Nelson,

K.C.B., was assisting in the blockade, and where he hanged four malcontents on a Sunday dawn—"had it been Christmas Day I would have executed them."

That summer, in a landing on the Mole at Santa Cruz, he was hit in the arm by a grape-shot; the limb was at once sawn off by the ship's surgeon, the torn ligaments being crudely dressed; the suffering was exquisite, a peculiar agony was the jar of the cold steel on the nerves.

Emma learned that the wounded Sir Horatio had sailed home to join the half-pay captains at Bath and to serve with his one eye and one arm, and vivid personality, as a fine peg for the blatant patriotism of print-and ballad-maker. The war had been so long, so disastrous, so costly, that the Government had need of all the possible heroes to gild the pill which must sooner or later be presented to a disgusted nation.

So popular was Sir Horatio that it was thought unwise to disturb an idol suitable for the mob; the protests of Captain Sir William Parker were ignored, and the affair of the *San Josef* glossed over.

It was an ugly time in England, with Radicals and Pacifists shouting, "no war, no famine!" with riots and risings, high prices, unemployment and poor trade, and certain swelling mutterings, not unlike those that frightened Maria Carolina, rising from secret meetings and street-corner knots alike.

The Government was very grateful to heroes, and Sir Horatio was graciously received by the King at his Investiture, and given a Reception at the Guildhall, where, in the presence of the Lord Mayor, Alderman John Wilkes, once something of a Jacobin himself, gave the hero of St. Vincent a gold casket and a handsome sword.

Emma exulted to read of all this; she began to think that she had predicted a glorious future for the little captain who had passed four nights in the Palazzo Sessa, and that she had some share in his fame. There seemed, however, little chance of seeing him again; he was looking for a cottage in which to settle down with his amiable, quiet wife, his Fanny, and there was no longer any excuse for him to write to the Hamiltons.

The British Minister's wife began to feel the strain of the Queen's incessant anxieties; there were ten thousand French in the north, twenty-five thousand along the coast round Genoa; the Toulon workshops were still building and fitting out warships, the crust of authority over the patriots of Naples began to wear as thin as the glaze over the cone of Vesuvius before an eruption. The Queen believed herself threatened by land and sea—and with no hope save in the British Navy—the name of General Bonaparte created a panic in Europe; the British Fleet in the Mediterranean seemed the last, the only weapon, in the hands of the old order, which was struggling for existence with a new order so dramatically successful.

Italian princelings were scattered, like the kings on a pack of cards, before a flip of the fingers of the red caps, the tricolour flags showed above the ramparts of ancient patrician cities; when all else in the Continent had fallen before the French, it seemed that Ferdinand Bourbon had little hope of maintaining his unstable throne—which, even in his own country, had no supporters beyond his corrupt favourites, the rabble of *lazzaroni* and the discredited Church that was already defeated in her great stronghold, Rome. There was, too, the danger from the sea; for what purpose was the huge armament being built at Toulon?

The spies of William Pitt reported to Whitehall that eighty thousand Frenchmen were to embark under General Bonaparte for Egypt as a step on the march to India; French officers were already at the Court of Tippoo Sahib, French agents were endeavouring to raise a revolt against the British in Hindustan.

The Admiralty advised Lord St. Vincent, as Sir John Jervis had been created, to dispatch a flotilla to the Mediterranean and to put it under the command of Sir Horatio Nelson, then in the mouth of the Tagus, on board *The Vanguard*, "to seek the armament preparing at Toulon" . . . in order "to take, sink, burn or destroy it."

With fourteen first-rate line-of-battle ships, Sir Horatio set sail for Naples, on his ship of seventy-two guns, with his square blue flag, his blue ensign fluttering from the complicated design of sails and rigging. He was hampered by losing sight of his frigates in a storm, by shortness of stores, by damage to some of the ships; he wrote to Sir William Hamilton, that he needed provisions, frigates, "the eyes of the navy," and "good pilots."

He thought that the French were off the Sicilian coasts and was determined to follow them "even if they go to the Black Sea."

. . . . . .

Sir William was distracted; Naples was not at war with the Directory, the French Resident was watchful and arrogant; the French troops were on the frontiers, and Ferdinand, when last he had in a panic conceded peace terms to Berthier, had promised not to victual British ships.

When the fleet put into Naples Bay, Sir William could promise no open help, though he had some useful information. The Frenchmen had passed Sicily, making for the south-east; it was known that General Bonaparte was on board one of the men-of-war.

As for obtaining an order for provisions, pilots and frigates, Sir William could do nothing; the King had shut himself away in an agony of fear, terrified of a rising in the city, terrified of the French, dreaming of the guillotine's being set up in the Piazza del Mercato, of his baroque splendours' being fired about his ears. Even Emma, with the Queen's friendship, even the Queen with her seat at the Council, dared do nothing; they had even to endure the action of the French Resident in sending openly to Rome news of the British Fleet's movements.

The two women could only cling together in the long, shadowed rooms behind the shutters that screened them from the June sunshine, vow vengeance on the French, and pray for success for Sir Horatio Nelson; chattering and weeping in unison, the daughter of the Cæsars and the daughter of Cheshire peasants, were perfectly in accord.

The Rear-Admiral of the Blue did not leave the *Vanguard*, which was anchored in the bay, but Emma wrote to him; "God bless you and send victorious. . . . the Queen desires me to say everything that is kind. . . . God bless you, me dear Sir, your affectionate and grateful Emma Hamilton."

And at the last moment, when the straining canvas was set to catch the wind for departure, another note from the Palazzo Sessa was brought to the ship by a boat rowing swiftly across the harbour. This note enclosed a message from the Queen, the few lines in Emma's hand bade the consecrated hero kiss the royal letter and send it back; it was signed "ever yours, Emma."

Sir Horatio sat down in his cabin, writing hurriedly, painfully with his left hand, peering with his one eye.

"My dear Lady Hamilton,

"I have kissed the Queen's letter, pray say I hope for the honour of kissing her hand when no fears will intervene. Assure Her Majesty that no person has her felicity more at heart than myself, and that the sufferings of her family will be a tower of strength on the day of battle, fear not the event, God bless you and Sir William, pray say I cannot stay to answer his letter here. Yours faithfully, Horatio Nelson, 6 p.m."

The ports of Syracuse were closed to the British Fleet, news came that Malta had fallen to the French, and that the Knights had supplied Bonaparte with provisions; the Republicans were sailing east.

Sir Horatio was now convinced that their destination was Alexandria; he sailed to the Eastern port to find the enemy had not arrived; he cruised round Syria, Crete, returned to golden Syracuse; the timid Bourbon was still neutral, still invisible; Sir Horatio had been gone nearly a month and his provisions were very low; he still had no light frigates; his fleet was blind and deaf. He wrote to patriotic Emma, pouring out his humiliations, his despair, but Emma and the Queen had saved him. Ignoring her husband, the pact with France, Maria Carolina had struck straight at her enemies; her hatred of the French found expression in the order she sent to the Governor of Syracuse. The British Fleet was victualled, watered and sailed with the first favourable breeze across the Tyrrhenian Sea.

Sir Horatio wrote to thank the Hamiltons for their exertions, "be assured that I will return either crowned with laurels or covered with cypress."

A captured enemy vessel told him that General Bonaparte had landed in Alexandria, the British had missed him by a day; Sir Horatio turned in pursuit and on the last day of July his spy-glass showed him the Republican Fleet anchored in the fairway before Aboukir Harbour; the tricolours brilliant in Eastern sunshine.

In Naples Emma moved through the dazzling fruit-scented heat, attired in her classic muslins, exhaling martial patriotism, a Bellona in a Dunstable straw-hat.

She felt herself a goddess indeed; comforting the Queen, who, on her knees, swallowed holy wafers and babbled to her saints, inspiring Sir William, who was a little overwhelmed by the crisis, driving through the streets where the *lazzaroni* shouted for her, and the patriots had a glance of contempt for *Emma Lyonna, la putana inglese,* practising naval songs in her strong ringing voice, defying the French, the rebellious Neapolitans, trusting in Nelson and the British—thus Emma, the big woman, nearly forty years old now, whose beauty was spilling over, like the petals of a loosened rose or the seeds of a split pomegranate. While Horatio Nelson strove for the hero's renown, she prepared for him the hero's reward.

II

RULE BRITANNIA

WHEN A GREAT MAN HAS A DARK CORNER
      IN HIM
IS IT TERRIBLY DARK?
                   —Goethe

THE VICTORS

'FOR GODS THERE ARE, THROUGH JOVE'S HIGH COUNSELS GOOD,
HAUNTING THE EARTH, THE GUARDIANS OF MANKIND.'

(QUOTED BY ROBERT SOUTHEY WITH REFERENCE TO LORD NELSON)

TO the little Englishman, making his plans in the main cabin of
the *Vanguard*, the moment was of supreme importance; in his
nervous excitement he felt as if his life were rushing up to a climax;
for years he had longed for an opportunity of winning glory, and
the chance that had come his way at the Battle of Cape St. Vincent
had only whetted instead of satisfying his appetite for reward and
fame. He was also animated by two other passions—an hysteric
loathing of the French people, whom he regarded as monsters
capable of all atrocities, and a genuine desire to please the two
beautiful women who, from the temptingly brilliant city of Naples,
had sent out their appeals and their encouragements.

One of these women was a Queen, of the finest blood in Europe
—the other was an Ambassadress and a famous beauty. The simple
and rather vulgar mind of Horatio Nelson was fascinated by these
words and all they meant to him. His life, up to the moment
when he sighted the French Fleet at anchor in the fairway before
Aboukir Bay, had not been happy. He had always been tormented
by two demons, ill-health and ambition.

If, then, on the eve of this great attempt at a great achievement, he had looked back, as men at such a crisis will look back
along the years, he would not have been satisfied with what he saw.

He was within a few weeks of his fortieth birthday, and had
from his continued ill-health, anxieties, and his two severe wounds,
the appearance of a man at least fifty years of age. Nothing in
those forty years had been quite as he would have wished it, except
perhaps his late London triumphs, and there had been a sting in
them; the glances and smiles of those who really knew the truth

of the *San Josef* incident and the justified complaints of Sir William Parker.

.   .   .   .   .   .

Horatio Nelson had been born in a very quiet part of the world —the village of Burnham Thorpe, in the county of Norfolk.

His early childhood had been passed in a place as dreary as the mind of man could conceive—an eighteenth-century rustic rectory, where the incumbent was both poor and fanatic. Horatio, one of a family of motherless children, was brought up by his father, the rector, in an atmosphere devoid of all pleasure and excitement, all gaiety or colour; he was always delicate and nervous and his character took an unstable turn from his constant fevers and agues.

The village of Burnham Thorpe was as dull as Hawarden; it was off the high road, a cluster of cottages, an inn, the church, the North Sea spreading a few miles away. The rectory was humble, the rooms dark and damp; trees that allowed little sun to penetrate through the small windows stood back and front. There was that constant wind and rain and perpetual mist that Emma had learned to know so well, when she had herded sheep on the Flintshire moors.

The Nelsons were scarcely gentlefolk; they made the most of a connection on the distaff side with Sir Robert Walpole, but they had little money and little influence and all of them were sickly, gnawed at by constant disabling ailments; Horatio in particular was a neurotic, undersized weakling, but animated by a spirit that flamed with a passionate desire to overcome circumstances. He received some local schooling in Norwich Grammar School, little more than sufficient to teach him to read and to write; he absorbed the grim theology of the evangelical section of the Church of England from his father, the Rev. Edmund Nelson. The clergyman's gaunt figure in his black gown and Geneva bands, preaching death and damnation from the village pulpit to rows of drowsy yokels, became merged in the boy's mind with that of God Almighty.

Not very intelligent, sensitive and quite self-absorbed, he accepted the God who was so crudely drawn for him by a dull and narrow-minded father. The loss of his mother was a deep personal grief and increased his nervousness. At the Norwich Grammar

School his schoolfellows jeered at him for his effeminacy because he wore neat clothes and kept a pet lamb.

An uncle in the Navy seemed to indicate a career for Horatio. At nine years of age he was sent from Norwich to Rochester where, homesick and miserable, he was sent on board the *Raisonnable*, then under the command of his uncle, his mother's brother, Captain Suckling, who had suggested to the Rev. Edmund that the boy was far too weakly to be sent to sea, but that a cannon-ball might supply the provision that did not seem to be coming from any other quarter.

The young boy was worked hard, he sailed on a Polar expedition and to the East; melancholy, sickly, his feeble constitution further shattered by the hardships he had undergone, he returned home at eighteen years of age, loathing the sea, loathing the Navy, and weighed down by a gloom only broken by his own indomitable force of will. An immense vanity that did not quite amount to pride, raised him above himself; in a half-delirium of self-assertion he vowed: "I will be a hero, I will brave every danger."

In 1777, he was sent out to Jamaica; a year later he got his own ship and cruised about looking for prizes; he liked the life, but he soon became desperately ill, and was invalided home to take the Bath waters, shrunken and half-paralysed by poisonous fevers. As soon as he could stand on his feet, he was sent on service in the Baltic; the nervous gloom and the black depression returned; he lived in a continual state of physical suffering; he worked very hard at his duties, was conscientious and anxious and much liked by the sailors; he was frequently and desperately sea-sick.

A touch of brightness came through his acquaintance with Prince William Henry, the King's son, who had been sent into the Navy to encourage recruiting for the senior service. In 1782 Horatio Nelson sailed for the West Indies, delighting in the company of the Royal Prince, in whom he discovered many brilliant qualities. He took some prizes, had a few brushes with the French, and returned to Portsmouth again, discouraged and depressed. A doctor thought he had consumption "and quite gave me up."

He had some abstract consolation, to which he clung tenaciously.

"I believe there is not a speck in my character, and true honour, I hope, predominates in my mind."

There followed a short stay in the Burnham rectory, visits to France, where he hated everything, save two very beautiful English ladies, the daughters of a Mr. Andrews, a clergyman. With one of these he fell in love:

"Had I a million of money I am sure I should this moment make her an offer of them."

But the beauty refused him, and he returned still more despondent to England. He got some childish pleasure from discovering that a French prisoner he had once taken was a great person, the Prince de Deux Ponts—but as for the French, "I hate their Country and their manners."

In 1784, when Charles Greville was taking Emma to George Romney's studio, Horatio Nelson sailed for the West Indies as Captain of the *Boreas*. The discomforts and miseries of fever-smitten Antigua bored him horribly; his one consolation was the company of the English ladies on the island, in particular of a Mrs. Moutray, who was most kind to him.

Through the sweltering heat and the hot, unwholesome damp days that followed the rainy season, "were it not for Mrs. Moutray who is very, very good to me, I should hang myself in this infernal place." It was there that he met and married his dearest Fanny; she was a certain Mrs. Francis Nisbet, a well-bred, pleasant, handsome young widow with a wealthy uncle and guardian, Mr. Herbert, whose stock of negroes and cattle was valued at £60,000 sterling. She was twenty-three years old and had a little boy, named Josiah, by her husband, a medical man, who had died in a lunatic asylum. He was married in March 1787; the ceremony was honoured by the presence of His Royal Highness, the Prince William Henry, who gave the bride away. The bridegroom's income had been assured by the kindness of his uncle, William Suckling. The future, though it did not look brilliant, was by no means dark. Horatio was really in love with his charming Fanny, who, on her side, had thought him at first odd, and then fascinating, and who was quite prepared to offer him all the esteem and affection she had to give anyone. "With the purest and most devoted affection I do love her," wrote the bridegroom to the benevolent uncle.

At this time Emma was already in Naples, and Sir William Hamilton holding up a candle as he gazed with infatuated admiration at her famous attitudes.

The year of his marriage the captain of the *Boreas* came home, and for a while there was no new appointment for the young captain. He had to live in the old, damp rectory with his wife and his father, eating his heart out because he felt himself neglected. He was much liked by his intimate companions, but was not popular with those in authority. He was apt to make trouble, to be difficult, quarrelsome and full of complaints; his nerves were always out of order; his wretched health handicapped him severely. Though he pestered the Admiralty for another ship, he was allowed to remain in the boredom of the Norfolk rectory, where "dearest Fanny" showed herself rather dull and uninteresting; she fussed about her health and could not understand her husband's furious desire to be again at sea. He tried to farm, he tried to take up country sports and pastimes—he detested them all. All his education had been at sea; everything he had learned he had learned on board a ship; here in his native corner of Norfolk he was out of place, disgruntled, and most unhappy. It seemed a poor failure of a life.

Then had come the news of the French Revolution and nobody heard of it with more genuine horror and rage than Horatio Nelson, next, war with a life of action again, Toulon and the *Agamemnon's* sailing into Naples Bay, where there was such a fine view of Vesuvius, and where Emma Hamilton entertained him so kindly. After that, the Battle of Cape St. Vincent, the sudden honour, the casket and the sword, two wounds, a fine advertisement of his services to his country, which made him dear to the common people at home and caused his name to appear on the ballad-makers' slips, and his figure to be seen in the prints sold in all the bookshops.

He still had his dismal moments: "I hardly think the war can last—for what is it about?"

All this success, however, had not been cheaply purchased. His rudely severed arm had meant much torment, when the only possible sleep had been purchased by opium; his damaged eye caused him continual suffering; every organ in his body was awry. Days and nights were made infernal by fevers, agues, headaches, and uncontrollable attacks of nerves. Still, his immense vanity, which was at once simple and cruel, led him on; disabled, maimed, handicapped as he was, he still strained for the impossible goal; the boyish boast: "I will be great" was again in his heart, almost on his lips. A saying which was attributed to him when he beheld the French in Aboukir Bay: "A peerage or Westminster Abbey," crystallized his thoughts. It was a schoolboy's dream—to be a hero, to be crowned by a beautiful woman.

.   .   .   .   .   .

Sir Horatio Nelson gave the signal for the attack on the afternoon of August 1st, 1798. Admiral François Paul Brueys d'Aigalliers, the French noble in command of the Jacobin Fleet, was unable to get his ships into the abandoned and neglected port, though he had offered ten thousand *livres* to any pilot who would conduct his flotilla into the harbour. He was, therefore, anchored in the open road, in what was considered a fine, if not an impregnable, position. There were thirteen French ships and four frigates; the guns numbered eleven hundred and ninety-six and the men eleven thousand two hundred and thirty; they were animated by much of that stern, fanatic enthusiasm which had enabled the Republicans to win so many stupendous victories on land.

Under Sir Horatio Nelson's command were the same number of ships, but slightly fewer guns and eight thousand and sixty-eight men. A north-west wind bore the British Fleet towards the shoals where the French lay anchored; at half-past six in the evening the guns of the *Goliath* under Captain Foley, broke the hot blue silence. By a brilliant and unexpected manœuvre the British, to use technical language, "doubled the enemy's van," that is, Captains Hood and Foley in the *Goliath* and the *Zealous* got between the French ships and the shore, thus escaping Brueys's gunfire, for all his cannon were pointed seawards, and in a few minutes disabled the French ships. With six colours flying, so that in case any were shot away, the flagship should not appear to have struck, Sir Horatio opened a murderous cannonade, which permitted the *Minotaur*, the *Bellerophon*, the *Defence* and the *Majestic* to sail on ahead into the heart of the enemy's squadron and anchor close to the French ships. The French gunners returned the terrific British fire, but intermittently, and, as it seemed, without much heart or direction. They had been discouraged by the unexpected flank attack that was so brilliantly executed.

Admiral Brueys who was in command of the Republican Fleet, was a Languedoc noble, in the prime of life, who had been specially selected by the young General Bonaparte for this responsible charge; he was bold and capable, had been trained in the famous "*gardes de la Marine*" under the Monarchy and had since well served the Republic. His fault was over-confidence; he had a superiority of 184 guns and 3,162 men over the British and had not believed that they would venture to attack him; he had made the best of his position in the fairway by anchoring in a strong line of battle, but there were no shore batteries to protect him, and the wind that filled his sails was blowing the British forward, nor had he thought it possible for the enemy to anchor in the shallow water between his van and the shore. There was a French garrison at Rosetta at the mouth of the Nile, but this was too far off to do other than view the engagement from a distance. The African coast was lined by Arabs and Egyptians, who stood on the sandy shore or on the roofs of their flat white houses, watching the Europeans slaughter one another, indifferent to the course of the fight, but hoping for a spectacle and some plunder.

They were not disappointed; the French fought tenaciously, but with the desperation of men who believed that, from the first, they were doomed to defeat. Admiral Villeneuve, who commanded the rear, had lost hope from the moment he observed Nelson's manœuvre, which had opened the attack, and the anchoring of the British ships between their enemies and the shore, which exposed the French to the fatal crossfire.

The swift eastern night fell purple over the yellow coast and the violet sea; it was broken by hundreds of lights; the constant red and orange flash of the gunfire spurting from the decks of the combatants, the groups of four lamps on the rigging of the British ships that were their distinguishing marks in the dark, the random lanterns of the Republicans, the reflections glowing in the dark waters, the bonfires kindled by the watching Africans and the dull gleam in their windows as they lit up their chambers. The frightful din of the combat filled the hot night with a frenzy of sound; the sombre boom of the cannon was broken by the ragged sounds of explosions, fierce shouts of command, the crackle of musketry, the crash of falling sails and rigging.

The courage of the French was as great as that of the British, their cause was at least as good, as they fought for an abstract idealism; but they knew that they were no match for the jail-birds, pressed men, and hardened ruffians, individually so wretched and base, but in combination composing an invincible navy, who affronted them.

Many, perhaps the majority, of the British sailors, were there unwillingly, their condition, as the two great mutinies had recently proved, was that of slaves; they knew little of what the war was about; the Frenchmen were mostly volunteers, animated by a lively patriotism, enthusiastically prepared to die for a lofty, if impossible, ideal. Yet the victory went to the nation always unconquerable at sea. The knowledge that France had never beaten Britain at sea was in every heart during the bloody struggle, stimulating Sir Horatio Nelson's men as it disheartened the Republicans.

The British losses were heavy; the great ships were so closely entangled that every cannonade swept off victims; three times the gunners on the *Vanguard* were dragged away dead, three times replaced by men naked to the waist, while, in the flares of uncertain light, the powder monkeys ran up, slipping in blood, with fresh ammunition or with pails of water to dash over the red-hot guns.

Each British ship made for a Frenchman, anchored close to her, and raked her at close range; the *Bellerophon* anchored by the starboard bow of *L'Orient* (formerly the *Sans Culotte*), the French flagship; so skilfully had the British movements been made that Nelson's battle-line remained unbroken as ship after ship moved forward, closing in upon the despairing, but obstinate enemy.

After an engagement of two hours the eighth French ship struck her colours; the flag of the Revolution dragged amid shattered rigging. Sir Horatio had scarcely received the news of the last surrender, when he was hit by a stray shot that sent him down on his own quarter-deck with the exclamation: "I am killed! Remember me to my wife!"

He was carried down to where the maimed and dying were

huddled in the cockpit, the ship's hospital, where the surgeon, with arms red to the elbows, worked among the filthy, bloodstained straw by the light of swinging oil-lamps. The Admiral insisted on taking his turn with the other wounded; he waited in total darkness; the wound had cast a piece of flesh down over his one good eye; when at length the surgeon lifted this, Horatio could see again, but only through a rain of blood. He believed that he was dying and again sent his remembrances to his wife, and called the chaplain. He also sent for Captain Louis of the *Minotaur* to thank him for the help he had given the flagship, and made other arrangements among his officers. The surgeon assured him that the wound was not dangerous and prayed him to be quiet, but with heroic energy the Admiral tried to dictate despatches. His secretary, Mr. Campbell, when he was called to this task, was so overcome at the blind and bleeding state of Sir Horatio, who appeared to be dying and yet was enthusiastic, that he could not take down the dictated words, on which the wounded man supported himself on his elbow, and, sightless as he was, endeavoured to trace a few words on the letter-case he took from Campbell's shaking hand, describing the state of the battle.

Close by, in the flame-split darkness another brave man was suffering martyrdom—Admiral Brueys, thrice wounded, had refused to leave his post; his tricolour sash soaked red by his own blood, the Frenchman lay along his ship's deck, beneath the shot-tattered colours of the Republic, and gave the only orders left to him to give—those to die unflinchingly.

Close beside him, in the glare and din, stood a boy of nine years of age, wearing the colours of France in his little cap and looking out for his father among the officers who hurried to and fro. A fragment from a bursting gun almost severed the dying Admiral's legs from his body; he gave orders that he was to remain on deck; it was plain to all on board the flagship that she, hemmed in by six British ships and a target for their incessant fire, could not last. The superb *L'Orient*, a three-decker that carried a thousand men and a hundred and twenty guns, towered above her assailants, like the bulk of a great beast brought down by a pack of hounds; a treasure of £600,000 sterling was aboard her; she was splendidly equipped and richly furnished. About half-past nine one of her sister ships, *Le Peuple Souverain*, dark and dumb, drifted helplessly out of the line; from *L'Orient* came only a slow, uncertain fire, as some dying gunner dragged himself to his task; then, dreadful, even in that dreadful scene, the cry went from vessel to vessel, from mouth to mouth. "*L'Orient* is on fire!" The vast and majestic ship began to be outlined in flames, pots of oil and buckets of paint were lying about on the deck, for the beautiful vessel had been in progress of refurnishing when the British had come after her; the flames soon licked these and then rose towering high, like infernal torches, to light the hideous scene. So fierce and sudden was the conflagration that it was impossible to use the fire-buckets or to take any means of saving the blazing ship—the funeral pyre for the mangled body of Admiral Brueys. The Republicans hurled themselves into the water, which was reddened by blood and illuminated by the reflection of flames, covered by huddled spars, tangled wreckage and the shattered bodies of men. The battle continued, but even amid the din of battle the climax of horror was the burning of the French flagship, and all the other ships' crews saw one another by the light of these murderous flames, which rose above them all till they seemed to lick the distant stars.

At eleven o'clock the fire reached the powder magazine of the *L'Orient*, and with a burst of sound so violent as to drown even the fury of the cannonading, the French flagship was blown up.

The magnificent structure was split into thousands of splintered fragments, which were thrown high into the air, mere specks against the vermilion-orange of the background; as the booming thunder died sullenly away, there was a silence that meant a lull in the combat. The nearest British ship, *The Alexander*, was desperately sluicing down her sails.

The pause in the tumult brought Sir Horatio, half blind, staggering on deck, leaning on the arm of his captain; the sight of the vast furnace before him caused him to forget everything but a rush of human feeling; he ordered the one boat he had available to be put out to save the possible survivors of the *L'Orient*. About seventy of the drowning Frenchmen were rescued by the British boat. Among them had been seen, for a second, the white face of the French boy, the son of the Commodore, Casa-Bianca, before he sank with his father.

There was something in this disaster that impressed even the most excited, the most hardened, the most inured to scenes of horror.

The light of the explosion had revealed other French ships drifting dismasted and helpless and silent. Even the brutalized victors felt a touch of pity for so complete a defeat; but, as an English sailor, Captain Miller, afterwards wrote: "All feelings of compassion were stifled by the remembrance of the numerous and horrid atrocities this unprincipled and bloodthirsty nation had committed, and when *L'Orient* blew up about eleven o'clock, though I endeavoured to stop the momentary cheer of the ship's company, my heart scarce felt a single pang for their fate."

The French did not accept their overwhelming defeat tamely. After a lull of horror the ships in the rear began firing again and fought on with heroic obstinacy, although little was left of them but damaged hulls. Throughout the night they struck one after the other. With the dawn two went aground; with the rising of the sun hardly a tricolour fluttered in Aboukir Bay.

One of the French frigates, in proud despair, blew herself up; ten mere riddled shells surrendered—five were sunk; the *Généreux* and the *Guillaume Tell* and two frigates escaped to the west. Over four thousand Frenchmen died for the Republic that night; those that were cast away on the shores were murdered by Arabs, who, in fascinated excitement, had crowded along the edge of the waves and watched the fantastic spectacle presented under the August night.

It was a great victory. It was, as Sir Horatio declared, more than a victory, "it was a conquest," and one not too dearly gained.

The British had lost, in killed and wounded, not many more than eight hundred men; none of their ships was completely disabled; the prize-money would be handsome (though the huge fortune on *L'Orient* was lost), the honour overwhelming.

The wounded hero, with his wan face and bandaged head, ordered a public thanksgiving on every ship of the Fleet and began his announcement of the triumph with the usual formula: "Almighty God, having blessed His Majesty's arms with victory——"

He was pleased with his men—how superior was "their discipline and good order to the riotous behaviour of lawless Frenchmen."

He did not mention the captain of the *Goliath* in his despatches
—was it the Sir William Parker episode over again? Glory was
not a commodity that Sir Horatio could afford to share. While
Captain Foley remained unnoticed, Nelson's friend and flag-
captain, Edward Berry, went to London to advertise extensively
and skilfully the glorious conduct and brilliant success of Horatio
Nelson; no one quite knew whether Captain Foley had acted on
his own initiative or not in the brilliant manœuvre which had
secured the initial success of the battle.

After victory, the fruits of victory! There were some gloriously
gratifying things to be done. There was the dead French Admiral's
sword to be sent to the City of London; there was a letter to be
dispatched to Sir William Hamilton.

"Almighty God has made me the happiest Englishman in
destroying the enemy's fleet, which I hope will be a blessing to
Europe. You will have the goodness to communicate this happy
event to all the Courts in Italy. My head is so indifferent that I can
scarcely scrawl this letter. I have intercepted all Bonaparte's dispatches going to France; his armies must break and will not get
out."

When General Bonaparte's letters were deciphered, they were
found to contain heartening news. The great Frenchman had been
quarrelling with his Generals; *L'Orient* had had a cargo of ingots
of gold and diamonds. The French hoped to seize Egypt, and in
time India. It was all wonderfully exciting. Sir Horatio's head
was splitting with the noise and his wound, loss of blood, and the
nausea of sea-sickness. He could not forbear, however, from
writing to the fair Ambassadress at Naples; the hero was panting
for his reward.

"My dear Lady Hamilton,
"You will soon be able to see the wreck of Horatio Nelson.
May it count for a kindly judgment if scars are marks of honour."

In Naples the suspense had been nerve-racking. So excited was
the Queen that it might have been thought that the French Fleet
was on its way to attack her capital, instead of having been engaged
on quite different business. Emma, too, was keyed up into a state
of almost intolerable tension, which, together with the August
heat, the terror of the King, and the agitation of Sir William, made
her almost lose control of her patriotic ambitions.

When the great news came at last through Captain Capel, on
his way with dispatches to London, she quite lost her control; the
Queen and Emma both fainted; but Maria Carolina soon revived
to give a display of violent hysterics. In a frenzy of enthusiasm
she expressed herself with the blatant manner only possible to an
excited woman. Kissing her relieved husband and clutching to her
bosom her astonished children, embracing everyone who happened
to cross her path, she ran about the palace exclaiming: "O, brave
Nelson, O God bless and protect our brave deliverer! O, Nelson,
what do we not owe to you, saviour of Italy! O, that my swollen
heart could tell him personally what we owe to him."

She laughed, cried, clapped her hands, wept and prayed at the
same moment. An unprejudiced spectator might have thought
that she had received the news she was to be Queen of the world,
in permanent security.

This excessive royal joy was equalled by that of the Hamiltons.
Sir William felt a great load off his withered heart and bent
shoulders. His nation had glorified itself by most emphatic action;
he felt himself deputy for a hero as he scribbled: "It is impossible
for any words to express in any degree the joy that the account of
the glorious and complete victory occasioned at this Court and in
this city."

Taking refuge in hyperbole, he declared to Sir Horatio that no
history, whether ancient or modern, recorded such a magnificent
action; and in his excitement he forgot that he had had the acquaintance of the victorious Admiral only for four days, and added: "You
may well conceive, my dear sir, how happy Emma and I are
at the reflection that you, our bosom friend, have done such
wondrous good in having humbled these proud robbers and vain
boasters."

Emma, of course, had to have her say. When the Queen could

be a little quieted, when she could contrive a moment or two to herself, she scrawled out her congratulations to Horatio Nelson:

"My dear, dear Sir, what shall I say to you? It is impossible I can write, for since last Sunday I am delirious with joy and assure you I have a fever caused by agitation and pleasure. Never, never has there been anything so glorious. I fainted when I heard the glorious news, and fell on my side and was hurt. I should feel it a glory to die in such a cause. No, I would not like to die till I see and embrace the victor of the Nile."

Characteristically, there was a postscriptum which related to millinery. Emotion had deprived Emma of the careful restraint that, under Sir William's anxious teaching, she had learned to keep over her essential vulgarity. Without Charles Greville to choose her clothes or Sir William to advise upon them, she went wildly astray. "My dress, from head to foot, is all a Nelson; even my shawl is blue with gold anchors all over; my earrings are Nelson's anchor; in short, we are be-Nelsoned all over."

She had found time, while the joy bells were ringing, and the Queen screaming in hysterics, and the Royal children clapping their hands, and Sir John Acton sobbing with relief, and the King grunting his approval, to run to the shops and to the dressmakers and to order these curious and unbecoming ornaments.

She had other pleasant tasks in hand, too; there was the Palazzo Sessa to decorate, there was a festival to arrange; by now she was an adept at festivals; there must be a supper and a ball, and of course, there were the hero's apartments to prepare, and the Italian orchestra must be taught to play "Rule Britannia" and "God Save the King" and some nautical airs.

The heat was suffocating; fans fluttered in all the palatial apartments, nets were drawn before all the windows; those who could, rested behind shutters during the heat of the day, but Emma was abroad, ordering this and supervising that.

She thought nothing of either trouble or expense; what did it matter if Sir William was already somewhat in debt, if she had lately been outrunning her income? This was not an occasion for economy or prudence.

Mrs. Cadogan, the smug mother, helped with the easy energy

126

of a woman used to these excitements. There was so much to be got ready—shawls for Emma's attitudes, the tambourines she used when she danced the tarantella, the lights for the alcove where she posed, her music to be looked out, wax candles to be laid in by the hundred, baskets and baskets of roses, peaches, nectarines, early grapes, roses, lilies and whatever else could be obtained to be ordered, fresh servants to be hired, new liveries to be commanded, wine in the cool cellars to be set ready to be brought up, fireworks to be prepared, and the whole household to be coaxed and scolded and drilled into an orgy of enthusiasm for "Britannia" and "Britannia's" hero.

.   .   .   .   .   .

Neither the Queen nor Emma, nor, indeed, anyone in the Palace or the British Embassy, noticed the cold and sullen calm with which the city of Naples received the news of the French defeat. The Neapolitan patriots were silenced, but not disheartened. Neither the crammed prisons, nor the increased troops, nor the thousands of spies, nor the efforts of the Giunta had been able to quell their spirits. While the Queen raved and Emma bustled, the patriots waited and endured.

The defeat of the French at Aboukir Bay which left General Bonaparte shut up in Africa with twenty-three thousand men, put an end to the hopes of the Neapolitans of a speedy deliverance from the Bourbon through intervention of French arms.

"Victory," said the victor, "is not a name strong enough for such a scene."

Nor despair a word strong enough for the emotion felt by those oppressed by the tyranny of Ferdinand, Maria Carolina and Sir John Acton, when they heard the news that had sent the Queen and Emma unconscious to the ground.

Unrepresented, silenced by a misgovernment as unjustified as it was intolerable, the Neapolitans went on cautiously and bitterly with their secret schemes for deliverance, while the alien Queen, with her foreign Minister, and her foreign *confidante*, rejoiced so grossly at the foreign victory.

THE PATRIOTS

'LA CONSACRAZIONE D'UN' EROICA CADUTA'

(BENEDETTO CROCE, ON THE FALL OF THE PARTHENOPEAN
REPUBLIC)

SIR HORATIO NELSON was fully occupied, as was Emma, with the fruits of victory. He could not at once set sail for Naples; dizzy from the wound in his head—the pain was so intense that he believed his skull was fractured—sleepless, continually sea-sick, shaken by the nervous reaction after the long pursuit and the tremendous battle, Sir Horatio showed an heroic energy in striving to get the utmost out of his victory.

The loss of his frigates, to his intense annoyance, prevented him from following up his success as he would have wished. Two French ships staggered away.

The British squadron had to be refitted, and it was only by the help of his faithful friends, Troubridge, Ball, Hood and Hallowell, that the Admiral was able to undertake this exertion. He also took upon himself to send an officer overland from Alexandretta to India with dispatches to the Governor of Bombay. He had complained of the bombastic tone he had found in General Bonaparte's letters; his were no ill match.

"I trust that God Almighty will overthrow in Egypt the bane of the human race. Bonaparte has never had yet to contend with an English officer, and I shall endeavour to make him respect us."

Lieutenant Thomas Duval carried these letters, announcing the victory of the Nile, overland; this done, the dispatches dictated, read through, and Captain Edward Berry sent off with them to be a forerunner of Sir Horatio's glory in London, the sick and nervous Admiral, shaken by his own fatigue and his own glory, set about putting his victorious fleet in readiness to sail.

Aboukir Bay through those blazing days of summer was a fearful sight with corrupting swollen bodies floating about and tangled masses of the wrecks of the noblest ships of France. On the shore the Arabs burned the dead bodies and searched the driftage for any iron it might contain. The *Swiftsure* hooked up a portion of *L'Orient's* mainmast out of the ugly medley in the polluted water, and Captain Ben Hallowell, a sardonic Canadian, ordered his carpenters to make a coffin of it, using both wood and iron.

When this rude casket, made of such strange materials, was finished, Captain Hallowell sent it to the Admiral with this note: "Sir, I have taken the liberty of presenting you with a coffin made from the mainmast of *L'Orient*, that, when you have finished your military career in this world, you may be buried in one of your trophies, but that that period may be far distant is the earnest wish of your sincere friend, Benjamin Hallowell."

Sir Horatio ordered the coffin to be placed upright in his cabin, where it might be constantly before his eyes.

It seemed that he might soon lie within it; he became extremely ill with fever brought on by fatigue, nervous tension, the blow on the head, and the queer kind of spiritual exaltation that was raging within his racked brain.

He wrote to Lord St. Vincent on a note of despair: "I never expect, my dear Lord, to see your face again. May it please God that this is the finish to that fever of anxiety which I have endured from the middle of June. Be that which pleases His goodness; I am resigned to His will."

The shattered man was, however, at what his contemporaries termed "the summit of glory" and had no material occasion for his gloom and misery, save only his wretched health. He longed to be at Naples, but not immediately could he accept Sir William's passionate invitation: "Come here, for God's sake, my dear friend, as soon as the Service will let you. A pleasant apartment is ready for you in my house and Emma is looking out for the softest pillows to repose the few weary limbs you have left."

.   .   .   .

Maria Carolina and the Hamiltons were not the only people to

6ecome hysterical upon the news of the victory of the Nile. A frenzy of rejoicing had swept through England. Captain Edward Berry was knighted for bringing the news; Lord Spencer wrote from Whitehall sincere congratulations on "the very brilliant and signal service you have performed for your country, the glorious action of 1st of August last, which most certainly has not its parallel in naval history"—while the destruction of the French Fleet moved Lady Spencer to strains that Emma could not have bettered:

"Joy, joy, joy to you, brave, gallant, immortalized Nelson. May that great God whose cause you so valiantly support take you to his refuge at the end of your brilliant career. All, all that I can say falls short of my wishes."

There were now likely to be laurels enough, armfuls of them, not only from his own country, but from all over Europe. Whatever reward he wished for he was likely to obtain, but the sick, nervous man was as unhappy as he had been in his neglected days of obscure struggle. Even his own sailors thought him strange in his manner, they reminded one another of the wound in the head, while the victor wrote to his wife, dwelling on his victory, his illness, his splitting head; he had continually to sink exhausted in his cabin, scorched with fever, light-headed from pain, but he was soon up again and his work was well and swiftly done. Three of the badly damaged prizes he burnt; he valued them at £60,000 and hoped that he might count on the Government for so much. The other six prizes were sent home under the escort of Sir James Saumarez; Captain Hood was left with six ships in Aboukir Bay, and not much more than a fortnight after the victory the British Fleet turned towards the brilliant city where Emma was making ready her grandiose welcome.

The voyage across the Mediterranean was difficult for the disabled ships. The *Vanguard* had been so badly damaged that for the last part of the voyage she had to be towed. Sir Horatio, lamenting that for four years and nine months he had not had a moment's rest for mind or body, lay in his cabin, struggling with nervous sensations more horrible than any wound. He felt as if "a girth were buckled taut over my breast, and I endeavour in the night to get it loose."

From the windows of the Palazzo Sessa, Emma watched the sea in a frenzy of impatience. In the weeks that had passed since the battle the Queen's hysterics had scarcely abated; she had written to the Neapolitan Ambassador in London: "I wish I could give wings to the bearer of the news, at the same time to our most sincere gratitude. The whole of the sea coast of Italy is saved, but this is owing alone to the generous English. This battle, or, to speak more correctly, this total defeat of the Regicides' squadron was obtained by the valour of this brave Admiral, seconded by a Navy which is the terror of his enemies. The victory is so complete that I can still scarcely believe it, and if it were not the brave English nation which is accustomed to perform prodigies by sea, I could not save myself from doubting it. . . . Recommend the hero to his master, he has filled the whole of Italy with admiration of the English. . . . All here are drunk with joy. . . ."

England was then to the Queen "that unique great and illustrious nation," that had beaten "the infernal French." Emma also referred to the nation described by the Queen as "*ces monstres nos voisons*"—"as cursed France!" "infernal French!" "the abominable French Council!"

While Maria Carolina was writing that everyone in Naples was drunk with joy, she overlooked some details that might have been considered likely to mar this delirium of delight. The British victory had decided her to plunge into war with France—but her fever-racked army was undrilled, unequipped and the only means of drawing the guns was by oxen, winter was coming on and nothing was ready. In brief, despite the Aboukir Bay success, the Queen had many difficulties to face before she could hope to meet the French on equal terms, but she troubled about none of them; well might Baron Alquier, who knew her well, write of her:

"The life of the Queen is nothing but a series of errors and regrets . . . tormented by a desire to govern . . . her habit of meddling has been nothing short of disastrous for Europe."

. . . . . .

The third week in September the *Culloden* and the *Alexander* appeared in the bay, giving notice of the approach of the flagship; the sight of the British colours in the harbour was the signal for an explosion of delirious joy among the Court party and the anti-French; the patriots were silent, regarding one another with sad, ironic looks, the aristocracy held contemptuously aloof.

In charge of the Neapolitan Fleet he had laboured so hard to equip, Prince Francesco Caracciolo watched the hubbub without comment. The French Resident, the charming aristocrat, General de Canclaux, whom the Directory had sent to Naples, on being ignored, had left his impossible post some time before. He had been succeeded by Mackau, his chargé d'affaires, a shrewd and fiery *sans-culotte*, who had given great offence by his efforts on behalf of the imprisoned patriots. Mackau had been replaced by Garat, a pedantic idealogue who was, however, honest and bold, and he had been followed by his secretary Lacheze. This man had now to stand aside and watch Maria Carolina, in spite of all promises and treaties, flaunt herself openly as an ally of Great Britain and an enemy of the Republic.

The Queen's conduct however, caused Lacheze no surprise, his unsuccessful efforts to obtain the release of the political prisoners had shown him her temper; he remained watchful, in touch with Rome, where Masséna had succeeded Berthier. Though it could hardly be said that General Bonaparte "had turned the Mediterranean into a French lake" and had cut the British trade-route with India, the French still occupied the whole of Italy save Venice, which was held by the Emperor, and the tricolour still floated above Valetta—twenty leagues from Sicily—Hompesch had surrendered Malta to General Bonaparte six weeks before the Aboukir Bay battle.

Lacheze, a violent Jacobin, had, however, much to gall him; there were five Portuguese vessels in the bay under the command of the Comte de Puységur, a French royalist; there had been the alliance with the Empire in May of that year; there was the murder of General Duphot in Rome; there was the flagrant violation of neutrality in the watering of the British Fleet at Syracuse —but Lacheze could do nothing but lower in the background and cry: "Tout est vieux en Europe et tout s'achemine vers la ruine, excepté la France!"

Cardinal Fabrizio Ruffo in Paris tried to persuade the Directory that the warlike preparations of His Sicilian Majesty were against the Corsairs, not against France, while the Directory decided to recall Lacheze, whose Republicanism was too violent to be any longer fashionable, and to send in his place General Lacombe Saint Michel to try moderate counsels.

Meanwhile Lacheze had to stand aside and watch the King and Queen of Naples receive the man who had destroyed the French Fleet.

.   .   .   .   .   .

On September 22nd in the golden weather that was beginning to have the thick, drowsy air of an Italian autumn, the *Vanguard* patched and shattered, came into the bay and was at once surrounded by hundreds of barges, gaily decorated by fluttering pennons, and by boats flying the English and Neapolitan colours, by music, and shouting, and huzzas; a richly decorated barge, which flew the arms of Britain, carrying His Britannic Majesty's Minister and his lady, came up alongside the battered man-of-war; the Hamiltons were accompanied by a band of musicians, who were energetically playing "Rule Britannia"; the stirring melody sounded extremely well on the French horns.

Emma was attired in the special dress she had had designed for the occasion—a blue shawl embroidered with gold anchors, the same nautical emblems, designed in gold, dangling from her ears, a long white dress with small buttons, on which were embroidered large initials of "N"·in gold, and a sash of the national colours.

Sir William was attired in a more orthodox fashion, in brocade, with powdered hair, in those breeches and laces and elegant fopperies that were fast becoming the mark of a past generation and a dead order of affairs.

With them was a thronging medley of secretaries and servants; lap-dogs and monkeys were scrambling over tables, on which were the last overblown, vivid Neapolitan flowers, flagons of iced sherbet, baskets of fruit, wine and sweetmeats.

Emma had been shouting directions with great energy as the barge made its slow progress across the bay, and as it neared the side of the *Vanguard*, it seemed as if her emotion would prove too much for her control; she began to strike one of her famous attitudes, clasped her hands and cast up her eyes, until the captain of the barge, fearful that it would upset, ventured to ask the patriotic lady to keep quiet, until he had manœuvred alongside the British man-of-war.

The Ambassador's lady subsided, but not for long; it was a great moment, and one that suited her and pleased her from the crown of her head to the tips of her toes.

She was swung on to the deck of the *Vanguard* (from which all traces of blood, fire and powder had been removed by scrubbing and cleaning), in the basket used for conveying lady passengers on board a man-of-war. Released from this grotesque contraption, she looked about her and saw standing before her the long-expected hero. With a shriek: "Oh, God, is it possible"—and bursting into the tears she could so readily command, she cast herself at the disfigured hero, brushed his breast, slid down his one arm, and then fell prone on the deck. Thus they met, Moll Cleopatra and Mark Antony from a Norfolk vicarage.

Sir Horatio found the scene deeply affecting. When Sir William scrambled up the side of the warship, Emma was raised between them and escorted down to the state cabin; they all wept together.

From the boats clustered in the bay rose shouts of "Deliverer! Preserver! Conqueror!" and strains of "Rule Britannia" and "God Save the King" came from hundreds of different instruments.

The *lazzaroni* lining the quay sent up cheer after cheer, and encaged birds were released as a Symbol of Joy, till the blue air was full of busy, winged things.

Emma was still sobbing, Sir Horatio and Sir William were leaning on each other, all overcome with emotion, when news came that His Majesty, King Ferdinand, with his Queen, was alongside the *Vanguard*; so the three must go on deck at once to welcome the Sovereigns of Naples.

As the hero and the beauty came up into the sunlight together, they would have been to an impartial spectator an ill-matched pair.

Easy living, freedom from care, plenty of rich food and fine wine, had broadened and coarsened Emma since the days when George Romney had been able to paint her as a wood-nymph or Ariadne. She had always been tall, and now she appeared enormous, the span of her shoulders vast, and her waist unbecomingly thick; her feet, always large, had not improved with the years, and she had developed the heavy, slightly wobbling walk of a middle-aged

134

woman who had run to flesh. She had lost, also, some of the
magnificent tresses which, in her own imagination at least, had
once fluttered round her heels; the famous chestnut locks had been
clipped close round the shapely head in the antique fashion, but
still hung richly in a profusion of curls; Emma might still be
termed beautiful, a goddess, a Juno, a superhumanly handsome
creature, though her complexion had coarsened from the lovely
rose in which George Romney had delighted, and was like a stain
on the broadening cheek; her nose had developed a slight aquiline
curve and the flatness of the face, the length of the neck, were now
distinctly visible defects. There yet remained the vivid colouring,
the magnificent lustrous eyes, the beautiful mouth, the woman's
triumphant air of being an acknowledged beauty. Her fame was
over her like a golden veil, her self-confidence disarmed criticism.
She was Emma, fashioned by twenty years of praise, by the adoration of Romney, by the homage of noblemen, by the friendship of
a Queen. She had for long held a position of authority. Her voice,
once carefully modulated to please Charles Greville and Sir
William, had become loud and insistent. She chattered Italian
with a Neapolitan accent, interspersed with English sentences,
touched by the tones of Flintshire. She gesticulated violently—at
every third or fourth movement she struck an attitude, graceful,
dramatic, incongruous.

No one had cared to inquire what her character had become
during these Neapolitan years. Her position had been that of a
friend of the Queen's and the wife of Sir William; not much of
grace or dignity, of honesty or generosity, could be expected of a
woman who successfully filled two such roles.

Many scandals had gathered round her; the nobility loathed her
as much as the *lazzaroni* liked her; her past and her present combined against her. It was said in the intellectual *salons* of Naples
that she owed her position, her domestic felicity more to Sir
William's blindness than to her own good conduct. To the
Italians, the British Minister resembled the well-known figure of
their national comedy.

The senile pantaloon's wife need not be faithful, since he so
stupidly dotes on her, that, while he is kissing one of her hands,
with the other she is passing a note to a lover.

Such as Emma Hamilton was, there she stood on board the *Vanguard* against her vivid background, beside the hero.

And the hero was satisfied with her; indeed, he wept with delighted, gratified vanity, when he found himself so dazzlingly rewarded by so beautiful a woman.

He saw no flaw in Emma. To him she was as beautiful as she ever had been to Charles Greville or George Romney; a superb creature, incontestably divine. Sir Horatio Nelson was himself of insignificant appearance, frail, even mean looking; but the haggard, lined face, the drooping, sensual underlip, the untidy tousle of hay-coloured hair, had already become symbolic of British sea-power. The little figure in the battle-worn, weather-stained blue uniform with the empty sleeve, white breeches falling over the shrunken legs, a patch over the inflamed eye, a cocked hat set on with a reckless air, was already known all over the world as a type of the naval glory of England. Ignorant of everything save his chosen profession, uneducated save in the school of war, scarcely a gentleman, and vulgar-souled, the hero had yet, for all his nerves, vanities, humours, and eccentricities, a brilliant air of being above his fellows, a flash of some genius and heroism that made him seem superior to better men.

.　　.　　.　　.　　.　　.

The King's gorgeous, cumbrous state-barge was alongside the *Vanguard*, rocking on the blue-gold veiled waters of the bay. Magnificent above all the magnificence in the harbour was the Royal scarlet pavilion on which were emblazoned all the complicated honours of the Spanish Bourbons. Good-naturedly pleased with the excitement, and relieved from the strain of months of panic and fear, King Ferdinand scrambled on board, an imposing figure with his rolling profile, his staring pale eyes, and full lips; His Majesty chattered voluble Neapolitan dialect, as he handed his Austrian Queen forward.

Sir Horatio could not understand a word that the Sovereigns said, nor had they a syllable of English. But no interpreter was necessary; it was understood that everything was joyful, fervent felicitations made the very air glow.

When the British officers landed on the great quay, beneath the semi-circle of flat-roofed houses, the colour of dead flowers, beneath terraces of agaves and arbutus, the high, dark pines beyond, with the Palace before them, and the great formidable fort above on one side, the Castle and the lighthouse on the other, the whole edged by the radiance of the Southern light, amid shouts of welcome and the flying flags, the flutterings of the released doves, and the playing of "Rule, Britannia," there was created an illusion that this was indeed the summit of felicity. It was Ulysses and his companions landing on the island of Circe, it was Rinaldo and his knights entering the garden of Armida, it was King Arthur and his fellows of the round table touching the shores of the Fortunate Isles; it was all this and more to Horatio Nelson.

At night the luxurious city blazed with illuminations, the rockets split into coloured stars in the purple air. In front of the Palazzo Sessa the initials of the victorious Admiral blazed in fairy-lamps; all the shipping in the harbour was outlined with strings of coloured lights; the music was incessant—every fiddler was scraping out "Rule Britannia" or the British National Anthem; fair fingers were plucking out these melodies on guitars and zithers, crowds were singing them in the streets, embracing the sight-seeing British sailors.

In the handsome apartments of the Palazzo Sessa Sir William's Etruscan vases, his antique bronzes, his cabinets of ivories and coins, were twined with laurel wreaths, and ribbons with the famous initial and every nautical emblem that Emma could think of. To her the most familiar of these was an anchor, and anchors there were in plenty, in ribbon, in gold cord, in paste, in flowers, hanging on her own broad white bosom and tangled in her own chestnut locks.

The conquering hero was flattered by the rescued Queen who, with her children clinging to her ample skirts, would have made a touching picture of beauty just rescued from distress, had she not been so obviously courageous herself. Her firm, jutting jaw, her sparkling eyes, the energy of her ferocious denunciations of the French were hardly suited to the language of a timid female, snatched from her enemies. Vengeance was the Queen's first desire.

Everyone was very happy; Sir William gave a great festival to celebrate the fortieth birthday of the British Admiral, a dinner with covers for eighty, a ball for nearly a thousand, for which he incurred debt to the amount of six thousand ducats.

All the Court party were there. There was everything that a lavish hand could provide, that a decadent society could enjoy, and a superb climate adorn. Count Francis Esterhazy also gave a huge ball. But the hero was still the son of the Norfolk parsonage; he believed himself a man like David, raised up by God to do his work, and sick and giddy as he still was, he doubted if the Calvinistic Deity, in whom he so firmly believed, would have been quite at home in the Neapolitan Court, and he viewed at first with disgust his surroundings.

The men seemed to him effeminate, the women depraved; he felt nauseated by the rich, unfamiliar food, he was sickened by the powerful wine, the pungent scent, deafened by the incessant music, the high voices of the women, the inane compliments of the men. He did not like what he could see of the government, corrupt, foolish, and treacherous. Nowhere did he find his own spirit of nervous energy; neither King Ferdinand nor the Queen nor Sir John Acton seemed to wish to do anything but laugh and feast and talk. Even the violent and active spirit of Maria Carolina seemed directed to random ends.

In the middle of all the gilded festival, wholly for his benefit, the hero wrote: "This court is so enervated . . . I am very unwell and their miserable conduct is not likely to cool my irritable temper. It is a country of fiddlers and poets, whores and scoundrels."

But the bilious attack passed; and he began to recover some health and spirit. In the golden rain of incessant adulation his simple vanity began to expand. He wrote to Fanny:

"All Naples call me *Nostro Liberatore*, and my greetings from the lower classes was truly affecting. I hope some day to have the pleasure of introducing you to Lady Hamilton, she is one of the very best women in the world, she is an honour to her sex; her kindness and Sir William's to me is more than I can express. I am in their house, and I may tell you it required all the kindness of my friends to set me up. . . .

"Celebrations from Lady Hamilton, celebrating my birthday to-morrow, are enough to fill me with vanity; every ribbon, every

button was Nelson; the whole service was marked, H.N., glorious
1st of August. Songs and honours are numerous beyond what I
can ever deserve. I send you the additional verse to 'God Save the
King,' and I know you will sing it with pleasure."

The pictures of the battle still hung in his disturbed mind and
clouded his spirits. Sometimes he felt a little uneasy that he
was not wholly pleasing the God with whom he had identified
himself. He regretted that the French ship, *Guillaume Tell* had
escaped.

"I trust God Almighty will yet put her into the hands of our
King. His all powerful hand has gone with us to the battle, protected us and still continues to destroy the unbelievers. All Glory
be to God."

To his father he wrote in an exalted strain:

"The Almighty has made me an instrument of human happiness
and I am daily receiving the thanks and prayers of Turks and
Christians."

in a half-understanding of his own weakness, he added:

"All my caution will be necessary to prevent vanity from showing itself superior to my gratitude."

The rewards came showering in. They were perhaps more
than any man had received before. On October 6th he was
gazetted "*Baron Nelson of the Nile, and of Burnham Thorpe in the
County of Norfolk.*" This was not what he had expected, but at least
it was a peerage.

There was an uproar among his friends in Naples that he had
not received an Earldom like Sir John Jervis or a Viscounty like
Admiral Duncan.

"Hang them," cried Lady Hamilton, in a fury of partisanship;
and the hero himself was ill-tempered at the meagre degree of the
honour. Was he, even after such a victory as that of the Nile,
still to be neglected and slighted?

It scarcely seemed so; there was another sword from the City
of London, valued at two hundred guineas. There was from Selim

the Third, the *Grand Seigneur*, who had lately joined the coalition
against France, one of the highest honours within the power of
His Imperial Majesty to bestow—a clasp of diamonds and an
aigrette of heron's feathers taken from a Royal turban, the *chelengk*,
the famous plume of triumph, and a huge pelisse of rich black sables.
The Dowager Sultana sent caskets blazing with brilliants, supposed
to be worth a thousand pounds; there were more brilliants from
Russia—this time round a portrait of the Tsar; from the King of
Sardinia, another potentate relieved from the fears of the dreaded
Republicans, a box, also heavy with diamonds; from the City of
Palermo a gold box and chain; from King Ferdinand, as an earnest
of greater benefits to come, an antique Royal sword; from the
Island of Zante a gold-headed cane, whilst soon came news that the
East India Company meant to vote him £10,000 and from various
other companies and funds were sums of money and pieces of plate.
There were also medals in gold for the captains, and in silver for
the other officers, gilt metal for the petty officers, and in copper
for the seamen and marines, struck by Lord Nelson's old friend,
Alexander Davison, whom he had appointed sole prize-agent for
the captures of the Battle of the Nile.

The College of Heralds was kept busy, getting together the
details of an elaborate coat of arms, the supporters of which had
augmented honours, flags, palms and tattered flags. When the
news began to come from England, it was indeed very gratifying to
the hero of the moment—London had risen to a fervour of
rejoicing over the news of the victory; everywhere there had been
illuminations, patriotic songs, flag-wavings, transparency scenes in
theatres and concert halls, showing the destruction of the French
Navy. No man, however vain, could have asked for more adulation.
He had, too, on every hand, through the good offices of Captain
Berry, now Sir Edward, a good advertisement. His loyal friend
acted as a first-class publicity agent and raised quite an agitation in
the country because the hero had not received at least an Earldom.
It was expected that the question would be mooted, when the Houses
of Parliament met in the following November.

Fanny, during all this, remained quietly at Burnham Thorpe,
enjoying the newly bestowed honours in the quiet company of her
old father-in-law and giving no hint how her mind or her heart

lay. There were plenty of local honours to cheer the old age of the
Rev. Edmund; there was a village collection for those wounded
in the battle, a fat pig roasted whole, big tankards of cider and beer
drunk by the gratified yokels, patriotic ballads sung in the sanded
tap-room of the local inn, a public banquet, a thanksgiving in the
village church; all this news coming in gazettes, prints, letters and
broadsheets to Naples, helped to make the very air the hero breathed
warm with praise. Emma, echoing all the delightful news with
cries of joy, was his constant companion, he was frequently with
the Queen, who added feminine allure to regal airs, and whose
very title was imposing to the parvenu Englishman. An Imperial
Archduchess, a Queen! These titles never lost their zest for
Horatio Nelson; he even accepted Ferdinand, with all his obvious,
crude faults, as an excellent person—it was enough that he was the
King. There were thousands of people in Naples who viewed with
bitterness and scorn the antics provoked by the Battle of the Nile.
There were those among them who noted that the face of the Queen
that smiled so graciously on Lord Nelson, showed "ferocity and
sensuality," while that of the King revealed "imbecility, cowardice
and frivolity." To these patriots, silent in the background of the
festival, "Giovanni Acton," was "corrupt, perfidious, flattering,
gifted with all the talents for intrigue" while to them, Sir William,
bending and scraping before his illustrious guest was the ridiculous
"scimia del ministro britannico."

And Emma? To these aristocratic and intellectual Neapolitans,
"the Divine Lady" was merely a woman of the streets and what
King Solomon found so hateful—a maid in the place of her
mistress.

.   .   .   .   .   .

In the Palazzo Sessa Lord Nelson began to recover gradually
his health and spirits, and further, to find himself more at home in
a world he had at first so detested. The enchantress had waved
her wand and everything had become of magical shape and
hue.

The hero had never known anything like it before; he was
dazed by the gorgeous ballrooms lit by hundreds of wax lights; the
triumphal arches with his name in a transparency, the caressing
foreign tongue whispering flatteries; the courtly melodies of

Cimarosa, alternating with the heady strains of "God Save the King," to which a new verse had been added:

> "Join me in great Nelson's name,
> Put on the rolls of fame,
> Him let us sing."

Above all—the praise, crude but to this man delicious, of a King, of a Queen, of Emma Hamilton, of dark-eyed ladies, of suave men of high birth.

His revulsion from "the fiddlers and poets, whores and scoundrels" soon passed with the headaches left from nights spent at the gambling-tables or in the ballrooms; he became overwhelmed by adulation, by the "kind attentions" of the Hamiltons; he had lost all sense of proportion when he wrote to his distant Fanny that Sir William and Emma "deserved the love and admiration of the whole world," because of their care of him.

In the debauched atmosphere of Naples, in the honey-sweet sunshine which fell over street after street of dusty stone houses devoted to pleasure, the British sailors became gladly demoralized; there were many Omphales ready to tame these fatigued demigods; an exhausted Hercules could find soft couches in plenty on which to repose; officers and men alike rowed across the crowded blue bay, landed on the busy quays, swaggered through cheering *lazzaroni* and picked lavish pleasures with fingers that soon grew unsteady.

.   .   .   .   .   .

To serve in the British Navy was believed to be one of the hardest tasks in the world; the recent mutinies at the Nore and Spithead had given a discontented public an odd glimpse into the private lives of sea heroes.

When the red cloths had been run up on the flagships of Lord Rodney and Earl Howe, the fighting men who were at once the pride and the scorn of Britain, became, for the first time and briefly, articulate.

The rude stalwarts who had received their copper medals for sweating at the red-hot British guns in Aboukir Bay, who had rendered possible these gaudy Italian rejoicings, were described by their own advocates as "scourings of jails, the friendless, the abject and the vile." The sailors on the fighting-ships were treated like felons, fed on biscuits as hard as flints, salted horse, Irish pork —some of which was kept so long that it was "polished like a cornelian," putrid water, rancid cheese and butter. Even these wretched supplies lay at the mercy of a cheating purser; on a line-of-battle ship this office was valued at £1,000 a year, the rum, contracted for from the Colonies, served out at the rate of two gills of ardent spirits per head per day, gave temporary relief at the cost of intense suffering. The pay was ninepence three farthings a day; this was usually in arrears and often made in paper of dubious value. The common seaman's share of prize money was small, he was seldom allowed on shore, and he was entirely at the mercy of officers and petty officers, who often treated him with great brutality; a flogging "to lay bare the backbone" was not uncommon.

When sick or wounded the seamen received the roughest treatment, and the least protest or complaint was regarded as insubordination, "Jacobinism," and the offender was liable to summary execution.

The sea voyages were long and there was little or no chance for the seaman to communicate with his friends, nor indeed for them to learn if he were alive or dead. This, in the case of pressed men, violently torn from their homes and occupations, produced a despair that often killed.

As some compensation for these hardships, the Admiralty not only permitted, but encouraged, vice and debauchery amongst both officers and men; when a line-of-battle ship put in at an English port, women of the street came on board in boat-loads and were allowed to disport themselves in the men's miserable quarters, and even to share the bunks occupied by the midshipmen.

Thus filth, disease, and excess extinguished what small chance of health and happiness tyranny might have left the sailor after— "mean, endless and unpitied hardships of food, clothing, and of pay which were aggravated by long years of the most brutal and cold neglect."

The two great mutinies of 1797 had wrung a few paltry concessions from Pitt's Government, on paper at least, but all the championship of Fox and Sheridan had not been able to do much for the men on whose conduct the safety of the country was admitted

143

to depend; men were hanged and transported in revenge for their blockading of the Thames, and the hanging of Billy Pitt in effigy.

Such were the heroes who had won the Battle of the Nile, who had refused to pity the Jacobins, perishing in the flames of *L'Orient* and who now reeled in and out of the wineshops and *bagnios* shouting "Rule Britannia" to the tinkle of mandolines.

The officers were mostly middle-class men, bred to the sea from childhood, ignorant of everything save their profession, brutal, vulgar, insensible, unbeatable at their work, greedy for prize money, for medals, for glory. They, too, took their share of pleasure where they could find it, and, scorning these soft foreigners, yet enjoyed strange delights in the intoxicating weather, in the care-free City of Sin, which stood so near the spot where Hannibal and the Carthaginian warriors had been enervated by Campanian luxury.

. . . . . .

The vague enchantment over Lord Nelson began to find a focus; when he was writing a dispatch, he put at the end that his letter was "a glorious jumble," because Lady Hamilton was sitting opposite to him; remembering that he was God's chosen captain, he added: "Our hearts and hands must be all in a flutter: Naples is a dangerous place, and we must keep clear of it."

He continued to complain of his health, "I hope," wrote Lord St. Vincent frankly, "the luscious Neapolitan dames have not impaired you."

In November came more exciting news; William Pitt had had to excuse himself in the Commons for the paucity of the reward given to the hero of the Nile, and the Commons, by way of amends, had voted Lord Nelson £2,000 a year; the College of Heralds was still busy with lions devouring tricolour flags, ruined batteries and palms, naval crowns and *chelengks*, while Lord Grenville had looked out a motto:

"Palmam qui meruit ferat."

True, there was a murmur from Fanny, in Burnham Thorpe, a protest from friends—why did not the hero return to where his family waited to welcome him?

When Lord Nelson had heard of the sable pelisse he was to

receive from Turkey, he had expressed the pleasure it would give him to see his Fanny wear it—but when it arrived in Naples, it was at once draped round the splendid shoulders of Emma, while the plume of triumph was sported in her luxurious locks.

The Court was beginning to smile at the junketings in the Palazzo Sessa, at the orgy of patriotism and hero-worship; all that was best in the city held aloof with bitterness or an ironic acceptance of the littleness of the tyrants. Prince Francesco Caracciolo occupied himself with his starved little navy, which was as efficient as his genius could make it, and watched in silence the flamboyant honours paid to the successful foreigners.

At the great banquets where covers were laid for eight hundred guests, where Lord Nelson had the place of honour, where all the talk was of the heroism of the British Navy, Prince Francesco sat silent, seemingly sunk in thought, refusing the elaborate dainties, crumbling his bread on the lace cloth. The displays the Neapolitan Court was making were not pleasant spectacles for a man who happened to be both a patriot and a gentleman. In the hearts of many men, placed as was Prince Francesco, arose the question of other loyalties, more important than the conventional loyalty due to an alien dynasty.

. . . . . .

The two women ruled everything; the Queen would have her way and gratify her spite with a war, Emma would have her way and gratify her vanity with a hero.

She was past the need of pleasing the gentlemen; she could aim at something more than a baronet or an earl's son—nothing but the victor of the Nile would satisfy her now.

From the moment that she had slid her substantial person, hung with toy anchors, on to the holystoned deck of the damaged *Vanguard*, she had meant to have him—the man, his fame, his trophies, his money, a share of the thanks from a grateful country. She saw at once his great weakness and her ability to satisfy it; whatever flattery he required she could supply; she really thought him a great man, but she added something to her own estimate of his worth; she was prepared to see him with his own eyes.

Ignorant of everything, save what profit could be made from

masculine passions, and the advantages to be gained from flattering a spiteful woman, the Patroness of the Navy was quite prepared to believe that Lord Nelson was God's elect and that the fight against the French Republicans was a holy war. But this aspect of the case did not much concern her; she wanted the successful man of the moment, as once she had wanted Greville and Hamilton.

Unfortunately for her, the hero was not a man to touch a woman's senses; mean in appearance, withered, yellow, mutilated and half blind, with rough manners, untidy in his dress and uninformed on every subject save the British Navy, weak in physique, continually sick, or coughing or gnawed by nerves, he was, at the age of forty, scarcely a better specimen of manhood than Sir William at sixty-five, and certainly not the sort of creature to enthral an Emma of thirty-eight, hearty and experienced. But she did not mind, she had found no difficulty in assuming love for her old husband, and she would find none in assuming an heroic passion for the battered Horatio. Besides, he was easy to get on with; mentally of her own level, socially nearer to her rank than Greville or Sir William, eager to accept her as she was, without trying to train her, or alter her; he could never tease her into acting the gentlewoman, for he did not know what a gentlewoman was, he would never check her vulgarity, wince at her noisy voice, complain of her garish clothes, for he would never notice these defects.

To him she was perfect; they were as easy in each other's company as the seaman after a long voyage was easy with the fat doxy waiting for him in the Wapping ale-house.

And each of them knew the jargon of the age, she from her cottage, he from his Rectory, had learned somehow all the sentimentalities, the moralizing, the tears, the poses, the affectations rendered popular by the writings of authors neither of them had ever read or perhaps heard of.

He could believe that God was with him in all he did, and she could babble about virtue and goodness with the air of a Julie or a Clarissa. She soon had him completely enchanted; she had not to use many of her arts before her personality had mopped up his, as a sponge mops up water.

He was soon as doting as Sir William, frantically and for ever in love, as besotted as General Bonaparte with his Josephine Beauharnais, quite lost to everything and everyone that did not circle round this woman.

What there was of heroism and genius in him, the fanatic courage, the half-insane energy, the power he had to lead and inspire other men, was not valued by Emma, who was no judge of greatness, but she resolved to use his position and his fame for her own ends. And the sum of it all was, that there was, by that autumn, a war with France, to gratify the Queen.

.   .   .   .   .   .

There were forty-five thousand Frenchmen left in Italy after the Battle of the Nile, and with General Bonaparte shut up in Egypt, these were disposed to keep quiet, and certainly had no intention of attacking Naples.

It was only obvious common sense to leave these dangerous enemies alone. But the Queen still had the picture of her murdered sister hanging in her cabinet with her own threat written beneath, and nothing could induce her to forgo what she thought would prove an easy vengeance. She appealed to the Emperor, who had just renewed war himself, for help; it was promised, but not immediately; winter was coming on and the imperial troops could not think of moving until the spring. Those who knew the leisurely methods of the Viennese Cabinet might doubt if they would stir then.

However, to console his mother-in-law, the Emperor sent her one of his more inefficient generals, the amiable and accomplished Bavarian, General Carl, Freiherr Mack von Leiberich, who a few years before had been in London arranging the campaign of 1794 with the Duke of York, his equal in incapacity, and who had seduced the brilliant Dumouriez from his allegiance to the French Republic.

The elegant imperialist arrived at Naples in a rich equipage with outriders, followed by a staff that occupied five carriages; with his charming manners, white, gold and scarlet uniform, and social graces, he was a great asset to the festivities to which Emma led her Nelson.

Naples was prepared to put eighty thousand men in the field, there was General Mack von Leiberich to lead them—so why not march straight on Rome and dislodge the insolvent, atheistical Republicans who were installed in the Eternal City?

Lord Nelson, then tacitly acknowledged as the arbiter of Neapolitan destinies, strongly pressed this plan; he advised the uncertain king, in language half of the Roman forum, half of the London pothouse, that he had two courses open to him, either to die, sword in hand (with God's blessing on a just cause) or to be kicked out of his kingdom.

This advice was the measure of the Admiral's infatuation; for to urge Ferdinand into an attack upon the French was stupid to a degree, showed a complete ignorance of the entire situation, and even a lack of ordinary intelligence.

If war was to be resolved on, it was only common sense to wait until spring should bring the Austrians and perhaps the Russians into the field as allies, before provoking an enemy for the moment cowed; nor was winter even in the South of Italy a desirable season for a campaign. Besides, Lord Nelson knew the state of the Court, the corruption, the muddle, the topsy-turvy finances, the inefficiency of every department; he had been told that the bulk of the population was seething on the point of revolution; he continually expressed a contemptuous opinion of every branch of the Neapolitan service, and often dwelt on the expense and difficulty of fitting out their costly, but neglected, fleet; he did not trust General Mack von Leiberich, nor indeed any foreigner, and in his quieter moments he must have seen that Ferdinand was a vicious fool and that Maria Carolina was worse, a meddling, vindictive, hysterical woman. But the first was a King, the second a Queen and Emma was their friend, so Lord Nelson urged on the crazy war.

He had always been fond of ladies though in a slightly shamefaced way, as one handicapped by both a religious training and an unattractive person; fourteen years before he had written, self-consciously—"they trust me with the young ladies, I am such an old-fashioned fellow."

Now he proved that there was one lady with whom he could not be trusted, when Emma lured him into starting a campaign in the autumn of 1798.

There was another force at work within him too—fanatical

hatred of the French nation. He had himself been startled by the
ferocity of his own thoughts when he had written: "Sometimes I
despair of getting these starved Leghorners to cut the throats of
the French crew—what an idea for a Christian!" he had added.
He had had many other odd ideas for a Christian yet perhaps not
unsuitable for a Christian trained by an evangelical parson who
believed in heaven above and hell beneath, and the chosen and the
saved.

When he heard that typhus had broken out among the French,
Lord Nelson rejoiced; every time he referred to his enemies, it
was in coarse violent terms that would have completely satisfied
the Queen of Naples: "Down, down, with the French, is my
constant prayer!" he wrote to Mr. Windham, the British Minister
at Leghorn.

The glow of the Nile victory was over all the Court; the Queen
had forgotten the Battle of Lodi three years before, when her
husband, in common with all the Princes of Italy, had desperately
cringed before General Bonaparte, when Prince de Belmonte
Pignatelli had followed the conqueror from one camp to another
in order to obtain an armistice. She had forgotten how Admiral La
Touche's grenadier had knocked at her palace door with the
ultimatum. She saw her troops, not only overrunning Italy, and
restoring the Pope, but seizing some of the Papal territory to which
she had long laid claim.

.   .   .   .   .   .

On November 21st there was, if not a formal declaration of
war, a manifesto issued in Naples stressing the insults to the Pope
and to monarchy lately offered by the French Republic, the seizure
of Malta, the occupation of Italy; to remedy these evils, the King
of Naples would march on Rome. General Lacombe, the newly
arrived French Resident, was fobbed off by the tale that all the
preparations were against the Dey of Algiers, but he was not
deceived. He had noticed the state of affairs in Naples, the crazy
administration, the forced levies, the deflated paper currency, the
toppling banks, the ruined trade, the deep discontent, the intolerable
taxes, the spoliation of the churches, the universal corruption, and
he wrote home of this crazy war—"This Court boasts of sixty

thousand men, they have not more than twenty-five thousand, and ought not to count on more than ten thousand."

The Frenchman also knew that the Neapolitan alliance with the Emperor was merely a defensive one, and that, despite the Queen's assertions to the contrary, it was most unlikely that the Emperor would move before the spring.

In brief, no nation could have been less prepared for war than was the Kingdom of Naples in the autumn of 1798. But Lord Nelson could not see what was so obvious to Lacombe; he viewed the situation entirely through the eyes of the Queen, and helped her and Emma to overcome the reluctance of Ferdinand, which arose from cowardice, not wisdom, to take the offensive. To the Englishman, the woman who had flattered him was "a great Queen" and Emma was a goddess—the beautiful woman who had been kind to him.

.   .   .   .   .   .

General Mack von Leiberich continued to inspect and parade the thirty-two thousand reluctant Neapolitans whom he had already flattered as "the finest troops in Europe," they were trained at San Germano, where Maria Carolina and Emma had shown themselves on horseback. The Queen ignored the fact that sixteen companies of her army, owing to the shortage of free men, had had to be recruited from jails.

"Be to us by land, General," said the Queen, with her dramatic air of a distressed wronged princess, "what my hero Nelson has been to us by sea."

It was a stimulating ideal, but Lord Nelson himself did not believe in the Bavarian, he had seen him blunder his manœuvres badly on the parade-ground, and declared that "he did not know his business."

"I have formed my opinion," he wrote, "I pray heartily that I may be mistaken."

Yet he was still strongly in favour of the silly march on Rome and hung over Emma entranced at her lusciousness, as she scribbled a note to Fanny, who might be beginning to wonder many things, and who had given a most disconcerting hint that she might come to Naples.

Scandal was again busy about the enchantress; Lord Nelson's old friend, Mr. Davison, wrote: "I cannot help again expressing my profound regret at your continuance in the Mediterranean," while Lord St. Vincent hoped "that the fascinating ladies of Naples would not seduce a man of mere flesh and blood, who would be unable to resist their temptations."

But Emma knew how to deal with such situations. Penelope must be kept quietly at home in the dull place that suited her so well, so Circe, grinning a little, wrote:

"Lord Nelson is adored here and looked upon as the deliverer of this country. He was unwell when first he arrived, but by nursing and asses' milk . . . quite recovered. . . . We only wanted you to be completely happy."

There were compliments to the Rev. Edmund and to "your ladyship" and the clever little letter concluded—"your ladyship's ever sincere friend and humble servant, Emma Hamilton."

There was an informal postscript.

"Sir William is in a rage with Ministers for not making Lord Nelson a Viscount. Hang them I say!"

"Deliverer of the country"; she had, indeed, got him to the point, that he looked upon himself, under God, as the Deliverer of Italy.

.   .   .   .   .   .

Five thousand Neapolitans seized Leghorn; Lord Nelson sailed to Gozo, captured it, planted the Bourbon flag above the rocks and returned to Naples, which was, he was convinced, the one place in the world that required his presence.

He had quarrelled with General Naselli over the question whether Naples was legally at war with France. Naselli declared it was not, and wished to allow the French shipping to leave Leghorn Harbour; after much shuffling on the part of Naples, the Englishman had his way, the French privateers were detained, the crews dismissed, their cargoes dispersed; these had largely consisted of grain for the troops.

Lord Nelson wrote wildly: "The enemy will be distressed, and thank God, I shall get no money. The world, I know, think money is our God; and now they will be undeceived, as far as relates to us."

There had been times when Lord Nelson had not been so indifferent to prizes, but he now had no need to worry about worldly affairs; there was a comfortable fortune awaiting him at home, and a royal treasury at hand for his immediate needs. On his return to Naples after the Malta interlude there were more rejoicings; sonnets fluttered thick as the released doves. An Irish Franciscan predicted that the English hero would take Rome with ships—despite geography. There were more balls, concerts, illuminations, fireworks, and then Ferdinand of Naples and General Mack von Leiberich departed for Rome, inspired by the tears and cheers of the Queen and Emma, and followed by troops both unwilling and untrained. The commissions had been sold to young fashionable men, incapable and frivolous.

As their route was across Neapolitan territory, their progress was unopposed, but the Bavarian General over-marched both men and horses and arrived at Castalana with his troops in a condition of utter fatigue.

The King entered Rome with his motley army, his artillery drawn by oxen taken from the plough; Championnet, the French General in command of the garrison, withdrew at the approach of the Neapolitans.

It was a flash of triumph for the old order, bells clashed, the orthodox rejoiced, the King, surrounded by his nobles, made a stately entry on horseback between Roman palaces lit by wax-tapers and hung with tapestries; there were plenty of orders, plumes, sashes and stars.

Ferdinand had promised protection to all who submitted, but for all that he put to death some French residents who made no resistance; his soldiery rewarded themselves for an uneventful victory by drowning the Jews in the yellow waters of the Tiber, and by the indiscriminate murder and pillage of supposed atheists and Republicans. While his troops were thus celebrating the triumph of Christianity with murder and rapine, the King gave himself up to receptions, eating and drinking, to issuing proclamations, and inviting the Pope to return to Rome "on the Wings of the Cherubim."

This show of friendship to His Holiness was not quite sincere;

there was a second plot in the drama of the struggle between the Allies and the French in Italy, and that was the secret struggle between Austria and Naples for the Papal territories. There was not only the question of driving the French out of Rome, but that of seeing that the Imperialists did not get much of the spoil. So King Ferdinand, as befitted a victor, began pillaging what Papal treasures the French had not sent to Paris; and the troops not employed in murdering Jacobins were busy packing up His Holiness's pictures, statues, tapestries and bronzes.

King Nasone had no great taste for these things himself, but they were worth money, looked handsome about a palace, and dear Sir William would no doubt be delighted to see wagon-loads of *objets d'art* coming into Naples.

The tricolour still waved over the squat, formidable round tower of Castel Sant' Angelo, but the King had silenced the French cannon by informing the garrison that for every shot fired he would put to death one of the sick Frenchmen in the hospitals.

Trees of liberty and red caps, with other republican emblems, were diligently removed from the obelisks that had once proclaimed the pride of people and Pontiff; the King sent messages to Naples ordering a public thanksgiving, and the Queen and Emma were able to embrace each other with tears of gratitude, while the cannons on the Neapolitan castles fired out salvos of joy.

But Lord Nelson was uneasy; he had no inkling that his own advice had been pernicious, but he could not bring himself to trust any foreigner. In between the bouts of sickness caused by mingled champagne and asses' milk, and when he could clear his mind of the dazzle of Emma's overwhelming femininity and drag his shaking limbs off Emma's silk cushions, he looked to the Fleet anchored in the bay. Despite the *Te Deums*, he thought it likely that the ships might yet prove useful. Events confirmed his poor opinion of Mack, as the Italians called von Leiberich; that general was supposed to have given himself chronic sick headaches by over-studying military science, but he was quite incapable of putting this hard-won learning into practice.

Nor was his present command a test of any man's capacity, since he distrusted, and was distrusted by, both officers and men, and the entire army mistrusted the King. Cowardice and treachery completed the work that inefficiency had begun, and the Neapolitans were soon starving, without clothes or weapons.

San Filippo, commanding nearly twenty thousand Neapolitans, deserted to three thousand of the enemy, shot through the arm by one of his own soldiers, and the Republicans came in for a good haul of booty, which more than balanced the losses they had suffered at Leghorn.

Mack von Leiberich, with the main body of disaffected, disloyal troops, himself disheartened and uncertain, abandoned point after point, despite superior numbers and many technical advantages, and fell back on Capua.

.   .   .   .   .   .

After three weeks of inaction in Rome, Ferdinand also began to feel uneasy; he kept his eye on his line of retreat, carriages, wagons, horses, mules were always ready for the signal for departure.

As the bad news came in, the King's nervousness increased; on December 2nd he cancelled a visit to a gala at the Alberti, on the 7th he was away to the Alban hills; his army had indeed completely collapsed; at least ten thousand men had been taken prisoner without making a show of fight; and Mack von Leiberich's disorderly retreat was turned into a flight by the desertion of hundreds of troops, who sacked the food-wagons and straggled southwards across the winter landscape robbing and destroying as they went.

During the twenty days of King Ferdinand's occupation of Rome, Championnet had been quietly getting together his orderly, seasoned, and disciplined battalions. He, a pupil of Hoche, was one of the best of the magnificent generals the Republic had provided to lead those armies which had overawed Europe; a gentleman, an idealist, cultured and humane, a fine leader and an excellent soldier; he was also young, of a fine presence and spoke Italian fluently.

His plans ready, he advanced on Rome, and re-occupied it without the least difficulty, and ordered the redirection of the packages and bales of Ferdinand's plunder "for the museums of France."

.   .   .   .   .   .

At Albano King Ferdinand heard with unspeakable fear of the downfall of his hopes; he had but one thought, to get back to Naples and the neighbourhood of the British ships. His frank cowardice gave his retreat an air of *opera buffo*. When he heard that Championnet was in Rome, Ferdinand asked the Duca d'Ascoli to change clothes and place with him. Attired in the royal uniform, the Duke went ahead, while Ferdinand followed, riding beside Prince Migliano Loffredo, and pleading in the dialect of a Neapolitan *lazzarone*—"not to be left behind."

When the carriages were reached, His Majesty took one of the plainest and sat on the left-hand side, pallid with emotion as he rolled over the ravaged country to Naples.

Lord Nelson heard with disgust of these disasters; the Neapolitans had, he declared, no honour to lose, "they seemed afraid of a sword or a musket," but they had lost everything also; he was sickened and alarmed, too, by the condition of the Court—"the state of this country is very critical; nearly all in it are traitors or cowards . . . in short, all are corrupt."

He wrote in ignorance; there were thousands of noble, brave, and honest people in the kingdom of Naples, but they did not belong to the Court party. Nor did Lord Nelson trouble his head about them; all not on the side of the King were to him "Jacobins" and worthy of destruction.

"Down with the French, ought to be written on the walls of every Cabinet in Europe," he wrote.

Yet he knew what this King was, and considered his followers the scum of the earth; but an unbalanced mind, one, indeed, almost overturned by nervous reaction and excited vanity, prevented him from seeing even a glimmer of the truth and even from reflecting that his poor opinion of the Neapolitans should have prevented him from urging on a war at the wrong time of the year, and a march on Rome that, in Ferdinand's hands, was bound to be a grotesque failure.

.   .   .   .   .   .

When the rattling carriage with the sweating King inside rolled into the courtyard at Caserta, the Queen who passed for a brave woman, sunk in a panic of terror into Emma's arms, fearing "les scènes de Varennes avec toutes leurs suites."

She might have known that in just such a fashion her wretched husband would return, but she behaved with all the abandon of one profoundly disillusioned, and went from one fit of hysterics to another.

Emma, far more level-headed, took counsel with Lord Nelson, who, uneasy and out of his depth, fretted in the Palazzo Sessa.

No one troubled about His Britannic Majesty's Minister; Sir William was now as much a part of the background as one of his own Etruscan vases; he too felt bilious and nervous, but Emma, with a hero to wait on, no longer fussed over him; he had to nurse her lap-dog, play with his monkey, turn over his cabinets of coins, curse the French, and long bitterly for the quiet days before the war.

With the perfume of Emma's presence over him, Lord Nelson rallied his spirits and tried to take stock of the situation; he liked to be a champion of distressed ladies, he tried to think what could be done for a panic-stricken Queen, with a baby at her breast, a crowd of small children, an incapable husband, a corrupt personnel; with a man like Sir John Acton filling all the big government posts himself.

The task was not easy, even with Emma as inspiration; Vesuvius was in eruption and the air heavy with gases and darkened by showers of fine ashes; the nervous tension was heightened by the sight of the great dark mountain with the flaming cones and gloomy spread of smoke; rumblings of earthquake shook the streets where the British sailors drank and idled; timid people spent the nights in their carriages, and the fishermen read in the livid skies the presages of mighty storms.

The news that came into Naples could hardly have been worse; Championnet and Macdonald had decided to advance on Naples; the foolish advice of Lord Nelson, the impulsive fury of the Queen had roused a nest of hornets. Von Leiberich's disbanded army moved in hordes over the country, destructive as locusts, bloodthirsty as only human beings can be; the towns of the Abruzzi fell without resistance into the hands of the advancing French; Macdonald and Championnet, commanding the best troops in the world, steadily fought their way through anarchy to the coast. In Naples and the surrounding country was utter panic; streams of terrified people followed the priests into churches crowded with images of saints, and, fearful lest God had forgotten them, hid or sent away their property, if possible, by sea.

The Queen and Emma, peeping from the great windows of the Palace, saw the square filled by *lazzaroni* begging for weapons with which to kill the French and the Jacobins; the educated classes remained desperately quiet, praying for the speedy arrival of the French; Maria Carolina urged on the secret police, the spies, but they slackened in their zeal, apprehensive of Championnet's approach. Yet the Queen contrived to have hundreds of suspects arrested, including the Minister of War.

General Francesco Federici told the King roundly to his face that he alone was to blame for this terrible crisis, Prince Caracciolo sat silent and pale at the dinner-table of General Berta, not even unfolding his napkin, nor drinking a glass of water. Sir John Acton began to pack a lifetime's plunder, Sir William to make agitated arrangements for the transport of the fine collection of Sicilian vases he had hoped to sell to the King of Prussia, and now intended to offer at a bargain price to the museum in Montague House.

Emma was everywhere, supervising everything with the air of a goddess who "rides the whirlwind and directs the storm."

On December 21st an ugly little incident brought matters to a crisis; one Ferrari, a Royal messenger, who was taking a letter to Lord Nelson, then on the *Vanguard* in the bay, was seized by the excited crowd, dragged to the Piazza Reale and there murdered while the King gaped from a balcony. The meaning of this was obscure; Ferrari, though in Royal employ, was dispatched as a spy and a Jacobin, either under some mistake, because he knew too much, or because, as the patriots said, the Queen had engineered a crisis for her own ends.

In any case, Maria Carolina used the incident to make out that she and her family and all the royalists were in danger of their lives, and to pretend that *émigrés* were being slaughtered in the streets of Naples.

The King remained in a state of passive terror; watching his wife, Emma and Nelson, for a signal, with the rapt attention of a dog who longed to know if it was to jump through a hoop, or stand on its hind legs.

Since his flight from Rome no one paid him any serious attention and the squibs crackled.

> "From his native shore
> Marched our King with men galore
> Whom he bravely led
> Swaggering from home
> Flourishing on Rome,
> He came, he saw, he fled."

.   .   .   .   .   .

The victor of the Nile decided on flight before the French as quickly as had poor King Big-Nose, when he was caught in Rome by the news of Championnet's advance. Lord Nelson still saw everything through the eyes of Emma; he believed that the mob was rising as it had risen in France in 1793; he could not understand that the vulgar people, the *lazzaroni*, were entirely on the side of the King and Queen, and that it was the intellectuals and the aristocracy who were against the Court.

It might have been considered the duty of the British Admiral after his once having undertaken to defend Naples, to remain in that city, to fortify it as best he could, and with the men, stores and ammunition at his command to defy the advancing enemy. Instead of doing so he resolved on instant flight, and he used the British Fleet to convey the Royal Family to Palermo across the Tyrrhenian Sea, and that despite hard, winter weather and the gathering of mighty storms.

The political situation was still in a hopeless tangle, the atmosphere full of suspicion, doubt, treachery and hysteric panic. It was still doubtful whether Naples was yet officially at war with France.

The King and Queen, their Court and friends, resolved to escape from this bloody chaos which Ferdinand's cowardice and Maria Carolina's vindictiveness had done so much to bring about. In this design Emma was the guardian angel and Lord Nelson the protecting knight. The Queen clamoured that the mob wanted to keep them as hostages; this was utterly untrue, but Lord Nelson believed it.

He made the fleet ready, and had already written to Troubridge:

"Things are in such a critical state that I desire you to join me without one moment's loss of time. . . .

"Everything is as bad as possible. For God's sake make haste. Approach the place with caution."

All his instructions were marked "Most Secret." He had so far deceived himself that he did not realize that he was helping a couple of cowards to flee from their posts, but rather saw himself as one who waited on great events. He arranged for barges and cutters to lie outside the docks and wharfs, men to be armed with cutlasses and the launches with carronades. He himself came on shore heavily armed, as if in fear of an attack, mounted to the Queen's room by a secret staircase, and found Emma, assisted by the always useful Mrs. Cadogan, in a state of tragic energy.

She was supervising the packing of all the valuables in the Palace; pictures, tapestries, bronzes, ivories, clothes, furs, were being thrown into boxes and baskets, and tied up in bales and marked "Biscuits" and "Salted Pork"; ornaments and jewels were swept into every possible receptacle. The same work had gone on at the Embassy; everything that was of the least value, from Emma's famous five hundred pounds' worth of diamonds to the cashmere shawls she used for her poses, was packed up and carted away.

For twelve nights in succession the energetic woman did not take off her clothes, only snatching a few minutes' sleep here and there, then and now, on a Pompeian couch or a satin arm-chair. Gems, curios and dresses to the value of £2,500,000 sterling passed through her hands in less than a fortnight. Under her vigilant eye all this booty was sent with the aid of the British sailors to the British ships. Nor did this amount of plunder blunt the avarice of the King and Queen; as if their design were to ruin utterly the unfortunate country they were abandoning, they took all the money out of the bank, all the treasure—much of it coined from private plate and ornaments that had been gathered together for war—and had this sent on board the *Vanguard*.

By not confiding their persons and their treasure to Prince Francesco Caracciolo, they offered the Neapolitan Admiral, who had been a personal friend of the King, a deliberate affront. Caracciolo was not only the best sailor in the small Neapolitan Navy, but one of the best sailors in the world. The English Admiral, Hotham, had publicly complimented him on his brilliant services in the Mediterranean; but now, in this atmosphere of universal suspicion

159

where nobody seemed to be trusted by the Royal party save the British, he was passed over, and the plunder of the Bourbons deposited in the charge of the British Admiral.

Efforts were made to keep these preparations of the flight secret, but the news leaked out. The *lazzaroni* were in despair, believing that their beloved King was abandoning them to be murdered by the French, as indeed he was; while decent citizens secretly rejoiced. An underground passage led from the Royal Palace to the Mole, and this was most useful in conveying away bag and baggage. When everything that was valuable and movable had been taken away, and news was coming daily of the quick advance of Championnet and Macdonald, the Royal Family took the final step and fled from Naples on the night of December 21st accompanied by Sir John Acton, the Hamiltons, the Prince Castelcicala, Prince di Belmonte Pignatelli and some other courtiers and ministers.

With the Queen were her children, the youngest of whom was an infant in arms, and one of whom, the Crown Prince, had with him his wife Clementine, the daughter of the Emperor; this Princess had to look after her delicate and sickly child, who was so backward in intelligence that Maria Carolina declared she believed it was an imbecile.

Lord Nelson watched over the whole proceedings with a solemn anxiety which, considering the circumstances, had an air of caricature. The whole affair was like the libretto of a melodramatic opera. From a city where they were not in the least danger, where indeed a large number of the populace were ready to fight for them, from an enemy who had not yet arrived and who might without difficulty be defied and kept at bay, King Ferdinand, his family, and Court, fled as if a thousand furies had been on their heels.

The use of the underground passage was an unnecessary touch of drama, perhaps the result of Emma's theatrical imagination. If they had gone away openly, there was no one likely to stop them. Nelson, cloaked like a Spanish conspirator, led the way through the passage, swinging a dark lantern, and the party—women and children huddled together, men nervously clutching their swords —came behind him, stumbling in the half-light, shivering in the damp. They emerged at the wharf to find a sharp gale blowing, tattered clouds scudding across a black sky, and the waters foaming high among the rocks. The party sat huddled in the *Vanguard's* barge, whipped by the winter wind; they were rowed by British sailors across the bay. When they reached the flagship they found it already crowded with other refugees, among whom was the Imperial Ambassador. The other British warships and some foreign merchant-men which had no wish to encounter the French were ready to accompany Lord Nelson. It was, however, by reason of the wind, impossible to leave the bay, and for twenty-four hours the *Vanguard* veered about the gulf, now and then taking on board other Royalists, whose barges came struggling up through the choppy sea.

Prince Francesco Caracciolo was in command of the *Sannita* which, though it was poorly equipped, he managed with superb skill.

The storm increased in violence and the ships were unable to pass Capri until dawn on Christmas Day. Several Neapolitan ships which should have accompanied the Royal party were unable to sail, because the sailors had deserted, not so much from disloyalty to the King as from loyalty to the families whom they would have been forced to leave behind to affront an invasion. The passage across the Tyrrhenian Sea was made only with the utmost difficulty. Emma kept up her spirits wonderfully; she bustled about, making up beds, providing linen, nursing the prostrate Queen, comforting her sea-sick children. Afterwards she wrote to her crony, Greville:

"All our sails were torn to pieces and all the men ready with their axes to cut away the masts, and poor I to attend and keep up the spirits of the Queen, the Princess Royal, three young Princesses, a baby six weeks old, and two young Princes. The King and Prince were below in the wardroom, my mother there assisting them, all their attendants being so frightened and on their knees praying."

Maria Carolina lay on the plank in her cabin, vomiting into the basin that one of the Neapolitan sailors brought, emptied, and returned, continuously. Her children were alarmingly ill; their only relief was rags, damped in vinegar, applied to their temples. Nelson, directing the passage of the ship with the utmost anxiety, declared that never before had he seen such a storm; at one moment it was doubtful whether they would make Palermo; nor were the British Admiral's spirits raised by seeing that the *Sannita* under Prince Francesco Caracciolo's command rode the tumultuous waves easily, despite the tempest, and kept alongside the *Vanguard* to encourage the King by its presence. High in the wind and rain the vermilion standard of the Sicilian Bourbons fluttered in the dark; the ship's lanterns were gloomy specks of light, half-submerged in the whirl of the tempest. In one of the cabins Sir William, who had been fretting himself to a string over the safety of his antiquities that he had seen packed on board a British merchant-man, and that for all he knew were by then at the bottom of the sea, sat, incapable of rendering anyone assistance, holding a pistol to his head, threatening, he said, to shoot himself if the ship went down, that he might not hear the guggle-guggle of the water in his throat.

The Imperial Ambassador also made other preparations for what he believed was his approaching end. He cast into the angry waves the snuff-box which bore the nude portrait of his mistress. He did not wish, he said, to go into the presence of the Almighty with such a profane article upon his person.

Lord Nelson, harassed and anxious as he was, did not fail to notice with admiration the brave conduct of the beloved Emma. While all the foreigners were groaning with fear and sea-sickness, the Patroness of the Navy showed herself worthy of her title; she was brave, efficient and cheerful, waiting on the Queen and the Royal children with real devotion. It was in her arms that one of the unfortunate little Princes died from exhaustion.

On the afternoon of Christmas Day, as the *Vanguard* battled round Capri, the little fleet sighted Palermo; the scarlet pavilion and the British flag were still flying from the topmast of the *Vanguard* as the battered ship lumbered into the harbour. The Captain of a Neapolitan frigate that then chanced to be in the road had to help the British ship into safety, while Prince Francesco Caracciolo showed his expert seamanship by sailing in swiftly over the tempestuous sea; but the skill that he showed on this occasion brought him neither admiration nor reward. It was, if anything, felt to be unfortunate that it should have been he and not the hero of Aboukir Bay to make this display of marvellous seamanship. In the wake of the Royal flight were the red flares of the Neapolitan ships then in the harbour, which, upon being deserted by their seamen, were burnt by Commodore Campbell in command of the Portuguese frigates.

Sick, dishevelled, and shaken with grief at the loss of her son, Maria Carolina landed on the quay at Palermo, attended by her frightened children and her ragged retinue. Emma, however, had kept up her spirits; she and Mrs. Cadogan had shown their superiority to a parcel of foreigners; indeed, so spirited had been her conduct that Nelson, writing an account of the Royal flight to Lord St. Vincent, gave her official praise:

"It is my duty to tell your Lordship the obligation which the Royal Family as well as myself are under on this trying occasion to Lady Hamilton. Lady Hamilton provided her own bed, linen, etc., and except one man, no person belonging to Royalty has helped the Royal Family, nor did her Ladyship enter a bed the whole time she was on board."

. . . . . .

The reception given to the fugitives by the Sicilians was, as the Queen bitterly remarked, what might have been expected—curiosity touched with suspicion and contempt. The Royal visit was entirely unexpected, and nothing was ready for the Queen's comfort. The accommodation available at the Royal Palace was of the most wretched kind. Always voluble, a prodigious letter-writer, and in need of a confidant, the Queen sat down the day after her arrival in Palermo and scribbled off two long letters to the Marchese di Gallo, the Neapolitan Minister at the Imperial Court, a man whom she disliked and whom she had violently abused, but to whom she now turned in her distress.

In her own breathless hysteric and vivid way, she described, in cipher and lemon juice, the sufferings that seemed to her without parallel, and despatched the letters to Vienna in the hope which underlay the hysteric scrawl that di Gallo would be able to persuade the Emperor to come to her assistance:

"The most unhappy of Queens, mothers and women, writes

163   M

this to you. I say the most unhappy because I feel everything so acutely and I doubt if I shall survive what has happened to me during the last forty days. We fled from Naples on Friday. The arrangements for burning the ships kept us till Sunday in the harbour, where we received deputations that came to harangue us to try and make us return, but never thought of arming themselves to defend us. Mack came on board Sunday morning, half-dead, weeping, exclaiming that all was lost, that treason and cowardice were at their height and that his only consolation was to see us on board Nelson's ship. The sailors fled from the ship; at last we had to put English and Portuguese sailors to replace them. At least 1,500 sailors fled in one night. We had at last to man the *Sannita* and the *Archimede*—without which Nelson would not sail, with foreigners. The Portuguese remained behind in the harbour to burn, to my eternal grief, our beautiful Navy, which has cost us so much. We set sail at eight hours of the evening. Our misfortunes which are such that I wish to die! To begin with the most essential, at Palermo people seemed pleased to see us but not enthusiastic. The nobles crowded round; they seem to have no desire but to obtain all they can and my heart tells me that if the Emperor does not soon put himself in action it will not be four months before we are forced out of Sicily as we were out of Naples. I would offer these vultures all the jewels and treasures which we have with us, if they would only leave us to live and die in peace. . . .

"Indeed, I feel desperate. I vow to you I do not think I can live in this condition. I do not believe I shall survive. In the name of God, arrange for my unhappy daughters to go to Vienna where marriages can be arranged for them or they can retire to the Convent of the Visitation. My daughter-in-law is very ill with her chest; she is not likely to survive. Their father, though I should not speak of that, does not seem to feel anything except what concerns himself personally and not much of that, or to realize that he has lost the best part of his crown and his revenues. He only takes notice of the novelties that amuse him, without thinking that we are reduced to a quarter of our revenue, dishonoured, unhappy, and have led others into the same unhappiness. Indeed, I am in despair, I do not think I shall survive. Everything displeases me here, all I love best has gone. The civilities here are such as would be given to a King who has lost everything. I think no more of grandeur, nor of glory, nor of honours, I only think to live retired in a corner."

After a pause for Emma's ministrations and a little repose, the unhappy Queen continued to put her troubles on paper:

"The details of all our suffering will make you tremble. It has really been beyond my strength to endure, and I feel that I shall not survive. Friday the 21st, following a revolt in the town, people killed and wounded under the windows of the King, talk of the people confiscating the Castles, the arms, and forbidding anyone to leave the City, flight was decided upon. What I suffered during the rest of this day cannot be expressed. There was a cold north wind as we left at night. I trembled like a leaf. Without my virtuous and attached Mimi I should have fallen a thousand times. Think of the horror of this, with six children and my young daughter-in-law and an infant at the breast! We arrived on board all rigid with cold and I half-insensible with unhappiness. We passed that first night without bed, without light, fire or supper. Saturday, the 22nd, began with a letter from the deputation, everyone demanding to speak to the King, who would see no one. The wretched day passed in this misery and my heart was torn. We tried everywhere to find what was necessary for so many children accustomed to every luxury, but in vain. At last on Sunday morning arrived poor General Mack. We received him, and he was much struck to see an unhappy, but honest, loyal, sensible family, seated like beggars on the ground. The sailors fled; even by offering them gold we could not keep them. At last four vessels, five frigates, ten galleons, twelve corvettes, ninety shallops were condemned to be burnt, proving the infamy of our sailors, who, though they cried 'Long live the King' continued to flee, and so condemned to the fire the fruits of so much trouble, so much money. Niza, the Portuguese Admiral, performed this work so cruel to me, and the *Sannita* and the *Archimede* left, the last with four hundred sailors, and the *Sannita* with two hundred, of which half were English and Portuguese, all the Neapolitans having fled. We raised anchor at eight o'clock in the evening. At midnight the bad weather commenced, but the storm did not really break till Monday, the 24th. We were all the voyage lying on the ground, eleven of us in the demi-poop, the women half-unconscious, two sailors kept bringing us vinegar and basins in which to vomit. At one o'clock after midday there came such a tempest that the sails were all torn to shreds, both in our vessel and that of Caracciolo. We began to think ourselves lost. The mast broke, the sailors were climbing about with hatchets to cut down the damaged rigging.

Louise was in her chemise on her knees, Amelia demanding a confessor who would come to give her absolution, Leopold the same. I felt so unhappy to think of what had happened and what must happen yet, that I saw death come without regret, trusting in the Divine Mercy and content to perish with my children. Towards two o'clock the danger ceased and Nelson said that in the thirty years he had been at sea he had never seen such a storm, a wind and tempest. When night came the sea was so heavy that everything had to be roped. We remained still on the ground. Tuesday, Christmas Day, the storm diminished a little, and at nine o'clock my son Albert, aged six years and a half, who had never suffered from convulsions, though so very delicate, suddenly took one so strong that, though he had never vomited, he died at half-past seven in the evening in the midst of us, despite all our remedies. Let any mother judge of my feelings. His dear little corpse stayed with us until five o'clock in the morning, when we arrived, and I hastened to disembark. The town of Palermo is large, the Palace uninhabited, inconvenient, cold, lacking everything, neither chairs, nor bed, nor sofa, nor anything. One half-furnished apartment, which was warmed, had to serve for my daughter-in-law and her child. The former is very sickly, but I hope to prolong her life. I have been bled, all my children are ill, nobody has yet recovered from the voyage. I have besides the frightful loss of my child and that of our realm. The King is well, the Prince the same. The Princess suffers with her chest and keeps coughing. My daughters and Leopold are sad, overcome, suffering, and think as I do. I have seen little here, but everything affects me, and I believe I cannot live long here; I am convinced that I shall succumb, and my death is indifferent to me, if I can see my six daughters and Leopold established in some religious institution in Austria. I see everything black. Give all these frightful and truthful details to the Empress, my daughter.

I feel everything, as I alone can feel. I foresaw all and no one would listen to me. Religion can alone support me. Italy is in the hands of barbarians, our commerce is ruined. Further, for the climax of unhappiness, the few effects and the goods we saved have been lost in the tempest. I do not even like to think how many honest people have perished—only the diamonds are saved. I should have preferred to have kept more useful furnishings. As for me, I am in true despair, convinced that Sicily will soon follow the example of Naples, and that we shall lose life and honour.

If the sea voyage were not so long I would try to get to Austria, but I fear too much to lose another child. The King passes my comprehension. He has already taken a little house in the country. Prince Jaci is his factotum. He goes each evening to the theatre or the masked ball and is gay and content, is irritated if anyone talks to him of Naples, will not give any audiences, will not show himself officially in any public place, he grumbles at anyone who mentions business to him and speaks as if nothing had happened; therefore they all despise him and do as they please. I am quite sure I shall perish here; I cannot live much longer and my children will remain without a mother, abandoned orphans. O blessed tempest, why do you not engulf us all?"

Throughout that winter the Queen continued to write to the Marchese di Gallo, a man whom she had scornfully declared to be "half a Frenchman," but on whom she now relied to urge the Emperor to assist her. These letters were all of the same tone, full of lamentations, descriptions of her miserable situation, and constant assertions that she "would not be able to survive."

The King had, as his wife so bitterly noted, slipped easily into his old comfortable ways. Avoiding his querulous wife and sickly family as much as possible, he settled down to the only kind of life he relished. As long as he had his boon companions and petty cash for his pleasures, he was content, and considered himself to be well rid of Naples.

"He is a philosopher," said Lord Nelson, adding with zest, "God bless him."

Emma and Mrs. Cadogan, cheerful and resourceful, did what they could for the Queen, but the winter was bitter, the Palace rooms gaunt and unfurnished. The Royal children went from one illness to another. It was believed that the Crown Princess, the Archduchess Clementine, was dying of consumption. She was kept alive only by a milk diet. The stone-floored Palace, with the long, uncurtained windows and undraped doors, lacked every comfort. There were no cushions, no easy chairs, no good beds; worst of all was the cold. The Queen's cries against the draughts, the chilly atmosphere, and the bitter winds rose to heaven.

The British ships, men-of-war, and the merchant-men rode in the harbour; the British sailors and refugees did what they could to accommodate themselves in Palermo. The polished, elegant Sicilian nobility viewed the Royal caravan with cynic amusement, those who hoped to get something out of the King hung round him, all others remained aloof; there was always somebody to give a masked ball, a company to perform at the theatres, enough singers and musicians to get up a concert.

Emma's indomitable energy soon produced a fair imitation of the delights of Naples; she did not relax any of the arts that fascinated Lord Nelson, and she was constantly his companion during these trying winter months, while her old husband sat shrunken in front of the smoking wood-fires cursing the mighty winds that blew from Etna and lamenting over the cases of vases which had been lost in the famous tempest.

Queen Maria Carolina, with her usual exaggeration, had greatly overstated the Royal losses on the passage from Naples to Palermo. Most of the booty besides the diamonds had been saved, and the only life lost had been that of the unhappy little Prince Albert.

.   .   .   .   .   .

Never had a city been more completely abandoned than Naples. When the populace saw that the harbour was clear of British shipping and that the Royal Family had fled, they soon discovered that they had been despoiled not only of every means of defence, but almost of every means of existence. There was no money in the Royal Treasury or in the banks, everything of value had gone from the Royal Palaces and museums; private property belonging to Royalists and foreigners had been taken away by British and allied ships. The army that had followed King Ferdinand to Rome and back was now split up into marauding *banditti*; there were not enough regular troops left in Naples to garrison one of the castles. The sailors who had deserted the Royalist ships were without officers and practically disbanded. There was no form of government; Prince Pignatelli had been left as Regent with the foolish injunction "to defend Calabria to the last rock."

On January 12th news came that General Mack von Leiberich, who had returned to Capua, had surrendered to Championnet, who refused his sword with the smiling remark that his Government had forbidden him to accept goods of English manufacture.

168

The leading citizens hastily got together in some attempt at law and order, and sent deputations to wait on the Regent, who put them off with evasive replies. On December 28th the anxious inhabitants of Naples saw smoke rising off the coast at Posilippo, and learned that the Portuguese Commodore, the Marchese di Niza, acting under whose orders no one knew, was burning the Neapolitan Fleet, which had been Prince Francesco Caracciolo's pride and occupation for years and which had successfully kept at bay the Corsair.

During the next few days the wintry seas about Castellamare and other places along the coast were illuminated with bonfires fed by Neapolitan ships. Some believed that the Portuguese Commodore had received his orders from Lord Nelson, some thought that this was the Queen's meddling, some thought that he had acted on his own initiative; the actual destruction of the fleet had been carried out by Commodore Campbell, a Scotsman in the service of Portugal. The wanton destruction of the Navy which had cost so much to build, and which had been a source of satisfaction to all honest Neapolitans, caused distress and indignation in the heart of every patriot. One of them wrote: "It was a pitiful sight to see the burning ships while the nation was robbed of its strength—so many tears, so much substance and wealth of the citizens were consumed. All night long they kept on burning, keeping the whole sea ablaze."

This strange act, which completed the defencelessness of the great city, increased the panic in Naples; there were reports that all the wood stored for shipbuilding and all the grain in the granaries at the Porta della Maddalena were also to be destroyed.

Deputations of the more responsible citizens waited in vain on the Regent, he would receive no one; petitions were ignored; Championnet was at Spavanise, a few miles off, and the tumult, tension and fear, in Naples became fearful; the militia, or town guard, paced before the threatened stores, while there were bread riots in the streets, and the citizens sat long hours in anxious conclave.

Anarchy was in sight; the situation resembled that of Paris in 1792, save that, in Naples, the mob was loyal to the sovereigns, and the aristocrats as well as the intellectual middle-classes, were republican in sentiment.

These people were hot against the Queen; it was said that she had been heard to declare that she would "leave Naples nothing but its eyes to weep with." Her hand was suspected in everything; the only hope of safety—of existence—seemed to be in the coming of the French.

By January 11th, Pignatelli had made ruinous terms with the French Generals; a two months' truce was purchased by ceding Capua with all its military stores and a line passing from Acerra on the Mediterranean to the mouth of the Ofanto on the Adriatic; the ports of the two Sicilies were to be declared neutral, and Ferdinand was to indemnify the Republic by a payment of ten million francs. After telling the city to raise the sum the French demanded, Pignatelli took flight, disguised, appropriately enough, as an old woman; when he reached Palermo, Ferdinand, for no particular reason, put him in prison. The *lazzaroni* were now rising; they were still desperately and blindly loyal; furious at the thought of the Frenchmen's succeeding without much difficulty, after getting arms from two regiments which arrived from Leghorn they began to parade the streets, shooting and sacking. Everyone in the confusion was fighting with everybody else, not quite knowing why or how; the prisoners in the Vicaria rose, the militia fired on the mob. The brilliant city was falling into the convulsions of anarchy, while Maria Carolina sat in her cold, marble room in the Palermo Palace, scribbling her lamentations to di Gallo.

King Ferdinand was better served in Naples than he deserved to be; the faithful *lazzaroni* seized and captured the Castel Nuovo and ran up the Royal banner, after carrying off all the arms and ammunition in the fort. The Castel dell' Ovo and Sant' Elmo fell both rapidly and easily into the hands of the people and all three forts soon displayed the vermilion pavilion of the Sicilian Bourbons.

The better classes believed that the Regent Pignatelli, acting on orders from the Queen, had arranged, before his flight, for the garrisons in the forts to give way to the people. The Royal adherents, in other words, the lowest, basest part of the population, then opened the prisons and began massacring everyone whom they suspected of Jacobin principles, including any young men whom they happened to see wearing trousers or short hair. The turmoil was not soothed by the news that, when the Regent had fled, he had taken with him the last five hundred thousand ducats of the public money.

On the 19th the mob barbarously murdered the Duca della Torre and his brother. Della Torre was a mathematician and geologist, whose cabinets of curiosities and scientific instruments were among the finest in Italy, and whose collections of antiquities rivalled those of Sir William Hamilton. He was a wealthy man and of an ancient family; he had wished to accompany the King to Sicily, but for some reason been refused permission. Like every other cultured gentleman in Naples, he was suspected of Jacobinism. The mob broke into his Palace, which they completely sacked, destroying among other rarities a priceless library, pictures by Raphael, Titian, Correggio and Giorgione valued at upwards of a hundred thousand ducats, an elaborate collection of mechanical instruments and a costly laboratory. The Duca and his brother, after the Palace had been stripped till nothing but the bare walls were left standing, were dragged to the *Marinella*, there shot, and burned in tar-barrels on bonfires.

When Maria Carolina heard of this, she was not disturbed. It rather brightened her own exile:

"I believe that the people were entirely right," she wrote to the Empress.

Some of the other news from Naples was not so gratifying to the Queen. The patriots by means of strategy had contrived to get possession of Sant' Elmo, and from the great fort they ran up the tricolour flag. From the ramparts they could see Championnet's camp-fires.

The Republicans marched on the city from every side; the *lazzaroni* fought in a fury of bravery worthy of a better King. It was only after three days of hand-to-hand struggling in the streets, which he had to clear by firing guns at close range, and wherein he was assisted by the batteries of the Patriots from the castles, that the French General was able to occupy Naples. All parties of decent people, though they named themselves Patriots, Republicans or Liberals, were united against the *lazzaroni*, and ready to make common cause with the French.

The next news that reached Palermo was sufficient to send the

Queen into a faint, falling on Emma's resplendent bosom. Championnet was completely master of the city; everyone, even the *lazzaroni*, was now subdued, and won over by a compliment to San Gennaro.

Championnet had been welcomed by the Patriots and a Republic with the pedantic name of Parthenopean had been proclaimed.

This name was in the popular, intellectual tradition, an echo of the classical idealism of the dead Gironde, a tribute to that enthusiasm for Brutus, Plutarch, and the heroes and heroines of Corneille and Racine, that had proved at once so stimulating and misleading to the children of the French Revolution.

But, childish and affected as the name might seem, it was not altogether inappropriate: Parthenope was the ancient name of Neapolis or Naples, so called from the name of a Siren whose dead body was cast up on this rocky coast.

The ideals that these desperate, exalted, honest, gifted men followed, might have been likened to the themes of the songs of the Sirens, seductive, luring to destruction—the echoes of a melody uttered by a Siren already dead.

General Championnet, an idealist himself, chose the most brilliant, unselfish, scholarly and single minded, of the intellectuals, professors, poets, doctors of medicine, scholars, and men of letters, to rule his new Republic. Naples being what it was, a worse choice could hardly have been made. The selection of a President was typical of the new government; Carlo Lauberg, in a French uniform, with the office of chief chemist to the Republican forces, seemed a fine combination of talent, efficiency and science; but he was an unfrocked monk, who had married, and fled from Naples some time before on account of his Jacobinism, he was, while honest and zealous, a fanatic, and the last person likely to appeal for long to the lazy, ignorant, superstitious, Neapolitans, while his election was an unforgivable insult alike to the Church and the Bourbon.

The mob had committed hideous excesses during the struggle with the French. In the middle of their patriotic efforts they had lost interest in the battle and had begun to loot the city indiscriminately, including the Palace of the very monarch for whom they so ferociously fought. While some of the *lazzaroni* were hurling stones from the house-tops on the French, others carried off the doors and window-frames from the Royal residence. Many of them had been heard to lament that if the fight in the streets with Championnet's troops had lasted only another day, the *lazzaroni* would have been able to enrich themselves for life by sacking the entire city. The French General lost a thousand men during the battle in the streets; it was believed that four times that number of *lazzaroni* were slaughtered.

But the brilliant city quickly recovered its gay spirits. A popular speech from the tactful Championnet, whose Italian was clear and easy, a present to San Gennaro, a guard of honour for the Saint, a few promises, a burst of sunshine, and the crowd was screaming; "Long Live the French"; in dark wine-shops and *bagnios*, where the British sailors had revelled away their prize-money, the soldiers of the French Republic refreshed themselves after their labours with the same zest and the same welcome.

The flags of the new Republic, red, blue and yellow, stitched together from cloths taken from the Church of San Martino were flying above the massive fortification of Sant' Elmo; the Carthusian monks feasted the patriots in the Certosa. On Sunday a *Te Deum* (despite the French atheism) was sung in the Cathedral, Championnet superintended the planting of a Tree of Liberty before the King's residence which his own loyal subjects had so zealously sacked; this was an elaborate affair, a huge pine-tree, uprooted in the neighbourhood with all its roots and branches, the famous Phrygian Cap crowned the topmost branch, while the new colours of the Parthenopeans were bound to the trunk with those tricolour ribbons the French always carried with them.

The King's supporters in Naples seemed as happy as Ferdinand himself, who was in Palermo not in the least affected by the news which sent the Queen into convulsions of rage; her husband shook it all off with his habitual good humour; he had two and a half millions of money into which to dip, several factotums to see to his pleasure, a nice little house in the country, and Sicily seemed to him in every way as desirable as Naples.

With a shrug he dismissed all thoughts of his lost Kingdom, but the Queen, thinking of that French-born Republic across the water, was ready to die of rage and shame—"I cannot survive" was

173

the burden of her letters to di Gallo, who was not able to stir the Emperor into action on her behalf.

· · · · · ·

The news of the French success across the water did not greatly affect Emma; she, too, like the King soon settled down to the new conditions. The Sicilian winter might be bitter, but it was soon over. Emma always knew how to achieve a certain comfort; the new mode of life suited her very well, for Lord Nelson, as a matter of course, had made his home with the Hamiltons; he was no longer a guest in their Palace, but one, as it were, of the family.

To the Sicilians the withered old husband, the buxom wife, and the draggled hero, were three very familiar characters, who always made their appearance in every farce and puppet-show, and whose antics were always highly applauded.

When she was in Naples, one of Emma's famous impersonations had been a young girl with a raree-show, she was now providing a raree-show in real life and one much relished by the spectators. She was enjoying herself hugely and cared nothing about what was happening in Naples or anywhere else; Sir William had rented a grandiose Palace containing fifty great painted rooms. There the three of them lived with Mrs. Cadogan in attendance and a swarm of hired servants installed.

As the Queen had persuaded herself that all her plunder had been lost in the tempest, so Emma was talking about nine thousand pounds' worth of valuables left behind at the British Embassy. The truth was that she had saved everything worth saving and had trunks of dresses, boxes of plate, cases of china and every kind of luxury with which to furnish her new abode, nor was it altogether unpleasing to her vanity to be able to pose as the heroine of a great tragedy and the confidante of a Queen in distress. She was not cowardly; besides, she felt sure there was no real danger—the British Fleet was in the harbour, and the hero Nelson was as much attached to her as the locket to her wrist; she kept open house for all the British in Sicily.

By March the lazy, cynic city of Palermo had by then learnt that a hero was dwelling in their midst, and presented Lord Nelson with the Freedom of the City in a golden casket. The Sicilians, at once subtler, finer and easier, than the Neapolitans, and completely indifferent to the Bourbon dynasty which to them was an alien tyranny, viewed with detached amusement the antics of the exiled royalties and of the foreigners, and saw to it that a large portion of the plunder of Naples should pass into their hands.

With Sir William, the convenient *mari complaisant* fast becoming decrepit, Emma found that the life at Palermo, which was even looser than that of Naples, suited her perfectly. She had, in a way, put aside her official position, and during this interlude she might forget she was the wife of His Britannic Majesty's Minister, just as easily as King Ferdinand forgot that he was supposed to be master of the Two Sicilies. When she was not encouraging the Queen in the draughty marble Palace, she was drawing closer her enchantments round the man whom she had long since marked as her own.

Their relationship was perfectly well understood by all, and, when the sudden spring adorned the gilded island with an intoxicating wealth of flowers, Emma had passed to Lord Nelson as she had passed to Sir William from Charles Greville.

His money was useful, too; the largesse given by a grateful nation went to foot the bills that Emma ran up. Sir William, who had become petulant in his new and humiliating position, had whined about the expense of keeping an open table for all the officers of the fleet in Palermo Harbour, and for all the British travellers who, even in this time of war, managed to straggle down into Italy; but there was no need for Emma to retrench; Lord Nelson's purse was now at her disposal; and she, feeling that practically the gratitude of the British nation was at her back to pay her expenses, became extravagant as she had never been in her life before.

Every evening there was a banquet, every night, gambling. There were wax-lights and liveried servants, costly dainties, and carriages and horses, silk and satin dresses for Emma. There was no longer Mr. Greville nor Sir William to keep her in check, to whisper to her how a gentlewoman behaved, there was only Lord Nelson to admire and applaud. Sometimes she would sit half the night at the green-baize tables, flinging down and taking up the piles of gold, while the hero, trying to keep up with the glittering activities of his Circe, would, drowsed with wine and fatigue, often fall asleep, nodding over the piled cards; as much as five hundred pounds was sometimes lost by Emma at these card parties, but she was often lucky and always good-humoured.

The news of this fantastic establishment in the Sicilian capital spread across Europe. The British Embassies and Chancellories, and the various Courts, were, or affected to be, scandalized.

The Admiralty thought that Lord Nelson might be better employed, the Foreign Office could hardly be gratified by the position occupied in Palermo by His Britannic Majesty's representative. But how was the scandal to be stopped?—an odd combination of circumstances had given the game into Emma's hands.

Fanny, Lady Nelson, was mute, and silently suffering, living patiently with the Rev. Edmund in Burnham Thorpe; her son, Josiah Nisbet, had made scenes in Naples, on his mother's behalf, but in vain. To her husband Fanny was not only in another world, but non-existent. The possession of Emma had given him a desperate courage; between that and the fumes of his own glory his head was turned, and he was ready to defy the world. According to the theology of Burnham Thorpe, Palermo was the headquarters of all the sins, and the Palace which Nelson shared with Sir William and Emma, a fit abode for the Scarlet Woman. By what jugglery the man who thought that he had been raised up by God to pursue a holy war against infernal monsters reconciled himself to his being the lover of his host's wife, he alone knew; but, in some way, he had so justified himself to himself; he felt neither remorse nor regret, and his clouded mind was ready to believe that there was something divine in the woman who had dazzled his senses so that their love for each other redeemed everything. Love, the infatuated man named his passion, and the word was misused; but it served, as so often before and since, as a cloak for passions with uglier names. It was fashionable to affect to believe that "love" redeemed everything, and these lovers had caught up this convenient theory as aptly as if they had been characters in a French novel: "I hate their country and their manners," Nelson had once written of the French; but it was the French model of "sensibility" and illicit passion glossed by the unchallenged divinity of love, that he was unconsciously following. The man who prayed so fervently to a Deity he had never understood, this product of a rustic parsonage was playing a part familiar to the frequenters of the cheaper French theatres, the admirers of the crudest French farces.

Curiosity, perhaps a touch of malice, brought English travellers who had contrived to straggle across the seat of war to Palermo and to the Palace where the British Minister and his wife entertained the hero of the British people.

One such tourist who was received thus at Sir William's palace, noted curiously how Emma came into the room "leaning on her old husband's arm, her tresses floating round her full bosom." Short locks were unpopular because of the Jacobins, and she had allowed her ringlets, once cropped in classical fashion, to grow again. Emma clasped her bosom with an affected enthusiasm, declaring that she was languishing for her beloved Naples, but the visitor noticed that her colour was high and that her health seemed excellent. She had, of course, a great deal to say about the political situation. Her speech was a mixture of Lancashire and Italian; she referred constantly to her "dear Queen" and lamented over the valuable properties she had left behind in the Palazzo Sessa. One of the tourists, Lord Montgomery, she claimed as a cousin and begged him to stay to dinner. The hero came forward from a dark corner where he had been sitting over his desk, and began to cross-examine the Englishmen as to what was happening in Naples, as they had lately come from that city. He insinuated, rather impertinently they thought, that they should not have stayed in the rebel city so long; whereupon Lord Montgomery, who happened to be of Liberal tendencies, replied hotly that he much admired the Neapolitan Republicans, adding that true patriotism seemed extinct nowadays, upon which Lord Nelson and his fair friend exchanged very significant glances. The two Englishmen half-amused, half-disgusted, came to dinner that evening in Sir William's great *Palazzo*, when Lord Nelson took the opportunity to buttonhole one of them with:

"Say, sir, have you heard of the Battle of the Nile?"—continuing, "that battle was the most extraordinary one that was ever fought, and it is unique, sir, for three reasons. First, for having been fought at night, secondly, for having been fought at anchor, and thirdly, by its having been gained by an Admiral with one arm."

177

The Englishman was not impressed; he thought the speech more fitted to after-dinner, when an extra glass of wine might have excused it.

There were other visitors who were not so tolerant. When the new British Ambassador at Constantinople, Lord Elgin, came through Sicily, he noted emphatically "the necessity of a change in our representative at Naples and in our conduct there."

Captain Troubridge, no Puritan and attached to Nelson, who had been left as Commander of the Mediterranean squadron, wrote urgently:

"Pardon me, my Lord, it is my sincere esteem for you that makes me mention it. I know you can have no pleasure in sitting up all night at the cards. Why then sacrifice your health, purse, even everything. If you knew what your friends feel for you I am sure you will cut all the nocturnal parties. The gambling of the people at Palermo is publicly talked of everywhere."

Nothing had any effect—Emma might do as she pleased. The place was a fitting background to her enchantment; every night there were serenades on the water of the bay; moonlight began to fall on the breaking blossoms of orange-groves, on the amber-coloured rocks of Palermo, on the rich palaces with the twisted iron balconies where the luscious creepers hung, on the magnificent church where Frederick Hohenstaufen rotted to dust in his Imperial Purple. Everything was different from anything that Lord Nelson had known before, even more gorgeous, unexpected than Naples had been. In Palermo everything was for sale, and there was the money at hand with which to pay. The Queen might complain of lack of comfort, but neither the King, the Hamiltons nor Lord Nelson felt any pinch. In the spring the gorgeous island was like a basket of flowers, of jewels round the fruitful slopes of the snow-wreathed volcano. Blossoms plentiful enough to wreathe all the vanished nymphs of Greece blazoned the fields of which Theocritus had sung. Was not this an earthly Paradise to those of the fogs, mists and damps? The art of man had cunningly enhanced nature; there were gardens where fountains flashed in trim *allées*, where temples shone white amid the perfumed boughs of syringa, oleanders and pomegranate; there were walks where

178

hedges of hornbeam, cut stiff as walls, cast a purple shade. There was the Palace in the Conca d'Oro in the Chinese style, where even the Christian chapel was hung with Eastern bells like a pagoda, and where the superb garden was laid out in the curve of the golden shell, where the corn-coloured cliffs rose bare into the violet sky and to right and left could be seen the blaze of the ocean. Within the toy-like palace were dainty contrivances for amusement, for enjoyment, a table that rose, loaded with dainties, through the floor, at the pressing of a button, alcoves where water slid over the backs of kneeling marble Tritons offering rose-leaves in a shell, lattices of scented wood through which the sunlight streamed in slats of gold, couches piled with cushions filled with swansdown. And, when flowers staled by their profusion, there were more costly ornaments to please the eye, crystal dishes filled with coral and pearl, a coffee-service painted with the portraits of the heroes of the Nile, some of Sir William's rescued treasures—a bronze satyr, a Pompeian vase, encrusted with masks, a Renaissance jewel that winked emerald and ruby.

And always there was Emma, with her Olympian beauty, her voluptuous curves, her jolly laugh, her unfailing kindness, her high spirits that filled the days with excitement.

She was so clever, too, at arranging those drama scenes that greatly pleased the victor of the Nile; Emma's histrionics vivaciously expressed something in his own temperament.

A Turk was sent by the Czar of all the Russias with a presentation snuff-box, and Lord Nelson received him in the Pelisse and Plume of Triumph sent by the Grand Seigneur. Emma worked this up into a gratifying scene. The Turk was afterwards entertained to dinner, when he took too much rum, and encouraged by Emma's smiles he leapt up, drawing his sword:

"With this weapon I cut off the heads of twenty French prisoners in one day. Look, there is blood remaining on it."

Emma kissed the sword and handed it to Lord Nelson.

Then there was the excitement of the arrival of cases from England, as much as fifty guineas' worth of prints of the Battle of the Nile, all the caricatures in the newspapers, ballads and other evidences of the great popularity of the hero, and the walls of the

Sicilian palaces began to be plastered with his exploits praised in his native tongue.

There remained a fear that Fanny might come out to join him; distasteful amid all this excitement as it was to write to her, her husband forced himself to pen such letters as would prevent this catastrophe.

"You would have seen how unpleasant it would have been if you followed any advice which carried you from England to a wandering sailor. I could, if you had come, only have struck my flag and carried you back again, for it would have been impossible to have set up an establishment either at Naples or Palermo."

But he was not for ever happy and was never content. Melancholia and sickness often overtook him for days together; he wrote in a fanatic, half-crazy strain to his friends:

"My only wish is to sink with honour into a grave, and when I do that I shall meet death with a smile."

These delights did not grace any definite action; nothing much was done by the Bourbons, the Hamiltons or Lord Nelson, to dislodge the French who seemed to be firmly established in Naples, where the aristocrats and the intellectuals were, with fervent honesty and energetic idealism, trying to build up a Republic, and this in spite of every handicap. The women had their petty intrigues to vex and confuse what Lord Nelson, unfamiliar with classical names, termed the Vesuvian Republic, but for the rest, the British Fleet idled, for no particular reason, in the Harbour of Palermo.

.   .   .   .   .

To one man at least the situation was intolerable. Prince Francesco Caracciolo had been wounded in his pride as a man, as a patriot, and as a sailor. He, who had devoted his life to the interests of the Neapolitan Navy, had had to see it almost utterly destroyed in a moment of panic and fear, he, who had been a loyal subject of the Bourbons, a personal friend of the King, had had to see himself set aside, while a foreigner had been overwhelmed with adulation and entrusted with the persons of the Royal Family and with all their treasure.

He saw that neither Lord Nelson, nor Sir William Hamilton, nor indeed any of the English, understood a jot of the political situation of his unhappy country; he saw that they were committing blunder after blunder, the results of which were tending to the utter ruin of the Kingdom of Naples.

Not only was Lord Nelson absolutely incapable of judging the political situation of Italy or of Europe, but he was, in the estimate of a man like Prince Francesco Caracciolo, of no birth—a parvenu. Indeed, Horatio Nelson, proud as he was of his connection with the Walpoles, was, even in the indulgent eyes of his own countrymen, scarcely a gentleman. He had had during his whole career to complain of being neglected as an outsider. Nor had he ever been able to acquire any veneer of breeding.

To a Neapolitan of ancient race, like Francesco Caracciolo, everything the Englishman did and said, jarred, and the flattery so grossly showered on him, that he so greedily accepted, was nauseating.

The burning of that fleet with which the Neapolitan Admiral had kept the coasts clear of pirates was a hard blow to Caracciolo, and it was reasonable to impute some of the blame for this frantic act to the all-powerful Englishman. Lord Nelson indeed, and no doubt with sincerity, repudiated Commodore Campbell's action and went so far as to say that he would court-martial him were he under his command, but the Queen smoothed the matter over.

In any case the fleet had gone and it was not easy to trust the word of one obviously in such a hysterical condition as was the English Admiral, nor to respect the good faith of the Queen. Indeed, in the exaggerated, often lying letters she was writing frequently to the Marchese di Gallo at Vienna, Maria Carolina described the destruction of the fleet as having occurred on January 5th; it had taken place on the eighth of that month, and the news did not come to Palermo till some days later.

It was not difficult, therefore, for Prince Francesco Caracciolo to credit the bitter rumour that the property of the people of Naples, and his own especial interest and pride, had been sent up in flames to satisfy the spite and fears of the Queen and the wild, random policy of Lord Nelson. No man of sense could have placed any reliance on the judgment of the Englishman after his advice to Ferdinand to march on Rome. Nor could the Italian aristocrat

181

respect either the behaviour or the morals of this son of a puritanical English rectory; manners were lax in Neapolitan Court circles, but the spectacle which the Hamiltons and Lord Nelson provided, while they raved of patriotism, glory, and virtue, was too much even for southern Italian broad-mindedness.

Not only was the thing scandalous to the squeamish, it was in its grossness, vanity, and lack of humour offensive to the well-bred.

No friends of Prince Francesco Caracciolo had fled with the Royal Family; only the moral scum of Naples had shared that shameful flight; round the King and Queen, as always, were the foreigners Maria Carolina had encouraged at the expense of the Neapolitan nobility; Tuscans and Austrians, flattering the Englishman Sir John Acton, who was amusing his exile by making arrangements to marry his brother's daughter. Francesco Caracciolo detested these people; across the sea in the abandoned city were his family, his friends, his fellow-countrymen, all he admired, all he loved. He knew their worth, the sincerity of their motives, the desperate situation in which they had been left, the odious tyranny under which they had suffered. These men, and Francesco Caracciolo himself, were patriotic in a fashion unknown to Lord Nelson and the Hamiltons; they did not expect honours, glory, stars, ribbons, praise, and pensions; they were prepared to risk all they had, to dare utter ruin and an ignominious and horrible death for the sake of an ideal—*la patria*. Republicanism was in the air; intelligent people everywhere were infected, sometimes to madness, by the hopes of a possible new order for mankind, by visions of liberty, tranquillity, the spread of intellectualism, humanitarianism, a reaching upwards to a universal felicity.

To such people the claims of Divine Right—all the intricate entanglement of dying, dead or corrupting systems of government that encumbered Europe—seemed disgusting and farcical. Francesco Caracciolo might well ask himself if any loyalty was due to Ferdinand Bourbon, who had twice forfeited his claims to kingship—(a claim at best founded on a dubious foreign conquest)—first, by utter misgovernment, secondly, by despoiling and abandoning his country in a moment of crisis.

After a few weeks at Palermo, Francesco Caracciolo requested permission to go to Naples to look after his affairs. This was granted, not without a sharp warning from Sir John Acton, and the Neapolitan Admiral arrived in his native city on March 2nd; he was warmly welcomed by the men trying to rule the kingdom. Carlo Lauberg, the President, chemist and mathematician, Pasquale Baffi, one of the finest Greek scholars in the world, Mario Pagano, the famous jurist, and Domenico Cirillo, a celebrated botanist, Gabriele Manthoné, a brave high-minded soldier, General Massa, the General Federici who had told King Ferdinand to his face of his faults, and such brilliant young aristocrats as Ettore Carafa, Gennaro Serra di Cassano, Prince Pignatelli di Strongoli, Prince Ferdinando Pignatelli, Prince Moliterno, the Duca di Roccaromana and many other like-minded patriotic aristocrats. Supporting these energetic, talented, and devoted men, were a group of fervent middle-class intellectuals, such as Vincenzo Cuoco, Vincenzo Russo and Ignazio Giaja, the poet, and several high-born ladies conspicuous among whom were Giulia Carafa, the Duchessa di Cassano, and Maria Antonia Carafa, Duchessa di Popoli, noble and beautiful sisters, who were prepared to risk all they possessed for republican ideals.

Francesco Caracciolo was welcomed also by the Madame Roland of this Gironde—the muse of the Parthenopean Republic, Eleanora Fonseca Pimentel, a poetess of merit, a cultured intelligent woman, who was then devoting herself to editing, with skill and enthusiasm, the official journal of the Republic—*Il Monitore.*

The Neapolitan Admiral thus found himself surrounded by all that was familiar, inspiriting, agreeable; in contrast to what he had left, which was alien, degrading, hateful. In Naples was all he liked, in Palermo all he detested. No man who possessed any reasoning power, and who was capable of a cool judgment, could have failed to see where his loyalty lay.

.   .   .   .   .   .

Emma had to console the Queen for more bad news from across the water; Francesco Caracciolo, loved, respected by all classes in Naples, the idol of the disbanded sailors who were longing for revenge for their burnt ships, had joined his friends and had entered the ranks of the Republican army as a foot-soldier in the National Guard.

Maria Carolina was beside herself with fury at this dastardly treachery, as she termed it, but she and Emma soon contrived to amuse each other with a new intrigue.

This consisted in fomenting, by petty means, royalist risings in Naples. The trick was to smuggle into Naples printed pamphlets, or leaflets, that were written by the Queen, but purported to be Republican proclamations likely to cause public indignation and trouble between the Neapolitans and the French; some of these false manifestoes gave out that Easter, and other great religious festivals were to be abolished, others gave notice of imaginary conspiracies against Championnet, which were likely to inflame him against the Republican middle-classes.

This stuff was slipped by Emma into the Minister's post-bag for Leghorn, from there it was distributed to English residents who sent it through the ordinary post to Royalist agents in Naples; these were mostly among the *lazzaroni*, who enjoyed any excuse for making mischief. Anyone of intelligence saw through the trick; only those, the very ignorant, whose mentality was the same as that of the Queen, were deceived. But some trouble was caused; French soldiers were murdered, when they were caught unawares, and constant disorders broke out among the *basso populo*. The Republican Government, as incapable as brilliant and honourable, was harassed and bewildered.

The Queen continued to be unhappy in this Sicilian exile; she quarrelled with everyone, and her lamentations were unending; her letters, ill spelt, ill written, testify not only to her condition of life, but to the state of her mind.

"My health is very poor. I inhabit a fresh, new apartment where nobody has ever lodged before, without tapestries or furniture and a cold to make one tremble. I had a high fever. At present I have a heavy cold on the chest which nothing can remove except the opium which I take at night to stupefy my sense a little. The King is quite well, I envy him. He is not in the least afflicted, only irritated to see me always in tears. My daughter-in-law makes me feel unquiet. She often has little fevers, sweats at night, and dry coughs. The other day she coughed up two handkerchiefs full of blood. She is horribly thin; she lives on a milk diet and keeps in bed. Francesco has a cough, very often fever, and I believe that another tragedy is preparing for me, and bow my head to Divine Will. I believe that I cannot endure many more misfortunes. My daughters are still ill from what they suffered on the sea, from the damp here, from the cold, and from the privation of all conveniences that we find here. My three daughters and Leopold are all this morning in my chamber so that the apartment where they sleep can be aired a little. There are fifteen beds in four rooms, where they pass the night. There is not a single covered wall in the place, nor a sofa, nor an arm-chair; nothing but white walls, a straw chair; and without a fireplace, the cold is enough to kill one. Also I have a cold that never ceases, and each evening causes me a little fever. I beg with tears in my eyes to remember that the greatest act of friendship you can do for me, that which will bring all my sincere and devoted gratitude, will be to find establishments for my daughters. That will allow me to die in peace and tranquillity."

A letter sent later continues in the same strain.

"For me my only hope is for a miracle sent by Providence; it is no more use relying on human means of succour, unless you can do something for us. If you can, you will be indeed our saviour. For me, I only desire to remain quietly at home, and far from the world. I vegetate in the narrow circle of my friends and mix no more with anything. I see that you and I have the same ideas as to the future of the Princess. This good young person is always in bed, takes milk four times a day, with opium pills, and despite that her dry cough never comes to an end. She is certainly in a consumption and coughs up blood in quantities, has abundant sweat, and always her young husband sleeps beside her. They ought to be separated. My health is always bad. I cannot recover. The blow has been beyond my forces, my strength to endure. Here everything afflicts me, and besides I lack everything. The little that I have left must be for those who have exiled themselves for us. . . . The King is charmed to be in safety. He economizes in a villainous fashion at our expense, torments us horribly, goes out to a theatre, the country, and is not in the least affected. The Prince and the Princesses are sick and suffering. My daughters and Leopold suffer, but try to console me. I am desperate, nothing can comfort me. The government here is in such a state that there is very little one can do. . . ."

In all the long correspondence there is no mention of the devoted Emma, and very little of the hero of the Nile. The one object of the correspondence was to goad di Gallo into teasing the Emperor to drive out of Naples those insolent Republicans with their tricolours, Trees of Liberty, and Phrygian caps, who made Maria Carolina feel ill every time she thought of them.

In May, in the ripe heat of the Sicilian spring, news came that another French Fleet had put to sea. It was believed to be making for the Mediterranean and Lord St. Vincent ordered Lord Nelson to join him at Minorca; the answer was a refusal to obey.

"I am sorry that I cannot move to your help. This island appears to hang on my stay. Nothing could console the Queen if I departed, as I promised not to leave them."

He added irrelevantly that his heart was breaking and he was seriously unwell.

On May 19th, however, he set sail on the *Vanguard*, writing immediately to Emma:

"You cannot conceive what I feel when I recall you all to my remembrance."

The French, through the laxity of the British blockade, slipped into Brest, and in not much more than a week Lord Nelson returned to Palermo. He was received with a fulsome flattery that would have made a sane man wince. When he was twenty-four he had written:

"I have closed the war without a fortune, but I trust, from the attention that has been paid to me, that there is not a speck on my character. True honour, I hope, predominates in my mind far above riches."

Yet now he did allow Maria Carolina publicly to crown him with honour on his return from an eventless voyage—he had not even seen the enemy. There had been a time when he had considered the wearing of epaulets on a naval uniform a little cheap; now he was pleased to wear Turkish aigrettes, sable capes, and that most unbecoming of honours, a wreath of laurel.

His fortune was being rapidly spent; Emma kept no check on

186

the expenditure and Sir William never asked where the money came from as long as the bills were met.

Long before, Lord Nelson had written of another woman, Miss Andrews: "Had I a million of money, I am sure I should this moment make her an offer of them." Had he had a million of money then it would have been at Emma's disposal.

.   .   .   .   .   .

The war began to take a turn against the Republicans; Russia took an active share in hostilities and captured Corfu; the Austrians defeated the French. Championnet and Macdonald withdrew from the City and Kingdom of Naples, leaving only small garrisons behind, and the few-months-old Republic was left totally defence-less.

To add to the peril of the unfortunate patriots who had hoped and dared so much, Cardinal Fabrizio Ruffo, a Cardinal but not a priest, had landed in Calabria as the King's Lieutenant to raise the country. As he advanced and the French retreated, he gathered together a horde of men who, in the name of the Roman Catholic faith and of Ferdinand of the two Sicilies, were prepared to follow him in an attack on Naples. Among these strange troops, whom he called the army of the Holy Faith, the *Santa Fede*, were the Cala-brese peasants, some priests and friars, criminals who had escaped from the galleys in the confusion of the times, bandits who had been roaming the country during the late disorders, and a large number of the disbanded soldiers who had broken up on Ferdinand's retreat from Rome.

The Queen's hopes began to rise high; she saw herself returning, and returning in triumph, to Naples, but she still needed the British hero and the British ships; all Emma's arts were to be employed to induce Nelson to return to Naples. It was true that Lord St. Vincent had ordered him to follow up the French squadron at Toulon, but the infatuate man did not long resist the pleadings of the enchantress and of the Queen. The Bourbons needed the British Fleet to overawe the already lost Republicans. Emma wrote to Lord Nelson:

"The Queen begs and conjures you, my dear Lord, to arrange matters so as to be able to go to Naples. For God's sake consider and do it. We will go with you if you will come and fetch us. Sir William is ill, I am ill, it will do us good. God bless you."

Not without some agony did Lord Nelson give way:

"I am full of grief and anxiety," he wrote to Sir William, "but I must go. It will finish the war."

He cared little whether it finished the war or not. All that mattered to him was that he was pleasing Emma and would be in her company. When he left for Naples in the middle of June, husband and wife accompanied him on the *Vanguard*.

. . . . . .

The islands between Sicily and the mainland had surrendered at once to Captain Troubridge, who had come up from Alexandria to join Nelson, bringing several ships with him. It was Nelson's wish to encourage the loyalty of the inhabitants of the islands by distributing food and money among them, many of them being in a state of famine, and, with a flash of his native intelligence, his rage rose against the Sicilian Court when he saw these reasonable demands refused.

"There is nothing," he said, "which I propose that is not as far as orders go implicitly complied with, but the execution is dreadful and almost makes me mad. I desire to serve their Majesties faithfully, as is my duty, and has been such that I am almost blind and worn out and cannot, in my present state, hold out much longer."

The assistance to the islanders was to be given only to the loyal remnant left after a complete purge of Jacobinism; this did not show any merciful spirit in either of the English officers. The Republicans made a desperate effort at defence.

The Queen heard with despairing fury that Prince Caracciolo had been elected head of the Republican Marine, the small remnant of the navy which had been destroyed by Niza and Campbell.

On April 8th the Prince issued a proclamation in which he put, with justification, the blame of his country's disaster on the English, who had "sacrificed every right to their own interests" and who were despoiling the fugitive King of the national treasure he had pillaged before his flight. With hopelessly inadequate means, the patriotic Neapolitan did what he could; flying the new flag of Naples, he put to sea to challenge the English off Procida.

The coarse and brutal Troubridge was cruising about the islands on the *Culloden* (a sinister name for such an errand) and encouraging not only the massacre of "Jacobins," but of all who had remained passive under Republican rule. Among these were some harmless old priests; the lonely islands had neither gallows nor hangmen and Vincenzo Speciale, the miserable Sicilian lawyer who represented Bourbon vengeance, asked Troubridge for these adjuncts of civilization. The English captain indignantly refused, on the ground that the British Fleet was being asked to do menial work, but he made no effort to save the priests nor any other of the innocent victims of the Bourbon re-action; "the villains increase so fast on my hands and the people are calling for justice; eight or ten of them must be hung." Lord Nelson promised help, adding in his reply: "Send me word some proper heads are taken off; this alone will comfort me." The King wrote in the same strain with a touch of his usual buffoonery, "the cheeses must be hung up to dry," with the help of the Russians and of God, all the rebels would soon be strung up, and so on.

The Queen expressed the same sentiments in her violent, dramatic style, the "vile, corrupt nation" must be punished; the traitors, Caracciolo, Moliterno, Roccaromana, Federici, etc., must be put to death. "I would have no pity used," "a massacre would not displease me," "the weeds must be hunted out, destroyed, annihilated."

In brief there was a plan for a wholesale scheme of vengeance; Emma approved, encouraged, was a busy go-between, quick at messages, and a clever interpreter; Troubridge wrote to her of the progress of the slaughterings in the islands and she fed him with the Royal flatteries so that the son of a Westminster tradesman, so oddly in charge of the fortunes of these Italians, wrote: "I feel highly honoured by Her Majesty's notice. I wish I could serve them more *essentially* and *quick* (sic)."

．　　　　．　　　　．　　　　．

On April 27th Prince Francesco Caracciolo was all day with his five gun-boats between the fire of the Royalists in the fort at

Castellamare and that of the British ships at sea; the next day
Macdonald arrived with reinforcements by land, a few corvettes and
Caracciolo's one frigate came to his help; the British were driven
off and the Bourbon colours captured from the fort. Neither the
Queen nor Lord Nelson was likely to forgive this success. On
May 16th Caracciolo again attacked the British at Procida, from
which fort the British ships had been called to meet the Gallo-
Spanish Fleet, which was then sailing into the Mediterranean.

He had eight gun-boats, six fire-boats, and some smaller vessels;
a spirited action was kept up all day; the new flag of the Parthenopean Republic was floating from the little fleet as it attacked the
coast defences.

The Conte di Thurn, a foreigner in the Bourbon service, in
command of the *Minerva*, sailed out to defend the shore, and
Caracciolo surrounded and nearly captured the frigate; Thurn
was saved by a stiff wind, which caught the sails of the patriots
and caused them to retreat.

The last success of the bankrupt, doomed Republic was that
gained at Torre Annunziata by General Schipani, assisted by the
fire from Caracciolo's gun-boats.

Misfortune closed round the adherents of the Parthenopean
Republic. Through Calabria Cardinal Ruffo's army of the Holy
Faith advanced on them. On the sea the British Fleet drew near.
The *lazzaroni* in Naples and the peasants round about began to rise
in favour of the Bourbons, to whom, at heart, they had always
been loyal. The fishermen along the coast began to murder those
they disliked on their own account. Captain Troubridge received,
with a basket of grapes sent for his breakfast, the head of a Jacobin
concealed beneath the leaves, and wrote on the margin of the
accompanying letter: "A jolly fellow."

Over the whole Kingdom of Naples the peasantry were rising
in their traditional manner and indulging in acts of hideous violence.
The Republicans did what they could, but their situation was such
that no one could do much.

Captain Edward Foote on the *Sea Horse*, with Neapolitan frigates and a small British vessel, with a few regular troops—
Russians, Turks and Austrians—was sent ahead to co-operate with
the land forces of Cardinal Ruffo and the Royalists. He had no

other instructions, he awaited news of Ruffo's advance and of the arrival of the British Fleet from Palermo.

Cardinal Ruffo advanced with his terrible horde of ruffians towards Naples. On learning of his approach, the Republicans threw themselves into the two great castles, dell' Ovo and Nuovo, while such French as remained in the city went up into Fort Sant' Elmo, which so magnificently commanded the city and bay. These forts were all very strong places, heavily fortified, and the design of the Republicans was to hold them until the French or Spanish Fleet came to relieve them, by driving off the British ships, and landing troops to defeat Ruffo. This was their only hope.

By Midsummer Day, after grim fighting at the Ponte della Maddalena, Cardinal Ruffo had forced his way into the city and taken possession of Naples in the name of King Ferdinand. As soon as they found themselves successful and knew that the gorgeous city was at their feet, Cardinal Ruffo's troops, the *Sanfedisti*, plunged into bloody excesses that horrified him, cynic and insensible as he was. He did his utmost to stop these scenes of carnage, but with little success.

Lord Nelson and the Hamiltons had not arrived and Ruffo was plenipotentiary for his master, the King of the two Sicilies. He, therefore, on his own authority, and acting in concert with Captain Foote of the *Sea Horse*—then in the bay—arranged an armistice with the Republicans. For five days the negotiations went on; a treaty was then signed by the representatives of five nations, Great Britain, Naples, Turkey, Russia, France. The most important article of the long capitulation was "that the troops composing the garrisons will remain in the fortresses till such time as the ships hereunder referred to, for the transportation of those individuals who desire to proceed to Toulon, shall be ready to set sail."

It had been arranged by the Cardinal, who was sick, anxious and exhausted, wishful not to estrange so completely the Republicans as to render the return of King Ferdinand impossible, and who was eager to avoid further bloodshed, that the lives of all in the three great forts should be spared, and that if they submitted they should either be allowed to return to their own homes or go on board transports provided for Toulon. The Cardinal also agreed that the garrisons should march out with the honours of war, with their arms and baggage, drums beating, colours flying, guns loaded, and each with two pieces of artillery. Antonio Micheroux, who also represented King Ferdinand, was emphatically for leniency.

The two generals in charge of the castles, Manthoné and Massa, signed the treaty on June 19th; two days later it was accepted by Méjean in command of Sant' Elmo, Captain Foote, for Great Britain, signed on the 23rd; the Turkish and Russian commanders had already signed.

Both Ruffo and Micheroux were sincere in their desire for some sort of issue from the bloody anarchy in which the country seethed. They knew that Ferdinand, in his wife's words, "cared no more for Naples than if it had been the country of the Hottentots," and they believed it their interest and their duty to supply his deficiences. Ruffo was sickened by the incredible excesses of his own followers that he could not check, he wished to save as many of the Republicans as he could; on this point all the Allies agreed with him. No one had any objection to the treaty whereby the important forts, the very keys of Naples, would return to the King, and the brave garrisons, together with any other people who might have taken refuge with them, would be granted their lives, on condition that they returned quietly to their homes, or, if they could not accept King Ferdinand as master, went into exile in France. Transports were to be provided for such as wished to go to Toulon, and Ruffo sent hostages up to Sant' Elmo who were only to be released, when the patriots should have reached French soil.

So far, so good; Cardinal Ruffo, disgusted, weary and shocked, was thankful that he had been able to make so honourable an arrangement with the remnant of the Parthenopean Republic, and Antonio Micheroux, a sensitive, and humane man, was relieved to know that some lives at least would be spared amid the slaughterings that marked the triumph of the *Santa Fede*.

Micheroux had, from the first, protested strongly against Ruffo's policy of arming the dregs of the nation and setting them on the Republicans and he had, before the surrender of Naples, been in favour of very generous terms for the vanquished. Both these men knew that neither the King nor the Queen would like any leniency

192

to be shown to the patriots, but, confronted by an appalling situation, they hoped that expediency would prove a fair excuse, even before the fury of Maria Carolina.

Captain Foote had signed the treaty without demur and nothing remained but to put it into effect, and this Ruffo proceeded to do, though he had received a letter from the Queen, confused, contradictory, yet clear enough in its refusal "to treat with criminal rebels at their last gasp . . . trapped like mice . . . low and despicable scoundrels."

. . . . . .

On the morning of June 24th, the Royal hostages were released from Sant' Elmo and the refugees began to leave Castel Nuovo where Massa had persuaded the Republicans, who wished to die fighting, to surrender.

By the evening of that day the British Fleet had anchored in the bay, with Lord Nelson and the Hamiltons on board the *Foudroyant*; shortly before a boat had brought a letter from Sir William to Cardinal Ruffo, informing him that Captain Foote had sent Lord Nelson a copy of the treaty and that the British Admiral disapproved of it and was resolved not to remain neutral.

Indeed, Lord Nelson, with the last light of the Midsummer Day, had beheld an ugly sight through his spy-glass, the white flags floating from the mast of the *Sea Horse* and from the formidable bastions of dell' Ovo and Nuovo, while from Sant' Elmo, dominating the whole city, fluttered the colours of the French Republic.

The British Admiral was intensely angry at this sight. He knew well enough the temper of the King and Queen of Naples, and, he declared, "as to rebels and traitors no power on earth has the right to stand between their gracious King and them," and he added that he thought the armistice "infamous."

He proposed to send Captains Troubridge and Ball to inform Cardinal Ruffo of his opinions and intentions, but Ruffo, deeply alarmed and agitated by this turn of events, came on board the *Foudroyant* that evening. As a man of intelligence and spirit, he at once refused to accept this dictation from a foreigner. Not only had he been given full power by the King, his master, but Lord

Nelson was not a subject of King Ferdinand and had not been put in command of either the army or the navy. Neither had Lord Nelson had anything to do whatsoever with the fall of Naples—that was entirely the work of Cardinal Ruffo and the amy of the Holy Faith. He, therefore, on every ground, considerd himself justified in standing by the capitulation which had been approved by Captain Edward Foote representing Great Britain, by France, by Turkey and Russia, as represented by the officers of these nations then in Naples.

When Lord Nelson learned that Cardinal Ruffo intended to stand by the capitulation, his fury flamed, and Emma was by his side to encourage him. She knew, perhaps even better than he did, the temper of the Queen. They had not been sent to Naples to make terms, but to inflict vengeance. Maria Carolina had not wished the British Fleet to sail against her capital in the hope of making some honourable compromise which would allow her a more or less peaceful return to her throne—no, she had wished it to go as the instrument of her vendetta against the Jacobins, Republicans and Frenchmen. She had said and written that a massacre would not displease her. To her the establishment of the Parthenopean Republic had been an intolerable affront, which nothing but blood and a great deal of blood could wipe out. Neither she, nor the King, nor Sir John Acton, nor any of the ministers who had fled to Palermo had stopped to think what the abandoned city was expected to do. It would seem that its inhabitants had been expected to allow themselves to be massacred for the sake of the Royal Family they had always loathed, and of that Government which had not only abandoned them defenceless to an enemy, but which had for years spied on them, imprisoned them, confiscated their property, and insulted them in every possible manner. As they had not done this, but taken advantage of the crisis to try and form their own government, to introduce law and order into chaos, to make some sort of workable constitution out of anarchy, they were to be treated as the most dastardly rebels and traitors.

Lord Nelson knew, Emma knew, and Sir William knew, when they consulted together in agitated anger on the *Foudroyant*, that the least talk of mercy to Naples would be abhorrent to the Queen. Nor was the King much less vindictive; his veneer of good-humour had soon been rubbed off. He had appeared indifferent to all his fortunes, he had amused himself in Palermo with the money plundered from Naples, issuing his little edicts that the women were not to cut their hair short or the men to wear fringes *à la Brutus*, but when the chance of vengeance came he was ready to take it.

He, too, wished the disobedient city to be punished—no thought of magnanimity, nor prudence, nor policy, nor of what their future reign was likely to be if they took this bloody vengeance when it was in their power, troubled either of these sovereigns. Nor did it concern them, nor Lord Nelson, nor Emma, that the most enlightened people in Naples, the bravest, the most cultured, the sincerest and the most honourable, had founded and run the brief Republic. There was only one man at this little conclave who had some humanity, some common sense, some dignity—Fabrizio Ruffo. He did not believe in the policy of blind cruelty that would turn Naples into a shambles. There had already been hideous deeds enough; the prisons were full of maimed and dying Republicans; the streets were piled with corpses. Cardinal Ruffo was not a particularly enlightened statesman, nor even a brilliant politician, but it did not seem to him that it was possible for their Sicilian Majesties to return and reign with even passable comfort and security in a city where the decent inhabitants had been given over to slaughter by the lowest of the population, where these ruffians and *banditti* who composed the army of the Holy Faith had been allowed to pillage and murder without let or hindrance. Besides, he was the victor and felt he had a right to decide what he should do with his victories. He had promised the garrisons that the terms of the capitulation would be observed and he intended to keep this promise, despite the King, the Queen, and Lord Nelson.

He declared nobly that to violate the treaty would be an abominable outrage against public honour, and that he would hold responsible before God whoever should dare to impede its execution.

Cardinal Fabrizio Ruffo expressed himself thus in forcible Italian that Sir William, harassed and peevish, and Emma, voluble and raucous, translated to Lord Nelson, who seemed to have taken upon himself the role of arbiter of the destinies of Naples.

His Eminence had a good case, which he put into eloquent

words; alone among the councillors of King Ferdinand he had some wisdom and humanity, was a little far-seeing as a politician, and a little magnanimous as a man. In everything he was a contrast to the British Admiral who listened to him with nervous rage.

The Cardinal, worn and excitable, came of one of the oldest, and proudest families in Calabria, had been Papal Treasurer, was brilliantly educated, witty, infidel, active, energetic, and subtle, with all the faults of an intellectual and of an aristocrat.

He was capable of ignoble actions, he was an opportunist, licentious, and extravagant, for no man could serve King Ferdinand without lending himself to some baseness. There had been some flaws and scandals in the career of Fabrizio Ruffo, but he was in everything the superior of the three people with whom he so passionately argued.

He was the only man that had done anything to regain Naples for the Bourbons and from the first he had advised moderation in dealing with the rebels. He had been firmly opposed to the Royal plan of vengeance, and had argued, as a matter both of humanity and of common sense, that Ferdinand's only reasonable policy was one of conciliation and mercy.

He had done his best to control the rabble of the *Santa Fede*, and had been sincerely horrified by the excesses committed by ruffians who were utterly beyond his control; all this he put before the three English people. His present case he thought simple.

The great object was to obtain the surrender of the three great castles which were capable of holding out for months, and which, in the event of the appearance of the Gallo-Spanish Fleet, might prove extremely difficult to deal with. This he had accomplished by means of an armistice which the representatives of five nations had approved and signed.

The garrisons were prepared to disarm, to evacuate the forts, most of them would exile themselves to Toulon; they had already released their hostages.

What was to be gained by breaking the armistice, by annulling or violating the capitulation? Obviously nothing but the delights of vengeance on helpless enemies.

But the two Englishmen remained obdurate, Emma, in her muslins, blowsed with fatigue and heat, fanning herself and sipping iced water in the great cabin of the *Foudroyant*, translated into French Lord Nelson's contemptuous refusal to see any point of view save his own, while Sir William repeated stupidly: "Kings don't treat with rebels." Ruffo argued that the treaty, once made, must be observed, in the name of common honesty. His honourable attitude was so odd to Lord Nelson that he began to suspect the Cardinal of Jacobinism, he was utterly under the sway of Emma, and behind Emma was the vindictive Queen.

Angered and indignant, Ruffo was rowed ashore to consult the other signatories to the treaty, the Russian and Turkish commanders, and Antonio Micheroux, King Ferdinand's other plenipotentiary.

All these men at once agreed that it would be impossible to violate the treaty, and made the emphatic statement that it was "useful, necessary and honourable to the arms of the King of the Two Sicilies and of his powerful allies, the King of Great Britain, the Emperor of Russia and the Sublime Porte, because without further bloodshed that treaty put an end to the deadly civil and national war, and facilitated the expulsion of the common foreign enemy from the kingdom."

It might have been supposed that here the matter would have ended. But there was still the strange trio on board the *Foudroyant* to be reckoned with, and behind them the Bourbon and the Hapsburg.

On the 25th Troubridge and Ball went on shore with the messages for the Commandants of the two rebel castles that Ruffo refused to send to them; these stated Nelson's refusal to honour the treaty, Nelson also asked Ruffo, if, supposing that he, Nelson, broke the armistice, would, he, Ruffo, assist an attack on the forts?

The Cardinal refused and wrote to the British Admiral, reminding him that Foote had signed the treaty in the name of the King of Great Britain, and that if he, Lord Nelson, broke it, he would do so on his own responsibility; and in such an eventuality he, the Cardinal, would put the enemy *in statu quo* and withdraw his own troops.

During the whole morning the messages went to and fro, then Fabrizio Ruffo came again on board the *Foudroyant*, which lay anchored within sight of the two great forts, which were flying the

flag of truce, and of the third, Sant' Elmo, from which the tricolour still floated in the sultry June air.

No one's temper was improved by the tension of the last few
days; Sir William was peevish, Emma bored and "fag'd," Lord
Nelson violent and domineering. The Cardinal showed all the
weary passion of the man who felt he was in the right and was
most unaccountably thwarted by the folly and cruelty of an upstart.

He haughtily questioned the right of Lord Nelson to dictate
terms to another country's General, as he, Ruffo, was, but the
three English people knew whom the King and Queen would
support.

There was a passionate discussion that lasted two hours, neither
side would give way; Emma was quite worn out with interpreting,
when her lover seized a piece of paper, and scrawled across it with
his left hand: "Rear-Admiral Lord Nelson, who arrived in the
bay on June 24th with the British Fleet, found a treaty entered
into with the rebels, which he is of opinion ought not to be carried
into execution without the approbation of His Sicilian Majesty."

Thus the attitude of Lord Nelson was clearly defined; Cardinal
Ruffo returned to Naples and, still considering the treaty binding,
wrote to General Massa, commanding in Castel Nuovo, advised
him of the English attitude, reminded him that Lord Nelson had
command of the sea, and broadly hinted that the garrison had
better try to escape by land, to which course he, Ruffo, would offer
no resistance.

Massa suspected this generous and desperate attempt to save
him from Nelson to be a trap to induce him to break the articles
of the capitulation and so deliver him to Royalist vengeance.

He sent a reply which showed his firm reliance on the honour
of the signatories to the capitulation treaty and his determination
to abide by it in every detail.

Ruffo, deeply conscious of his dreadful situation, agitated and
distracted, made yet another attempt to save the men for whose
lives he believed himself responsible. He tried to induce the two
rebel garrisons to come out, by sending a herald with a renewal of
his offer, and proclaimed that he would shoot anyone that meddled
with them or with their property.

Again the patriots refused to listen.

The Cardinal now found that his authority was being undermined by Royalists, who, encouraged by Nelson, and followed by armed *lazzaroni*, were arresting suspected persons and taking them by sea to Procida, where they would be out of the jurisdiction of Ruffo.

These people were also tearing down the Cardinal's humane proclamation, which he had pasted up all over the city, forbidding any interference with private citizens and commanding respect for the white flag; the English and their emissaries were indeed encouraging the rabble to rise against the Cardinal as a "Jacobin."

The Queen, on hearing the news from Naples, had at once written her mind to Emma; along a copy of the treaty she had scribbled her indignant comments on every article; she shared Lord Nelson's opinion that it was "infamous."

"June 25th, 1799.

"My Dear Lady,—I have just received your dear letter without date from the ship, with the Chevalier's for the General. . . . The General writes the wishes of the King, who incloses a note under his own hand for the dear Admiral. I accede entirely to their wishes, but cannot refrain from expressing my sentiments to you. . . . The rebel patriots must lay down their arms and surrender at discretion to the pleasure of the King. Then, in my opinion, an example should be made of some of the leaders of the representatives, and the others to be transported under pain of death if they return into the dominions of the King, where a register will be kept of them; and of this number should be the Municipalists, Chiefs of Brigade, the most violent Clubbists, and seditious scribblers. No soldier who has served shall ever be admitted into the army; finally, a rigorous severity, prompt and just. The females who have distinguished themselves in the revolution to be treated in the same way, and that without pity. . . . The Sedile, the source of all the evils, which first gave strength to the rebellion, and who have ruined the kingdom and dethroned the King, shall be abolished for ever, as well as the baronial privileges and jurisdiction, in order to ameliorate the slavery of a faithful people who have replaced their King upon the throne, from which treason, felony, and the culpable indifference of the nobles had driven him. This is not pleasant, but absolutely necessary, for without it the King could not govern quietly his people for six months, who hope for some recompense from his justice, after having done everything for him. Finally, my dear Lady, I recommend Lord Nelson to treat Naples as if it were an Irish town in rebellion similarly placed."

On the 26th Nelson, fortified by this letter, himself sent into the castles copies of his manifesto that Ruffo had refused to handle.

The Cardinal, on learning of this, put his troops *in statu quo*; he still hoped that the Republicans would come out and surrender unconditionally, thus relieving him of the onus of breaking the capitulation.

Neither of the Republican Commanders, however, took any notice of Ruffo's desperate moves and clung to the articles of the treaty, which they were resolved to observe scrupulously.

Riots and panic broke out in Naples as Ruffo withdrew his troops to their original positions; thousands of fugitives streamed out of the city fearing a renewal of the civil war.

News came from Capua that the French and Jacobins had beaten the Royalists and were marching on Caserta; the hostages held by the French sent out messages to say that, owing to the delay in carrying out the terms of the treaty, they were in danger of their lives.

Ruffo put these matters before Lord Nelson, begging him to take some decisive action; he himself expected nothing but a flare up of the hideous conflict.

.   .   .   .   .   .

The terrible situation suddenly changed; on the same morning, June 26th, Captains Troubridge and Ball came ashore, waited on the Cardinal and gave him a letter written in French by Sir William, and dated early in the morning of that day:

"Lord Nelson begs me to assure your Eminence that he is resolved to do nothing to break the armistice that your Excellence has accorded to the Castles of Naples."

Suspicious but relieved, the Cardinal asked the two captains to authorize the following declaration, which he had written in Italian:

"Captains Troubridge and Ball have authority on the part of Lord Nelson to declare to His Eminence that his Lordship will not oppose the embarkation of the rebels and of the people who compose the garrisons of the Castles Nuovo and Dell' Ovo."

Ball signed this declaration, Troubridge would not; of course, neither of their signatures would have had any value; Ruffo argued with the Englishmen, wanting a more precise undertaking, but had to be content with Hamilton's and the dictated paper which he sent by ten o'clock to Antonio Micheroux with a covering letter, saying that Lord Nelson had consented to carry out the capitulation, and that he, Micheroux, was to proceed to carry out the treaty; the two documents were sent to assure the safety of the garrisons, but Micheroux did not use them, as the Republicans trusted in his "simple word," as he put it himself. Acting in good faith, Antonio Micheroux did as Ruffo directed; the garrisons marched out, only the Russians giving them the stipulated honours of war; those patriots who chose exile were given safe conducts and allowed to embark on a transport waiting to take them to Toulon, others returned to their homes in Naples.

The British sailors took possession of the castles; the transports did not sail, but were anchored between the guns of the castles and those of the British ships; on June 28th, the members of the garrison who had gone home were arrested and taken back to the castles—this time to the dungeons.

.   .   .   .   .   .

On the 29th, Sir William wrote from the *Foudroyant* to Sir John Acton at Palermo, touching on the tiresome disagreement between the Cardinal and Lord Nelson—"however, after good reflection, Lord Nelson authorized me to write to His Eminence this morning early, to certify to him that he would do nothing to break the armistice . . . with the rebels." Hamilton added that Nelson had promised "any assistance of which the fleet was capable" (presumably in embarking the rebels) and added complacently—"This produced the best possible effect. Naples had been upside down in the apprehension that Lord Nelson might break the armistice; now all is calm." In conclusion Sir William added the banality: "If one can't do exactly what one wishes, one must act for the best and that is what Lord Nelson has done."

On the following day Hamilton again wrote to Sir John Acton, coolly exposing the cheat. "Lord Nelson, concluding that his Sicilian Majesty has totally disapproved of all that the Cardinal has done in contradiction to his instructions as regards the rebels of the castles, and those rebels further being on board of twelve or fourteen transports . . . Lord Nelson has believed himself sufficiently authorized to seize the transports and have them anchored in the middle of the British Fleet. . . . I have reason to believe that we have Cirillo and all the greatest traitors on board the transports and that the *coup* will have been totally unexpected."

Thus the Britannic Minister, writing of the cleverness of his wife's lover to the lover of the Queen.

To Lord Grenville in Whitehall Sir William sent an inaccurate, garbled account of the affair, which suffered both from the fact that a mind always weak was breaking up as the result of age and fast living, and from the Minister's desire to put a gloss over a most dishonourable affair to the Home Government.

Sir William, nervously anxious to put himself right with his Government, wrote a "separate and secret" dispatch to Lord Grenville, in which he enclosed some of the Queen's letters to Lady Hamilton which he found did "so much honour to the Queen's understanding and heart" and a copy of Cardinal Ruffo's capitulation, to which document Sir William applied Lord Nelson's term "infamous." In his letter the Minister (writing from the *Foudroyant*, July 14th, 1799) mentions that he thinks of returning to England on "the first ship that Lord Nelson sends downwards" —probably this was to protect himself from the possible humiliation of a recall, as Sir William seems to have had no sincere intentions of return. The vindictive nature of the Queen's comments on the capitulation is sufficiently shown by the last paragraph of her letter. No doubt Sir William's object in sending this paper was to cover himself in case of possible censure, but his taste in humanity was not as fine as his taste in antiquities if he believed that Maria Carolina's cruel spite could be accepted by anyone as showing either "understanding" or "heart."

After using the expressions "real insolence," "infamous," "absurd," "real wickedness," "vile," "base," and other such terms about the rebels the Queen summed up her sentiments in her usual breathless style and with her usual fury.

"This is such an infamous treaty that if by a miracle of Providence some event does not happen to break it or destroy it I count myself dishonoured and I believe that at the cost of dying of malaria, of fatigue, of a shot from the Rebels, the King on one side and the Prince on the other ought immediately to arm the Provinces, march against the Rebel city and die under its Ruins, if they resist, but not remain vile slaves of the scoundrelly French and their infamous Mimics the Rebels.

"Such are my sentiments; this infamous capitulation if carried out afflicts me far more than the loss of the Kingdom and will have far worse consequences."

Almost as great as the bitter wrong done to the garrisons of the castles was the wrong done by Lord Nelson and the Hamiltons to Fabrizio Ruffo. Ruffo had seen what was right and had tried to do it; against terrible odds he had endeavoured to be just, merciful and wise. And these other three, with the Queen behind them, had overwhelmed him, had broken his resistance, had traded on his fundamental weakness. He was no hero and did not believe in heroism; forced to an issue, he could not risk ruin by offending the King and Queen; beyond a point he could not suffer for a good cause. He saw the trick—the use of the word "armistice" instead of "capitulation," he knew how little Lord Nelson was to be relied on, he knew Sir William's quality, he knew Emma was on board the *Foudroyant*, managing husband and lover for the Queen's ends. But he pretended to be deceived; he even helped to deceive Antonio Micheroux by making out that the English letter had undertaken more than it really had; he abandoned the men whom he had tried so hard to save, because he could not face the consequences of a longer resistance. He knew that on every hand he was being intrigued against, that his estates, his rewards, his life, might have to answer for his humanity, and he gave way. Like Pilate he washed his hands, and while the shameful betrayal was taking place, he went to the Cathedral to celebrate a *Te Deum*, cynic misery in his heart, the ornate service sounding like jeering mockery in his ears.

He wrote to the Queen, asking, on the score of fatigue, to be allowed to resign his post. Maria Carolina replied with vague, false flatteries; as he was well aware, she suspected and disliked him. To her, as to the Hamiltons and Lord Nelson, humanity, wisdom, and magnanimity seemed to be Jacobin qualities.

.   .   .   .   .   .

An actor in the scenes that were taking place in Naples, while Emma was singing "Rule Britannia" on board the *Foudroyant*, has left an account of them.

Guiseppe Lorenzo, of a respectable lower middle-class family, was a clerk in one of the regiments of the Republican Guards. On the arrival of the *Santa Fede* Lorenzo obeyed the signal given from Sant' Elmo and rallied with some others of the guards to the defence of the city, which was being desperately undertaken by the Marchese di Monterone and the Duca di San Pietro di Maio, seconded by General Wirtz with a legion of Calabrese and a few cavalrymen. After fiercely disputing the ground inch by inch, the Republicans were driven back, some threw themselves into the Castello del Carmine, others dispersed, seeking for shelter from the advancing hordes of Cardinal Ruffo's troops.

Lorenzo and a companion, Gennaro Grasso, ran to the house of the elder Lorenzo, where they changed their uniforms for civilian clothes, and hastened out again, with the intention of trying to get into the Castel Nuovo, over which the flag of the Parthenopean Republic still waved; they changed their minds, however, on the advice of Grasso, and made their way to the barracks of their regiment, which was attached to the convent of Monte Oliveto; they found this crowded with soldiers and other refugees.

Exhausted by fatigue they cast themselves across a table in the guard-room and slept; after three hours they were awakened by shouts of "*Evviva il Re*," the war-cry of the rabble. Springing up, they found that all their companions had disappeared and that the corridor outside was crowded by a horde of armed people, all, including women and children, waving weapons and shouting fiercely. The two young men escaped by a side door in the guard-room to the convent.

A lay brother who knew Grasso hid them all night in his cell, and in the morning shaved off their military side-whiskers and gave them monkish habits and rosaries.

He had hardly done this, when the mob, searching through the convent, broke into the cell; they were, however, satisfied that the soldiers were genuine monks, and one man, remarking the pallor of Lorenzo, asked him kindly if he felt ill. But as they were leaving, a barber who had formerly been employed by his family recognized Lorenzo. Barbers and hairdressers were all violently against the Republicans, who wore their hair short and unpowdered, thereby diminishing considerably the trade of the *coiffeur*. This question of long hair became a very important one. A man could change his trousers for breeches and turn his red waistcoat, but he could not at once grow his hair. Locks and queues of tow and horse-hair were resorted to, usually in vain; the garb of a monk remained the only disguise that offered much hope of escape.

This barber followed Lorenzo with threatening looks, muttering in his ear: "Your life is in my hands." As Lorenzo hastened his pace, the barber gave him a vicious thrust with the butt end of his musket that threw the young man to the ground; he picked himself up, and, together with Grasso, contrived to struggle through the press and out of the building. Hurrying along, almost at random, with their hoods over their faces, the two soldiers found themselves in the centre of the city, which was being sacked by the victorious *lazzaroni*, who were destroying the houses of so-called "Jacobins" and everything that was in them. They were dragging out the clerks from the banks and shops and murdering them; Lorenzo observed bands of ruffians driving along groups of naked women and children; at the street-corners were already heaps of corpses, piles of heads and of human limbs, recently hacked off.

Half-crazed by horror, the two young men decided to take refuge with an uncle of Lorenzo's who was a monk in the convent of Santo Tolandino, quite close to the Castel Sant' Elmo; this person not only refused to receive them, for fear of compromising himself, but jeered at them, saying: "Do you think Ferdinand IV will lose a kingdom with as little fuss as if it were a handkerchief?"

The two youths turned away, and went on a desperate search for help, followed by insults and suspicious looks from the swarms of Ruffo's men who passed them. They tried in vain to persuade another relative of Lorenzo's, who lived near the little Porta di San Lorenzo, to take them, and were forced to retrace their steps across the city; they found themselves pushed by the immense crowds on to the Piazza di Mercato, where the congestion was so great that it was impossible to pass through. The Tree of Liberty, which had been put up by the Republicans in the middle of this square, was being degraded in the most bestial fashion by the Calabrese and the *lazzaroni*, and this in the presence of a great number of women, who assisted at the spectacle. A large number of prisoners were being conducted in front of the tree, "just like cattle to the butchers," and were being shot at. Most of them were not killed at once. Dead, or half-alive, they were decapitated; the heads were rolled on the ground as an amusement and formed the ball in a kind of game.

The two fugitives managed to push through this horrible crowd, and got away by the Porta Alba. They were again held up before the convent of San Pietro di Maio, against which the Calabrese were directing a fusillade, declaring that the Jacobins were shut up inside it.

A good woman, the wife of a tailor, took them into her shop, believing them to be monks. Soon after, she went out to explore the streets, to see what was happening, and returned trembling, having been censured by the crowd for sheltering two Jacobin monks. Almost at the same instant the shop was invaded by armed men. The chief of them began to interrogate the fugitives and demanded to see their papers; the presence of mind of Lorenzo saved them. He was able to throw away secretly the two gold earrings he had in his portfolio, and to show the holy relics on his person which had been given him by his mother shortly before her death.

The ruffians then were persuaded that these were genuine monks, and the chief of the gang offered their help in exchange for a consideration. Lorenzo had in his pocket ten *piastre*, but he did not dare show this for fear of exciting the cupidity of the mob, and therefore refused the assistance. When they had escaped this peril, Lorenzo, who had never ceased to remind his friend what stupid advice he had given him and how much better it would have been if they had gone into Castel Nuovo, tried to think how it would be possible to get into the fortress, after all, and they set out to cross the city again with this purpose in view.

They saw on all sides the same tragic scenes; in the Piazza Trinita Maggiore they saw people being massacred, by shooting and stabbing by bayonets. Further they saw being murdered a certain Guiseppe Merendo, a poor, honest man who had lost his reason, and who insisted on coming out of his house with the French cockade in his hat.

In the same Piazza, Calabrese and brigands were seated on top of bodies to eat their meals.

When the two young men reached the church of Santa Maria Nuovo they were arrested by the armed people who were guarding the house of the President, Molinare, and who suspected them of being Republicans. Lorenzo, however, showed such wit, and gave such meek, holy, and learned answers to their captors that the mob were half-persuaded they had before them two poor lay-brothers of Monte Oliveto, and when a man appeared on the balcony of the President's house and declared that the two friars were really two members of the Civic Guard, those who had arrested them exclaimed that the gentleman must be mad or mistaken. This personage, who had recognized the two young men, insisted that he was right, he knew them very well, and they were soldiers and Jacobins.

Lorenzo continued to argue that he was a true religionist, and he and his companion were conducted before the Castello at the Bridge of the Maddalena; a rabble of ruffians accompanied them; Lorenzo arguing tranquilly that he was really a monk. His companions disputed this. One of the *lazzaroni* cast a cord round Lorenzo's neck three times, and drew it so tight that he felt his eyes starting from his head, as if all the nerves of his forehead were bursting. He felt the effect of this for eight days afterwards.

As a last resort he slipped the ten *piastre* that he had in the hand of a *lazzarone*, who was at his side. He soon saw that he had done right, for from that moment this wretch became his protector.

When they reached the Bridge of the Maddalena, they found that most of those who had been conducted in front of the Castello had been massacred, not only men and grown-up people, but women, children, old men, girls, and on two carts, like so much butcher's meat, were piled the bodies that were thrown immediately into the sea, nearly all still half-alive.

A group of armed men came forward and wished to take the two newcomers from the hands of those who had brought them to treat them in the same manner, but those who had captured Lorenzo and his companion insisted on conducting them in front of the Castello. The Calabrese officer at last took them into the presence of the Cardinal.

Fabrizio Ruffo was at a half-gunshot distance, surrounded by all his staff and many officers. The Calabrese presented to him the two monks and informed him of the case.

Ruffo turned to Lorenzo and asked:

"Ah, well, who are you? Are you really monks?"

Lorenzo was about to reply, when the Cardinal pushed him back with both hands, and said: "Stand away from me, and then talk," as if he feared, when Lorenzo came to approach him, that he was going to be the victim of a desperate attack.

When Lorenzo was about ten paces from the Cardinal, Ruffo repeated: "Speak now." The young man said: "We are not monks—that is the truth."

He gave him then the whole story, from the moment they had been routed on the Bridge of the Maddalena, told him they were not conspirators, but only men who had been engaged in a humble capacity as secretaries in the Civil Guard.

The Cardinal then wanted to know why they had been arrested. The crowd shouted out they were certainly two perfidious Jacobins. There was then an argument between the Cardinal and the crowd —the Cardinal wanted to set the prisoners free, the crowd to shoot them. At last Ruffo, knowing the fate that would have been theirs, if he released them, said to his officers:

"Put these where the others are, in a safe place."

The crowd then broke out into a furious orgy of hate, biting their fingers at the two victims they had lost, and screaming out: "Ah, dogs, if we had known you were not monks, we should have carved you in pieces!"

Lorenzo felt, however, a little assured, as if he were in the power of justice. He and his companion were taken first to a provisionary depot of prisoners, and then to the courtyard of an empty palace in the Via de' Portici.

The escort which accompanied the column of prisoners was

captained by a Calabrese priest, armed with two pistols and a sword, who amused himself by telling the prisoners they were all being taken off to be shot, and at every forty steps made the column pause, telling them this was the place where they were to meet their end, and then marched them on under the pretence of finding a better spot in which to murder them.

Lorenzo made the great mistake of beginning to address this priest as "citizen," having been accustomed for several months to use that form of address:

"Citizen, in the name of charity, tell me where we are going?" The terrible priest replied:

"Ah, scoundrel, how is it you have the courage to call me citizen? I am your enemy, and I assure you I am taking you to be shot," and added some foul words and gave him a blow in the side that caused a severe wound.

Lorenzo was sent from one prison to another, from Portici to the Granili, from the Granili to the Corbletta Stabia, and from there to the prison of Santa Maria Apparente. His descriptions of the sufferings of the victims of the Bourbons, of the spoliation and extortion committed by officials and jailers, of the insults and torments inflicted by the *lazzaroni* on the prisoners, are almost incredible.

"The Neapolitan people," he wrote, "were tormented until the last moment of imprisonment."

He was, however, once allowed to see his father, and had a visit from his uncle, the monk, who showed himself so affectionate towards him on June 14th. He remained in prison till the first fury of the reaction had passed. Judged and condemned at the end of the year, he was exiled for ten years, and left for France and arrived at Toulon on January 1st, 1800.

He is thus described:

"Giuseppe Lorenzo of Naples, son of Alexandro, about twenty-two years of age, five feet eight inches, dark chestnut hair, regular features, chestnut eyebrows, dark-blue eyes, straight nose, clean-shaven."

.   .   .   .   .   .

Emma found life on board the *Foudroyant* trying. It was a great tax on her energy and resource to have to manage husband and lover at once in the restricted space of the man-of-war. Still, she did her best, as she always had done, to please the gentlemen. Sir William was coaxed, Lord Nelson flattered, and everyone on board ship kept in a good humour as well as she was able to do it. Even in the boiling heat with the continuous and hideous excitement and turmoil going on, she preserved her cheerfulness and continued to keep one object in view—the pleasing of the Queen by a clean sweep of all the rebels, by means of herself and Lord Nelson. Not only would this be, in her opinion, in itself a most meritorious action, it would bring more reward and glory to both the hero and his supporters.

She had always hated politics and she found the whole situation extremely tiresome; she would much rather have been in the Palazzo Sessa or in the rambling old palace at Palermo, sitting at the faro-table gambling away Nelson's prize-money, or posing in a well-lit alcove with wreaths of flowers, shawls and vases. She neither understood nor cared anything about the real situation in Naples, Italy or Europe, but she hoped it would soon be over, that she could go back to the old, jolly life with an obedient husband doddering at her side, a tame hero in her train.

Whenever she could get a few guests on board, she gave dinner-parties and afterwards performed on the harp, singing patriotic airs or odes written by Court poets in praise of Lord Nelson. Often in the evening the big woman would hold a concert on deck, gathering the sailors round her in a semi-circle to provide the chorus for her singing of "Rule Britannia." Her powerful voice went across the heavy night to where the transports, then turned into prison-ships, were anchored in the middle of the British Fleet; there the patriots, who had emerged from the castle trusting in the sworn words of five nations, languished in misery, chained down in the heat and darkness, without any comfort for mind or body, without a spark of hope, while through the portholes would come the strains of the strident British anthem and the ringing voice of the Patroness of the Navy.

Every day boats rowed out from the quays to the transports and took aboard numbers of the prisoners. They were delivered to the Giunta and speedily tried, if the farcical preliminary to rapid executions could be called a trial.

Negotiations continued with the French Commandant at Sant'
Elmo. This man, Méjean, chanced to be a scoundrel. It was
therefore not difficult to make terms with him. It would have been
possible for him to have obtained, even from the Queen, the lives
of several Republicans. This much concession the Court was
prepared to grant in return for the surrender of the formidable
castle. But Méjean asked for nothing and even betrayed those
Neapolitans who were among his own men, and who could have
claimed the right of protection of the French uniform. It was
said that he accepted large sums of money from the Sicilian Court
for this service.

When the garrison marched out of Sant' Elmo, many of the
French officers tried to disguise as fellow-countrymen the Neapolitans who had served with them, but Méjean walked up and down
the ranks, pointing out the Republicans to their enemies.

.   .   .   .   .   .

Another excitement was provided for the party on board the
Foudroyant. Prince Francesco Caracciolo had been, ever since he
had joined the Republicans, an object of the Queen's peculiar spite.
She had accused him of base ingratitude in forsaking her husband's
service; but in truth the noble Neapolitan owed nothing to the
Sicilian Court. His honours were hereditary and his position he
had won for himself by hard work—he had never accepted pension
nor favour from King Ferdinand. Still, however, the Queen persisted in regarding him as a monster of base ingratitude and perfidious disloyalty. Apart from these feelings she was afraid of him.
He knew, as she said in one of her letters, "every gulf and inlet"
in the long Neapolitan coast. He was far too dangerous a man to
be suffered to escape, and, whenever she ran over any particular
objects of her vengeance, she always mentioned Francesco Caracciolo.

When the Prince saw there was no more fighting possible, he
had left the castle secretly and, in disguise, gone to some of his
mother's land outside Naples, where he had hoped to remain concealed until he was able to get out of the country.

Cardinal Ruffo, had endeavoured to save Caracciolo, a man
whom he had always liked and admired. He tried to convey to

him certain passes which would enable him to slip out of Calabria, but he found it impossible to reach the fugitive Prince, who was betrayed by a servant into the hands of the Royalists, and after two days in one of the abominable prisons of Naples, corrupt as the grave and melancholy as hell, Francesco Caracciolo was brought on board the *Foudroyant* and delivered to Lord Nelson, a man who had once been his companion-at-arms and who had affected to admire him. "We all love Prince Caragholillo or whatever his name is."

Heavily chained, ragged, unshaven, and almost fainting from lack of food and water, Francesco Caracciolo stood on the quarter-deck of the British vessel. He was mute with the silence of one who knows both that his case is hopeless and that his judges are contemptible. His fate had, indeed, been decided, before ever he was dragged on board the British ship. The Queen had written

"I am very sorry about the flight of Caracciolo, for I believe that such a ruffian on the sea may be dangerous to the sacred person of the King. Therefore I could wish him put beyond the power of doing harm."

Both Nelson and Sir William Hamilton agreed with the Queen's views, which they proceeded at once to put into execution. As soon as it was known on board the *Foudroyant* that Caracciolo had been arrested, Sir William Hamilton asked for him, quite ignoring Ruffo, whose tendency to humanity he knew and dreaded, and appealing directly to Sir John Acton. Nelson made two applications direct to Cardinal Ruffo for the custody of Caracciolo. Ruffo kept Caracciolo out of Nelson's hands as long as he could, but when the Royal letters arrived from Palermo giving Nelson full powers, the Cardinal retired bitterly to the background, and Caracciolo was given to his enemies.

It was on June 29th when the Neapolitan Admiral was brought on board the *Foudroyant*. On the 27th of that month Hamilton had written to Sir John Acton:

"Caracciolo and twelve others of those insolent rebels will shortly be given into Lord Nelson's hands. If I am not mistaken, they will be sent cautiously to Procida to be judged there, and as they become condemned they will return here for the execution of their sentence. Caracciolo will probably hang from the yard-arm of the *Minerva*, where he will remain exposed from daybreak till sunset to set such an example as is necessary for the future service of His Sicilian Majesty's Marine in the heart of which Jacobinism has already made such great progress."

This course of action having been decided upon, it would appear that it was a waste of time to submit Francesco Caracciolo to the form of even a brief court-martial, but this was done; judicial murderers often like to be nice in their methods.

Hamilton wrote again to Sir John Acton soon after Caracciolo had been dragged on board the flagship. The mincing senile *dilettante* wrote with the callousness of a man entirely without heart:

"Here we have the spectacle of Caracciolo, pale, with a long beard, half-dead and with downcast eyes, brought in handcuffed on board this vessel, where he is at this moment with the son of Cassano, D. Giulio Pacifico the priest and other infamous traitors. I suppose justice will be immediately executed upon the most guilty. In truth, it is a shocking thing, but I, who know their ingratitude and their crime, have felt it less painful than the numerous other persons present at this spectacle. I believe it to be a good thing that we have the chief culprits on board our ship now that we are just going to attack Sant' Elmo, because we shall be able to cut off a head for every cannon ball that the French throw into the City of Naples."

Lord Nelson immediately ordered a court-martial on Caracciolo to take place on his flagship, that is, British ground. When, a few months previously, he had been irritated by Commodore Campbell's burning of the ships, he had declared that he would have court-martialled him had he been under his command.

Francesco Caracciolo was no more under Lord Nelson's command than had been the Englishman in Portuguese service, but all such considerations were now brushed aside. Nelson was responsible, first, to Lord Keith, the Commander-in-Chief of the Mediterranean, and, then, to the British Government; he was a subject of King George III and not of King Ferdinand, who had not even officially given him the position of Generalissimo of his forces or Admiral of the Sicilian Fleet, an office which was nominally held by the Crown Prince. Lord Nelson had, therefore, not a shadow of any authority to take any action whatsoever against any Neapolitans or subjects of the Sicilian King. The full extent of his duty would have been to hand the prisoners over to the representatives of King Ferdinand, but he knew, and the Hamiltons knew, indeed, all the British Fleet and all the Royalists knew, that he could do what he liked in the way of ferocity against the patriots with the full applause and approval of the Sicilian Court.

Conte di Thurn, a foreigner in the Bourbon service, was sent for by Nelson, and with five senior officers formed a Council of War, to try, as Thurn put in the report he sent to Ruffo that evening: "Cavaliere Don Francesco Caracciolo, accused as a rebel against His Majesty, our August Master, to be tried and awarded punishment adequate to his crime."

The court-martial was held in one of the cabins of the *Foudroyant*. It lasted two hours. The prisoner had no one to speak in his defence and was not allowed to call any witnesses. When he was asked what he could say for himself, he replied that far from deserting the King, as he was accused, the King had deserted him. No proper report of the proceedings was taken. The prisoner could hardly hold himself upright from exhaustion. "He seemed half-dead with fatigue," noted Hamilton. He made one request—to be judged by English officers, saying that Thurn was his personal enemy and they had lately been engaged in a bitter civil war. No notice was taken of this request. He was judged guilty by a majority of votes, four of the officers voting for death and two against.

When Lord Nelson received this verdict he ordered Thurn to inflict on Francesco Caracciolo the most ignominious possible death—he was to be hanged at five o'clock of the same day at the yard-arm, and left hanging till sunset, at which hour, the cord being cut, he was to be let fall into the sea.

It was one o'clock when Thurn received this order from Nelson; in another half-hour he put Francesco Caracciolo on a boat, took him on board the *Minerva*, the ship on which Caracciolo had fired and which he had nearly captured in the action off Procida, and put him *in cappella*. Not only was the mode of death the most degrading possible, but the last proviso contained for the seaman a peculiar horror. Nelson himself had a dread of being thrown uncoffined into the sea. Besides, it meant that the Prince, a Roman Catholic, would be denied not only the last rites of the Church, but all Christian burial. He would, indeed, be treated as a dog, and his carcass as carrion. Conte di Thurn, himself no friend of the prisoner, was a little uneasy at the severity of the sentence. He ventured to point out to the British Admiral that it was usual to give condemned prisoners twenty-four hours' respite, in which, in company with a priest, they could attend to their soul's welfare. Sir William Hamilton ventured to second this request, but Nelson refused to listen to it.

During the time between Caracciolo's leaving the *Foudroyant* and the hour of the execution, which had been placed at five o'clock, two requests came from the prisoner—one that he might have a priest, another that he might be shot instead of being hanged. Lord Nelson refused both.

He could have saved Francesco Caracciolo. The death of this brave man and the deaths of the garrisons of the two castles that were held by the patriots were directly owing to his action. He, too, had the entire responsibility for the hideous details of the execution.

At five o'clock precisely in the late, blazing Neapolitan afternoon, the starved, hunted man, stumbling from fatigue, was brought on the deck of the *Minerva*. The rigging of the British ship was dark with seamen waiting to see the spectacle of a Neapolitan patrician hanged at the yard-arm of a Neapolitan ship. None of the bitterness of an ignominious death, none of the full taste of complete failure was spared Francesco Caracciolo. He died like a brave man, finding a smile for a midshipman who wept to see his fate, glancing even in that moment with interest at the design of a British ship riding near. The noose was adjusted, the haggard, thick-set man run up to the yard-arm, where he kicked out his life in the blue air.

Sir William scribbled away to Sir John Acton, fit recipient of such letters:

"All that Lord Nelson thinks and does is dictated to him by his conscience, by his honour, and I believe that in the end his decisions will be acknowledged as the best that could have been taken."

Yet there was something about this terrible action that struck uneasiness even into the withered heart of the British Minister:

"For the love of God," he added, "contrive that the King comes and lives on board the *Foudroyant,* that if possible his Royal Standard be run up. The die is cast. Now we must be as firm as we can."

At sunset the body of the Neapolitan Admiral was cut down and flung like offal into the darkening waters of the bay.

.   .   .   .   .   .

Emma had kept out of the way. She had seen to it that there was no record of the proceedings on that occasion. Ugly stories were told about her. One was that she and Nelson had taken a boat and rowed round the *Minerva,* staring with coarse curiosity at the corpse of Francesco Caracciolo; another was that on having a sucking-pig for supper she had begun to weep, declaring that it reminded her of the man that had been just executed—but afterwards, recovering her good spirits, she made a hearty meal, devouring even the animal's brains. It is likely enough that these stories are not true, but there were some women of whom they would never have been said. She had played her part; she had been the Queen's most efficient instrument, always at her husband's ear, always at her lover's ear, urging that they must please the adorable Queen. And the Queen was not unmindful of these services.

Whilst Caracciolo in his misery was waiting for death, Emma Hamilton scribbled three letters to the Queen, which have not survived, but the Queen's answer is in existence. It runs:

"I have received with infinite gratitude your dear, obliging letters, three of Saturday's and one of anterior date bearing the list of the Jacobins arrested, who formed part of the worst we have had. I have seen also the sad end of the crazy Caracciolo. I comprehend all that your excellent heart must have suffered and that augments my gratitude. I see perfectly what you point out to me and am filled with gratitude for it."

Probably Emma had mentioned that her exquisite sensibility was a little hurt by all the horrors that were happening around her.

216

On shore the executions were beginning; the garrisons of the castles were the first to suffer.

Gabriele Manthoné asked if it was true that the King had annulled the capitulation; when told that it was so, he replied: "Then I maintain that he is a tyrant," and refused to speak again.

General Massa, who was hurried from the court-martial to the square where he was to be executed, said with ironic bitterness: "Make haste, make haste, I have so little time to lose." He had before lamented that through relying on the word of five nations he had betrayed his own garrison.

"Had I not got," he said, "men and ammunition and arms and provisions? I could have held out for months, or, at the worst, I could have blown myself, my fellow-soldiers, and the Castle into the air, and met a noble, not a felon's death."

One by one they were beheaded in the broiling heat and amid the insults and jeers of the *lazzaroni* drunk with blood.

So indecent were the ghastly antics of the crowd that the *Bianchi* (*padri confortatori*), the Brothers who, in Christian compassion, waited on the last moments of those who were condemned as criminals, protested.

These monks said that these unfortunate "rebels" were hurried to their end so swiftly, that there was no time to think of their souls. The Bianchi also complained that the dead bodies were left for hours at the mercy of the mob, and that the most horrible scenes took place. It is impossible to dwell on the orgies of obscene cruelty, of cannibalism, in which the vile crowd indulged.

In thus loosing the basest of the savage populace on those who had endeavoured, in the face of every difficulty, to maintain an ideal, in thus hurling the brave, the noble, the gentle, the cultured, the learned, the young, and the beautiful, to glut the foul passions of the mob—passions, too, like her own, the Queen gratified at last her lust for vengeance; one wish of hers was fulfilled; Naples was treated "like a rebel Irish town"; many of the atrocities committed in that city were the same as those which were being committed by Sir Ralph Abercrombie's troops in Ireland. The mutilation of the dead, the eating of human flesh, the use of human heads as footballs, were common to both the Bourbon vengeance of Naples, and William Pitt's vengeance on Ireland.

As a meddling, vindictive woman is universally loathed more deeply than a masculine tyrant, the victims of this fury found a focus for their scorn in the Queen; she was not more detestable than her wretched husband, than the worthless Sir John Acton, but she appeared more hateful because she was a woman; her sex gave an added air of meanness, of degradation to these ignoble horrors.

Already the patriots had quoted against the Queen the French verses written to her sister, Marie Antoinette, about the violated treaty:

> "Monstre échappé de Germanie,
> Le désastre de nos climats!
> Jusqu'à quand contre ma patrie
> Commettras-tu tes attentats?
>   Approche, femme détestable.
> Regarde l'abîme effroyable
> Où tes crimes nous ont plongés!
> Veux-tu donc, extrême en ta rage,
> Pour consommer ton digne ouvrage
> Nous voir l'un par l'autre égorgés?
> Plus prodigue que l'Egyptienne,
> Dont Marc Antoine fut épris,
> Plus orgueilleuse qu' Agrippine
> Plus lubrique que Messaline
>   Plus cruelle que Médicis."

The attack was ferocious and extravagant, but these terms might more justly be applied to Maria Carolina than the Queen to whom the stern reproaches were addressed.

.   .   .   .   .   .

Nothing was gained by the massacres in Naples, by these savage executions, save the gratification of Bourbon cruelty. It was a lesson to a world that had been shocked by the excesses of *La Terreur Rouge* in France, that *La Terreur Blanche*, as had indeed already been proved in La Vendée and Marseilles, that the old order could be as savage, as base, as insane, as any *sans culottes*, drunk and starving from the slums. While among the followers and instruments of the Bourbons could be found men like Charette,

Speciale or Mammone, it was merely ironical for any Royalist to appear shocked at the record of the Jacobins.

The odium of these atrocities was cast on the British, "ferocious wolves of English," who became detested by all save the basest class; the final political result was to drive the country into the arms of France, to make Naples feel that anything was better than the renewal of the Bourbon rule.

The ruined men who were thus martyred would, had they been exiled, have been no trouble to the Neapolitan government, but, put thus infamously to death, they became in their turn potent symbols of future vengeance.

The fanatic Garat, who had been the French envoy at Naples, exclaimed with just fury:

"You say the dead do not return, that you murder these men to be rid of them! Indeed, in this way you will never be rid of them. The dead do return, in more terrible guise than ever the living came back—they come to demand payment for their spilt blood!"

Nothing had been gained by the judicial murder of Francesco Caracciolo, which Lord Nelson had intended as a frightful example to the rebel Jacobins, and those French, "the mere mention of whom made his blood boil." Caracciolo, ruined and a prisoner, would have done no harm to the Bourbons alive; dead, he became a national hero, a reminder of what had been done, an earnest of what might be achieved.

"The consecration of an heroic fall," neither the Bourbons nor the British were fine enough to see that aspect of the fall of the "*figli di Parthenope*"; in this desperate sacrifice lay the germ of Italian unity, of Italian liberty; those who died for *la patria* in 1799 prepared the way for 1806, for 1860, when Garibaldi and his patriots chased the Bourbons and their parasites for ever from the fair countries they had befouled.

In the Piazza dei Martiri—named after these martyrs—in Naples, the mighty Lion of 1799 at the base of the memorial column is wounded but still grips eternally the fasces.

On June 28th, Captain Foote, whom it was convenient to have out of the way—he had signed the violated capitulation in the name of Great Britain—sailed to Palermo to fetch the King, while

Emma was making herself useful by collecting lists of prisoners, which she sent to the Queen. She wrote to Maria Carolina every day and the lists of condemned persons passed to and from the women, till one would have thought that they would have felt their fingers befouled by blood.

The Queen had long had a list by her of those on whom she would take vengeance if the Republic fell; among them was the editress of *Il Monitore*, the elegant and gifted poet Eleanora Fonseca Pimentel; she had found refuge in the castle and then had been taken on board the transports. She was among the number of the remnant of prisoners who were at last told they could depart; she had given a guarantee never to return to Naples and not to interfere in politics, and it was believed she might be allowed to sail for Toulon. This was not to be. She had written several scathing articles against the Queen and the Royal Family in the columns of *Il Monitore*, and no pity could be extended to a severe critic of Maria Carolina.

The Royalist guards came on board the polacca, arrested her and lodged her in the prison that the Bianchi protested against entering, because of the filth, foul air, and condition of the captives.

On July 8th the King came on board the *Foudroyant*; at the same moment as this grand eloquent reception was taking place, and while he and his smug courtiers were overwhelming the Hamiltons and Lord Nelson with noisy gratitude, prisoners were still being rowed across the bay from polaccas to the prisons in Naples.

This was a very pleasant sight for His Majesty, who listened with relish while Sir William, who was flustered but relieved that the worst was over, explained how cleverly Lord Nelson had stopped the transports just as they had been about to sail for Toulon, and how he had acted so promptly in getting Caracciolo out of the hands of Ruffo (who must be a Jacobin at heart) and in having him hanged before there was time for anyone to interfere. And there was Emma, blooming, but a little fagged from the heat, to drop her curtsy and to receive the messages from her adorable Queen.

The *Foudroyant* was now to be a Palace and a Court, since His Majesty, for all the triumph of the *Santa Fede*, dared not go ashore.

The Royal vengeance was hurried on. The accounts of this made a pleasant diversion to amuse His Majesty, when he was at his ease after supping with Emma and Nelson and Sir William. It was ordered that these hangings and beheadings should all take place before twelve, because soon after that hour there was a drawing of the lottery and the good King did not wish to deprive his subjects of the excitement either of the executions or of the lottery.

When Emma went on deck to obtain a little air in those stifling July days, when the sun beat down from sunrise to sunset on the brilliant waters, she could see the boats going to and fro, taking loads of prisoners from the polaccas to the town; she could see the outlines of the prisons where people of all ages and of both sexes festered alive in filth and disease.

She knew what was taking place in Naples. She constantly received from people she had known and from people who were strangers to her, but who realized her influence, applications, supplications and entreaties; she took no heed of them, and there is no record that she made any effort to save anyone or even that she was the least affected by the circumstances in which she found herself. She only wished that the whole affair was over and that she was back again in the rich, luxurious life she liked so well.

On July 19th, she wrote thus to her old friend and love, Charles Greville, who must have seemed a long way from these strange events in which the girl in distress that he had rescued from the London streets was taking so prominent a part.

"On board the *Foudroyant*,
"Bay of Naples, July 19th, 1799.
"Dear Sir,

"We have an opportunity of sending to England, and I cannot let pass this good opportunity without thanking you for your kind remembrance in Sir William's letter. Everything goes on well here. We have got Naples, all the Forts, and to-night our troops go to Capua. His Majesty is with us on board, where he holds his councils and levees every day. General Acton, Castelcicala, with one gentleman of the bedchamber, attends His Majesty. Sir William, with Lord Nelson and Acton, are the King's counsellors, and you may be assured that the future government will be most just and solid. The King has bought his experience most dearly, and at last he knows his friends from his enemies, and also knows the defects of his former government and is determined to remedy them. But he has great good sense and his misfortunes have made him steady and looking to himself. The Queen is not come; she sent me as her deputy and I am very popular, speak the Neapolitan language, and am considered, with Sir William, friends of the people. The Queen is waiting at Palermo and she is determined, as there has been a great outcry against her, not to risk coming with the King, for if it had not succeeded on his arrival and he not being well received, she would not bear the blame, nor be in the way. We arrived here before the King some fourteen days and I have privately seen all the Royal parties, and having the head of the *lazzaroni*, an old friend, who came on the night of our arrival and told me that he had ninety thousand *lazzaroni* ready at the holding up of his finger, some supplied with arms. Lord Nelson, to whom I interpreted this, has got a large supply of arms for the rest, and they were deposited with this man. . . .

"We gave him only one hundred of our marine troops and these brave men kept all the time in order and he brought the heads of all this ninety thousand round the ship on the King's arrival, and he is to have promotion. I have through him made the Queen's party and the people at large had prayed her to come back—she is now very popular. I send her every night a messenger to Palermo with all the news and letters and she gives me the orders in the same way. I have given audiences to those of her party and have settled matters between her nobility and Her Majesty. . . .

"In short, as I can judge, it may all turn out fortunate. The Neapolitans have had a dose of Republicanism. What a glory to our good King, to our country, to ourselves, that we, our brave fleet, our great Nelson have had the happiness of restoring the King to his throne, to the Neapolitans their much loved King, and being the instrument of giving the future a solid and just government to the Neapolitans. . . .

"The guilty are punished, but the faithful are rewarded. I have not been on shore but once. The King gave us leave to go as far as Sant' Elmo to see the effect of bombs. I saw at a distance our spoilt house, the town and villa that had been plundered. On Sir William's new apartment a bomb burst. It made me low-spirited I don't desire to go back again. We shall, as soon as the government is safe, return to Palermo and bring back the Royal Family, for I can see not any permanent government till that event takes place. . . .

"I am quite worn out, for I am interpreter to Lord Nelson, the King and Queen, and altogether feel quite shattered, but if things go well it will set me up. We dine now every day with the King at twelve o'clock and the dinner is over by one. His Majesty goes to sleep and we sit down to write in the heat. On board you may guess what we suffer. My mother is at Palermo and I have an English lady with me used to write and helping to keep papers and the things in order. We have given the King all the upper Cabin, all but one room that we write in and receive the ladies who come to the King. Sir William and I have an apartment in the ward-room, and as to Lord Nelson, he is here and there and everywhere. I never saw such vigour and activity in anyone as in this wonderful man. My dearest Sir William, thank God, is well, and of the greatest use now to the King. We hope Capua will fall in a few days and then we shall be able to return to Palermo. On Sunday last we had prayers on board. The King assisted and was much pleased with the order, decency and good behaviour of the men, the officers, etc. Pray write to me. God bless you, my dear Sir, and believe me, Ever Yours affectionately, Emma Hamilton.

"It would be a charity to send me some things, for in saving all for my dear and Royal friend, I lost my little all. Never mind."

Not all the men had been so decent and orderly as those whom the King admired, when he saw them at their Protestant prayers on the clean-scrubbed deck of the *Foudroyant*. One, John Jolly, had been shot by Nelson's orders for insubordination, and a sailor for the same reason had been strung up to the yard-arm.

Emma, when she had gone ashore, had noticed nothing but the damage to her own property, but Naples at that moment was almost what Ruffo had bitterly said it would become—"a heap of stones," and the blood was drying on the hot pavements. The hangings, and beheadings, went on day by day; the flower of Neapolitan civilization, all that was enlightened, cultured, scholarly, humane, suffered the most hideous, degrading, and painful of deaths in the packed square of the Mercato, where the mob, drunk with blood-lust, blasphemed and rioted under the fierce sun, in the sour stenches.

Emma went on compiling her lists of prisoners and condemned, the Queen checking the names off with those other lists she held herself. The two women estimated that there were still eight thousand left in the prisons; no one counted those who had been massacred, killed in the street fights or driven into exile.

.   .   .   .   .

The King, strolling on the deck of the British man-of-war after one of his afternoon naps, saw a dark object in the bright, fouled waters of the bay that roused his curiosity. He peered through his spy-glass and was soon shrieking in terror. Coming rapidly towards the ship, visible to the waist as if he walked through the polluted waves, was the body of Francesco Caracciolo, bolt upright, with his long black hair hanging round his livid swollen face. Frightened and convulsed were the superstitious crowd—Ferdinand and those with him; only one of the priests recovered sufficient wits to say —"Caracciolo has returned from the dead to beg the King's pardon."

This slightly reassured Ferdinand, but he immediately ordered that the corpse have Christian burial.

The body of Caracciolo was drawn up on board one of the Neapolitan ships, rowed ashore in the twilight, and buried in the little church of Santa Maria delle Grazie a Catena, built by the fishermen's savings, on the shore of Santa Lucia, where the sailors and fisherfolk, who had greatly loved the man who had so long defended their coast, and who had lived in the great house in their quarter, laid him in his native soil beneath a humble grave-stone on which was written "Francesco Caracciolo, 1799."

The Brothers belonging to the fraternity of Santa Maria delle Grazie a Catena helped to bury the body of the Captain who had carried the flag of Naples to the shores of Tunis, and one of them gave it a benediction. The porter of the monastery had known Francesco Caracciolo since, as a boy, he used to run wild around these rocky coasts, and the old man recalled how the Prince had been called "the madcap," with his streaming black hair, quick limbs and merry laugh.

Long after the curious searched in vain for a trace of the grave of the woman who queened it on board the *Foudroyant*, while

Francesco Caracciolo was furtively buried by his humble friends in the sea-shore church, this inscription might be read:

Francesco Caracciolo
Ammiraglio della Repubblica Partenopea
Fu dall' astio d'ingeneroso nemico
Impeso all' antenna il 29 Giugno, 1799.
I Popolani Di S. Lucia
Qui Tumularono L'onorando Cadavere.

On August 5th, Emma wrote again to Charles Greville:

"*Foudroyant,*
"Bay of Naples, August 5th, 1799.

"As Sir William wrote to you to-day, my dear Sir, I will only say that the Kingdom of Naples is clear. Dasta and Capua have capitulated, and we sail to-night for Palermo, having been here seven weeks and everything gone to our wishes. We return with a Kingdom to present to my much loved Queen. I have also been so happy to succeed in all my company and everything I was charged with. The King is in great spirits. I have received all the ladies for him and he calls me his *Grande Maîtresse*. I was near taking him at his word, but as I have had seven long years service in Court I am waiting to get quiet. I am not ambitious of more honours. We have had the King on board a month and I have never been able to go once on shore. Do you not call that slavery? I believe we shall come home in the spring. It is necessary for our pockets and our bodies want bracing. . . .

"Your sincere and affectionate Emma.

"My mother in Palermo is longing to see her Emma. You can't think how she is loved and respected by all. She has adopted a mode of living that is charming. She has a good apartment in our house, always lives with us, dines, etc. Only when she does not like it. For example, at great dinners, she herself refuses, and has always a friend to dine with her and la Signora Ambasciatrice Inglese is known all over Palermo, as she was at Naples. The Queen has been very kind to her in my absence, went to see her, told her she ought to be proud of her glorious daughter who had done so much in these last suffering months. There is great preparation for our return. The Queen comes out with all Palermo

225

to meet us, a landing place is made, all suppers, illuminations all ready. The Queen has prepared my clothes. In short, I am fagged, I am more than repaid. I tell you this that you may see I am not unworthy of having been once your pupil. God bless you."

.   .   .   .   .   .

There was a faint shadow over all this glory in the thought of Fanny's waiting in Burnham Thorpe Vicarage, and the letters, which became with each one more peremptory in tone, from Lord Keith, reminding his second-in-command that he could not for ever keep the British Navy in the Bay of Naples.

As early as June, while the question of the rebel castles was distracting Naples, Lord Keith, newly Commander-in-Chief of the Mediterranean Fleet, had ordered Lord Nelson to "send such ships as you can possibly spare off the Island of Minorca to await my orders."

Lady Hamilton's lover disobeyed, evading his superior's commands by declaring that the safety of the Bourbon Kingdom demanded his presence off Naples. Urged again, and more emphatically, he put forward as an excuse for not moving the Fleet that the French were still at Capua, giving it as his unasked-for opinion that it was better to save the Kingdom of Naples and risk Minorca, than to risk Naples to save Minorca. Taking no notice of this advice or comment, Keith retorted by a peremptory command:

"Your Lordship is hereby required to repair to Minorca."

By this time he had heard or guessed something, perhaps a little too much, of what had been happening in Naples: "Advise those Neapolitans not to be too sanguinary. Cowards are always cruel," he wrote. "Give them fair words and little confidence."

Again Lord Nelson disobeyed. He sent four ships to Minorca, but he could not be expected himself to leave the Bay of Naples where the celebration of the anniversary of the Battle of the Nile was to take place on a grand scale; he had, however, to endure other annoyances besides Lord Keith's vexatious dispatches. Above all there was the question of Fanny. Nelson, when he had got an opportunity through Captain Hardy's going on leave to England, had sent tactful messages to his wife and requested that she would

send Lady Hamilton some presents. Fanny had obeyed and dispatched a cap and 'kerchief such as were fashionable in London.
She had given him scraps of news; she had ordered for him a suit
of fine clothes for Her Majesty's birthday and that the expenses of
his new chariots were alarming:

"Nothing fine about it, only fashionable . . . .
    Three hundred and fifty-two pounds for harness, etc., for one
    pair of horses."

Lord Nelson cared little about matters of expense; the present
from the East India Company—£10,000—had just been paid to
his English bank, and he was glad of the chance of distributing it
among his friends and relations; not only was he, where money
was concerned, generous by nature, but it was a good opportunity
of keeping his family quiet and of swaying them in his favour. £500
was to be given to his father, £500 each to his two brothers;
there was plenty left over for his sister and for Fanny, to whom he
wrote pleasantly, begging her to distribute the money, promising
to return as soon as his health permitted, but carefully emphasizing
the poor state he was in. He was able to send Fanny also a glowing account of the celebrations of the famous August 1st, when the
King had dined on board his flagship and the whole of the bay
had been illuminated, so that by night it might have seemed as if
the town and villages were all housing prosperous and happy
people from Procida to Sorrento. At night the outlines of the
prisons were hidden, the scaffold and the block concealed in the
shadows, and the murdered bodies washed ashore on the rocks were
invisible.

"A large vessel," wrote the gratified hero, "was fitted out like
a Roman galley. On its oars were six lamps, in the centre was
erected a triumphal column with my name, at the stern were
elevated two angels supporting my picture. In short, my dear
Fanny, the beauty of the whole was beyond my powers of description. More than two thousand variegated lamps were suspended round the vessel, an orchestra was fitted up and filled with
the very best musicians and singers. The scene of beauty was in a
great measure to celebrate my fame. . . . (Describing their
previous distress etc.) But Nelson came, the invincible Nelson, and

they were preserved and again made happy. This must not make you think me vain."

More congenial even than writing his own praises was the task of writing to dear Mrs. Cadogan about the beloved Lady.

"Our dear Lady is also, I can assure you, perfectly well, but her time is so much taken up with excuses from rebels, Jacobins and fools, that she is every day most heartily tired. Our conversation is, as often as we are liberated from these teazers, of you and of your other friends in the house at Palermo, and I hope we shall very soon return to see you. Till then, recollect that we are restoring happiness to the Kingdom of Naples and doing good to millions."

The honest dame must have been highly gratified to receive this letter from so great a hero, and to hear that dear Emma was "doing good to millions." Perhaps by then Mrs. Cadogan had learned to read and write.

One of the "Jacobins and fools" who pleaded with Lady Hamilton was the famous Domenico Cirillo, a man respected and beloved by all who knew him, a famous physician and a celebrated botanist. From the dark cabin of the polacca where he writhed in heavy chains, he wrote a letter in English to Lady Hamilton, reminding her of their one-time acquaintance, protesting, and with truth, that he had done nothing to serve the Republic, but, not being a man of politics, had endeavoured to live quietly under any government that might be in Naples, and had spent his time administering to the sick of all denominations and opinions.

This elegant and courteous appeal, written in such bitter extremity, from such a man would have sickened with remorse and pity the hearts of most women. There is no record that it disturbed that of Emma Hamilton. Nelson scrawled at the side of the letter that Domenico Cirillo was a fool who might have been saved if he had not been obstinate.

The meaning of this obstinacy was that, when the high-minded man discovered at what price of humiliation he was expected to buy his pardon, he refused. He went to his felon's death shortly afterwards as precisely dressed as prison conditions allowed, wearing a jaunty French cap with a bow. Like all the other Republicans, he died bravely—"*da forte*" as General Massa said. Many of the Republicans preferred death to shouting "*Evviva il Re.*"

Emma was able to tell the Queen that Eleanora Fonseca Pimentel, whose anti-Royalist articles had so infuriated Her Majesty, had been duly hanged in the Mercato, the dreary square before the Church of the Carmine, after drinking a cup of coffee and quoting a line of Horace.

Hanging, as practised in Naples, was not an easy death. The victims mounted a long ladder, had the rope put round their necks, were then pushed off by a man seated at the top of the gallows, an assistant, the *tirapiede*, then leapt out on to the feet, swinging, struggling and fighting with the victim, into space, while the man who had been at the top jumped on the shoulders of the dying person. In this manner was the elegant and cultured Eleanora Fonseca Pimentel destroyed. As she mounted the ladder, she saluted the bodies of her friends which were lying below; some had been hanged, some beheaded. She had in vain asked as a favour the latter mode of death, to which, by reason of her noble birth, she was entitled.

But the ignoble gallows suited the rage of the Queen and the humour of the mob; the *lazzaroni* liked to see the three figures, victim, hangman, and assistant, swinging about at the end of the rope; it was a fine chance for ribald jokes.

The corpses that the brave woman hailed as she climbed the ladder were those of the high-minded young aristocrats, who had worked ardently for the Republic, Giuliano Colonna and Gennaro Serra. For the space of the summer day the remains of the poetess swung in the Mercato, the butt of the insults of the *lazzaroni*, Emma's friends whom she had been so pleased to see crowding in their barges round the *Foudroyant*, and whom Lord Nelson had supplied with British arms.

.   .   .   .   .   .

The fall of Capua, to which Emma had alluded in her letter to Greville, was the final defeat of Ettore Carafa.

After an heroic defence of the fort, lack of provisions compelled him to capitulate; he surrendered on the condition that the garrison should march out with their property, arms, and with military honours, while he himself and some of his officers were to be allowed to join the French then in camp at Ancona, but again it was a question of "the King does not make treaties with rebels."

The capitulation was broken and Ettore Carafa, the young, bold and splendid patrician, was sent in chains to Naples, where he was kept in a foul, unlit prison, fastened by an iron collar round his neck to the wall. Brought out to die in the rags of the French uniform that should, by all the rights of nations, have saved him, since he had taken service with the French Republic, he lay on his back with unbandaged eyes; as he said contemptuously to the headsman: "Tell thy Queen that Ettore Carafa knows how to die," his beautiful head was struck off.

The relation of this heroic death gave the good-humoured King Ferdinand a chance for a joke. In his dialect of the streets, he chuckled: "So the young Duke knew how to flourish to the last!"

The Giunta continued its work; many people were beheaded in spite of heavy bribes; those who said that they had come out of the castles on Lord Nelson's word were told that the King had annulled all promises of clemency.

.   .   .   .   .   .

On August 5th the *Foudroyant* returned to Palermo, bringing, as Emma had grandiloquently said, a present of a Kingdom for the adored Queen. The daughter of the Hapsburgs was on the quay-side to receive this gift; behind her came a vast crowd, first, her own particular following and sycophants, flatterers and underlings, and then the cynics of the Sicilian nobility, who hoped for either pickings of the plunder or at least a spectacle, and then the rabble of Palermo, agape for a raree-show. These people, like the *laz-zaroni* of Naples, cared little who was the ringmaster as long as there was a circus.

Emma and the Queen fell into each other's arms with tears, embraces and exclamations of joy. The work was done. Naples had been ground down again under the heel of Bourbon tyranny. The enlightened, intellectual and honest people, who had made a

desperate stand against ferocious misgovernment, had been either
murdered or exiled. The British Navy, with no credit to itself or
to the nation it represented, had made a semblance of restoring
Bourbon rule in South Italy. Caracciolo was dead, so were men
like Gabriele Manthoné, General Massa, Mario Pagano, Baffi,
Pacifico. All who had ventured a word, a gesture, a look against
the Bourbons had been punished; a noble and beautiful youth,
whose gaiety had charmed even his jailers, had been beheaded for the
alleged crime of knocking the head off a plaster statue of Carlos III,
an offence really committed by the King's dear friends, the *lazzaroni*.
No trick, no subterfuge, no chicanery had been spared to give the
Queen her glut of vengeance. Even those who had passively lived
under the short Republic, who had merely suffered the French
out of indifference or timidity or liberal-mindedness, had been
slain, exiled, or ruined. No one could complain that Maria
Carolina had not found in Emma a willing tool, that Hamilton
had not loyally supported his wife, and that Lord Nelson and his
captains had not been most efficient executioners for the Bourbons.
Now the rewards began to come in.

"Those excellent Sovereigns," as Nelson afterwards named
them in a frenzy of snobbery, were lavish in their gifts and noisy
in their gratitude. The Queen had written about the festivities
on August 1st:

"My very dear Lady,

"You will scarcely believe how very desirous I felt to be with
you on the 1st of August at table with our hero and all his fellow
heroes, companions and officers. I should have given so heartily
the hip, hip, hip, that in spite of the cannon's roar my voice would
have been heard, so deeply is my heart penetrated."

Not having been able to assist at the banquet on board the
Foudroyant, she had done her best in making preparations for a
great festival in Palermo. It happened to be also the feast of
Santa Rosalia, which gave a popular air to the whole rejoicing.

There was something for everyone, and the Queen had chosen
her gifts with great tact, for they were exactly what suited the
recipients. To Emma, still lamenting "the goods" that she had
left behind in the Palazzo Sessa, there were cartloads of dresses

valued at over £3,000, a gold chain set with the Queen's portrait, surrounded with diamonds forming the words "Eternal gratitude" in Italian, and another expensively mounted picture of King Ferdinand supposed to be worth a thousand guineas.

Sir William had another jewelled picture of His Majesty. The value of the dresses and of the pictures was supposed to be something like £10,000.

For Lord Nelson there was a gift extremely to his taste—the Sicilian Dukedom of Bronte, "thunder" in English; it had a gratifying sound to a hero's ear. His Majesty assured the new Duke that his revenues would be in the neighbourhood of £3,000 sterling a year; Lord Nelson at once, with his usual lavishness about money, wrote to his father that he should have a charge of £500 on the estate. He was immensely pleased at his reward and hoped to make his tenancy "the happiest in Sicily."

. . . . . .

The *festa* of Santa Rosalia, which coincided so happily with the rejoicings for the conquest of Naples, was the most important social event in the lives of the Palermitans, the most important religious festival of the year for the people. Against the background offered by the superb city, where the Saracenic and Norman palaces rose in a medley of baroque splendour above gardens filled with the delicate fronds of the pepper-tree, the glow of the pomegranate, and the metallic sharpness of palms, took place the fantastic celebrations of the young virgin of Charlemagne's blood, who, hundreds of years before, had fled from some such scene as this, to die in holy seclusion in a grotto on Monte Pellegrino.

One of Emma's excursions had been out to a rugged mountain from which the glitter of Palermo could be seen below among the dark groves and golden rocks, and where in a dark hollow of the ancient hill was the shrine of the royal maiden. On the spot where Santa Rosalia had drawn the last sigh of her pure breath reposed her statue in untainted white marble. Her gown of solid gold, her golden coronal, her golden book, cross, staff and skull, had all been given by Bourbon kings, who had also offered the marble cherub who presented a golden lily to the dying saint.

Above the grotto, the mountain soared to a peak where stood

232

another statue of Santa Rosalia, in grey limestone, before an oratory; above her was a beacon tower built to flash warnings along the coast on the approach of those corsairs whom Francesco Caracciolo had beaten back to the African shores.

The festival of the patroness of Palermo was usually held from July 11th to 15th; but this year the rejoicings were continued until the British Fleet arrived from Naples.

The weather was superb and the Sicilians were adepts at this kind of pageantry, which suited so well the luxurious promenade of the *Marina*, or Porto Borbonico, which rivalled with its sea-wall, carriage-way, Ionic temples, huge statues of Bourbon kings and rich locust-trees, the fashionable Chiaja of Naples. Here the patricians on the hot summer nights had displayed their carriages and horses, their clothes and jewels, while they talked over the bloody scenes taking place in Naples, and here a gigantic display of fireworks was arranged in honour of Santa Rosalia, who had died a pure maiden in a mountain grotto, and of Lord Nelson, who had achieved so much success by slaughtering his fellow-men in the name of God and King Ferdinand.

There were plenty of novelties to amuse Emma, who had now got "Jacobinism" off her mind, and could rest and enjoy all the fun. The saint's car moved in procession down the Toledo from the Porta Felice to the Porta Nuova; it was seventy feet long and eighty feet high; and towered above the tall façades it passed. It was drawn by thirty-two oxen and preceded by a squadron of Sicilian cavalry, while about it pressed a crowd, delirious with enthusiasm, casting the brilliant flowers of Sicily beneath the gilded hoofs of the sweating white beasts. The car itself, mounted on a wheeled float, was in the form of tiers of seats on which were grouped liveried court musicians, above them a temple rose where groups of angels held up tabernacles; these were surrounded by festoons of blossoms, flags and holy pictures. The gigantic structure was crowned by a monstrous figure of the virgin saint, attired in silver, and half veiled by a transparency of tissue clouds; beneath her a group of children from the foundling hospitals, attired in brocade, struck up hymns on zithers and guitars, when the Court band came to a pause.

This monstrous temple took two hours to jolt and stagger down the Toledo, where the air was thick with the blue smoke of incense and the perfume of the crushed flowers. If Emma was a delighted spectator of this scene, which was so much to her taste, how much more exciting did she find the spectacle on the *Marina*! There, seated beside Lord Nelson and Sir William and their Majesties in the Ionic loggia, built for Spanish viceroys, she viewed against "the oriental sapphire" of the night the famous fireworks. A huge fantastic palace had been built on the sea-front; the façade, which showed transparencies depicting the glories of the Bourbons and Lord Nelson, was lit skilfully from behind.

The surviving vessels of the Neapolitan Navy, among them the Conte di Thurn's vessel, from the mast of which Prince Francesco Caracciolo had been hanged, lay in the harbour, flying the Bourbon flag. These were outlined by tiny fairy-lamps that made the rigging appear to be of strings of stars. They began the display by firing their cannon; the echoes from the mountains were much admired by the Royal party. The ships then sent off water-rockets and bombs, which burst under the sea with great effect; after half an hour of this amusement, the sham palace was suddenly lit up, while fountains of fire spouted in front of it; as these faded into sparks, a garden of flame was disclosed, palm-trees, orange-trees, flower-vases glittering on a fiery parterre.

The palace then broke into suns, stars and wheels of coloured fire, which consumed the entire structure. But the show was not over. From the ruins of the firework building rose two thousand rockets, interspersed with bombs, squibs, serpents, and devils in leaping fire.

As this display faded, another took place over the sea, where fire-balls broke in showers of gold and silver over the dark waves that extinguished them, while on the *Marina* appeared enormous banana-trees swaying in a rich green flame.

The climax of the pyrotechnics was the siege of a castle during a thunderstorm, where bombs, lightning, thunder-bolts, and fire-balls exploded together in one supreme conflagration.

After this there was mounting into ornate carriages, drawn by the beautiful Sicilian horses, and Emma between husband and hero was taken to the Flora to hear the music amid the roses, the mulberry and pepper-trees, under the shade of cypress and palm.

Then a parade along the streets to see the illuminations, where Lord Nelson shared the honours of initials and transparencies with the saint.

The next day there was horse-racing in the street, and the car was again dragged down the Toledo, this time adorned with dozens of wax tapers; the day after more races and a vast company pressing into the fantastic splendour of the Duomo, where Norman and Saracen kings lay in robe and crown, and where thousands of wax lights, hung from the roof, seemed like a heaven full of stars.

Then, the public fountains were hung with lamps, the relics of the saint, exposed in their silver case, were carried in procession across the excited city, and more fireworks, music, and firing of cannon.

The Queen did not allow these rejoicings to come to an end; on September 3rd, while the hanging and beheading were taking place daily in Naples, while the prisons there were crowded with dying and hopeless victims, a splendid country fête was celebrated in some gardens at Colli outside Palermo, where Saracenic pavilions stood among orange-groves. The great moment of this festival was based on one of the famous attitudes. A Temple of Fame had been erected, in which were life-size figures; the principal of these represented Lady Hamilton as Victory, holding a laurel wreath out to Lord Nelson, who was being led up to the Goddess by Sir William Hamilton. At the climax of the gala, when music, wine and mutual compliments had brought everyone into a state of high excitement, the King advanced, took from the wax figure's hand the wreath of laurels—which was then discovered to be sewn with sparkling diamonds—and placed it on the untidy, tow-coloured hair and wrinkled brow of the British hero. Wreaths of the same nature and value were also available for Sir William and the Patroness of the Navy. The festival then proceeded with every detail of extravagance that a theatrical mind could conceive and a large purse execute. There were dances, dramatic scenes, fireworks, torchlight processions, refreshments in Sicilian-Gothic casinos, beneath the leaves of the magnolia, the papyrus, and the citron, and, on the bosoms of all the ladies and on the shoulders of all the men hung, amid the ribbons and the jewels, ornaments glorifying the hero of the Nile.

* * * * * * *

The news that Lord Keith had followed the Gallo-Spanish Fleet to Brest, and had therefore left Lord Nelson in command of the Mediterranean station, could hardly damp these arduous festivities. Whatever commands were sent to him, whatever responsibilities were laid upon his shoulders, he refused to leave his Emma and his Queen, the golden flatteries, the luscious sunshine of the sweet, brilliant autumn days in Palermo. Two duties claimed him; he should have proceeded to the blockade of Malta, and he had undertaken that not a Frenchman should leave Egypt.

Writing home, he stressed his poor health; he was almost blind and truly very ill, told his wife that he scarcely expected "to rub through the winter," that he never hoped even "to see Bronte." In the same letter he begged her to send him prints of his famous exploits, such as the boarding of the *Saint Nicholas*. He wanted also some of the caricatures, and a good laced hat and a plain one, but always he emphasized his ill-health. "I am heartily tired of war, I am fagged and tired out."

The naval side of his work was done well; no laxity was allowed among his men. A sailor who had been insolent to his officer was hanged at the yard-arm "in the usual manner," and the Fleet was efficiently run, but Lord Nelson could not bring himself to leave the baroque city of golden stone and Saracenic towers nor Emma's luxurious palace, where long tables were nightly strewn with gold pieces, where there was always champagne to drink and delicate food to eat, rich and fantastic gardens to walk in, and Emma herself with her lustrous eyes and her red lips and her loud laugh and her incessant flattery.

There was also always La Favorita, the Eastern villa with the casino hung with bells in the midst of the rich gardens, with the secluded walks leading to the enchanted bay of Mondello.

There, between the yellow Doric temples, in the shade of the dark trees backed by the golden rocks under the ilex, the plane, the olive, and the flowering laurel, Emma wandered in her Sicilian satins, leaning on the arm of the hero in his faded British uniform.

The interior of La Favorita contained tributes to the glory of Lord Nelson and the enthusiasm of Emma and the Queen.

There was a chamber *à la turque*, furnished with luxurious divans by the grateful Sultan, there was a Pompeian room, designed by

Sir William for the repose of his wearied countryman and adorned with ornaments from the buried city, there were mosaics in the "Saracenic style," and there were, in every possible place, prints, caricatures, and paintings of the bravest of men, Horatio Nelson, and of the fairest of women, Emma Hamilton.

The eccentric casino had an underground ballroom, cool and dim, corkscrew staircases leading to a belvedere on the roof, called the temple of the winds, from which the ornate gardens could be viewed, stretching beneath the yellow cliffs.

Lord Nelson liked this atmosphere, this background, he enjoyed it with the fierce enjoyment of the rustic nobody who suddenly comes to Court, with the relish of Christopher Sly, snoring in the Prince's bed. He liked the air that was heavy and rich with incense and the perfume of bursting fruit; he liked the nights that hardly passed without the bursting of fireworks among the stars that hung in the heavy, purple, Sicilian heavens; he relished the concerts of music, the trill of mandolines and of guitars, above all he liked the sensation that the most beautiful woman in the world belonged to the bravest man alive and that a whole Kingdom lay at their disposal; he was passionately "lost in love."

The Queen, with the hysteric energy that nothing could exhaust, made no pause in her constant flatteries, in her showers of gifts. To everyone who had served her to achieve her vengeance, there were portraits with diamonds, jewelled snuff-boxes, watches, any and everything else given.—Lord Nelson thought her "good and great."

.   .   .   .   .   .

Sometimes there was an unpleasant letter to write to Fanny which jarred on this. One in particular had to be penned in a panic, when Lady Nelson suggested coming to visit Lisbon. Her Lord assured her that it was the dirtiest place in Europe and "more unwholesome than the worst part of Portsmouth." He tried to quiet her by writing of the home they would have when he returned, "a neat house near Hyde Park, on no account on the other side of Portman Square."

On October 18th came bad news. General Bonaparte had contrived to slip across the Mediterranean and to land in France. Nothing could have been more vexatious to the Allies. It was

Lord Nelson's peculiar business to see that this dreaded enemy did not return to France; the fact that he had done so made the Battle of the Nile fruitless; but the Admiral was not ashamed of his disobedience and negligence—"no blame lies at my door," he asserted.

. . . . .

Emma enjoyed herself thoroughly. As she had no imagination but plenty of courage, she had no fear of the future. She was as happy as a child glutting itself with sweetmeats and never guessing that the bottom of the bag might be near. She was not even troubled by thoughts of what the British Government might be thinking of Sir William's conduct, or of what the British Admiralty might have to say about the lingering of the Mediterranean Fleet in Palermo Harbour; she did not trouble herself about what Josiah Nisbet might be saying about his stepfather's behaviour, which had provoked him beyond the restraint of good manners; the golden episode was coming to an end, but Emma did not realize this, and it was without any fear of the future that she lapped up these Sicilian delights, as an overfed cat deigns to lap the rich cream in the porcelain saucer.

Emma had recently had an agreeable addition to her establishment; this was Miss Cornelia Knight, something of an authoress in a genteel way, who, with her mother, Lady Knight, had shared the flight from Naples. Soon afterwards Lady Knight had died, kindly ministered to by the efficient Mrs. Cadogan, and the shrewd, well-bred Cornelia had been left in the charge of the British Minister's lady who kindly promised to see her safely to England, when the occasion for that trip should arise. Cornelia had soon established herself in the queer household and acted as a secretary to Emma. She was a neat, precise, fairly intelligent young woman who was quite clever enough to sacrifice her prudery to her interests. In brief, she saw nothing whatever wrong in the fantastic admiration Lady Hamilton showed for Lord Nelson; it seemed to her quite natural that her dear friend should feel thus ardently for so great a hero.

Miss Knight, then, in these Palermo days, fetched and carried, and listened and coaxed and flattered, and was altogether a very useful adjunct to the extravagant household.

These delights were too brilliant to last; Emma at last noticed, first, with vexation, then, with alarm, signs that they were coming to an end. In January Lord Keith returned to the Mediterranean command; this time Nelson could not refuse to meet him at Leghorn; he received what he might have expected—a cold and haughty greeting. Keith said nothing about the Bay of Naples business, nor did he mention Emma, but his manner conveyed that he had heard a good deal.

The two Admirals came to Palermo together; Lord Nelson had already written to Emma:

"Having a Commander-in-Chief I cannot come on shore till I have made my manners to him. Times are changed. It has been no fault of mine that I have been so long absent. I cannot command, and now only obey."

The Queen held no festival to amuse and dazzle Lord Keith, who spent over a week in the Sicilian capital and marked it with a disenchanted eye; he happened to be a gentleman, and that made it awkward for everyone.

Another blow fell. Sir William was recalled. Lord Grenville had decided, soon after receiving the dispatch describing the capitulation of the rebel castles, that the old dilettante could no longer retain his post. The old man received this news in a spirit of bitterness.

"I have, after thirty-six years' service to this Court, been either kicked up (or down) out of my post. It gives much uneasiness to this Court and poor Emma is in the greatest distress."

Arthur Paget, a gentleman and distinguished diplomat, a product of Westminster School and Christ's Church, Oxford, was sent to take Sir William's place. He also viewed Palermo, the Hero and the Beauty, the King and the Queen, with the cold eye of disenchantment. His dispatch to Grenville would not have made pleasant reading to the Hamiltons or their guest:

"I am sorry to say that Lord Nelson has got more or less into all his nonsense. His Lordship's health is, I fear, sadly impaired, and I am assured that his fortune is fallen into the same state, in consequence of great losses which both his Lordship and Lady Hamilton have sustained at faro and other games of hazzard."

Keith wrote even more emphatically:

"The whole was a scene of fulsome vanity and absurdity all the long eight days I was at Palermo."

The Queen, too, began to weary as if all the glory had become tarnished, like a mirror a breath had been blown on.

The joys of vengeance began to nauseate even Maria Carolina. An uneasiness, a fear not untouched by a vague remorse, depressed the melancholy, excitable woman. It was apparent, even to her intelligence, that never again could she set foot in Naples, that the Bourbon rule in South Italy was over, and over in shame and disgrace. Even in the midst of a relentless war the slaughtering in Naples had roused and sickened Europe; the good opinion of everyone in every part of the world had been lost. The Queen never paused to think reasonably on any subject, but it began to be apparent even to her that the recapture of Naples with the help of the British Navy and the enthusiastic co-operation of the Hamiltons had led to nothing except the creation of an almost universal hatred; nor were her own circumstances much improved. The letters she continued to write to di Gallo in Vienna were still full of lamentations and complaints. Of her husband, His Sacred Majesty, whom she wished to set up as an absolute monarch, an arbiter over the life and death of thousands of other people, she wrote with the utmost contempt:

"The state to which we have been reduced has rendered him excessively avaricious. He directs the Royal house and all the accounts. We lack everything. When the Kingdom of Naples was reconquered every demand on the Royal purse was satisfied, but I, my daughters, son, and my daughter-in-law, we have only the half of what was owing to us. He paid no pension, no minister, nothing to anybody. Everyone is complaining. I know not how to remedy it. It is a tyranny and nobody can stand it. He will not hear of going back to Naples and says he will live and die in Sicily, from which country he will not budge. This is a true calamity. As for affairs, I have them very heavily on my heart and they are black on all counts. I suffer mostly from the violent severities that are being used. The number of guilty was so enormous that they had to be used according to justice. My heart is oppressed."

In the next letter the moment of regret, real or assumed, had passed, and Maria Carolina noted vindictively:

"Justice has been done on Cirillo—he was insolent to the last. The two sisters, to the great scandal of the public, had seven years of exile. What an end is mine, after having passed the good, beautiful, best years of my life in one long sacrifice! But one must bow one's head to the Divine will. Buy me a fine pelisse with large warm sleeves but not very expensive; it is for the warmth and not for the luxury that I need it. I suffer so much from the cold. My finances are much restricted. Whatever expenses the King undertakes, he always takes good care to cut mine down. He counts every farthing. It is incredible and passes all imagination. I only hold to life by a thread."

The two sisters to whom the Queen referred were the two Duchesses, Giulia and Maria Antonia Carafa. By huge bribes they had contrived to save their lives and had received what the Queen considered such a scandalously light sentence—seven years of exile. These two women had behaved with great devotion during the last dreadful days of the existence of the Parthenopean Republic, working among the sick and wounded, and in the end, like heroines of antiquity, with cropped hair and bared arms, helping the men who were defending the Mole.

There was also another woman against whom neither the King nor the Queen would relax their *vendetta*. This was that sad little heroine of romance, Luisa Molinos, or Sanfelice, who, to save a lover, had betrayed a Royalist conspiracy, under the rule of the Republic, in consequence of which some Royalist conspirators, members of the Bacher and Della Rossa family had been shot in the courtyard of the Castle Nuovo.

While the Queen was writing to di Gallo about her heart's being distressed by the horrors that were taking place in Naples, this poor young woman, beautiful, gentle and nobly born, was lying under sentence of death in the degradation and misery of one of the vile Neapolitan prisons.

The little Crown Princess, who had been so ill and so uncomplaining, demanded the life of Luisa Sanfelice as a favour from the King, when she gave birth to an heir to the throne, but it was roughly refused.

241

After agonizing delays and desperate attempts on her own and her friends' part to save her life, after being tried, condemned, twice *in cappella*, and sent to Palermo and then back to Naples, Luisa Sanfelice was, nearly a year after Queen Carolina wrote the above letter, beheaded on September 11th, 1800, amid the public rejoicing and illuminations for the birth of another Bourbon Hapsburg. She was the last and the most pitied of the victims of Maria Carolina's *vendetta*; in her case, in that of Francesco Caracciolo, and in those of Carafa, Massa and Manthoné, there was, even for the taste of the Royalists, too apparent an element of bitter, implacable, personal revenge. The odium of all these events was cast with added bitterness on the British. Ruffo, in a letter to Sir John Acton, stated that the English would always be hated in the country, because "of the destruction of the Navy, which had not only been in itself a great loss but had spoiled the bottom of the Gulf."

But the sun still shone in Palermo and there was one more supreme honour for Emma. Off Malta, Lord Nelson had performed one of his dashing, heroic exploits. After a stern fight he had taken one of the ships that had escaped from the Battle of the Nile, *Le Généreux*, which was conveying troops and provisions to Malta. This was a useful as well as a showy piece of work; the troops numbered two thousand and there was a great store of provisions and ammunitions for the relief of La Valetta. The engagement indeed deserved the word "glorious"; it had been thirty-two small to eighty large guns and Lord Nelson was justified in writing under the entry in his journal: "Thank God."

Even this gratifying success did not, however, bring Lord Nelson into the good graces of Lord Keith, who gave him a reception by no means to the hero's taste. Nelson wrote to Emma:

"Had you seen the way that Peer received me I know not what you would have done, but I can guess."

Lord Keith had heard and seen too much at Palermo; the official account of the engagement off Malta, which he sent to the British Admiralty, Lord Nelson considered likely to be so little favourable that he wrote privately to Lord Grenville. Anxious as he was to put himself right with the powers at home,

Lord Nelson could not risk disobeying his superior in command
who had ordered him to take command of the squadron now off
Malta and had pointedly said: "that Palermo was an inconvenient
place of rendezvous."

The two officers quarrelled on this subject, Nelson insisting
that his state of health was such that nothing but staying with his
friends for a few weeks would enable him to survive. He had
written to Emma a little earlier that year: "to say how I miss your
house and company would be saying little. It is true that you and
Sir William have so spoiled me that I am not happy anywhere
else but with you, nor have I an idea that I ever can be."

This was true enough; it was also true that he was ill—reckless
and nervous away from Emma. She seemed to support him with
her energy, her self-confidence, her brilliant flatteries. He had
succeeded in getting for her another reward beside those bestowed
on her by the grateful Queen. She had helped, with a few pounds
from Sir William's store, the starving Maltese, and had also
exerted herself to obtain food for the refugees from the islands.
This service was exaggerated by Lord Nelson into one sufficient
to justify a demand for a handsome recognition from the Emperor
Paul, who was then Grand Master of the Order of St. John of
Jerusalem.

Nelson wrote to the Czar of All the Russias thus:

"The laborious task of keeping the Maltese quiet in Malta,
through difficulties, which Your Majesty will perfectly understand, was principally brought about by Her Majesty, the Queen of
Naples, who at one moment of distress, spent £7,000 belonging
absolutely to herself and children, by the exertions of Lady Hamilton, the wife of Sir William Hamilton, my gracious Sovereign's
minister to the Court of the two Sicilies. If your Majesty honours
these two persons with the Decoration of the Order, I can answer
that none ever more deserved the Cross, and it will be grateful to
the feeling of still Your Majesty's most faithful and devoted
servant, Bronté Nelson."

These services of Lady Hamilton's were greatly exaggerated.
She had never spent large sums of money on any cause, nor was
she a woman likely to give away in charity what she would have
found useful for herself, but Paul did not concern himself with the

rights or wrongs of the matter; the little Cross of Devotion of the Order of St. John of Jerusalem was sent to Palermo together with a pleasant letter signed by His Imperial Majesty.

This honour brought a new excitement; it was necessary that all enrolments in the Order of Malta should be recorded at the College of Arms, London, so Emma began to occupy herself with the questions of her birth and ancestry. This business was likely to take, and in fact did take, a long time, and it was a pleasant if agitating occupation to get together some story for the Heralds and to dream of the day when she would be able to quarter her own arms. With a view to stopping any inconvenient enquiries in her native place, she described herself as the daughter of Henry Lyon of Preston, in the County of Lancashire, instead of Neston in the County of Cheshire.

.   .   .   .   .   .

Sneering and bitter against Keith, Nelson loitered in Palermo: "Great changes are coming on and none that I can see for the better. We of the Nile are not equal to Lord Keith in his estimation, and ought to think it an honour to serve under such a clever man." He directed the blockade of Malta from Palermo; the Island capitulated April 1800.

While he was ashore his ship captured the last survivor of the Battle of Aboukir Bay, the *Guillaume Tell*; Nelson was not pleased that he had missed this glory by being ashore and his ill-humour was augmented by the news from London. There was the dispatch of recall from Lord Spencer:

"It is by no means my wish or intention to call you away from service, but having observed that you have been under the necessity of quitting your station off Malta, on account of your health, it appears to be much more advisable for you to come home at once than to be obliged to remain inactive at Palermo while active service is going on in other parts of the station."

Nelson and the Hamiltons visited Malta in state, then returned to Palermo.

Lord Keith was told that Nelson should be permitted to take his passage in the first ship home, but the Scotsman had no frigate available.

Could not this be made an excuse to travel with the Hamiltons? Emma had done what she could to put off the day of departure. She had made things extremely unpleasant for Arthur Paget, "Cursed Paget," as the Queen called him, even to the extent of rendering it difficult for him to find rooms in which to lodge. He had been detained at Naples by the intrigues of the two women, who made it a tedious business for him to get a passage across the Tyrrhenian Sea; Emma and the Queen had contrived that any official reception should be much delayed, that it should be of a humiliating character when it took place.

The cool young diplomat was neither flurried nor confused by these crude tactics. On March 25th, he wrote to Lord Grenville:

"From what I can collect there does not seem as if there were a shadow of anything like order or regularity in any individual department in the state. I have seen and conversed with the persons at the head of them all; they all complain at the situation of affairs. . . .

"I hear that the *Giunta* (Commission which carries on the government of Naples) is composed, with one or two exceptions, of a corrupt, bad set of men. Law and justice are neither practised nor understood. . . .

"It is not to be told the pains that were taken by Lady Hamilton to set the King and Queen and the whole Court against me, even before I arrived. I was represented as a Jacobin and a coxcomb, a person sent to bully and to carry them back to Naples, and it is enough to know the character of the people here to be sure that all the jargon has had its effect."

In Arthur Paget's opinion matters could not have been worse. The events of which the Hamiltons and Nelson had been "the mainspring," in their own words, and which, as Emma declared, had "given happiness to millions," had left the country, in Paget's opinion, in this state:

"Every department of the state, ecclesiastical, civil and military, has assumed the most untoward appearance. Instead of religion there is an excess of bigotry, corruption has succeeded to justice, and the fact of calling in foreign troops in itself proves what the state of the army must be. . . .

"I really don't know whether any good can be done with the

present generation. So corrupt and so insensible to all principles of honour and morality do I think it. A total reformation on the largest and most comprehensive scale ought to take place . . . all the honest, trustworthy people either have been murdered or are in exile or in prisons."

And with an oblique but emphatic reference to the actions of the Hamiltons and Lord Nelson, he wrote:

"Nothing good or useful can be effected by the introduction and direct interference of foreigners."

After twelve months' residence in Palermo, Paget summed up the situation in the following words:

"When I look around me and reflect upon the persons employed in the different departments of the government, I do not understand how the thing goes on at all. The fact is that General Acton will not employ people who are not blindly devoted to him and he has certainly brought himself to think that it is a well-governed state. I always return to a position I formerly made. There is neither army, navy, commerce, justice, agriculture or religion, or roads in these Kingdoms, and as long as General Acton remains at the head of affairs I despair of seeing any change for the bettering of them. He will listen to none but those who flatter him; at the same time there is not a man in this Kingdom fit to hold his situation."

Such was the opinion of a cool, cold and impartial observer of the Court and Kingdom of Naples after the suppression of the Revolution and the meddling of Lord Nelson and the Hamiltons. Beyond the badly governed city there was anarchy; at Castelluccio the infamous brigand, Mammone, and his *banditti* ruled without interference and the outrages committed by him and other outlaws passed from the horrible to the grotesque in their crazy ferocity.

In the Castel Sant' Elmo political prisoners still rotted naked in the damp dungeons; one reckoning stated that forty thousand families had some of their members thus imprisoned and were not able to obtain either their release or their trial.

Over the face of Italy, nay, of France and of Europe, wandered the starving Neapolitan exiles, begging their way, dying by the

roadside. Petitions from the innocent and the wronged lay un-
opened in the bureaux of Sir John Acton's secretaries; such
resources as the country had were strained to offer rewards to Nelson,
Troubridge, Ruffo, Thurn, and others who had been the executors
of the King's will and the Queen's vindictiveness.

Cardinal Ruffo received the Abbey land of Santa Sofia at Benevento, which was worth an annual pension of fifteen thousand
ducats. Perhaps when he enjoyed this handsome estate, he sometimes thought of the capitulation of the castles, the thirty pieces of
silver and the potter's field. Thurn, who had presided over the
court-martial which had condemned Caracciolo, and a certain
Scipione La Mara, who had helped to betray him, were both
rewarded with annual pensions. La Mara received, too, the splendid
house and rare botanic gardens that had belonged to Domenico
Cirillo. There were few spoils left in the devastated Kingdom; such
as they were, they were distributed to the unworthy and the base,
the servile courtiers, the abject tools of tyranny.

.   .   .   .   .   .

Nothing would suit the Queen but that she must go to Vienna
to see her daughter, the Empress; even Sir John Acton complained
of this considerable and unnecessary expense. Somehow, although
the Queen was always complaining of poverty, and even begging
for a fur coat from her own ambassador, money could be found
for useless extravagance; Maria Carolina was restless and impatient,
and had no wish to be left in Palermo without dear Emma, obliging
Sir William, the heroic Nelson and the British Fleet, so it was
arranged that the whole party should travel together overland as
far as Vienna.

Emma's spirits, dashed by the recall, rose at the prospect. She
was always accommodatingly good-humoured at changes of circumstance. Everything had been delightful both in Naples and in
Palermo, but then the future might be delightful too. She began
to visualize a triumphal progress across Europe with a doting
husband on one side, a Queen on the other and a hero in her train;
she foresaw dazzling receptions at every Court they passed, and
then in the future was London. There, she believed, she would
conquer everyone, even the Queen of England, and become a

very great lady indeed. It was hardly possible to believe that, after all the flatteries she had enjoyed in Naples, she would get the cold shoulder in her native city; of course, in England there was also Fanny; but Emma and her lover always thrust that figure out of their minds; the mistress, always resourceful, was sure that the unwanted wife could be somehow dealt with, when the moment came.

Unpleasant news from London there certainly was; with the bundles of newspapers, caricatures, and prints of the great victories and portraits of the one-armed, one-eyed hero, were reports of Mr. Fox's stern denunciations in the House of Commons of the Neapolitan barbarities. The orator had not been careful in his choice of expressions; publicly and vehemently he had denounced a campaign promoted by "murders so ferocious, cruelties so abhorrent that the heart shudders at the recital"; he flung out the ugly story of the violated capitulation for the Commons to digest; he made the Tories sullen, the Whigs excited, by his fierce account of the miserable victims savagely murdered and the way the British name had been disgraced; the ferocity and stupid cruelty and treachery of the darling, laurell'd hero, Lord Nelson became the topic of the drawing-rooms, the coffee-houses, and clubs.

There was, too, the question of Emma to be discussed in London; her past was too well known for anyone to take a generous view of her relationship with Lord Nelson, and the spectacle of the patient wife, waiting in the little Norfolk vicarage with a stately old father, touched the public imagination; popular feeling began to run high against the hero of the Nile.

When rumours of these things came to Palermo, Lord Nelson was defiant and bitter. He fiercely condemned Fox for not having behaved with "the wisdom of a Senator or the politeness of a gentleman or an Englishman," and, he added: "The rebels came out of the castle as they ought, to be hanged, and I hope all those who are false to their King and Country will be hanged."

He sent this statement to his faithful friend Alexander Davison (the army contractor, afterwards imprisoned for fraud), who had before been so useful with the Press and told him to get it in the papers. The case was, however, not such that any publicity could make much play with; still, Emma was there, Emma, stout-hearted cheerful and energetic, and the future could be thrust aside, though it began to assume a hideous shape.

.   .   .   .   .   .

On St. George's Day, the last year of the old century, April 24th, 1800, the Queen of Naples with her daughters and retinue, Sir William Hamilton, Emma, Mrs. Cadogan, Miss Cornelia Knight, a French maid and several Italian servants, sailed for Leghorn in two battleships, which Lord Nelson had taken from the squadron blockading Malta.

This short voyage was done in the grand style; Maria Carolina and Emma had much the same tastes; they loved to live in a state of theatrical display, and the state cabins were soon made fit for the reception of a queen, of a beauty, and of a hero. Apart from all comforts and luxuries provided by the Queen there were plenty of trophies; the figurehead of the *Guillaume Tell*, which was a painted plume of feathers, a stand of arms from the *San Josef* and the flag-staff of *L'Orient*; in the corner was a *memento mori*, the coffin presented by Captain Ben Hallowell to Lord Nelson. Despite this, however, they were very gay and merry. Miss Cornelia Knight composed some verses for the occasion, which were frequently sung during the voyage:

"Come, cheer up, fair Emma! forget all thy grief,
For thy shipmates are brave, and a Hero's their chief.
Look round on these trophies, the pride of the main;
They were snatched by their valour from Gallia and Spain.

Behold yonder fragment: 'tis sacred to fame;
'Midst the waves of old Nile it was sav'd from the flame—
The flame that destroy'd the new glories of France,
When Providence vanquish'd the friends of blind Chance.

Those arms the *San Josef* once claimed as her own,
Ere Nelson and Britons her pride had o'erthrown,
That plume, too, evinces that still they excel—
It was torn from the cap of the famed *Guillaume Tell*.

Then cheer up, fair Emma! remember thou'rt free,
And ploughing Britannia's old empire, the sea,
How many in Albion each sorrow would check,
Could they kiss but one plank of this conquering deck."

249

These were halcyon days, a fit epilogue to the Neapolitan and Sicilian romance; the tempest seemed stilled while Emma's ship rocked on the ocean.

When Emma beguiled her leisure by turning over the romances, novels and magazines, the packets of prints and newspapers, sent from England by Lady Nelson, she could not avoid some thought of the future, but always her confidence was unabated.

Not so with Lord Nelson; he was truly sick and suffering; his mangled body gave him continuous torture; he was agitated by the fear of an approaching blindness; only his vanity and his passion for the gorgeous woman who scarcely ever left his side held him to life. When he thought of the waiting Fanny, he became nauseated with agitation; home-sickness pierced him; behind was the "apple-tree, the singing and the gold," before, the foggy common place of England.

. . . . . .

Emma's courage and her lover's nerves might well indeed have been shaken by the situation, which was one to which neither could be blind. Three months before, Captain Troubridge had taken upon himself to write to Lady Hamilton informing her, as he put it, "of the ideas that were going about on things which may appear to your Ladyship innocent, and which I make no doubt were done with the best intention, but which your enemies will give a different colouring." And Troubridge had warned her of definite scandals, which had gone to Pisa and from thence to London. "You may not know you have many enemies. I therefore risk your displeasure by telling you."

The lovers had seen, too, some of the ill-natured English prints, some of the spiteful paragraphs in the English papers. While Emma laughed, Lord Nelson groaned; he viewed the future in dark colours.

When the British arrived in Leghorn Harbour, the party landed and were accommodated in one of the more stately hotels; there, while the Queen and Emma fussed and shouted, and the medley of servants ran about with the unwieldy travelling comforts, the worst possible news was brought into the town by a sweating courier.

Young General Bonaparte, who had been allowed by Lord

Nelson to escape from Egypt, was marching again on Italy, at the head of a magnificent army, which he seemed to have raised from the ground like the ancient hero, Cadmus, by a stamp of his heel; he had taken the tricolour flag across the Alps and broken the Imperial forces at Marengo. While Lord Nelson had been enjoying the fame of Aboukir and assisting the Bourbons to revenge themselves on Naples, the French General had displayed the heroic activity that was making him the dread and admiration of Europe. Even the destruction of the French Fleet had not ruined his designs; he had defeated the Mamelukes, taken Gaza, stormed Jaffa and returned to Paris in October; while the punishment of the patriots was continuing in Naples, General Bonaparte had accomplished a *coup d'état*, known as the 18th Brumaire (November 1799), which re-organized France, restored Christianity, gave an amnesty to political offenders, and raised General Bonaparte to the position of First Consul in a Government founded on the Roman model.

To give a lustre to this new France, which had arisen from that now completed episode, the Revolution of 1789, the young General had resolved to wipe out the tarnish of his arms due to the Italian disasters and the successes of Suwarrow.

Marengo, where the forty thousand French, brought through the St. Bernard Pass, had fallen on the flank of General Mélas, and Hohenlinden, Moreau's victory, more than counter-balanced any advantages that the Allies might have derived from the Battle of the Nile and the recovery of Naples.

The French advance, and the French victories, made the captured trophies, so jealously stored in Lord Nelson's cabin, appear slightly foolish, and both the bloodshed in Naples and the rejoicings in Naples seem useless and ridiculous.

III

HERO'S LEGACY

BELIEVE ME, MY ONLY WISH IS TO SINK WITH HONOUR
TO THE GRAVE;
AND WHEN THAT SHALL PLEASE GOD, I SHALL MEET
DEATH WITH A SMILE.
—Lord Nelson

THE SAILOR'S RETURN

MARIA CAROLINA was in despair at the news of the French advance; she remembered 1796, when at Lodi, Mondovi, Lonato, Roveredo, Arcola and Rivoli, General Bonaparte had overturned the Imperialists and the Princes of Italy, and Naples had had to cringe to him for terms. Of what use had been the illusive successes which had been gained by the Bourbons and the British Fleet, while the conqueror of Italy was shut up in Egypt if the First Consul was again to march into the peninsula?

The Queen thought of her Sicilian retreat; could not the British warship take her back to Palermo? Lord Nelson was willing to consent, but dispatches from Lord Keith arrived from Genoa; his orders were that all the men-of-war were to join his squadron.

Emma, the Queen, implored—just one ship—if not for Palermo, then for Gibraltar.

Lord Nelson sent the request; it was refused and Lord Keith, in the worst of humours, arrived from Genoa and presented himself before the odd company in the Leghornese hostelry, the re-called Ambassador, the invalided Admiral, the Queen, the Princesses and their retinue, taking this senseless journey to Vienna.

George Elphinstone Keith, the Scots patrician who had seen such long and honourable active service, was a man of intelligence, courage, breeding, and one whose career had been adorned with brilliant exploits; he had a pretty shrewd knowledge of the state of affairs in the Mediterranean, where he had been for some while second-in-command to Lord St. Vincent, which officer he had succeeded on his retirement in 1799. As Captain Elphinstone he had served under Lord Howe, under Lord Hood before Toulon, and had commanded a squadron off the Cape of Good Hope. Three years before he had been promoted to Vice-Admiral and made an Irish Peer with the title of Baron Keith of Stonehaven Marischal, the last title because his mother was the niece and heiress of the line of the last Earl Marischal.

When he arrived to take command of a perilous situation at Leghorn, he was a man of fifty-four years of age, of wide experience and sound judgment, resolute and self-contained, the last man in the world to be influenced by romantic or sentimental considerations. Handsome and robust, of a virile and energetic appearance, he viewed without sympathy or compassion the strange party that was awaiting his pleasure in the painted rooms of the Leghorn hotel.

Lord Nelson, indeed, made an effort to keep up appearances. In the presence of Miss Knight (he perhaps knew she was keeping a diary) he mentioned that he hoped during his stay in London that he and Lady Nelson would see a good deal of the Hamiltons, and he added that they would "probably dine together, that he and Lady Nelson would retire to their rest while the Hamiltons would be going to one of their musical parties." This pitiful attempt at placating the proprieties did not soften Lord Keith. He rapidly summed up the four people whom he saw before him. Hamilton, the tired, battered dilettante, the elegant figurehead who had meddled with such horrible results in politics was, in Lord Keith's opinion, senile. Withered and yellow, Sir William set about lamenting anything that interfered with his personal comfort; his private misfortunes he seemed to feel more deeply than he did any of the bloody events of Naples or of the war; he complained that in the great storm off the Neapolitan coast the ship, bearing his collection of vases to London, had been wrecked and only a few cases rescued; he occupied himself with his wife's pet dogs, with his own pet monkeys, and protested against everything; Lord Keith paid him no attention.

Emma was loud-voiced and dominant, directing the whole party as if she were indeed Britannia and they the waves; Lord Keith had at Palermo taken a dislike to the Patroness of the Navy. He considered Lord Nelson so wrapped up in this enervating atmosphere "as to have lost all zeal for the public service."

The Queen was, as always, hysterical and dramatic. She flung herself on her knees before the British Admiral and begged, with all her habitual gestures of a wronged princess, for the loan of a British ship to take her back to Palermo.

The situation was, indeed, unpleasant; General Bonaparte was supposed to be only a day's march from Leghorn. Emma tried to add her persuasions to those of Maria Carolina. Striking one of the most effective of her attitudes, Beauty in Distress, she besought Lord Keith to grant Her Majesty's request. The Scotsman was unmoved; the quartet seemed to him disgusting and disgraceful. He told the Queen, with no attempt at civility, that she could either go on to Vienna as quickly as possible by land or else return to her dominion in one of her own Neapolitan frigates, of which there were several in Leghorn Harbour, but none of which Her Majesty dared to trust.

Upon this, in Lord Keith's words, Her Majesty had "a sort of convulsive fit." The British Admiral took no heed of these feminine wiles, of the ravings of Sir William or of the sulks of Lord Nelson, nor of the screamings and flutterings of the Princesses and their attendants. He strode out of the hotel, out of the town, and sailed away towards Genoa with all the British battleships, leaving the stranded party to do what they could.

. . . . . .

There was nothing to do but continue the journey by land. On July 15th the cavalcade started out, taking over a day and a night along the bad road to reach Florence; it was impossible to stay at the Tuscan capital because of the advance of the French; they had to jolt on again, a slow, unwieldy procession. At Loreto there was an accident to the Hamiltons' cumbrous coach—a broken wheel, that detained them, nervously fretting, for three days, tormented by the news of Bonaparte's approach, by the monotone of Sir William's lamentations that he was dying, by the Queen's hysterics and the disorder of the Princesses and their retinue, who were in a state of panic lest any moment they should have their throats cut by those monsters, the French. As the procession struggled along again in the sweltering heat over the broken road, they passed some Imperialistic stragglers, who informed them that General Bonaparte was not two miles away.

After this there was not even the relief of pauses for repose at the wretched, flea-infested, filthy inns; they had to travel night and day in the greatest discomfort under the blazing Italian heat, until they were out of the territory which belonged to the House of Hapsburg, the Archduchy of Tuscany, and into the Papal States.

Emma and Mrs. Cadogan were the most cheerful of the disordered crowd. They had the quality, not uncommon to their class, of what is known as "rising to the occasion." They were always handy and good-humoured in a crisis, while Lord Nelson was sick and agitated, the Queen almost unconscious from terror.

At Ancona things were a little better. An Imperial frigate was ready to convey the Queen to Vienna. It was handsomely furnished with temptingly soft beds, silken tapestries and Persian carpets; but the crew looked sullen and menacing, and the Queen declared they were all Jacobins who would murder the royal party as soon as the ship set out to sea. The only other available vessel in the harbour was Russian, and Maria Carolina decided to sail under the Czar's flag to Trieste.

While they stayed at Ancona their spirits rose; the terrible menace of the French seemed to recede into the background. The Queen opened her baggage to distribute largesse. She had brought a fine booty with her; snuff-boxes in gold and diamonds, jewels, watches, chains, rings, and money. The Imperialist soldiers, then in garrison at Ancona, were each given a florin, with which to drink her health. It was quite like old times. There were cheers and *vivas* and mutual congratulations.

But once on board the Russian ship, things were bad again. It was all excessively uncomfortable—the ship dirty, badly equipped, inefficiently run. The expert sailor in Lord Nelson revolted at the condition of the Czar's vessel, which was, in his opinion, scarcely seaworthy. The captain, overcome by sea-sickness, did not put in an appearance, and the second-in-command was a Neapolitan who did not seem pleased at the sight of his rightful Queen; indeed, he behaved himself like "the most insolent of beings." It seemed touch and go whether they would make Trieste or not, but luckily the sea was as calm as a mill-pond and they landed on August 2nd.

There was a fine reception in the Austrian Port, people shouting in the streets, illuminations at night, admirers crowding round the British hero whenever he showed himself abroad. Three weeks' journey took them across the mountain roads to Vienna, and there their reception was everything that either the Queen, Nelson or Emma could have wished.

The old imperial city lay heavy and weary under the rich September sun. It seemed neither dead nor alive, but stagnant. It was very different from the violent life of Naples, from the lively splendours of Palermo, the cities which had known so many different governments, revolutions, upheavals and wars. Here there was an air of Imperial stability, even if it was the stability of decay.

When everything else in Europe had changed, when the greatest transition that mankind had ever chronicled was taking place in the world, Vienna remained of yesterday. Still in the enormous baroque palaces that seemed too vast and grandiose for human needs, built from the spoils of long wars and for plumed and laurelled heroes, moved men and women in brocade and jewels, with powdered locks, hooped skirts and diamond-hilted swords. Here were no patriotic songs, no strains of "Rule, Britannia," no flourishings of the "Marseillaise," no hymns of the Liberal or Republican, but the music of Mozart and of Haydn sounding like the elegy of a dying age.

Queen Marie Antoinette's nephew wore the diadem of the Cæsars; his wife was his cousin, Maria Carolina's daughter.

Into this rich calm, cynic yet smiling, war-weary yet serene, the Queen of Naples slipped naturally into place, a link in the Imperial chain of the Hapsburgs, daughter of Maria Theresa, an Imperial Arch-Duchess. In the enormous *salons* where stone giants upheld the canopied ceilings and thousands of perfumed wax-lights glittered before mirrors twice the height of a man, Maria Carolina queened it as if she had never lain seasick in the cabin of the *Vanguard* or gone on her knees at Leghorn to Lord Keith. Because of her, Emma was accepted by the pale, powdered ladies, whispering over the disaster of Marengo, by the defeated or helpless Generals in their white, gold, and scarlet uniforms, by the elegant ministers already foreseeing the peace of Lunéville.

Emma was eyed a little curiously perhaps; the great gilded city, where everyone was a little fatigued, a little melancholy, where everything was very fine and subtle, was a curious setting for the flamboyant charm and noisy vitality of Lady Hamilton; her vices were those of the peasant, the vices of the Austrians were the vices of an aristocratic decadence.

But there was the presence of the hero to gild over everything. The British Admiral was a picturesque and fascinating figure, with his one arm and his one eye, the faded, stained blue uniform, and the cocked hat set defiantly on the mop of unruly hair that never seemed to take a curl nor to accept a ribbon.

An Empire which had found the French invincible was likely to make much of the man who had destroyed the navy of the Republic, even if that victory had been fruitless.

There was a repetition of the Neapolitan and Sicilian fêtes; the Englishman set the fashion; the ladies tried to give their frocks a Nelson touch, an anchor in the hair, a bust of Britannia at the bosom, the British colours on the shoulder; the shops displayed nautical designs, intended to honour the British hero; his carriage was followed when he went abroad, and women held their children up for him to bless. Emma was for ever beside him; her florid beauty graced the festooned box, when he went to the gala at the Opera House, and she helped to acknowledge the cheers that greeted him as he bowed to the audience.

At the banquet given by Prince Esterhazy in the style made popular by Prince Eugène nearly a hundred years before, when there were heyducks and hussars in attendance and healths were drunk to the sound of trumpets and cannon, Emma was beside the hero in her satin, jewels and brocade. She had long left behind the simplicity so carefully taught her by Charles Greville, the classic robes so precisely designed for her by Sir William Hamilton; she now appeared, as far as attire went, a woman of fashion, and in these rich and modish clothes lost much of her beauty and all of her distinction.

Haydn waited on the Hamiltons and Lord Nelson in the handsome mansion where they stayed, and Emma displayed her ringing voice and dramatic gestures in singing a verse in honour of the hero, while the master accompanied her on the spinet.

But the aristocratic English in Vienna were sensitive to what they considered the ridiculous figure that the famous beauty cut; if the Viennese ladies could tolerate her with a smile and a shrug, her own fellow-countrywomen could not. She seemed to them strident, ill-bred and tiresome, while her relations to her doddering husband and to her maimed lover offended the tastes of the English colony in the imperial city. She was always at her lover's side; while Sir William followed with her lap-dogs, the hero would carry her pocket-handkerchief.

"He has the same shock-head and the same honest, simple manners," wrote Lady Minto. "He is devoted to Emma. He thinks her quite an angel and she leads him about like a keeper with a bear."

Lord Harris had expressed himself more emphatically: "It is really disgusting to see her with him. She is without exception the most coarse, ill-mannered woman I ever met with."

Emma's lack of breeding indeed offended that fastidious society; she had the bad taste to play cards while Haydn was performing, and her raucous voice rose through the tender melodies of the exquisite music, as she cleared up nearly £400 from the baize table while the concert was in progress.

Nor were the manners of the hero as much admired as they had been by the Queen's party in Naples. The English considered him very much the parvenu; ladies smiled behind their fans, and the gentlemen lifted their brows to see the little man strutting about wearing, whenever he went abroad, every ribbon, order and star he possessed, while in his cocked hat was stuck the Grand Seigneur's aigrette; this ornament was thought in Vienna very ugly and not valuable. The son of the Norfolk parsonage had not the air which could carry off baroque splendour against the background of Vienna; what might have appeared splendid on a Duke of Lorraine, a Prince of Savoy, was on him merely foolish.

But neither of the pair seemed to notice that they had caused offence or laughter. They acknowledged cordially and with no touch of ironic humour, the cheers of the people, and they received as their due the formal compliments of the great world.

.   .   .   .   .   .

The day came when the Hamiltons must be on their homeward way and Emma had to leave the Queen. It was the end of a strange partnership, an odd friendship. After so many years of intimate association, neither woman knew if she were really fond of the other or not; it had always been a question of expediency; the Queen had thought to make of Emma a political cat's-paw, and Emma had willingly kissed the hand which had held out to her the bounties that had made life a fairy-tale to the former London servant-girl. Now it was over. Out of it, this odd friendship, the Queen had had her vengeance on Naples, the British Fleet for months between Palermo and Naples, vengeance executed on some of her rebellious subjects. She knew that she could hope for nothing more from Emma Hamilton, whose flighty mind was already fixed on other schemes. She was nervous, melancholy, weighed down by premonitions of ultimate disaster as she bade good-bye to Emma, who, after all, had not been so very useful once Lord Keith had come on the scene.

On her side, the British Minister's wife had two coach-loads of fine dresses, some jewels and treasures, and the glory of being able to go back to England boasting that she had been the intimate friend of the Queen of Naples. Then with tears, protestations, hysterics, and promises for the future, the two women parted—the Queen to remain with the Hapsburgs, Emma to go in the great coach with her husband and Lord Nelson northwards towards Prague.

The meeting with Fanny was coming nearer. Ulysses had written to Penelope that he had asked his friend Davison to take a house in London, that he hoped to meet her there, that she must expect to see a worn-out old man.

.   .   .   .   .   .

The next stopping-place was Dresden, where they were received very civilly by the British Minister, Mr. Hugh Eliot, and his wife, and where they made a worse impression than they had made in Vienna. There was a shrewd, sharp-minded Englishwoman, Mrs. St. George, to watch and to note what they looked like and what they did and to put down her observations in a journal she was keeping.

This lady went on October 3rd to dine at Mr. Eliott's beautiful villa; Lord Nelson was present, the Hamiltons, and Miss Cornelia Knight, famous for her *Continuation of Rasselas* and *Private Life of the Romans.* These famous people, whose praises had been celebrated all over Europe, appeared slightly obscured in the cool estimation of the English gentlewoman. She wrote:

"Lord Nelson thinks of nothing but Lady Hamilton, who is totally occupied by the same object. She is bold, forward, coarse, assuming and vain. Her figure is colossal, but, excepting her feet, which are hideous, well-shaped. Her bones are large and she is exceedingly *embonpoint*. She resembles the bust of Ariadne; the shape of all her features is fine, as is the form of her head, and particularly her ears. Her teeth are a little irregular, but tolerably white, her eyes light blue with a brown spot in one, which though a defect takes nothing away from her beauty and expression. Her eyebrows and hair are dark and her complexion coarse. Her expression is strongly marked, variable and interesting, her movements in common life ungraceful, her voice loud yet not disagreeable. Lord Nelson is a little man without any dignity. . . .

"Lady Hamilton takes possession of him and he is a willing captive, the most submissive and devoted I have seen. Sir William is old, infirm, all admiration of his wife, and he never spoke to-day but to applaud her. Miss Cornelia Knight seemed a decided flatterer of the two, she never opens her mouth but to show forth their praise; and Mrs. Cadogan, Lady Hamilton's mother, is what one might expect. After dinner we had several songs in honour of Lord Nelson, written by Miss Knight and sung by Lady Hamilton. She puffs the incense full in his face; but he receives it with pleasure and sniffs it up very cordially. The songs all ended in the sailors' way, with 'Hip, hip, hip, hurrah,' and bumper with a last drop on the nail, a ceremony I have never heard of or seen before."

Mrs. St. George also accompanied the travellers to the Opera House, where she was amused by Lady Hamilton's obvious flattery of herself and noticed "she and Lord Nelson were wrapped up in each other's conversation for the best part of the evening." She thought that the hero resembled, in his person, the Russian Suwarrow, infamous for his cruelties.

On the following day Mrs. St. George received a strange invitation; it was from Lady Hamilton and requested the presence of the English lady to see the British hero dressed up for the invitation to Court he was expecting to receive from the Elector; thus Mrs.

263

St. George describes Horatio Nelson as she found him, arranged and posed by Emma:

"On his hat he wore the large diamond feather or ensign of sovereignty given him by the Grand Signior, on his breast the Order of the Bath, the Order he received as Duke of Bronte, the diamond star including the sun or crescent given him by the Grand Signior, three gold medals obtained by three different victories, and a beautiful present from the King of Naples. On one side is His Majesty's picture, richly set and surrounded with laurels which spring from two united anchors at bottom, and support the Neapolitan crown at top; on the other is the Queen's cipher which turns so as to appear within the same laurel and is formed of diamonds on green enamel. In short, Lord Nelson was a perfect constellation of stars and orders."

On October 7th, Mrs. St. George was allowed to see the famous attitudes which had so entranced Sir William Hamilton and pleased the romantic tastes of Goethe.

"Breakfast with Lady Hamilton and saw her represent in succession the best statues and paintings extant. She assumes their attitudes, expressions and drapery with great facility, swiftness and accuracy. Several Indian shawls and chairs and antique vases, a wreath of roses, a tambourine and a few children are her sole apparatus. She stands at one end of the room with a strong light to her left and every other window closed. Her hair (which, by-the-by, is never clean) is short, dressed like an antique, and her gown a simple calico chemise, very easy with loose sleeves to the wrist. She disposes the shawls so as to form Grecian, Turkish and other drapery, as well as a variety of turbans. Her arrangement of the turbans is absolute sleight of hand, she does it so quickly, so easily and so well. It is a beautiful performance, amusing to the most ignorant, and highly interesting to the lovers of art. The chief of her imitations are from the antique. Each representation lasts about ten minutes. It is remarkable that, though coarse and ungraceful in common life, she becomes highly graceful and even beautiful during this performance. It is also singular that in spite of the accuracy of her imitation of the finest ancient drapery, her usual dress is tasteless, vulgar, loaded, unbecoming. She has borrowed several of my gowns and much admires my dress, which she cannot flatter as her own is so frightful. Her waist is absolutely between

264

her shoulders. After showing her attitudes she sang, and I accompanied; her voice is good and very strong, but she is frequently out of tune. Her expressions are strongly marked and various, and she has no shape, no flexibility and no sweetness. She acts her songs, which I think the last degree of bad taste. . . .

"To represent passion with the eyes fixed on a book and the person confined to a spot must always be a poor piece of acting *manqué*. She continues her demonstrations of friendship and said many fine things about my accompanying her to sights. Still she does not gain on me. I think her bold, daring, vain even to folly, and damped with the manner of her first situation, much more strongly marked than one would suppose after having represented majesty and lived in good company fifteen years. Her ruling passion seemed to me vanity, avarice and love for the pleasures of the table. She showed a great avidity for presents and has actually obtained some at Dresden by the common artifice of admiring and longing. Mr. Eliott says 'she will captivate the Prince of Wales, whose mind is as vulgar as her own, and play a great part in England.' "

After the dress rehearsals and the expectancy of more festivals and more flattery, it was a severe blow to both Lord Nelson and Lady Hamilton to discover that the Electress would not receive Emma—"On account," noted Mrs. St. George, "of her former dissolute life."

To avoid a downright refusal to meet the wife of the British Minister, the Electress resolved to hold no Courts while Emma continued in Dresden.

Lord Nelson, in furious disappointment, cried to the British Minister: "Sir, if there's any difficulty of that sort, Lady Hamilton will knock the Elector down, and damme, I'll knock him down too."

On October 9th there was a great breakfast at the Eliotts' given to the Nelson party. Lady Hamilton repeated her attitudes with great effect.

Mrs. St. George wrote:

"All the company, except their party and myself, went away before dinner, after which Lady Hamilton, who declared she was passionately fond of champagne, took such a portion of it as astonished me. Lord Nelson was not behindhand, called more vociferously than usual for songs in his own praise, and after many bumpers proposed the Queen of Naples, adding, 'She is my queen, she is queen to the backbone.' Poor Mr. Eliott, who was anxious the party should not expose themselves more than they had done already and wished to get over the last day as well as he had done the rest, endeavoured to stop the effusion of champagne, effected it with some difficulty, but not till the lord and lady, or, as he calls them, Antony, and Moll Cleopatra, were pretty far gone. I was so tired I returned home soon after dinner, but not till Cleopatra had talked to me a great deal of her doubts whether the Queen would receive her, adding, 'I care little about it. I had much sooner she would settle half Sir William's pension on me.' After I went Mr. Eliott told me she acted *Mina* intolerably ill and danced to the *Tarantola*. During her acting Lord Nelson expressed his admiration by the Irish sound of astonished applause, which no written character could imitate, and by crying every now and then 'Mrs. Siddons be ——!' Lady Hamilton expressed great anxiety to go to Court, and Mrs. Eliott assured her it would not amuse her, but the Elector never gave dinners or supper. 'What,' cried she, 'no guzzling!' Sir William also this evening performed feats of activity, hopping round the room on his backbone with arms, legs, stars and ribbons all flying about in the air."

Mrs. St. George added on October 10th:

"Mr. Eliott saw them on board to-day. He heard by chance from a King's messenger that a frigate waited for them at Hamburg, ventured to announce it formally. He says: 'The moment they were on board there was an end of the fine arts, of the attitudes, of the acting, of the dancing and the singing. Lady Hamilton's maid began to scold in French about some provisions which had been forgot in language quite impossible to repeat, using certain French words which were never spoken but by men of the lowest class and roaring them out from one boat to another. Lady Hamilton began bawling for an Irish stew and her mother set about washing the potatoes, which she did as cleverly as possible. They were exactly like Hogarth's *Actresses dressing in a barn*.

"This evening I went to congratulate the Eliott's on their deliverance and found them very sensible of it. Mr. Eliott would not allow his wife to speak above her breath and said every now and then, 'Now don't let us laugh to-night; let us all speak in our turn; and be very, very quiet.' "

While the hero and heroine, who in their own opinion had "done good to millions," were returning home, two young Neapolitans, ruined and in exile, who by some chance had escaped the massacres and the judicial murders in Naples, were writing in Milan their accounts of the late Revolution. One was Vincenzo Cuoco, who was completing in the Northern city the manuscript he had begun in prison. In eager words that flowed one after another from his pen, he gave the Republican side of the glories that Nelson and Emma were still celebrating. He sketched the Neapolitan Revolution as it had been seen by a young man of intelligence, culture and high ideals. "I intend to write the history of a Revolution that should have formed the happiness of a nation, but that instead reduced it to ruin."

Cuoco in his first paragraphs surveyed the state of Europe. There was a tremendous desire everywhere for liberty, liberalism, humanitarianism—"the English would have broken into a revolution if they had not disdained to imitate the French." Cuoco described the Queen of Naples as the linchpin of European coalition against France, and indicted her court as "irresolute, vile, perfidious," the King as "a feeble enemy and a faithless friend." Sir John Acton he dismissed as a miserable adventurer, "the minister who came from a State that had no marine, to create one through Naples."

Skilfully and clearly the young exile sketched the state of the kingdom under the foreign domination of the Queen and Sir John Acton, the horrors of the prisons, the deplorable state of every department of the government, the great folly of the advance on Rome, the worthlessness and the obstinacy of General Mack.

When he described the flight of the King, he wrote: "With the Royal Family went the most precious furniture from Caserta and Naples, the greatest rarities from the museums of Portici and Capo di Monte, 20,000,000 ducats, perhaps more, in cash, and precious metal not yet counted, the spoils of a nation that remained in poverty."

The people watched the Court go "without displeasure and without joy." After describing the arrival of Championnet and the setting up of the Republic, the pleasure given to the populace by observing their religious festival ("what was religion to the mob but holidays?") Cuoco went on to describe the arrival of Francesco Caracciolo from Sicily.

"This raised our hopes. Caracciolo was worth a fleet. How daring and courageous was his combat with the English, undertaken with a few poor ships."

Cuoco described the arrival of the army of the *Santa Fede*. He had himself witnessed atrocities that he felt incapable of putting on paper. "Altamura was a heap of ashes and bloody corpses." In Naples hell opened—all that was good, great, industrious was destroyed, "and those few illustrious men, who escaped as by a miracle from the wreck, wandered without family, without country, homeless on the face of the earth; 80,000,000 ducats were lost in industry, the same amount in furniture, in private fortunes confiscated, and in confiscated goods. The product of four centuries was destroyed in a moment. Works of art stolen in the anarchy were sold cheaply to the English. The Court hoped to find security in the poverty and ignorance of the country."

This is what Vincenzo Cuoco in his garret in Milan wrote of the beautiful Emma and her heroic lover: "In the affair of the castles the Queen sent Lady Hamilton to Naples with messages to Nelson. To please the Queen the Hamiltons lent themselves to dishonour, so did Nelson. His honour, and that of his arms, that of his nation —this is what the world did not expect and what the English nation should not have suffered." Cuoco added: "I have read a letter from one of Nelson's secretaries: 'We commit horrid villainies to put again on his throne the most stupid of Kings.' Oh, the English know how to pity their victims!" With inexpressible anguish and bitter wrath the young Neapolitan wrote down his recollections of those summer days in Naples, when Emma had "fag'd" on board the *Foudroyant* and Lord Nelson had been secretly arming the assassins, those *lazzaroni* who had British weapons with which to do their bloody work.

Vincenzo Speciale was sent from Sicily, and he began with "a butchery of human flesh in Procida." When the Giunta was in Naples, Speciale tricked, under profession of friendship, Nicola Fiani into a confession and then sent him to death. "All sense of humanity seemed to be gone from those who judged the Republicans." Conforti, under promise of life, wrote a treatise on *The*

Pretensions of the Sicilian Bourbons to the Roman State and was then executed. The wife of Baffi, the famous Greek scholar, was treated with revolting cruelty.

None of the Republicans showed signs of cowardice. When Gabriele Manthoné was dragged before Speciale, the soldier said: "I capitulated," and refused to speak other words. When Cirillo was brought before the Giunta, the judge demanded:" What were you before the Republic?"

"A professor of medicine."

"And what are you before me?"

"Before *you*? A hero!"

Cuoco commemorated in his anguished lines the great courage of Carlomagno, Granalé and Nicola Palomba.

"I shall send you to death," said Speciale to Palomba. "I shall die," replied the prisoner, "but *you* shall not *send* me to death"— and he threw himself from the window of the judge's room.

Grimaldi escaped from his Russian guard after a month in irons and ran for a mile; when he was overtaken, he disarmed two soldiers before he was captured half-dead.

Cuoco gave a special note to Francesco Caracciolo:

"He was, without contradiction, among the first men of genius in Europe. The nation esteemed him, the King loved him; but what could the King do? He was envied by Acton, hated by the Queen, therefore always persecuted. Acton did not spare him any species of mortification. Caracciolo was among those few to whose genius can be added the purest virtue. Who loved his country better? Who did more for her? He created the Neapolitan Marine in a short time. He died a victim to the jealousy of Thurn and the cowardice of Nelson. When his sentence of death was announced to him, he was on the bridge discussing the construction of an English ship, and tranquilly continued his observations. A sailor who had been ordered to prepare him for execution was overcome by grief; he wept at the fate of the man under whose orders he had served for so long. 'Cease,' said Caracciolo. 'But it is pleasing that if I must die you should weep for me.' Caracciolo's body was seen suspended like a criminal's from the masts of the *Minerva*; his body was thrown into the sea.

"The King was on board Nelson's vessel; after two days the body of Caracciolo appeared beside the vessel under the eyes of

Ferdinand. It was recovered by the sailors who greatly loved him and he was buried in the church at Santa Lucia, near to his house. In despite of those in power he was laid to rest amid the tears of all the poor of that quarter."

Vincenzo Cuoco was misinformed as to the date of the King's arrival on the flagship and the appearance of Caracciolo's body.

The last pages of his little book Cuoco devoted to eulogies of his murdered friends—Domenico Cirillo, and Conforti, who had always supported the Court against the pretensions of Rome and who had saved the King 50,000,000 ducats by his reforms, Mario Pagano, Ettore Carafa, Russo, Eleanora Pimentel, Scotti and Federici.

The young exile concluded with this stern indictment: "The King, misled by false counsel, brought about the ruin of the nation. The Republicans had pure intentions, warm love of country, and courage. What will be the future of Naples, of Italy, of Europe? I know not. A profound darkness surrounds all the future."

At the same time Francesco Lomonaco was writing a report to Lazare Carnot, who had just taken Berthier's place as French Minister of War, heading his report "From the Neapolitan Patriots to Citizen Carnot, Minister of War, on the Secret Causes of Principal Events of the Neapolitan Catastrophe, on the Characters, Conduct, of the King, the Queen of Sicily, and the famous Acton."

The young Neapolitan began by a quotation from Tacitus. "A picture of horrid events sufficient to make humanity tremble will surely interest everyone possessed of sensibility."

"Citizen, I do not write for idle curiosity, but to place in true perspective the arbitrary and ferocious character of the King, the ruin of the most beautiful spot in the world, horrors such as mankind have not seen before. Many times the pen has fallen from my hand, my reason has nearly overturned, my paper been wet with bitter tears at the recollection of those tragic events. What I have to relate will recall the conduct of the imbecile Claudius, the dissolute Messalina and the vile Sejanus—the martyrdom of a nation."

The author then added that he wrote to satisfy the curiosity of Citizen Carnot as to what happened after the French left Naples;

he proceeded to attack Méjean, who had tried to cover up his own
bad conduct by calumny. "I will now relate the truth of the fate
of those heroes who threw themselves into the fire of the Revolution.
A holocaust of inhabitants of the coast and the islands was made
by the ferocious English, armed in all their fury. Tortures were
inflicted on the patriots; what horror, what barbarity! The streets
of the city of Naples were strewn with corpses. After the departure
of the French sounded the hour of the destruction of the Republic."
Lomonaco then came to a passionate denunciation of the violation
of the capitulation, telling Carnot "of the Sicilian despots, the
cruel Nelson," referring to "a St. Bartholomew, but one more
horrible than that which took place in Paris. Switzerland, Holland,
England herself, and all the civilized nations were shocked; did
not the English Whigs, Fox and Sheridan, raise their voices in
protest? I cannot describe the atrocities that took place, the
memory of them moves me too deeply. The patriots may be
compared to the Gracchi."

Lomonaco then proceeded to celebrate the self-sacrifice and
illustrious heroism of his friends, the men already mentioned by
Cuoco, to make a list of the names of 135 victims, most of whom
were beheaded, some few condemned to perpetual imprisonment in
the fosse or living graves of the castles.

"Heads of citizens were stuck up all over the country; the
Queen was the most perverse and dishonoured of the daughters of
Maria Theresa, dissolute in every way, maddened by boundless
ambition, blind incredulity, bigotry, vulgar in her sentiments,
intriguing, voluble, only firm in cruelty. Acton was gifted with
all the talents of intrigue, never had a fine idea in his head or a
generous sentiment in his heart; corrupt, perfidious, flattering, the
British Minister was a ridiculous old ape. While still at peace
with France the Neapolitan Court supplied arms and provisions
to Nelson. Ferdinand was a puppet in the hands of England, a
prisoner on board Nelson's ship. As well expect loyalty from wolves
as from these metallic souls. The crimes of the English are worthy
of Attila, what of the theft of the Dutch Fleet, the murder of Wolfe
Tone and the other brave Irish? The English behaved in the matter
of the Castles with barbarous bad taste. Nelson was bought by
Sicilian gold and the pompous title of Duca di Bronte. Cruel

tyrant!—as the intrepid Fox said in the English Parliament—
Nelson behaved with black treachery, dazzled by the flatteries
and gems of the despots, of which last he made an insolent display.
Infamy covers his abominable memory! How excellent in contrast
to him was the brave Caracciolo, the *Duilius* of the Republic, slain
by the jealousy of the barbarous Nelson! Would not this be a suitable inscription for Caracciolo's tomb: Here lies one who always
watched over the glory of his nation."

The two little works, written in the agony of defeat, in a frenzy
of indignation for murdered friends, penned in poverty and exile,
published by charity, never came to the eyes of Emma or of her
hero and would have been dismissed by them as libellous nonsense
had they chanced to see them.

But their story is not complete, unless it relates how the famous
pair appeared in the eyes of survivors of those slaughterings in which
they had assisted with such a firm conviction that they were
"doing good to millions."

. . . . . .

While the half-starved exiles in Milan were penning their
accounts of that Neapolitan summer, Lord Nelson was buying a
black lace shawl in Hamburg for Fanny, and Emma, helped by
Miss Cornelia Knight and Mrs. Cadogan, was looking over her
gowns to see which would be most suitable to wear at the many
public receptions that a grateful nation was sure to give the
Patroness of the Navy. She did not despair of going to St. James's;
her glory would surely blaze away the virtue of prudish old Queen
Charlotte, as the sun burns up straw.

At Hamburg all was very pleasant again. They met the exiled
Dumouriez, General of the Gironde, the victor of Valmy, and the
poet Klopstock, who first celebrated and then abused the French
Revolution in a series of terrific odes; this author introduced the
party to a Lutheran pastor, and the Christian hero signed his name
on the flyleaf of his Parish Bible; it was to be treasured as that of
"the Saviour of the Christian world."

By November 6th the trio were at Yarmouth, depressed and
vexed by a stormy passage and by the reports that a humiliating
peace was in sight.

The journey had cost them over £1,000; Lord Nelson had paid

the expenses of everyone with a lavish hand, but he only cared for money to spend it, never to hoard it, and Emma had been for long the mistress of his purse.

There was a hearty British welcome awaiting them. Their carriage was drawn by some of the mob to the inn where they were staying, where the Mayor and Corporation, important with the splendours of the occasion, were waiting to offer Lord Nelson the Freedom of Yarmouth. When he appeared on the balcony of the inn's best room to bow to his admirers below, Emma was blooming by his side. Her dress was appropriate, white muslin with flounces embroidered with gold anchors, and medallions bearing the emblems of Nelson and Bronte.

After that they all went to the parish church for a thanksgiving service. "See the Conquering Hero Comes" was played. Emma was in her element and highly delighted as Lord Nelson escorted her among the Protestant pews. There was some compensation after all for the regretted joys of Naples, and she believed that she was going to have a very pleasant time in England as the Patroness of the Navy, as the Britannia in classic robes whose spirit had hovered over the Battle of the Nile. In the evening there were patriotic songs, bawled out in front of the inn, bonfires, congratulatory messages; but Lord Nelson found time to sit down and write to Fanny:

"We are at this moment arrived. We shall set off to-morrow noon and be with you Saturday for dinner. Sir William and Lady Hamilton beg their best regards and accept your offer of a bed."

The next day they set out on the last stage of the journey, after distributing largesse and taking a cordial farewell of the town of Yarmouth. At Ipswich there was another triumph, and all along the highroad the cottagers turned out to curtsy and cheer in the November mists. The journey came to an end at Nerot's Hotel in St. James's Street. This was the appointed rendezvous where, after three years, Fanny and the old father must be met and the old life somehow taken up or somehow broken.

London looked very dull and shrunken, very drab and shabby, after Naples and Vienna, even after Prague and Dresden. It took all the shouting of the dirty crowds who ran behind the carriages, all the cheering of the people who opened the tall windows and leaned out, waving handkerchiefs, to gild the commonplace scene for Emma and Lord Nelson.

This long-dreaded meeting with Fanny took place against a dull background—the prim, public parlour of the hotel with its conventional furnishings and chill autumn light. Fanny herself was very quiet, perhaps also a little drab, as befitted a respectable woman of forty-two years of age. Her clothes were fashionable, but they were not such as Emma wore; a lace cap fastened under the chin, a fichu folded neatly over her shoulders; Lady Nelson had a certain elegance, but no ostentation; she was attired in good taste; but that was a quality her husband did not admire; her face was unsmiling, a little downcast. She knew herself to be in an impossible position.

What all Europe knew could scarcely be concealed from Lady Nelson; she had had plenty of time in which to turn over her son Josiah's indignant tales of those Neapolitan days. She knew that she had lost her husband. The question was, could she win him back? Was there a possibility of a renewal of their old life? She had nothing on her side except the power of convention; there was nothing on which she could rely save the technical fact—she was his wife.

Her husband entered, accompanied by the Hamiltons. There was Edmund Nelson, who was now old, a little frigid, a little embarrassed, hardened into his narrow virtue, an odd father for a hero. The mutual effusiveness saved the delicacy of the situation; Lord Nelson thrust into his wife's hands the lace trimmings he had bought at Hamburg; Emma was easy, self-assured; she felt as she had felt now for many years—that she held all the winning cards.

She filled the genteel parlour, as she had filled the Palermo palace of dusty golden stone; Fanny Nelson was a farthing rushlight beside her blaze of self-confident charms; Edmund Nelson withered in the brazen light of this trophy that his too-celebrated son had brought home; Sir William minced and chattered and flattered before the wife and father of his wife's lover, who had for some time been paying his bills.

· · · · · ·

274

It was soon clear, even to Emma's optimism, that the attitude of everyone who mattered was as hostile as that of the mob, which could do nothing but provide a gratifying background of huzzaing and flag-waving, was enthusiastic.

Lord Nelson had done much to please the Government of William Pitt; he had provided just that lustre which the Minister required to gloss over a long, costly, badly managed war, which had proved disastrously expensive to the country in money, materials, and men. Without such naval victories as the Battle of the Nile, without such heroes as Horatio Nelson, the Government would have had nothing to offer to a war-weary, discontented, and, to some extent, revolutionary-minded people. There had been, certainly, blacks spots in this blaze of glory; there had been Captain Foley's story, Sir William Parker's story, Captain Edward Foote's story—but all these might have been ignored; indeed, it had always been the Ministry's wish that such tales should be ignored and that the people should be allowed to have their hero without a blemish.

But what could not be swallowed was, first, the relationship of Lord Nelson with Emma, and secondly, the atrocities at Naples out of which the Whigs had made so much party capital.

A large section of English society believed that, by the violation of the capitulation of the castles, the honour of Britain had been smirched; that Sir William had behaved, not only in a cruel and foolish, but in an illegal fashion; the hanging of Prince Francesco Caracciolo was termed bluntly by many "a murder." Though even these things might have been denied and excused by the Tories, yet Emma could be neither denied nor excused.

There had been one chance for Lord Nelson of obtaining social forgiveness for the long dalliance in Naples and Sicily, for his disobedience to orders while in the Mediterranean, for his flagrant infatuation for another man's wife. If he had returned at once to Fanny and kept the Hamiltons at a distance, he might have been received and applauded, even by the Court. But he had done nothing of this; his relations with Emma continued, and almost openly; he made no effort to disguise his infatuation. It could be in the mind of every reasoning person, only a question how long Fanny would endure the intolerable position.

If Emma had been a gentlewoman, if she had even learned some of the arts of a great lady, she might have contrived to keep her lover and render herself inoffensive to society. It was not a prudish nor a squeamish period, and it might have been supposed that, where a husband was pleased, everyone else might have been charitable. But there was too much against Emma; her past was too well known in London (where it could be said without much chance of contradiction that she had been, and indeed still was, a kept woman who had passed successively to five protectors), and her manners and her appearance, which had not, strangely enough, been improved by fifteen years at Court and the warm friendship of a Queen—testified to facts, which even her friends could scarcely deny, and to which her enemies could easily add a host of fiction, slanders, and libels.

Sir William was so obviously senile, so completely hoodwinked, or so successfully pretending to be, that it was not difficult to suppose that Emma's behaviour had been indiscreet while she was at the Court of Naples. There were cynics who refused to believe that the robust and blooming beauty had waited till Lord Nelson sailed into Naples Bay on board the *Vanguard*, before she had taken a lover to console herself for an old, doddering husband. Then, also, Lord Nelson himself was of very modest birth; he had no friends or relations to speak for him, no high-placed acquaintances to give him countenance. The only great personage whom he had ever known—His Royal Highness, Prince William—seemed to have forgotten the Boreas days, and held aloof, and no one else came forward.

Miss Cornelia Knight, prudent and well-bred, looked round, sensed the atmosphere, and took her departure from the Hamiltons' *ménage*, with a shocked haste.

"Most of my friends," she sniffed, "were very urgent with me to drop the acquaintance. Things became very unpleasant."

Even Captain Troubridge, who had flattered Emma at Naples and willingly been Lord Nelson's lieutenant in the severities of 1799, stayed away and warned his friends to do so also.

Lord St. Vincent, who had, perhaps in irony, given Emma her famous title of "Patroness of the Navy," but who afterwards described her and her lover as "a pair of sentimental old fools," considered the whole situation impossible. As he put it, not without kindliness: "Lord Nelson is evidently doubtful of the propriety of his conduct. I have no doubt he is pledged to get his Lady Hamilton received at St. James's and everywhere, and that he will get into much *brouillerie* about it."

The opinion of the more tolerant was summed up by Lord Holland, who thought that Nelson's conduct in Naples showed a violation of good taste and judgment, and that it was "owing to the ascendency that an artful and worthless woman had obtained over a mind ignorant of the world."

Even while Fanny stayed with her husband, the fashionable world ignored the Hamiltons, who had taken a fine house in Grosvenor Square, where Lord Nelson was daily entertained. Fanny tried to push her complaisance too far; she undertook more than she could carry through; she accompanied her husband and the Hamiltons to a box at the theatre. The sight of the obvious relationship between Emma and her hero was too much for the neglected wife and she fainted and had to be taken home. For once Emma had to stand aside while another woman struck an attitude; she had to experience also the new sensation of watching her hero receive glory that she was not invited to share.

The victor of the Nile was again triumphantly received at the Guildhall; there were gaudy arches, shouting crowds of Londoners, and a sword from the City, this time gold-hilted and studded with diamonds. There was the installation of Lord Nelson in the House of Lords with traditional ceremony, but the three moved in a void as far as London society was concerned; all doors that were worth knocking at were closed to them; Emma's hopes of being received by the Queen, if indeed she had ever seriously cherished them, vanished when she learned from her indignant lover at the dinner-table in Grosvenor Square of the reception he had met with in St. James's. Charlotte had cut him dead with a coolness only possible to the completely virtuous when confronted with vice. The King had given him only a few curt words, turned his back on him, and then spoken for half an hour to a General of little importance. It was, indeed, an ironical situation.

Horatio Nelson had showered on him those honours and glories which it had been his wildest dream to obtain and which he had always considered it would make him supremely happy to receive; all his life he had yearned and worked for exactly those rewards which he now enjoyed, yet they were rendered unpalatable, almost repulsive, by social ostracism; he began in his sick disillusion to loathe London and long for Naples. He wrote to Emma during a brief stay at Greenwich, where he attended the funeral of a friend: "Although I have had my days of glory, yet I find this world so full of jealousies and envy that I feel doubtful of even a little future comfort." Depressed and exasperated by what he termed "the cold looks and cruel words of my enemies," with a sigh of homesickness for Sicily, he said: "I would sooner stay abroad for ever."

Towards the end of the year one invitation was extended to the trio whom London ignored; William Beckford invited them down to Fonthill. In a letter to Emma, couched in the fulsome tones which brought back a glimmer of the pleasures of Naples, he wrote: "I exist in the hopes of seeing Fonthill honoured by his victorious presence, and if his engagements permit him to accompany you here we shall enjoy a few comfortable days of repose, uncontaminated by the sight and prattle of drawing-room parasites."

Lady Nelson was not included in the invitation. William Beckford was probably the only man who, in inviting Lord Nelson to stay with him, would have asked Lady Hamilton also and ignored the wife. Fanny remained alone that Christmas in the Arlington Street lodgings to which they had moved from Nerot's Hotel, a sad commentary on the grotesque situation.

Leaving behind them an ungrateful London, and trying to forget the slights and injuries they had received, the Hamiltons and Nelson started again on one of their odd journeys. It was a triumphal progress, as usual. An escort of mounted yeomanry, "freedoms of the city" here and there. In the words of a contemporary "the illustrious naval hero was everywhere received with an ovation worthy of him, the anxiety of the townspeople trying to get a glimpse of him beggaring description."

The climax of all this enthusiasm was a reception at Fonthill. As soon as they reached the park gates William Beckford's own special corps of volunteers was ready to receive them, and a burst of music, swelling to the familiar strain of "Rule Britannia," floated through the wintery trees. At the door of the comparatively modest mansion which William Beckford had had built, close to the famous abbey he was erecting, the author of *Vathek* stood ready to bow before his guests, and, as they ascended the steps, the strains of music changed from "Rule Britannia" to "God Save the King."

The house was crowded with flatterers, dependants, and such people as curiosity had induced to countenance the entertainment offered by the host, under a social ban, to the three people whom London would not receive. The crowd of guests, swarming out of every corridor and chamber on to every gallery and window-place, greeted the Hamiltons and the hero with loud acclamations. It was almost Naples and Palermo all over again. Emma was triumphantly herself.

A spread table, such as is usually described as "a magnificent collation," awaited them; there was more music, more cheers and plenty of that "guzzling" which Emma had missed so terribly at the Court of Dresden.

This was only the beginning of the excitement. Great preparations had been made for a festival on the morrow, an out-of-door affair though the season was scarcely appropriate. In order to have the famous abbey as complete as possible for the great occasion, William Beckford had had gangs of men—seven hundred it was said—working by torchlight for weeks, and the next day the admiring guests were taken out to see what was known as "the wonder of the West," a huge Gothic abbey which, when it was viewed through the bare trees of the park, was visible in all its grandeur, the gargoyles, pediments, and pinnacles imparting to it the more salient features of an enormous monastery; the hall was spacious and lofty, the tower, which was in the centre of the building, was visible at a distance of four miles. Three wings stretched from it, eastward, northward and southward, each totally unlike the others, yet each constituting in itself "an elegant and commodious residence."

While the grand climax of the visit was being prepared behind a high screen of timber that hid everything from the guests, festivities entirely to the taste of Emma were taking place in

279

PATRIOTIC LADY

Fonthill mansion. She gave her famous attitudes, to the applause of all—one especially was admired as being so perfectly just and natural as to draw tears from several of the company. This pose represented "Agrippina exposing the ashes of Germanicus in a golden urn to the view of the Roman people."

As the afternoon passed on, printed programmes were distributed to the guests, and there was much mystery and expectancy in the air. When the short day came to an end, carriages escorted by the Fonthill volunteers in their smart uniform came to the door, and the guests took their places and were driven down the road towards one of the great avenues leading to the abbey. The language of a contemporary is needed to describe the scene that followed:

"At a particular turn every carriage stopped and one long, loud, ringing shout of amazement and delight burst from every throat. The enormous body of visitors found themselves in an instant transported as by magic to a fairy scene. Through the far-stretching woods of pine glittered myriad on myriad of variegated lamps forming vast vistas of light and defining the distant perspective as clearly as in sunshine. Flambeaux in profusion were carried about by bearers stationed wherever they were most needed. The Wiltshire volunteers, handsomely accoutred, were drawn up on either side. Bands of music, studiously kept out of sight, were placed at intervals along the route, playing inspiring marches, the whole effect being heightened by the deep roll of numerous drums, so placed in the hollows of the hills as to ensure their reverberation's being heard on every side. The profound darkness of the night, the many tinted lamps—some in motion, others stationary, here reflected on the bayonets and helmets of the soldiery, there seen through coloured glass, and so arranged as to shed rainbow hues on every surrounding object—the music, now with a dying fall, now waking the dormant echoes into life with marshalled clangour, riveted to the spot the lover of striking contrasts.

"Gradually the procession drew near to the Abbey itself, the tracery of its splendid architecture relieved by strong shadows, the inequalities of the building marked out by myriads of lights, and revealing, to the wondering eyes of the spectators, battlements and turrets and flying buttresses. No grander feature was there in the whole edifice than the tower shooting up three hundred feet, the upper part lost in total eclipse. Reared above the main entrance fluttered the national banner, and by its side the Admiral's flag, catching light enough as they flapped in the night breezes to display their massive folds to advantage.

"All present stood entranced. The moment the Abbey was fully disclosed, everyone, animated by a common impulse, sprang from his carriage and walked towards it; when the 'conquering hero' attended by his host entered the walls, the organ thundered forth a resounding peal of welcome, which shook the edifice to its foundations; while notes of triumph resounded from galleries and corridors around.

"From the Abbey they adjourned to the Grand Hall, which had been arranged for the banquet. An entire service of silver and agate of medieval pattern was laden with the fare of other days. On the board, and against the walls of the room stood wax-candles six feet high in silver sconces, while huge blazing logs of cedar, dried and prepared for the occasion, and continuously renewed, contributed to the material comfort.

"The banquet ended and the guests, well-nigh surfeited with the fanciful and gorgeous display they had witnessed, were desired to pass up the grand staircase. On each side of it stood, at intervals, men dressed as monks, carrying waxen flambeaux in their hands. The company were first ushered into a suite of sumptuous apartments hung with gold-coloured satin damask, in which were ebony cabinets of inestimable value, inlaid with precious stones and filled with treasures collected from many lands—then through a gallery two hundred and eighty-five feet long into the library which was filled with choice books and rare manuscripts, and fitted up with consummate taste, the hangings of crimson velvet embroidered with arabesques of gold, the carpets of the same colour—the windows of old stained-glass bordered with the most graceful designs.

"At last the guests reached the oratory, where a lamp of gold was burning by itself, shedding just light enough to display to advantage in a niche, studded with mosaics and jewels of great price, a statue of St. Anthony by Rossi. Here again the illusion of the monastery was well maintained. Large candelabra, in stands of ebony inlaid with gold and multiplied by huge pier-glasses, formed an exquisite perspective and enhanced the surpassing brilliancy of the scene.

"When the entire company was collected in this marvellous gallery, a stream of solemn music came floating through the air, none knowing from whence it issued. Beckford had always thought the effect of music heard under such circumstances irresistible. After gazing their full on the multitude of delights that met them at every turn, the guests were requested to retire in the direction opposite to that from which they had come. But, before they were allowed to depart, spiced wine, sherbet, lemonade and ice-water in flagons of ruby-coloured glass, and carafes of rose-water and little cases of attar-of-roses freshly imported from Shiraz and choicest fruit in baskets of gold filigree were handed round.

"It was long after midnight before the visitors could tear themselves away. But their host would not permit them to linger in case they should retire with their impressions impaired by familiarity. So that, before the lamps began to wane, several bands, accompanied by the mighty organ, struck up their most exhilarating airs, and as these yet hung upon the ear of the departing guests, the night breeze wafting their melodies through the air till distance drowned it, they left the Abbey grounds scarce able to believe that they had not been enjoying an Arabian night's entertainment instead of an English one."

．　　　．　　　．　　　．　　　．　　　．

There was, however, a keen business proposition behind this fairy-tale splendour. William Beckford had an ambition odd in one so eccentric, so gifted and so fastidious—he wanted a dukedom.

He considered that he had lived down what some people unkindly called his "former infamy," and he had thought out an extraordinarily complicated scheme by which he hoped to attain the desired honour. Sir William Hamilton was sadly in lack of money and Emma also would like a peerage and a pension. Could not every scrap of possible influence and the great hero of the Nile's prestige be used to obtain this end? William Beckford thought so, and he had already, through his agent, made a suggestion to Sir William Hamilton a few weeks previously—that, if in recognition of his services to Great Britain in Naples he could obtain a duke-dom, he, Beckford, would give, first, Sir William, then, his widow, a handsome present on condition that he was made the heir to the honours which Sir William would have no son to inherit, and which would, through Beckford's relation to the Hamiltons, remain in the family.

Emma was much excited and elated by the offer, and both her husband and Lord Nelson approved of it. The eager lady, with her usual energy, had gone so far as to ask for and obtain an inter-view with Henry Dundas, who, Mr. Beckford declared, "was the best of the tribe"—that is, the Ministry. The object of this inter-view, and one which Emma had not hesitated to put before the Minister, was that her husband's and her own services in the Mediterranean were worthy of a peerage.

Mr. Beckford had another scheme connected with this, whereby he hoped to obtain the Duke of Hamilton's consent to the transfer to Sir William of his dukedom, then likely to become extinct, in which case Emma would be a Duchess, receive a pension for life, and the millionaire-owner of Fonthill eventually become a Duke. All this complicated and quite unfeasible and impracticable arrange-ment was discussed between the four in the intervals of the Fonthill festivals.

Despite all the splendour Emma was distressed to see that her lover was very ill at ease; he seemed in a state of continual nerves. Once, driving in the grounds, he insisted on being set down and walking home.

The party returned to London on December 27th; Lord St. Vincent, who met them on the road, remarked on the hero's lowness of spirit. "He appeared and acted as if he had done me an injury and felt apprehensive that I was acquainted with it. Poor man, he is devoured with vanity, weakness, and folly. He was strung with ribbons, medals, etc. yet pretended that he wished to avoid the honours and ceremonies he everywhere met with upon the road."

Soon after he had left Fonthill Lord Nelson learnt that he had been appointed Vice-Admiral of the Blue. His ship was the *San Josef*, the flagship of the Spanish Admiral at the Battle of Cape St. Vincent.

The Hamiltons returned to Grosvenor Square still in an agitation over the peerage, and the hero to Fanny in the Arlington Street lodgings. The meekest of women would not have been in the best of humours after such open neglect, and, well-bred as Lady Nelson was, the inevitable moment came when her temper and her patience snapped. After a fortnight of this impossible life a reference to "dear Lady Hamilton" made the slighted wife retort with justified indignation: "I am sick of hearing of dear Lady Hamilton. You must give her up or me." Her husband retorted, as he was bound to retort, with an unforgivable sentence: "Take care, Fanny, what you say. I love you sincerely, but I cannot forget my obligations to Lady Hamilton nor speak of her otherwise than with affection and admiration."

"Then my mind is made up."

Fanny left the room and the house.

This action on his wife's part would, Lord Nelson knew, involve him in endless social difficulties and make his position with the Hamiltons almost impossible; but he could not bring himself to conciliate the unwanted woman; he even felt a relief of his nervous tension in seeing her go; an obsession such as his admitted of no restraint, no obstacle.

The situation was saved for a short while by his having to leave to join his ship at Plymouth. On the road he wrote Fanny a civil note, in which he sent "kindest regards" to his father. Before he had reached Plymouth, however, his agitation and anxieties had brought on a severe attack of illness. Covered with sweat and yet half-insensible from cold, he sat in his halted carriage panting for air with the windows down.

When he reached Plymouth, he was in no state to see anyone, avoided company and remained shut up in his room, bathing his eye in cold water and enduring as best he could the pain that racked his mutilated body. Emma wrote to him a budget of trivial news; the dog "Nile" he had given her had been lost, she had caught a cold looking for it, Fanny had gone to Brighton. The infatuated man wrote back coarsely: "Let her go to Brighton or where she pleases. I care not. She is a great fool and thank God you are not the least like her."

284

Emma had her own trouble, and a considerable one. It was the same as that which had caused her lover's agitation, illness and collapse of spirit; but she remained cheerful and arranged the new house, 23, Piccadilly, which she and Sir William had rented, with her usual gusto. One of the many stories that were going round the gossips about the hero and the siren concerned this house; one of the men engaged by the landlord of the place was going over it with an upholsterer and a servant, when he observed "an emaciated, weather-beaten person, rather shabbily dressed, follow us from room to room with seeming anxiety. At length he said, 'Pray, gentlemen, what is it you are about?' I answered, "We are taking a list of fixtures in the house to annex by way of schedule to the lease.' 'Oh, oh!' he replied, 'if that be the case I think you should include me in the list.'

And fixture in the house of the Hamiltons Lord Nelson had continued to be until he was forced to go to Plymouth.

Soon after, however, they had taken possession of their new abode, Emma was seized with a sudden indisposition which caused her to be confined to her room for several days.

Sir William was assured by Mrs. Cadogan that it was nothing serious, and the old man himself spoke of his wife's illness as "a foul stomach," and commented complacently on the bile she had thrown up in her frequent attacks of vomiting. Indeed, he believed, or pretended to believe, that Emma was suffering from the surfeit of good cheer—"that fare of olden days"—she had consumed during the Fonthill revelling. But she, Mrs. Cadogan, a few other confidants, and Lord Nelson, who wrote every day from the *San Josef*, off Plymouth, knew better; the climax of most secret anxiety and anguish was approaching.

On January 29th Emma gave birth to a daughter, which she contrived to keep for a week in the house under Sir William's nose and then to take away in a coach to a woman who had already been prepared to receive it, a Mrs. Skipton at 9, Little Tichfield Street, Marylebone, quite close to the handsome church where Emma had married Sir William nearly twenty years before. This business over, Emma, recovering in health and spirit and greatly improved in figure, mingled once more in the noisy society which she encouraged in the Piccadilly house.

285

She had arranged with her lover before he had gone to Plymouth a crude little fiction. They invented a Mr. and Mrs. Thompson —Mrs. Thompson was supposed to be in touch with Emma, who was to report all news of her to Lord Nelson, who, in his turn, would relate everything to Mr. Thompson, who was supposed to be continually with him. By this very transparent subterfuge Emma told her lover of the birth of the child, and received every day notes of hysteric joy and enthusiasm on these lines:

"I believe poor, dear Mrs. Thompson's friend will go mad with joy. He cries, prays, and performs all tricks, yet dare not show all or any of his feelings, but he has only one to consult with. He swears he will drink your health this day in a bumper, and damn me if I don't join him in spite of all the doctors in Europe."

In the transport of his infatuation, which had thus come to a climax in the birth of his first child, or, at least, of the child that he implicitly believed to be his, the hero of the Nile wrote in strains from which good taste and good feeling as well as common sense were entirely absent; the ferocity he had shown at Naples appeared in the fierce words of a letter written to "Mrs. Thompson": "Your good and dear friend does not think it proper at present to write with his own hand, but he hopes the time may not be far distant when he may be for ever united to his only love. He swears before Heaven he will marry you as soon as possible, which he fervently prays may be soon."

Such a prayer has an ugly sound coming from one who prided himself on his orthodox Christianity. Two lives stood between him and any possible union with Emma Hamilton.

Emma and Mrs. Cadogan manœuvred through all this excitement and hysteria with their usual robust good-humour. They were adepts at anything in the nature of intrigue. Emma was glad to have the child, because it was a strong hold upon her lover; it was the last handful of incense on the altar of his vanity, one that this time did not enhance his glory as a hero, but deliciously gratified his pride as a man. She had held him securely enough before; now he was certainly for ever hers, and she was happy in her dream of being a Duchess—twice over a Duchess, for there was the Sicilian Dukedom.

Sir William was very old and daily failing; Fanny had always been delicate and was reported as "being tortured with rheumatism" —she was also unhappy, perhaps heartbroken. Emma had good prospects.

The invincible Nelson was at sea again—probably there would be more victories, more honours, more stars and ribbons, more prize money, more pensions from a grateful country. Emma would never have any need to economize; she began to throw the money about with both hands.

.   .   .   .   .   .

But though his wife might dream of a golden future, Sir William began to feel the economic pinch; despite all the assistance he had received from his wife's lover, he had returned from Italy loaded with debts, which began to accumulate unpleasantly. To satisfy insistent tradesmen Emma was obliged to sell and pawn some of the diamonds she had received from her husband and from the Queen of Naples. She had totally forgotten all those nice economies and delicate adjustments of household expenses which Greville had so carefully taught her. She had forgotten, too, how to live within her allowance. Her account at Coutts's fell to a few shillings and she owed on her personal account £700. Sir William gave his wife £150 on account and began to look round for something to do to better his fortunes. He had no more Etruscan vases or treasures to sell; his household effects were not worth so very much and were rapidly being sold or pledged for current expenses.

Emma's extravagance seemed to have suddenly run beyond all bounds. She still tried to live as if she had the treasury of Naples to dip into. The large ornate house was always full of people, the kind of people who will go anywhere for drinks and food and noisy talk; covers were laid every night for twelve or fourteen persons; there were continual concerts at which Emma performed or entertainments at which she gave her attitudes; there were carriages, horses, and liveried servants to keep up. Sir William was tired of the din, of the riots, and the increasing vulgarity of Emma. He protested, he made scenes, he was peevish, but his wife took little heed. To her he was only a piece of furniture and one that was rapidly becoming worn out.

Mr. Hugh Eliott, the Minister at Dresden, had expressed the

opinion that the Prince of Wales might be interested in Emma. He was a man who admired buxom charm, and now at this unpleasant juncture of Sir William's fortunes, the suggestion arose (nobody knew quite where) that the Prince should be entertained in Piccadilly and view the famous attitudes of which he had doubtless heard so much. The cynics, of course, suggested that Sir William, under a social cloud, hampered by debt, uncertain of the continuation of his pension, slighted owing to the scandal of Caracciolo's hanging and the Naples murders, was anxious to secure the highest influence in the land, that of His Royal Highness, the Prince of Wales. And how could he secure it?—except by interesting His Highness in the fair and marvellous Emma. There was nothing very extraordinary in the idea. Sir William had taken the fair tea-maker of Edgeware Row in return for the payment of his nephew's debts, and possibly the highest personage in England might take her, albeit she was slightly blowsed and tarnished, in exchange for money and possibly a peerage.

The unhappy Admiral of the Blue, a prisoner on the *San Josef*, at least took this view of the situation, and, when he heard of the proposed visit of the Prince of Wales to the Piccadilly mansion, his letters became incoherent with jealousy and alarm. Fearful lest the Prince might do exactly as he had done himself, seduce his host's wife, or allow her to seduce him, he wrote of his future sovereign: "He is dotingly fond of such women as yourself and without one spark of honour."

There was not the least sign that His Royal Highness, with his own favourites and always surrounded by easy dames, was in the least interested in Emma, who was so long past her first beauty and so notoriously the property of another man; but Nelson continued to torment himself: "He will make every means to get into your house. I know his aim is to have you for a mistress. The thought so agitates me that I cannot write. I am in tears—I cannot bear it."

These continual anguished reproaches were too much for Emma's equanimity. She retorted by simulating a little jealousy herself. Why had he said that the West Country women wore black stockings? How did he know? He defended himself passionately: "Suppose I did say the West Country women wore black

288

stockings. What is it more than if you were to say—what puppies all the present young men are?"

Sir William insisted that there was an absolute necessity of asking the Prince of Wales to dinner, and he wrote to Nelson that "Emma has acquiesced in my opinion."

At this bitter news the wretched lover wrote a letter, crazy in its uncontrolled jealousy and couched in terms more proper to a fond husband writing to a virtuous wife than from a man like Horatio Nelson to a woman like Emma Hamilton. "Your character will be gone. Good God, he will be next to you and telling you fond things. Oh God, that I was dead. I tremble and God knows how I write. I am gone almost mad. It will be in all the newspapers with pictures. I am mad, almost blind. He will put his foot near you; he wishes, I dare say, to have you alone. God strike him blind if he looks at you. This is high treason and you may get me hanged by revealing it. Oh God, that I were. Will you sing to the fellow, and the Prince will be unable to conceal his passion. Does Sir William want you to be a wanton to the rascal? Will you sit alone with the villain for a moment? No, I will not believe it! Oh God, Oh God, I lose my senses. This is what no real, modest person would suffer, and Sir William ought to know that his views are dishonourable."

All this dramatic excitement was baseless; the Prince did not come to dinner at 23, Piccadilly. The excuse was that Emma was unwell and His Royal Highness does not seem to have pressed the point. But the emotional letters continued; Horatio Nelson, who read nothing and went nowhere where he could have met intellectual or literary people, was full of the cant of his age, and expressed himself in terms that would have done justice to a hero of one of those circulating-library romances descended from Richardson, Diderot, Rousseau, Sterne or Mackenzie.

When Captain Troubridge preceded him to London on leave, he wrote: "It rushed into my mind that in ten hours he would see you. A flood of tears followed. It was too much for me to hear." Sometimes the more natural tone of the quarter-deck would prevail. Of one lady whom he was pressed to visit he said: "I am told she likes a drop and looks like a cook-maid"—expressions that some had been unkind enough to apply to the divine Emma herself.

He was particular not to arouse his mistress's jealousy by even looking at another woman. His infatuation had reached, with the birth of a child, a pitch that was painful to himself and all others; his letters were passionate, sensual, outspoken.

At the end of February he had three days' leave; Emma received him with cheerful self-confidence and took him round to Little Tichfield Street and showed him the baby, whom he played with in what could only be described as "a transport of delight."

Lady Nelson writing from Brighton made her timid offers to come to town, but was repulsed. Emma, with her usual atrocious taste, made fun of "Tom Titt" as she called the abandoned wife: "Tom Titt does not come to town. She offered, but was refused. She only wanted to do mischief to all the great Jove relations. They are a vile set, Tom Titt and cub, hated by everybody."

By the 27th the lover was back again in his dull ship and Emma was absorbed in her gay life. The letter he wrote immediately showed a tinge of disappointment. Was Emma getting too absorbed in extravagance and dissipation, putting their great love second to her own amusement? It seemed rather like it. Instead of spending the evenings alone with him, she had gone out to routs and parties, including one with a lady who was very coarsely described. It was true, of course, that Emma was enjoying herself hugely and thinking more of Emma Hamilton than of Horatio Nelson. Adoration of such a type to such a woman was bound to be a little tedious and boring, but she kept her hold on the hero, sending down to the *Saint George* (to which he had been transferred) love-letters by the hand of a servant. These provoked an outburst of enthusiastic affection: "My own dear wife, for such you are in the eyes and estate of Heaven, there is nothing in this world I would not do for us to live together and to have our own dear little child with us. I firmly believe that after this campaign I will give up the sea, then we shall set off for Bronte. Unless all matters accord, it would bring hundreds of tongues and the slander of the Court if I separated from her, which I would do with pleasure the moment we can be united. I want to see her no more. Therefore we must manage till we can quit this country or your uncle dies. I love you, I never did love anyone else. I never had a dear pledge of love until you gave me one, and you,

290

thank God, never gave one to anyone else. My beloved Emma and my country are the two dearest objects of my fond heart, a heart sensible and true."

For the harmless, helpless Fanny there were cruel, harsh lines. "I neither want nor wish for anyone to care what becomes of me, whether I return or am left in the Baltic. . . . living, I have done all in my power for you, if dead, you will find I have done the same. Therefore, my only wish is to be left to myself. Wishing you every happiness."

Emma took no notice of any of these agonies of love, but behaved exactly as she wished to, enjoying herself up to the hilt. She still was ignorant enough of the ways of the world, or at least of the London world, to suppose that the Beckford scheme might be carried through, that she might find herself in this manner possessed of a pension of £2,000 a year for life and the title of Duchess.

Sir William also had sufficiently lost touch with reality in his own country to put some faith in this impossible intrigue; but he continued to pester the Government with demands for compensation for the losses and expenses he had sustained during the Neapolitan trouble.

Emma, who had left the walls of the Palazzo Sessa bare, talked about £9,000 worth of clothes and jewels which had been left behind before the royal flight; and Sir William had got an extraordinary dossier of imaginary expenses. A Mr. Peebles, to whom had been promised one of Mr. Beckford's pocket Boroughs, interfered in the affair and tried to push it forward while Nelson used all his influence with Mr. Addington for the same end; Sir William Hamilton canvassed all his kinsmen and clan, and every possible string was pulled, but in vain. Beckford, Sir William, Emma, Nelson, all were in bad odour at Court; there were no pickings for any of them from the well-gnawed bone of Court favour.

Sir William began to be seriously troubled by the state of his affairs and by the reckless extravagance of his wife, but she was faultless in the eyes of the man who wrote from sea in an ecstasy about the little Horatia: "I never saw a finer child produced by any two persons. It was, in truth, a love-begotten child. I am determined to keep him (the mythical Mr. Thompson) on board, for I know if they got together they would soon have another, and after our two months' trip I hope they will never be separated. Then let them do as they please."

But he could not resist complaining of the Piccadilly extravagance, reports of which came to him as he fretted and idled on his flagship, but he wholly blamed the old man—who was not responsible—and totally exonerated the wife, the real offender.

"What," he wrote, "can Sir William mean by wanting you to launch out into expense and extravagance? That he, that used to think a little candlelight and ice-water would ruin him, should want to set off at £10,000 a year, for a less sum would not afford concerts and the style of living equal to it!"

Nor did Lord Nelson like the idea that the Hamiltons should retire to a house to be lent them by Sir William's kinsman, the Duke of Queensberry: "If you were to take the Duke's house, a house open to everybody he pleases, you had better have a move at once. You never could rest. Why did not the Duke assist Sir William when he wanted assistance, why not have saved you from the distress which Sir William must have every day been in, knowing that his excellent wife sold her jewels to get him a house."

Here Nelson probably echoed Lady Hamilton's own account of the affair. She certainly had sold and pledged some of her jewels to keep tradespeople quiet, but in return Sir William had made over to her all his property, including plate, furniture, ornaments, pictures, and paintings. Soon afterwards some of these paintings, part of his valuable collection, had to be sold. Among them were some portraits of Emma herself.

"I wonder Sir William could do it," wrote Nelson. "Sooner than sell a picture of you, I would have starved."

Other pictures of Emma were standing face to the wall in the odd gallery which George Romney had built at Pineapple Place, Hampstead. The painter himself, completely insane, was dying in the care of his patient wife in his native northern air; it was as well, perhaps, that he should not have painted another portrait of Emma.

The scandal swelled, besmirching all with whom it came in contact except Emma herself, who remained unperturbed and cheerful, well-fed and flourishing. She had the countenance of the Rev. William Nelson, his wife and children, who were quite clever enough and quite tolerant enough to take a very liberal view of the connection which might benefit the entire family so considerably; the sisters, too, were friendly with Emma, the old father alone held aloof and refused to have anything to do with the enchantress; he remained faithful to his daughter-in-law and his son, and to the conventions that he had always so sternly taught.

.   .   .   .   .   .

Early in the first year of the new century, 1801, Lord Nelson was ordered to sea. The neutrals of Northern Europe had leagued together in what they termed "Armed Neutrality"—a piece of impertinence which brought down on their heads the wrath of Great Britain. From Denmark in particular—this country having refused to allow her ships to be searched for war materials—an explanation was demanded. The Danish Cabinet was believed to be under the influence of the First Consul.

A squadron set sail in March from Yarmouth Roads; the command of this Baltic expedition was given to Vice-Admiral Sir Hyde Parker, greatly to the fury of Lord Nelson, but after his conduct at Naples and Palermo the Lords Commissioners of the Admiralty did not see fit to trust him with the Chief Command. He was, however, inevitably the leading spirit of the expedition, burning with energy and that spark of fascinating heroism which gave him such a hold over his fellow-officers and the men who served under him.

Emma, in the midst of her Piccadilly splendour, soon had good news: "My dearest friend, that same Deity who has on many occasions protected Nelson, has once more crowned his endeavours with complete success. *Saint George, April 2nd,* 1801, *nine o'clock at night. Very tired after a hard-fought battle.*"

This was "the great and glorious" victory of the Battle of Copenhagen, which taught the Danes a lesson—that it was dangerous to challenge the majesty of Great Britain—at the cost of 943 officers and men killed and wounded and very heavy damage to the British battleships; the British had gained a few batttered Danish ships, only one of which was worth retaining as a prize.

The Danes, who had fought with conspicuous heroism and devotion, lost 1,600 killed and wounded. To Nelson and not to Sir Hyde Parker was undoubtedly due the victory, but the hero had gained his glory in his usual manner, by flagrant disobedience to orders. It had been, from first to last, a superb piece of work, but one not likely to commend him to the Lords of the Admiralty. And Sir Hyde Parker had the wording of the dispatches which contained the reports of the battle.

.   .   .   .   .   .

The Battle of Copenhagen had been carried out in dashing style, with several of those heroic, dramatic touches that so endeared Lord Nelson to his fellow-countrymen; the conflict had begun soon after ten in the morning; the Danish Fleet was close under the batteries of their own coast, and stretched for nearly four miles under Elsinore and Cronenberg Castles, which crowned the rocky shores of the strait. Lord Nelson, though worn out in mind and body by the incessant labour of watching his ships through the Channel—unknown and therefore dangerous to the British sailors—had offered his services for the attack.

After three hours of a fierce engagement, Sir Hyde Parker, who had been unable to get to the assistance of Lord Nelson by reason of a contrary wind and tide, signalled to his second-in-command to retreat.

Lord Nelson who had just remarked "that it was warm work but that he would not be elsewhere for thousands," ignored the signal to "cease action" and ordered his own signal for "close action" to remain flying.

"I have only one eye," he remarked. "I have a right to be blind sometimes."

He put the spyglass to his sightless eye and exclaimed: "I really do not see the signal! Keep mine nailed to the mast!"

By early afternoon the Danes were too distressed to continue firing, and Lord Nelson, who did not entertain for them the hatred he felt for the French, but rather regarded them as "brothers," sent an officer ashore with a flag of truce and an offer of an armistice, his object being as he declared, "humanity."

The slaughter had been, on both sides, horrible; some of the

British losses were due to the pride of one of the officers in command of some of the troops on board one of the warships; these men were useless and might have been sent out of danger, but were instead drawn up on deck to be shot down by the enemies' guns.

Lord Nelson went on shore and continued his negotiations in person with the Crown Prince; these were conducted in a lofty, chivalrous strain, oddly different from that used during the Naples business; but there was some high-feeling between Lord Nelson and the Danish Commander-in-Chief, and afterwards between Lord Nelson and Sir Hyde Parker. "I may be hanged," the disobedient second-in-command had said; he had himself hanged men for a less offence against discipline.

But Lord Nelson had again been successful; if the country had gained little but glory at this battle and paid for that dearly, glory was very necessary at this juncture of affairs, and the defeat was supposed to have acted as a useful warning to Denmark not to league with the enemies of Great Britain.

Sir Hyde Parker was recalled and Lord Nelson appointed Commander-in-Chief; there followed a brush with Russia, whose intentions were dubious, and this gave Lord Nelson an opportunity of making a statement which sounded ironic enough to those who remembered Naples—"the word of a British Admiral . . . was as sacred as that of any sovereign in Europe"; perhaps Ferdinand IV was not a European sovereign.

The death of the Czar Paul ended all fear of a Northern Coalition against Great Britain.

Emma celebrated the victory at Copenhagen by dancing a tarantella so vigorously that she exhausted several partners, including Sir William, a Neapolitan duke, and a black servant.

.   .   .   .   .   .

A severe illness followed the nervous tension of the Baltic expedition. Again Lord Nelson believed himself dying, but he had his dreams; he and Emma would escape to Sicily; they would live under the chestnut-trees at Bronte, they would enjoy again the golden friendship of a king and queen, all the glories of the old Neapolitan, Sicilian days would revive. Once more there would be fireworks breaking against the cones of Etna, decorated boats floating in the purple waters of the bay; he and Emma walking amid the orange groves, beneath the cypress trees, beneath the Sicilian moon; a dream, but one that kept the battered man alive, tormented by fear of total blindness.

On the way home his illness increased; he was constantly seasick: "I cast up what everyone thought was my lungs," he wrote.

On July 1st, 1801, he landed at Yarmouth. His brother Maurice had died during his absence, and to his blind wife Lord Nelson was, as always where money was concerned, most generous. He sent £100 at once to his sister-in-law and offered to look after her lavishly during the future, but to his own wife he could not be generous. She wrote a frank letter giving him news of his father: "I will do everything in my power to alleviate his infirmities. What more can I do to convince you that I am truly your affectionate wife?" But he would have none of Fanny. It was London for him and the Piccadilly house.

Emma, with her usual resource, arranged a holiday. They must all away to Box Hill with the Rev. William and his family as chaperons. Then there was a rural episode at the Bush Inn at Staines, where Sir William spent his days angling in the Thames, and Emma made everything delightful for Lord Nelson amid the rural pleasures; the idyll was broken up by the scare of an invasion. The First Consul was concentrating at Boulogne what he termed "the army for the conquest of England."

The lovers had again to part; Lord Nelson was given the command of a patrol of light vessels that was to cruise about in the Channel watching out for signs of the enemy. This was dull work, and he tried to enliven it by an attack on Boulogne, which was, however, unsuccessful. He was constantly seasick, and only his daily letters to Emma and her answers provided any spark of interest in the dreary days.

But Emma, as usual, had found something interesting to do. She was looking for a house. When Nelson had a few days on shore at Deal in September, she came with Sir William and the lap-dogs and the liveried servants in the heraldic carriage to meet him at the inn, "The Three Kings."

There they drank champagne, the best champagne, and discussed the future, all in high spirits. Emma had found a house at Merton. Emma thought it cheap, but the deposit demanded was £6,000, and Lord Nelson was in nearly as bad a financial condition as Sir William Hamilton; Copenhagen had brought in a mere Viscountcy and there were many claims on the other rewards which had seemed so handsome. But Emma was to do as she pleased.

Nelson was forced to put to sea again, bowed and shaken by that separation from Emma; but she, on her part, had a congenial occupation, the purchase and furnishing of Merton.

This was a modish, dignified mansion of the correct suburban style, palladian, with a flat, white front, trim lawns round about and a sweep of gravel with neat posts and chains; bargain as Emma thought it, to complete the purchase it took all the money that Lord Nelson possessed; he considered it well spent. He would not have her stint in anything; she spent £1,000 on furniture, encouraged by letters such as these: "I come on board, but no Emma; no, no, my heart will break. I am in silent distraction. The four pictures of Lady E. H. are hung up, but alas I have lost the original! We part, only to meet very soon again. It must be. It shall be. My dearest wife, how can I bear our separation? Love my Horatia and prepare for me the farm, Amen, Amen."

He was the more disconsolate and wretched, because it seemed to him in his seasickness and loneliness, as his little fleet patrolled the coast through the autumn mists that filled the Channel, that he had been forgotten once more, slighted, and overlooked, that Copenhagen had not been adequately rewarded. His sole interest besides Emma was the furnishing of Merton; she had everything that was his, the keys of his plate chest, his tea-urns, breakfast-sets; there was nothing for Fanny beyond a wife's pension.

Old Sir William endured as best he could this lavish spending of another man's money on the house he was to inhabit; he got away as often as possible from the bustle of the women and sat fishing in the Wandle, which meandered near the grounds of Merton, while Emma and Mrs. Cadogan with a host of servants and dependants rushed here and there fixing up hangings and trophies, arranging furniture, pictures, and statuary with great gusto and delight. Merton was to house all the trophies collected by Nelson's heroism and Emma's beauty; it was to be a temple consecrated to their combined achievements.

.   .   .   .   .   .

The Peace of Amiens released Nelson from his dreary patrolling of the coast. He hastened back to Merton, ignoring the huzzas and triumphal arches on the way in his eager desire to be beside his Emma again. In his mind hung brightly the golden dream of Naples. He and Emma would some day, perhaps soon, escape to Bronte, where, in an enchantment, Duke and Duchess, friends of the King and Queen, with little Horatia growing up beside them, they would revive all those joys which a few years before the little sailor had found so intoxicating. It was a desperate and pathetic project, "a search for lost time."

For a while there was perfect felicity at Merton; the sick man was supremely happy again with Emma, admiring Emma and Emma's cleverness at arranging everything, recovering in the breezy incense of Emma's flattery, enjoying the solid comforts that Mrs. Cadogan provided—all these things for a while were enough. But the world would break in—he had to take a seat in the House of Peers; he made a little speech that had no great effect, the visit to London forced him to notice that everyone still held aloof from him and Emma, everyone, that is, save those who had nothing to lose and something to gain by hanging round Merton; it is odd that he should have considered anything else possible; his passion had put everything out of focus for him.

But there was something worse than the mere cold shouldering of society. A personal affront was in preparation. Lord Nelson soon learnt that the Battle of Copenhagen was to be ignored. The City of London voted its thanks to the Army and Navy then in Egypt, but did not mention the Danish defeat. Nelson wrote to the Lord Mayor protesting, and sent a copy of his letter to St. Vincent, who was dry and unsympathetic. Nor was the victory mentioned in the King's speech and there was to be no medal.

Nelson, encouraged by the outraged Emma and the peevish whimperings of Sir William who feared for his pension, and despaired of his dukedom, raged. He even interviewed the Prime Minister, but all was in vain. The hero came face to face with what were evasively termed, "private reasons." The reasons were not so very private; nothing could have been more flaunting than Emma, and Lady Nelson was there for all to see. Over one of his brief, harsh letters: "I have done my duty as an honest, generous man, living, I have done all in my power for you, if dead, you will find I have done the same." She had written—"This is my Lord Nelson's letter of dismissal." Yet she brought herself to write to him again; a plea for reconciliation arrived at Merton.

It was, despite everything, magnanimously worded: "Do my dear husband, let us live together. I have now to offer you a warm, comfortable house. Let everything be buried in oblivion, it will pass away like a dream." The letter was endorsed—"Opened by mistake by Lord Nelson, but not read."

In giving his wife a handsome allowance, Lord Nelson thought that he had done everything. Out of his income, which was no more than £3,000 a year, she had £1,800; lavish as he was in financial dealings, he grudged Fanny's pension, because he could easily have spent it on Emma. When Merton was completely paid for and furnished, there was more selling of diamond boxes to meet current expenses, and this time they were some of the prize trophies which had celebrated the victory of the Nile.

Yet Emma held a miniature court at Merton. Sometimes she had the Piccadilly house open as well. Her housekeeping was often as much as £100 a week, and her table was seldom laid for less than twelve people. Sir William became more and more peevish and difficult. There were frequent quarrels, as the old dilettante, who could never quite forget that he had been born and bred a gentleman, ventured to protest against the senseless, extravagant vulgarities that both Emma and her lover enjoyed so much. Things became so bad that the harassed old man, tasting at last the lees of his wretched bargain with his nephew, wrote a paper not without pathos, either in its refusal to see the truth or in its resolve to be conveniently hoodwinked.

"I have passed the last 40 years of my life in the hurry and bustle that must necessarily be attendant on a Publick character. I am arrived at the age when some repose is really necessary, and I promised myself a quiet home, altho' I was sensible, and said so when I married, that I shou'd be superannuated, when my wife would be in her full beauty and vigour of youth. That time is arrived, and we must make the best of it for the comfort of both parties. Unfortunately, our tastes as to the manner of living are very different. I by no means wish to live in solitary retreat; but to have seldom less than 12 and 14 at Table, and those varying continually, is coming back to what was become so irksome to me in Italy, during the latter years of my residence in that country. I have no connections out of my own family. I have no complaint to make, but I feel that the whole attention of my wife is given to Lord Nelson and his interest at Merton. I well know the purity of Lord Nelson's friendship for Emma and me. And I know how very uncomfortable it wou'd make his Lordship, our best Friend, if a separation shou'd take place, and am therefore determined to do all in my power to prevent such an extremity, which wou'd be essentially detrimental to all parties, but wou'd be more sensibly felt by our dear Friend than by us. Provided that our expenses and house-keeping do not increase beyond measure (of which, I must own, I see some danger), I am willing to go on upon our present footing; but, as I cannot expect to live many years, every moment to me is precious, and I hope I may be allow'd sometimes to be my own master, and pass my time according to my own inclination, either by going (with) my fishing-parties on the Thames, or by going to London to attend the Museum, Royal Society, the Tuesday Club, and Auctions of pictures. I mean to have a light chariot or post-chaise by the month that I may make use of in London, and run backwards and forwards to Merton or to Shepperton, &c. This is my plan, and we might go on very well, but I am fully determined not to have more of the silly altercations, that happen too often between us, and embitter the present moments exceedingly. If really we cannot live comfortably together, a *wise* and *well concerted separation* is preferable, but I think, considering the probability of my not troubling any party long in this world, the best for all wou'd be to bear those ills we have rather than fly to those we know not of.—I have fairly stated what I have on my mind, there is no time for nonsense or trifling. I know and admire your talents, and many excellent qualities, but I am not blind to your defects, and I confess having many myself. Therefore let us bear and forbear.

"For God's Sake."

But Emma knew how to gloss even this over and things went

on as before; the wife not only lived openly with her lover, treating her old husband as part of the background, but she introduced little Horatia into the household under some tale that it was a little protégée of hers, the child of a friend; under the same excuse she had got Sir William Hamilton to pay the expenses of little Emma for so many years; now no one knew what had become of Emma the second; she had disappeared like other inconveniences of the past. Lord Nelson did not know of her existence and Sir William never troubled about her any more than he troubled about little Horatia; it was part of his code to accept the inevitable, the disagreeable with an air of breeding. Besides, he was too old and tired to concern much about anything; for Emma he had sacrificed not only his honour and his domestic happiness, his official position and his dignity, but even, what perhaps he valued most of all, his taste.

The man who had taken such keen pleasure in arranging the spacious rooms of the Palazzo Sessa with Tuscan vases and antique busts, with the relics of Pompeii and Herculaneum, whose collection of treasures had been world famous and whose taste and judgment had never been disputed, was now forced to live in what was half an old curiosity shop and half a raree-show.

Emma had collected together all the portraits, some masterpieces, some poor daubs, painted of herself that she could lay her hands on. Under dozens of names and in dozens of attitudes she smiled or frowned, laughed or languished, from the walls, which were also crowded with prints of all the exploits of Lord Nelson that the busy woman could get together; every victory was represented dozens of times over in the crude drawings of hack draughtsmen. There were also genuine trophies—the flagstaff of the *L'Orient*, pieces of French ships fished out of the water after engagements, figureheads and coats of arms from Bonaparte's frigates, busts of Lord Nelson, on which Emma kept laurel leaves freshly plucked from the shrubberies, cameos of Emma, gifts from the Royal Sovereigns of Naples—a proper museum of dead glories.

The few decent people who joined the racket that filled Merton found this display ridiculous and disgusting; but no one could stop it. Once Sir William had given up his attempt as he expressed himself, "to bring his wife up roundly," no one else could interfere.

Emma, triumphant over the deserted wife, carried the war into the enemy's camp. As is usual with her type, she wanted to have not only the rewards of vice, but the halo of virtue—so a hack writer was employed to compose stories to defame Lady Nelson and to create the impression that her bad-temper, selfishness, and coldness had caused her husband to leave her.

Among Emma's eager, even obsequious, admirers, was Nelson's brother, the Rev. William, his wife and daughter, who were frequent visitors to Merton, where their respectable presences helped to testify to that "purity" of Emma's attachment to Lord Nelson in which Sir William so firmly believed.

.   .   .   .   .   .

In the year 1802 Edmund Nelson died, unreconciled with his famous son—death put an end, too, to George Romney's insanity. Two links with the past were snapped for Nelson and Emma—no more letters from the old vicar, no more portraits from Romney's brush.

Lord Nelson became restless and melancholy, his blindness seemed increasing, his old internal trouble returned; he was always sick, in pain, nervous. The resourceful Emma was, as usual, ready with a distraction. Why should they not all go to the estate in Wales where Charles Greville in his late, sober middle age was busy improving the land he hoped soon to inherit? Those famous estates with which Miss Barlow had dowered Sir William long ago.

That summer they all set off, highly gratified by a fine reception at Oxford, where Lord Nelson received an honorary degree and the city's Freedom in a gold box. This satisfaction, however, was set off by a severer mortification. Most ill-advisedly, they called at the grandiose pile of Blenheim, the monument of a nation's extravagant gratitude to another hero, who had not hesitated to present a heavy bill for services rendered.

They were not received, but a cold luncheon was at their service; Emma, dismayed and furious, a goddess of wrath on the vast stone steps of the monstrous palace, shouted: "Had I been a Queen, you should have had a Principality after the Battle of Aboukir, so that Blenheim should only have been as a kitchen-garden to it!"

They left the luncheon untouched, and Nelson, sick with mortification, vowed that he had not yet "finished gathering his laurels."

The episode was not without its ironic touch. The hero who had founded the Churchill fortune, was scarcely more scrupulously moral than Lord Nelson, though he had chanced to be in love with his wife. Perhaps some of Horatio Nelson's honest, puritanical yeoman ancestors would have refused to receive Colonel John Churchill, when he travelled in the train of the King's mistress, Lady Castlemaine, as her avowed lover.

There were continuous, if petty triumphs, brass bands and official welcomes from small towns and cheering rustics until they reached Wales. There, on Sir William's estate at Milford, all the tenantry came out; there were the usual manifestations of joy at the appearance of the hero and the beauty, and the old pantaloon who ran behind them carrying the lap-dog and shawls.

Emma hoped that Lady Nelson and the fashionable world would hear of these receptions, and that it would "burst some of them."

She again met, after all these years, Charles Greville; he acted as their guide over the estate of which he was steward. He had not married his heiress after all, but he was on the verge of securing the fortune for which he had sold Emma. He had done quite well for himself in a small, comfortable way and the selfish, withered, fastidious man could view with irony and relief the blowsy, vulgar woman who had once been his wood-nymph and his Ariadne; he had, after all, secured the best of the bargain.

. . . . . .

Next spring Sir William died, his wife holding one hand, her lover the other; he had been so long old and useless and tiresome that his going made little difference to anyone. His will left Emma comfortably off and expressed a belief in the purity of her affection for Nelson and in Nelson's honour that was either the last ironic gesture of a broken man of the world or a profession of senility. Emma had all her late husband's goods and chattels as left in the house in Piccadilly, she had a revenue of £800 a year on the Welsh estate, a legacy of a like amount, while good Mrs. Cadogan was provided for by £100 a year and a legacy of another £100.

Nelson immediately added to this £1,200 a year, so that Lady Hamilton enjoyed an income of £2,000 a year, the contents of the Piccadilly house, and the free use of Merton, with the servants, carriages and horses and other luxuries that Nelson had paid for.

Now was the opportunity for Circe to whisk her Ulysses off to the enchanted isle. Bronte had not brought in the promised revenues, but it was always there—a dukedom and a palace beneath the blazing blue of the Sicilian sky. Yet they hesitated, each perhaps conscious in a different fashion that it was too late to search for the "Fortunate Isles."

They had ceased to care how they affronted London opinion. They could not, after all, be more ostracized, more cut off from decent society than they were. And to retire to Sicily meant that Emma would give up the life she enjoyed very much, and Nelson all hope of the further glories after which he hungered. They put off the exile for which they had so often sighed; and then, before Sir William had been more than a few weeks dead, came war again and once more the threat of invasion for England. News of a huge army concentrating on the French coast came to the ears of the Cabinet in London. Again, and this time it seemed with more reason than ever, England feared a landing of French troops under General Bonaparte.

Lord Viscount Nelson was appointed in May 1803 to the *Victory* as Vice-Admiral of the White to command in the Mediterranean Sea. His first duty was to cover Toulon and to prevent the French Fleet from leaving the harbour there. During this dull, monotonous work, which lasted for months, he became ill and melancholy again, homesick for Emma, for Horatia, for Merton, endeavouring to console himself with her pictures hung in his cabin, and as usual with him when he became dispirited, thinking that he had not long to live, and seeing all eclipsed by darkness.

But Emma was quite happy and busy at Merton. She had everything her own way now, with no peevish Sir William to fuss over. The future, to her robust optimism, looked encouraging. The Beckford project had fallen through, and she had not yet received the pension she considered her right both as Sir William's widow and in return for the services she had rendered Britain when in Sicily; but one of the lives that had stood between her and the hero had gone, and Fanny was supposed now to be ailing, broken with rheumatism and dispirited. Emma was quite confident that her lover would return with fresh glories; this time they would not be able to deny him a Dukedom—and who would share it with him but Emma?

While he was off Capri, writing to her at every chance he got of sending a letter, pressing a lock of her hair to his lips, she was bearing him his second child—this time without much trouble at concealment. He sent Horatia a watch with a priggish, old-fashioned letter such as his own father might have written, and for Emma there was a curious novelty—a muff made of the beards of mussels. The big, opulent, easy-going woman accepted this homage placidly; both her children took smallpox in the midst of the war fever, and little Emma died and was laid in Paddington Churchyard close to the house where Emma Hart had carefully noted down how she had spent her small weekly allowance given her by Mr. Charles Greville.

In the fierce excitement of that year of the renewed war and the dread of invasion no one bothered much about Emma. At times, as the news from Paris reached London, there was something of a panic, General Bonaparte gave a tawdry gloss to his project and an increase to his own splendour by being crowned Emperor of the French in Notre Dame; Spain joined him; the future looked black for Great Britain, a long struggle seemed in sight, and everyone was tired of the wars, save those who made money out of them.

> " 'Twas in that memorable year
> France threatened to put off in
> Flat-bottomed boats, intending each
> To be a British coffin
> To make sad widows of our wives,
> And every babe an orphan."

Lord Nelson was doing his utmost for his country, fretting to be at his old, heroic job of fighting once more, and longing to return with an armful of trophies for Emma. He did not forget her interests; he had never ceased to work for rewards, pensions, and honours for Emma. Off Naples he tried to renew the old relationship with the Queen, but Maria Carolina was distant. The flighty woman had had all she could hope for from both Emma and Nelson, and the man whose head she had once turned with coarse adulation was obliged to write home bitterly that things were not as they had been, and that it was only with great reluctance that Her Majesty had been induced to sign a paper stating that she believed Lady Hamilton was entitled to some reward from Great Britain for the services she had performed in Naples. His Francophobia had not diminished since he was last in these waters; upon the British Resident's offering him the services of a friendly Frenchman, he replied that the members of that nation were all alike and that he would not have one on board any of his ships, save as a prisoner; "forgive me," he added: "my mother hated the French."

.   .   .   .   .   .

In 1805 Spain declared war and in the spring of that year Lord Nelson performed magnificent service to his country by heading off the Toulon Fleet under Admiral Villeneuve, which was making for the West Indies in co-operation with the Spaniards; he intercepted the enemy, forced them to turn back, and the Indies were saved. But there had been a deep humiliation; the four treasure-ships that would have proved so rich a prize to Lord Nelson's "band of Brothers" were denied them, and Sir John Orde was sent to Cadiz to reap this fine harvest.

Nelson's lamentations were pointed with a heavy sarcasm: "I had thought—I fancied—but, nay; it must be a dream, an idle dream;—yet, I confess it, I *did* fancy that I had done my country service; and thus they use me!" That year, too, saw the end of the Emperor Napoleon's project for invasion of Britain. Attacked landwards by Austria and Russia, he was obliged to withdraw his forces from the French coast; the tension was relieved in England.

Arthur Wellesley, who had just returned to England, met Lord Nelson for the first and last time, when he returned home after the check to Villeneuve, and did not like him; the reserved, aristocratic soldier was offended by the sailor's fiery boastfulness, which marred the conversation.

"If I can call it conversation—for it was almost all on his side."

Even after his last service he was still ignored by society; how could it be otherwise when all his thoughts were of Emma? With her at Merton he was desperately happy in the last mellow days of summer. There was Horatia, there was old Mrs. Cadogan, there were his brother and his sister-in-law and some old friends to come and go: Emma wondered what he was going to get for his services in the Indies; were there no more honours, trophies, ribbons, crosses, rewards?—it seemed not. The King took no notice of him, the last victory had meant no more than the barren honours of the Viscountcy, the thanks of Parliament.

The thought of money, of Horatia's future, troubled him, but he tried to put it all aside, Emma could make him even forget how broken he was in body and that he was nearly blind, the menace of complete darkness was always before him; he dreaded the day when he should no longer be able to see the beauty of Emma—to him still without a blemish—or the infant charms of little Horatia. These September days in Merton could be, they knew, only an interlude; Viscount Nelson was in command of the Mediterranean Fleet, and might at any moment be recalled to his post, he had been allowed only a little space in which to repose, there was still Admiral Villeneuve with his Gallo-Spanish Fleet to be chased and beaten.

Horatio Nelson was the only man who, during the long war, so weary, so costly, so mismanaged, had achieved that spectacular glory which alone can make war acceptable to a nation, and he had been handsomely rewarded. Yet, by an odd irony, the titles, swords, medals, the pensions and formal thanks had been given with an aloof coldness that destroyed half their value. The people might shout warmly for their hero—symbol of the sea power of the country—but it was clear that in choosing Emma, Lord Nelson had chosen social isolation.

Not for a second did he regret his choice, but the price exacted for his great loss was a bitter one for a man brought up in such firm respectability, at heart such a snob, so narrowly religious, so avid of worldly honours, to pay.

Never did he see himself in the wrong, and Emma he always found flawless; to what then could he impute the fault? He vaguely and bitterly blamed "the world" that would not see the dazzling merits of his Emma, that would not recognize the exalted nature of his attachment to her, the brilliant services she had rendered to

her country. Everyone was wrong and he and she were right; he
had, however, to admit defeat, victorious everywhere else, he could
not make English society accept Emma.

This was a horrible blow to a man already sunk by disease,
wounds, and the effect of continuous excitement on a mind always
delicately balanced. Yet he was fiercely happy in a heart-rending
fashion; for his happiness had the desperate zest of a child at a
forbidden, entrancing game. His joy in Emma, in all that Emma
did, was, or had, was of that pathetic quality only possible to simple
people, a passion so intense as to burn up gradually the very springs
of his life.

He appreciated, in an agony of delight, the home she had made
for him, the children that she had given him, the flatteries she
offered him, the trophies she had arranged for him; he alone of
her lovers did not find her crude, a little vulgar, in need of training.
Emma in satin or feathers, Emma as a wife, Emma playing the
harp, Emma carving his meat, Emma in any pose, anywhere, was
to him perfection.

One side of him, too, gloried in their connection, in the sheer
advertisement-value of it; when he thought of the Wandle, purling
so charmingly past the Merton lawns, and himself and Emma idling
there, he reflected—"Emma rowing her one-armed Admiral!
What a subject for the caricaturists!"

Society might treat him as it would, he had, besides a genius
for fighting, a genius for publicity.

.   .   .   .   .   .

While the love-sick hero agonized at her side, Emma was calm.
Though she had that deep streak of cruelty, of malice which had
shown in Naples and in her treatment of Fanny Nelson, she was
always outwardly easy and good natured, and even her very
vindictiveness was more due to ignorance, selfishness and greed
than to active spite. She hit out at all who offended her or who got
in her way, in everything she was shallow, but when she was not
crossed, and to those who served her, she was very agreeable. Her
lazy voluptuous personality warmed the very air her lover breathed.
She did not love him, she had never loved anyone save only, perhaps,
for a short while, Charles Greville, the middle-aged gentleman

now so decorously aloof from her life, her nephew-in-law, perhaps she was only at her old game of pleasing the gentlemen which by now she knew so well, but whatever the game, it satisfied her lover.

And she was satisfied, too; she had always been confident, courageous, clever at seeing her own advantage, and now, as they were together in Merton, she had none of his worries, or fears, or nervous dreads.

After all, she was not so deeply stung by the hostility of a society that had never received her; looking back down the years she might consider it more remarkable that she had escaped Bridewell than that she was not admitted to St. James's Palace.

Amy Lyon had done pretty well for herself; her life was as she liked it, "everything that money can buy," and she had never wanted anything that money could not buy.

It was, gorgeous as well as a comfortable life at Merton and she knew plenty of jolly people who were not squeamish at coming to eat and drink at her lover's expense, to flatter and to admire.

She was not troubled even by the loss of her beauty; she had been as prodigal of that as Horatio Nelson had been of his money; at forty-two years of age she was all to pieces, for she had always put her appetites before her charms, but she did not care if a big, heavy, highly coloured woman with broad features and coarse complexion had taken the place of Ariadne and Cassandra, she looked impressive enough by candle-light, with her magnificent eyes and thick dark hair, and a few glasses of champagne would bring oblivion of any regret.

Besides, it was difficult to believe that her luck was at an end; Sir William had gone, and God Almighty might any moment remove "the impediment," poor Fanny, who did not know how to please the gentlemen, and then she would be the hero's wife —and, after he had had another of his victories, they would not be able to refuse him a Dukedom. It was a good prospect.

And even if the unwanted wife persisted in surviving, and Horatio succumbed to his complication of diseases—why, there were others, that amusing old satyr, the Duke of Queensberry, for instance.

Emma's lovers had always so obligingly provided a successor; under Sir Harry's roof she had met Charles Greville, who in his turn had been at such pains to arrange things with Sir William, who had been more than easy with Lord Nelson—so surely, Emma, being still Emma, need not bother about the future.

So her lazy content soothed his restlessness in those last days of August; a Saint Martin's summer, the sequel to those blazing Sicilian days. The quiet English weather had a wistful charm; the mellow sunshine fell tranquilly on the shaven lawns, the emblematic laurels, the grey rippled stream, where Sir William used to fish, the garden of late flowers, where Horatia ran and laughed in her muslin frocks.

There was a sweet flavour of domesticity about this illicit union, Emma, flamboyant as a siren of a Wapping inn over the card-tables at night, could be homely and cosy over the tea-cups in the morning with the child pulling at her skirts, as another child had pulled over twenty years ago, at the flounces of a girl crying in a Hawarden cottage.

It had to come to an end, these two had often played at melodramatics, and here real drama touched them; early in September Lord Nelson was recalled to his command. He could not have disobeyed now, as he had disobeyed in Sicily, the orders to leave Emma, nor did he wish to; he was wrought up into a state of exaltation that could find relief only in heroic action; but the parting was an agony. Social recognition came at last, from an unexpected quarter; always ready to irritate the Court and the Government, the Prince of Wales invited Lord Nelson and his lady to Carlton House, where he amused himself by looking them over, afterwards allowing without any sign of regret Emma to depart; Mr. Eliott had been mistaken when he had predicted that Emma would be a great success with His Royal Highness, and Lord Nelson's desperate jealousy had been causeless.

The Prince and the peasant beauty met a few years too late; he was a little faded, she a little over-ripe.

The couple returned to Merton where there was the final leave-taking; while the baggage was made ready, the carriage ordered, and the household in a confusion of preparations for the hero's departure for the war, he was kneeling by the child's cot, in a transport of sentimentality, patriotism, and adoration of that strange God whom he had so curiously identified with himself, the God in whose name he had sanctioned the Naples massacres, hanged Caracciolo, beaten the French, and saved the Sicilian Bourbons from the consequences of their own crimes and follies, the God to whom he had prayed to unite him to Emma by removing Fanny, and in whose sight he believed Emma was his wife.

To this crude Deity he addressed this strange petition: writing it down as he drove from Merton: "Friday night at half-past ten drove from dear, dear Merton, where I left all that I hold dear in this world to go and serve my King and country. May the great God whom I adore enable me to fulfil the expectations of my country and if it is his good pleasure that I should return, my thanks will never cease to be offered up to the throne of his mercy. If it is his good providence to cut short my days upon earth, I bow with the greatest submission, relying that he will protect those so dear to me, that I leave behind. His will be done. Amen, Amen, Amen."

At Portsmouth, where he had a frantic reception from the people, to whom he had always been a hero, he did and said some things that seemed to show a mind half-unbalanced by excitement, grief and self-sacrifice.

He had been to look at Ben Hallowell's coffin made from the wood and iron of the *L'Orient*, which was stored in a warehouse and remarked that he thought he might want it on his return; his usual boastings had a sublime air: "I shall outdo my former achievements, but I shall not return to enjoy the glories I acquire."

2

MORALIZING STARS AND PREACHING TOMBS

'IL DESIR VIVE, E LA SPERANZA E MORTA'
(PETRARCHA)

'COULD THE LOVER HAVE A SIGHT OF HIS ONCE ENCHANTING FAIR
ONE, WHAT A STARTLING ASTONISHMENT WOULD SEIZE HIM! "IS
THIS THE OBJECT, I NOT LONG AGO PASSIONATELY ADMIRED! I
SAID, SHE WAS DIVINELY FAIR; AND THOUGHT HER SOMEWHAT
MORE THAN MORTAL . . . FONDLY I LOOKED UPON THE GLITTERING
METEOR AND THOUGHT IT WAS A STAR . . . BUT HOW IT IS FALLEN!
FALLEN FROM AN ORB, NOT ITS OWN! . . . LIE, POOR FLORELLA!
LIE DEEP AS THOU DOST, IN OBSCURE DARKNESS. LET NIGHT, WITH
HER IMPENETRABLE SHADES, ALWAYS CONCEAL THEE. MAY NO
PRYING EYE BE WITNESS TO THY DISGRACE, BUT LET THY SURVIV-
ING SISTERS THINK UPON THY STATE, WHEN THEY CONTEMPLATE
THE IDOL IN THE GLASS"'
(HERVEY'S 'MEDITATIONS AMONG THE TOMBS')

'HOWEVER, WHATEVER HAPPENS, I HAVE RUN A GLORIOUS RACE'
(LORD NELSON)

THE news struck England with the alarm of an unexpected
calamity, with the joy of an unparalleled glory. It was felt by
everyone—felt most keenly by the simple and the ignorant—that
the peculiar island renown had been incredibly heightened. The
enemy, an arrogant, insulting godless enemy, who had dared to
threaten shores free for hundreds of years from the menace of an
invader, had been utterly destroyed, and in that destruction a hero
had been sacrificed. Lord Nelson had been slain at Trafalgar, thus
providing a page of British history that would never need a commentary. As no sacrifice is complete without the offering of a

living victim, so no victory blazes so brightly as that where the victor is slain.

The country was shaken by an event that was at once splendid, tragic, and noble enough to increase the national fame; the islanders' naval genius had found for ever its supreme expression. The man who had left Merton under a social cloud became a demigod, one of those half-fabulous creatures who shake the thunderbolt and stride the cloud.

Everything concerned with him became at once more worthy and larger than his eccentric life and dignified by his honourable deed. Lord Nelson was dead and for a while a cold bleak wind seemed to wither Emma waiting at Merton, which became suddenly the store-house of a dead man's possessions—from his clothes and slippers in the pleasant bedroom to the mast of the ship that had taken Napoleon to Egypt, the coloured prints of former victories, and the laurelled busts that stood in the hall crowded with trophies. Here was a chance to strike an attitude more effective even than that of Agrippina displaying the ashes of Germanicus to Rome, which had so delighted William Beckford and his guests. But there was no longer anyone to applaud; the big, robust woman sat down, without dramatics, to read with anxiety, with grief, and with an odd tingling of an emotion new to her—regret, the newspapers that related the glorious fight in Trafalgar Bay.

.   .   .   .   .   .

On October 6th, Lord Nelson had written: "I verily believe that the country will soon be put to some expense on my account; either a monument or a new pension and honours"; on the 9th of that month he sent his old friend, the honoured and valiant Cuthbert Collingwood, a plan of battle that he termed "the Nelson touch"; he had already used this expression in a letter to Emma, and told her how when he explained "the Nelson touch," it was like an electric shock. Some shed tears, all approved.

This plan, however, was not original; it had already appeared in a book of naval tactics written by John Clerk twenty years before, and when Lord Nelson came up with the enemy he did not use the tactics that had so moved his officers.

The Gallo-Spanish Fleet was sighted on October 21st; the

wind was blowing up for a storm and the sky becoming overcast; Admiral Villeneuve, who had been present at the Battle of the Nile, was not a very spirited or energetic commander, and the men under him were depressed by international rivalries, by the memories of past defeats, by long, tedious inactivity during blockades in forts; they were out of condition mentally and physically, and, moreover, hampered by all those formal rules of naval warfare that the genius of Lord Nelson had long since dispensed with; worst of all, the French officers were at feud among themselves; Dumanoir and Villeneuve being on particularly bad terms.

In size of ships, in weight, in numbers of men they had the superiority; among the four thousand soldiers on board were expert Tyrolese riflemen. The signal for attack was made soon after daylight; Collingwood had the command of the lee line, his ship was the *Royal Sovereign*.

As the British canvases swelled in the increasing West breeze, Lord Nelson sat in his cabin, under the portrait of Emma, and in his awkward, left-hand scrawl wrote out a prayer of unexceptional sentiments, and a codicil to his will, in which he left Emma, Lady Hamilton, as "a legacy to my King and country" and which was signed by two witnesses.

When his cabin was being cleared for action, he asked that Emma's picture should be treated as that of his guardian angel and he went on deck wearing a miniature of her under his uniform.

He seemed sure of a victory, and as expectant of death as if he were about to seek it; this was, however, the less remarkable as he had so often considered himself doomed.

The enemy, under the skilful direction of Villeneuve, spread out in order of battle, and the *Victory* ran up against the cloudy sky the signal which was considered not only inspiring but sublime. "England expects every man to do his duty."

The first word would have been *Nelson* had that been in the code.

His companions begged Lord Nelson to hide the four stars embroidered on his coat, but he refused, and continued to walk his quarter-deck, a clear target for the riflemen crouching in the French rigging.

Intermittent sunshine glittered on the splendid ships of the enemy as they opened fire shortly before noon; the long billows rolling into Cadiz Bay carried forward the British ships, Collingwood and Nelson leading; Collingwood was first under fire, and the action immediately became fierce and desperate; the *Victory* was in the very heart of the battle exposed to a continuous fire; she was frequently struck; broadsides were aimed at her rigging, the marines on deck were shot down; Lord Nelson's secretary was killed; a shot flew past the Admiral as he was talking to Captain Hardy. This punishment had been endured without reply; fifty men had been put out of action, and much of the rigging disabled before the flagship opened a return fire, and ran into the *Redoutable*, which met the *Victory* with a broadside and a crackle of musketry from the snipers in the rigging.

This practice of putting musketeers in the tops of battleships was considered foul play by the British, who likewise condemned another practice, of which they accused the French—that of firing red-hot balls. This device had, however, been used by the British Admiralty against the mutineers of 1798, and the warfare was savage enough on both sides for complaints of individual ferocity or unfairness to be as useless as unsubstantiated.

The *Téméraire* (Captain Eliab Hervey) closed with the *Redoutable* on the other side, and she in her turn was engaged by a Frenchman, so that the four great half-disabled ships were jammed together on the darkening sea, beneath the increasing hurry of the clouds.

A shot from the mizzen-top of the *Redoutable* struck Lord Nelson shortly after one o'clock, and he fell down on the stain left by his secretary's blood.

With a handkerchief over his well-known face and the four stars he was carried to the surgeon's room, where in the light of a swinging lantern, pressed on by mutilated and expiring men, he lay in agony and anxiety for more than three hours; dying at half-past four in the afternoon; soon after the British victory was complete; twenty French ships had struck and there were many prizes, though many more were lost through disobedience of Lord Nelson's last orders, which were—to anchor against the gale then rising.

Only these things had been in his mind as he lay dying—Emma

and the glory of the victory; once he had whispered—"Don't throw me overboard."

It is possible that into his distressed and clouded mind had crept some memory of Francesco Caracciolo. But his ever-present anxiety was Emma, and after Emma, his daughter.

He suffered greatly; slowly bleeding to death in the foul air, amid the cries and groans, the curses and laments, of those who died horribly for the glory of Britain; his whisper was for lemonade, for the waving of a sheet of paper, that stirred the stagnant atmosphere. He thanked his God that he had done his duty, he was glad that he had given the French "a drubbing," he thought that he had "*not* been a *great* sinner"; when he learned that it was another glorious victory, he seemed to die at peace; the last cannonade of the defeated enemy sounded as he was sinking into darkness and with his last breath there was silence among the shattered fleets blown upon by the swelling gale.

.   .   .   .   .   .

The news shook England; coaches, carriages, horsemen stopped one another in the streets and on the highroads; strangers spoke to one another; there was a general cessation of normal life, as if the country had been dealt a heavy blow and drew a deep breath of pain. Then from everywhere suddenly appeared mourning scarfs, funeral serge, brocade, streamers of crape; everything was bordered with black. Shop-windows, on the instant, became full of weeping Britannias, funeral urns, mournful lions—every possible symbol of victory and mourning. No one talked of anything else but this; A great victory had been won in Trafalgar Bay; Villeneuve's Fleet had been shattered, but Lord Nelson had been in that supreme moment of success killed by a shot from the enemy's rigging.

Then the nation heard with desperate excitement that the *Victory* was coming up the river with the hero's body, preserved upright in a cask of spirit.

Emma, still waiting at Merton, was left very much alone. Of all her lovers and protectors none was left now but him, who was neither lover nor protector—Charles Greville, who had recently inherited the price for which he had transferred her. But Emma had her consolation. When the first paroxysm of tears and grief was over, it was consoling to know that the hero had left her as a legacy to the nation, and that she, and she only, had been the beloved of the man who, so shortly before despised and neglected, though made use of, had now become a national hero such as had never been known before—so a mourning nation did not hesitate to proclaim.

She soon heard the famous details, how he had insisted on walking his quarter-deck in the thickest of the fight with the famous stars and orders embroidered on his coat, of the bloody fight between the *Victory* and the *Redoutable* and the end of it and his last words: "They have done for me at last—my backbone is shot through."

He had not forgotten her: "I have to leave Lady Hamilton and Horatia to my country. Remember me to Lady Hamilton, remember me to Horatia. Tell Mr. Rose I made a will, left Lady Hamilton and Horatia to my country. Take care of dear Lady Hamilton, poor Lady Hamilton. Remember that I leave Lady Hamilton and my daughter Horatia as a legacy to my country. Never forget Horatia."

In the child's little cabinet at Merton lay his letter, dated: "*The Victory*, off Toulon." He had sent this with the watch that she was to wear on Sundays and very particular days, when she had behaved exceedingly well and been obedient.

"I shall only say, my dear child, may God Almighty bless you and make you an ornament to your sex, which I am sure you will be, if you attend to all Lady Hamilton's kind instructions. Be assured that I am, my dear Horatia, your most affectionate father, Nelson and Bronte."

.   .   .   .   .   .

Britannia mourned her hero in the manner of great nations. It was more easy to honour Nelson now that death had separated him from Emma. His body was placed in the famous coffin made from the *L'Orient's* mainmast and enclosed in a superb casket. It lay in state for five days at Greenwich, surrounded by all the things the dead man had loved in life—his coronet, the Turkish plume, the shields, and trophies befitting a hero. Then it was removed down the river from Greenwich with every pomp that the simple vanity of Horatio Nelson could have desired, drums and fifes playing the "Dead March in Saul," trumpeters sounding the 104th Psalm, Admirals, Vice-Admirals, Captains, and Chaplain, the State Barge which had belonged to Charles II to put the coffin on, the Lord Mayor and Corporation of London, Regiments of Foot, squadrons of cavalry, pieces of cannon, pensioners, and seamen from the *Victory*, all in mourning with black neckerchiefs and stockings, the *Victory's* flag torn and bloodstained, the Heralds, the City Companies, the Knights Bachelors, the Knights of the Bath, members of the House of Lords, six Dukes of the Blood Royal, and His Royal Highness the Prince of Wales. In Christopher Wren's gloomy monumental cathedral the hero was buried with every circumstance of splendour that the occasion and the time could devise; Flaxman was to design the tomb and Sheridan to write the inscription on it; all the principal cities of the United Kingdom were to have a monument; everything that could be done was to be done.

The heir to the hero's reward was his brother, the Rev. William Nelson. He received an earldom, a pension of £5,000 per annum, and a gift of £120,000 in cash; it was a handsome expression of national gratitude, a pleasant consolation for the loss of a brother.

Lady Hamilton received without dispute the diamond star, £2,000 in cash, £500 a year for herself, £400 a year for Horatia, the whole totalling a fortune of £25,000, including Merton and its contents which also were left to Emma and valued at £10,000 to £12,000.

When the grief and the excitement and the hysterics had worn off and Emma turned round to count her gains, she found herself not so ill-provided for. Between husband and lover she had an income of £2,140 a year, and a handsome house, full of valuable furniture and effects. But she hoped for far more. Surely, in the tremendous excitement of the victory of Trafalgar the Patroness of the Navy would not be forgotten? The hero had deliberately left her as a legacy to his country—surely this was a request that could not be ignored. Even before the funeral she had learned of his dying request to his country. Captain Hardy had given Earl Nelson a codicil to his brother's will, written in a note-book and directed to one of his friends, George Rose, who, even before the magnificent funeral in St. Paul's, had written to Lady Hamilton:

318

"You will learn from the Captain that Lord Nelson, within the hour preceding the commencement of the action in which he immortalized his name, made an entry in his pocket-book strongly recommending a remuneration to you for your services to the country, when the fleet under his command was in Sicily after his first return from Egypt, on which subject he had spoken to me with great earnestness more than once."

This note, which took the form of a codicil to his will, enforced the claims that Lady Hamilton had always made with regard to her services in Naples; it declared that Lord Nelson had personal knowledge that Emma had obtained the King of Spain's letter in 1796, upon which Sir John Jervis *might* have acted against "the arsenals of Spain or her fleets"; it was not Lady Hamilton's fault that nothing was done.

The second service was that of securing the breaking off of Neapolitan neutrality, whereby the British Fleet had been watered and provisioned at Syracuse before the Battle of the Nile.

"Could I have rewarded these services, I would not now call upon my country; but as that has not been in my power, I leave Emma, Lady Hamilton, therefore, a legacy to my King and country that they will give her an ample provision to maintain her rank in life.

"I also leave to the beneficence of my country my adopted daughter, Horatia Nelson Thompson; and I desire she will use in future the name of Nelson only.

"These are the only favours I ask of my King and country at this moment when I am going to fight their battle. May God bless my King and country, and all I hold dear! My relations it is needless to mention; they will, of course, be amply provided for.

"Nelson and Bronte."

This might be accounted a document at once noble and pathetic, and the legacy one that the country should have been delighted to honour. Indeed, continual reproaches have been cast on the various Ministries, the Queen, the Prince Regent, and all who refused to grant the hero's dying request.

All sentiment was on the side of Lord Nelson, all reason against him; in truth the annoying part of the business was not that such a request should have been ignored, but that it should have been made.

This famous codicil, for all its noble air, was, in fact, written by a man completely blinded by an obsession.

The writer was a married man whose wife, as he himself admitted, had no fault and he expected his country to provide not only for her, but for his mistress and his natural daughter.

Any government that had pensioned Lady Hamilton and Horatia would have created an embarrassing precedent. It was computed that nearly sixteen hundred men had perished at Trafalgar; all of these from the spruce officer to the shabby pressed seaman might have had adored unlawful loves and cherished misbegotten children, whom they would have been thankful to leave to a grateful country.

There remained the question of Lady Hamilton's services in Naples; those, whom she had, ever since her husband's death, importuned for pensions and rewards, knew that these services were non-existent.

The Spanish letter had been sent in the ordinary way by the Queen to Sir William, and Emma had been only the go-between, while in the more important matter of the Syracuse outfitting of the British Fleet anyone that knew anything of Neapolitan affairs must have been aware that Maria Carolina, with her seat in the Council and her predominant influence in the Government, was perfectly able and willing to break the treaty with the French without any urging on the part of Emma Hamilton. That Lord Nelson should have stated solemnly his belief in these services, and his sense of their value was consistent with his long efforts to obtain something from the country for Emma and a proof of his complete infatuation, which caused him to be incapable of reason or judgment on any subject connected with Emma. The painful situation had another aspect; even if Lady Hamilton had made great efforts to forward the cause of Great Britain, these efforts were diminished by the clamour that she made for their recognition; the patriotism that has such a decided cash value ceases to be a virtue. For all she had "fag'd" in Naples Emma had been well paid, with jewels, dresses, the Cross of Malta, with festivals, flatteries and countless spoils; when both her husband and her lover had gone, she was left with a comfortable little property and a fair income, while her child was provided for; she scarcely, therefore, presented a pathetic figure and those who might have been moved to pity her were hardened by her crude extravagance and her quick recovery from grief.

Madame Le Brun had been in London soon after Sir William's death and had noted that Emma, a colossal figure in crape, seemed for all her streaming black veils to care little about her loss, and it was noticed that soon after Trafalgar the concerts and parties were continuing at Merton. It might also be argued that, in as far as heroism can be rewarded, Lord Nelson had been duly honoured; he was much admired for dying with the word "duty" on his lips, but, if he considered that he, in common with every man under his command, was merely doing his duty, by what reasoning did he suppose that he could leave not only his family but Emma and Horatia to the care of a country which had already lavishly recognized his success?

The situation, that Emma was, for the rest of her life, to endeavour to exploit, was wildly illogical.

A man cannot be a single-minded hero, who thinks that dying for his country is a mere act of duty—not only for himself, but for others—and at the same time expects extravagant rewards, honours, and applause, and, to crown all, to leave, as a final insult to an innocent wife, a mistress and a child to be provided for from public money.

Nor can a woman be a pure patriot, glad to work for her country's good, indifferent to everything but her national glory, and at the same time be observed openly scheming to obtain the utmost in money for her services.

At first Emma's hopes ran high. In the intoxication of reflected glory and in the expectancy of the substantial gratitude of her country she almost forgot her loss. Lord Nelson had been so often away from Merton that life there went on very well without him.

Soon the fortunes of Napoleon shone again; Arthur Paget, whose arrival at Palermo had been so distasteful to Emma in the old days, sent a dispatch from Vienna with such bad news, so graphically expressed, to Whitehall that Pitt, already a sick and disappointed man, died of the blow. The victory of Austerlitz did much to balance the victory of Trafalgar, and when the smoke of the cannons that had fired Lord Nelson's funeral salute had faded away, when all tears were dried and the crape bands untied, the black bows taken from the standards and a businesslike reckoning made up of the whole of the affair, it was felt that the hero had been sufficiently honoured and sufficiently paid. Lord Nelson would never be able to be useful to the British Government, and they had done, they considered, all that could be expected of a country grateful, but harassed; there was the tomb in St. Paul's, there were, in several cities, monuments.

The new Earl, formerly the Rev. William Nelson, behaved correctly to the woman whom he had flattered eagerly in the days of her glory; he took a common-sense view of his brother's uncomfortable loss. He accepted the memorandum in the note-book as a late codicil to the will, but as it did not deal with practical matters, he did not ask for probate of it, but gave the few lines which left Lady Hamilton as a legacy to his country to one of Nelson's friends, a certain Sir William Scott who "talked a great deal about you and said that you have great claims on the Government and they all sincerely wished they would do all they ought," as little Charlotte, the new Earl's daughter, wrote.

The second Earl Nelson, who could certainly afford to be generous, since he had received a large fortune and earldom through no exertion of his own, also brought the matter to the notice of the new Premier, Lord Grenville, read it to his Lordship and strongly pointed out to him the parts relative to Lady Hamilton and the child.

But in spite of so many good intentions and fine promises nothing was done. Queen Charlotte set her face against Emma, as always. The Government knew well enough that Emma's services to Britain in Naples had been greatly exaggerated and they held it to be only a rather lamentable proof of Lord Nelson's strange infatuation for his mistress, that he had borne witness to what he must have known was not true. And as for the £9,000 worth of clothes and jewellery and all the other properties that Emma was supposed to have lost on the occasion of the flight from Naples, no one who had seen the dresses and treasures which had arrived in London could have believed that story. In brief, the Government set its face against Emma's claims.

It might be not unreasonably supposed that, even allowing that Emma's fascination would no longer prove profitable to her pocket, she was reasonably well provided for, besides it was a question of creating a precedent. There might be a succession of heroes who would expect not only their own widows, but those of other men, provided for out of the public purse.

Emma had her friends who bombarded the Government in her favour and she was herself already an expert at a kind of super-begging-letter writing, but none of these arts availed her. Her behaviour was not such as to arouse compassion. She continued to live with sumptuous luxury, both at Merton and in Piccadilly, and she had not then either a husband to give her an air of respectability or a lover to pay her debts.

Grotesque slanders began to be spread of the Neapolitan and the Sicilian days, and other slanders, perhaps not so grotesque, of her present mode of life.

Everything about Emma's story begins to diminish in interest after Trafalgar; for everything she had lived for had slipped through her fingers, save money, and that too, was flowing away even faster than time.

She did everything that might have been expected of her; most of the incidents of this part of her career were those common to daughters of Joy, when Joy begins to take his departure. She entertained all those who cared to accept her tasteless hospitality; she appeared in public to faint when Barham sang "The Death of Nelson," to collapse when, in "Hearts of Oak," Miss Wheatley's pretty voice rose on the strain of "Rest, warrior, rest."

She began to spread about the tale that Lord Nelson had left Merton for the last time at her patriotic urgings; it was she, and she only, who had given the hero to his country and made possible the victory of Trafalgar. She related a story that had only too clear a ring of truth; on the final parting Lord Nelson had said— "Brave Emma, good Emma, if there were more Emmas, there would be more Nelsons!" Through all the flamboyant episodes there was a steady fall downwards.

"Lives" of Nelson appeared in which he was depicted as an impossible hero, and in which she was very delicately handled; his love-letters (hers had been, mercifully, destroyed) got somehow into print; Emma said that they had been stolen from her; memoirs were written under her directions by a hack; these made racy reading and were composed of that mingled truth and falsehood that pleases most. In these pages, for instance, her first strayings from virtue were gilded with a noble air—she had sacrificed herself to the amorous naval captain in order to save a fellow-countryman from the press-gang; there were other lively anecdotes in these lively pages.

The name of Emma began to be whispered in connection with some publications even less creditable; libels, some of them of a peculiarly abominable description, were circulating in print on the Queen of Naples. These contained details that it was thought could not be known except to someone who had lived in Her Majesty's intimacy—Emma was pointed out as the source of these foul publications; as she had already employed a hack to libel Lady Nelson, might she not have done the same to defame the Queen of Naples, whose neglect she so resented?

These pasquinades, exposing the private life of Maria Carolina to the jeers of Europe, circulated all over the Continent and were employed as some of the fiercest weapons against the Queen in her final downfall, when the French again took possession of Naples. If Emma's hand guided these secret attacks, she indeed took, what one of her biographers terms, "a base and terrible revenge."

Showing a brave front to her misfortunes, Emma went her way with a certain cheerfulness. There were great suppers, dinners, receptions to an easy-going crowd who ate and drank at her expense, and rewarded her with applause; there were concerts and attitudes and dancing of the tarantellas; but there were now no heroes to clap their hands. Put what face on it she would, Emma was entering the courtesan's purgatory—middle-age; her beauty, withered more by reckless living than by the years, had almost gone; her health, ruined by excesses, was failing.

With the death of the man who had for long not been her lover, Charles Greville, the last of her lovers had gone. The gossips said she was angling for the tarnished dukedom of her late husband's kinsman, the eccentric old Duke of Queensberry. He certainly was kind to her and lent her one of his houses at Richmond. It was from there, Heron's Court, that she wrote on December 4th,

1808, to His Grace, asking him for £15,000 as the price of Merton and of all its heroic trophies. The offer was refused, but Emma continued to live in the neat mansion on the sloping banks of the Thames, among the willows and formal gardens, the tidy houses and well-kept roads of the pretty suburb.

She was credited with one more attempt to please the gentlemen —it was reported that Prince Leopold of Saxe-Coburg admired her, and that she tried to make terms with him, but that her poverty and his money were both insufficient to strike a satisfactory bargain.

So Emma lived alone with Horatia, who had come to a difficult age, and with whom her mother quarrelled, taking the usual tone of disappointed self-sacrifice adopted by parents bored by their children.

Her worldly prospects began to be very clouded. Kind and well-to-do friends, examining her affairs, found them in almost hopeless confusion. She owed £8,000 and had anticipated £10,000 of her revenues by mortgaging the income to different persons. All that these zealous gentlemen who were so anxious to help Emma could do, was to take over Merton and all her assets with the intention of selling them for her benefit and that of her creditors, and to allow her £2,300 for her expenses. A little chastened by this crisis in her worldly affairs Emma sat down at Richmond in the neat retreat by the waters of the Thames, where the swans glided and the willows drooped, and wrote her will, which opened with a curious passage: "If I can be buried in St. Paul's, I should be very happy to be near the glorious Nelson whom I loved and admired, and as once Sir William, Nelson and myself had agreed, we should all be buried near each other if the King had not granted him a public funeral, it would have been that three persons so much attached to each other in virtue and friendship should have been laid in one grave when they quitted this ill-natured, slanderous world. But 'tis past and in Heaven I hope we shall meet. If I am not permitted to be buried in St. Paul's, let me be put where I shall be near my dear mother, when she is called from this ungrateful world."

Everything went, bit by bit, all the portraits, all the trophies, "Dear, dear Merton," the christening cup Lord Nelson had sent to Horatia, the bloodstained waistcoat that he had worn at Trafalgar. It was a sad spectacle, but who could have prevented it? Who could have saved Emma from herself? Even if "the cold-hearted Grenville" had given the insistent petitioner a few thousands out of the Secret Service Fund and a handsome pension, it would only have delayed for a while the inevitable end.

For two years longer Emma resided at Richmond, punctually receiving the money paid to her by her husband's nephew, Colonel Robert Fulke-Greville, who had inherited the Welsh estate.

In 1811, she was living in lodgings in Bond Street, where she wrote a second will:

"September the fourth 1811.

"I Emma Hamilton of No. 150 Bond Street London Widow of the Right Honourable Sir William Hamilton formerly Minister at the Court of Naples being in sound mind and body do give to my dearly beloved Horatia Nelson dau^r of the great and glorious Nelson all that I shall be possessed of at my death money jewells pictures wine furniture books wearing apparel silver gold-plated or silver-gilt utensils of every sort I may have in my house or houses or in any other persons' houses at my death any marbles bronzes busts plaster of Paris or in short every thing that belonged to me I give to my best beloved Horatia Nelson all my table linen laces ornaments in short everything that I have I give to her any money either in the house or at my bankers all debts that may be owing to me I beg that she may have I give to Horatia Nelson all silver with inscription with Viscount Nelson's name on or his arms I give to her wou'd to God it was more for her sake I do appoint George Macham Esqre of Ashford Lodge in the County of Sussex and the Right Honble George Rose of Old Palace Yard Westminster my Ex^{ors} and I leave them Guardians to my dear Horatia Nelson and I do most earnestly entreat of them to be the Protectors and Guardians and be Fathers to the Dau^r of the great and glorious Nelson and it is my wish that H.R. Highness the Prince Regent or if before my death he shall become King that he will provide for the said Horatia in such a manner that she may live as becomes the dau^r of such a man as her victorious Father was and as His Royal Highness often promised me that he wou'd have me remunerated when he had it in his power for the services that I have rendered to my King and Country and as I have never been remunerated nor ever received one sixpence from Government let me on my knees beg of his Royal Highness to provide for the said Horatia Nelson the only child of the Great and Glorious Nelson and I beg after my death that a copy of this my last will and testament may be sent to His Royal Highness the Prince Regent or if he is King it may be sent to His Majesty for His high worth honour and probaty and the friendship which he had for Nelson will induce him to protect his child for me H.R.H.ˢ always shewed me the greatest kindness and for the sake of Sir William Hamilton whom His R. Highness so highly honoured that he will provide for the orphan Horatia when my head is laid low she will want protection therefore to God Almighty to His R. Highness and to my Exᵒʳˢ do I most earnestly recommend her on my knees blessing her and praying for her that she may be happy virtuous good and amiable and that she may remember all the kind instructions and good advice I have given her and may she be what her great and immortal Father wished her to be brought up with virtue honor religion and rectitude

Amen   Amen   Amen   I do hereby annull all wills made by me formerly and I beg that this may be considered as my last will and testament written with my own hand this September the fourth 1811, Emma Hamilton.—If I shall have any money in the Funds or landed property at my death I give to the said Horatia Nelson all and everything belonging to me and if she shall dye before she shall be able to make her will I give all that I have bequeathed her to the daurs of Mr. John and Amy Moore my late Aunt and Uncle and now living in Moore Street Liverpool and I pray to God to bless them but I hope my dear Horatia will live to be happy and marry well and I hope that she will make her will as soon as I am dead for I do absolutely give her all I have I still hope Mr. Macham and Mr. Rose will see to the educating of Horatia and that she may live with Mrs. Macham's family till she is disposed to some worthy man in marriage I forgot to mention that I also give Horatia all my china glass crockery ware of every sort that I have—

"Emma Hamilton.   (L.S.)

"Signed sealed published and declared by Emma Lady Hamilton as her last will and testament in the presence of Thomas Coxe A.M.—William Haslewood of Fitz Roy Square, Middlesex."

Even in this will Emma did not admit the truth about Horatia.

She continued to insist that the child was Nelson's, but not hers, hinting with that odd mixture of drama and bad taste which seemed her special tone that her mother was too great to be mentioned, that her father, mother, and Horatia had a true and virtuous friend in Emma Hamilton. This might have been considered as an insinuation that the Queen of Naples was the child's mother, did not a brief consideration of dates render such an idea impossible.

This curious document reveals Emma as still obsessed by the idea that the Government owed her both gratitude and money, and reveals her as still possessing, or as fancying she possessed, the remnant of Sir William's *objets d'art*. Perhaps this was a delusion; the interest that she believed the Regent took in her seems to have been imaginary, nor is there any evidence that George IV had any "friendship for Lord Nelson."

.   .   .   .   .   .

Mrs. Cadogan died (1813) and Emma lost a useful, steady friend, a tireless servant; she continued in the various apartments she occupied to live luxuriously; she could not resist either the gratification of her appetites or the lure of the gambling-table.

She remained hopeful and cheerful; a good meal, a soft bed, a fine dress, a bottle of wine, and gay company and the day was always bright for Emma.

But there came an ugly day when Colonel Robert Fulke-Greville ceased to pay the £800 annuity from the Welsh estate. He had heard that it had been mortgaged, and that if he paid it to Emma he might be liable to be called upon for it again by those to whom she had sold it. This produced real distress; everything went, the last jewels, the remnant of the treasures, and, when these were gone, there was a flight to lodgings at Fulham, where Emma lived for a while in retreat with Mrs. Billington, the actress.

But in 1813 Emma could no longer evade her creditors; she was arrested for debt and went to the King's Bench Prison. No great severity was exercised. She was allowed to live at 12, Temple Place, where she was within the rules of the Bench, and where she had a fair measure of ease and liberty. From there she wrote a sad little letter redolent of the old glories.

328

"31st July, 1813.
"12 Temple Place:
"Saturday.

"My Dear Sir Thomas,

"Will you come to-morrow to meet our good pope and Mr. Tegart. It is the first of Agust (*sic*), do come, it is a day to me glorious, for I largely contributed to its success, and at the same time it gives me pain and grief, thinking on the Dear lamented Chief, who so bravely won the day, and if you come we will drink to his immortal memory. He coul'd never have thought that his Child and my self sho'd pass the anniversary of that victorious day were we shall pass it, but I shall be with a few sincere and valuable friends, all Hearts of Gold, not Pincheback, and that will be consoling to the afflicted heart of your faithful Friend.

"Emma Hamilton."

This letter stamped "Twopence—unpaid," never reached the person to whom it was addressed, and was marked "Gone away"— an expression which might have suited many of Emma's friends.

In the spring of 1814, through the renewed kindness of Alderman J. S. Smith, Emma was released from King's Bench Prison, but other creditors were waiting for her, among them a coachbuilder who was determined in his suit. Emma had still her friends, but no one could any longer do anything for her entangled affairs; time, her worst enemy, had triumphed.

She had passed from the courtesan's purgatory to the courtesan's hell, every expedient had been tried, every device exhausted. There was nothing for it but flight. Mrs. Cadogan was dead. There were few to assist, or even to be interested in, "The Divine Lady."

One July evening a harassed, ageing woman, panting from her weight, but gaily dressed, stood on the Tower Wharf holding by the hand Horatia, then a charming, clever girl fourteen years old, keen and dark; the servants were with them, a decent quantity of luggage, and generous Alderman Smith was there to see them off.

The spot had memories for Emma; here beneath the towers of the ancient fort she had met her first lover amid the bustle and licence of the press-gang ship.

She was still cheerful, though the features, once compared to the noblest profile on the superb Sicilian coins, were now lost in coarse

flesh, and the body, once of such "antique" grace, was now shape-
less beneath the finery; she lived for the moment only and the future
did not seem so dark; the Country would surely do something,
Colonel Fulke-Greville could be appealed to, and there were monies
due to her under old "Q's" will.

But, as the ship put off down the Thames, Emma, fanning
herself in the best cabin, was leaving them all behind, for ever.

Lord Nelson under the gilt dome, looming behind her, George
Romney in the Westmorland churchyard, Sir William—"Pliny
the elder," and Charles Greville, the man who had moved her
heart and stirred her senses more than any, but whose cold relations
with her had for long been only those of a nephew with an aunt
—all, all left behind and for ever.

.   .   .   .   .   .

When Emma landed in France, the country she had always so
detested, and to which she had done every possible ill-turn, she
put up at Dessin's, one of the best hotels in the country, celebrated
for good service, fine cooking, and handsome, well-kept apartments.

Soon after her arrival in Calais Emma wrote to one of her
friends, the Hon. George Rose, President of the Board of Trade,
who had tried in vain to obtain some pension for her; the letter was
characteristic in its account of a quiet life likely to impress and
move an ungrateful country, in the self pity, the sham philosophy,
and in the usual bankrupt's cry——"my virtues, not my vices
have undone me."

"Hotel Dessin, Calais,
"July 4, 1814.

"We arrived here safe, dear sir, after three days' sickness at sea
—as, for precaution, we embarked at the Tower, Mr. Smith got
me the discharge from Lord Ellenborough. I then begged Mr.
Smith to withdraw his bail, for I would have died in prison sooner
than that good man should have suffered for me, and I managed
so well with Horatia alone, that I was at Calais before any new
writs could be issued out against me. I feel so much better from
change of climate, food, air, large rooms, and *liberty* that there
is a chance I may live to see Horatia brought up. I am looking
out for a lodging. I have an excellent French-woman, who is
good at everything; for Horatia and myself and my old dame, who

is coming will be my establishment. Near me is an English lady, who has resided here for twenty-five years; who has a day-school, but not for eating and sleeping. At eight in the morning I take Horatia; fetch her at one; at three we dine; and then in the evening we walk. She learns everything; piano, harp, languages grammatic-ally. She knows French and Italian well, but she will still improve. Not any girls but those of the first families go there. Last evening we walked two miles to a *fete-champetre pour les bourgeois*. Every-body is pleased with Horatia. The General and his good old wife are very good to us; but our little world of happiness is in ourselves. If, my dear sir, Lord Sidmouth would do something for dear Horatia, so that I can be enabled to give her an education, and also for her dress, it would ease me, and make me very happy. Surely he owes this to Nelson. For God's sake do try for me, for you do not know how limited. I have left everything to be sold for the creditors who do not deserve everything; for I have been the victim of artful mercenary wretches, and my too great liberality and open heart has been the dupe of villains. To you, sir, I trust, for my dearest Horatia, to exert yourself for me, and that will be an easy passport for

"E. H."

Emma's situation in the French town was dismal compared to what it had been in Naples or London, but not by any means uncomfortable or dramatically sordid, the £400 left by Lord Nelson to his child was regularly paid every quarter, Emma was still entitled to some of her revenue from the Hamilton's Welsh estate; the Duke of Queensberry had left her an annuity of £500 a year for life, legal disputes were going on about His Grace's will, but it was considered certain that Lady Hamilton would receive at least some of the money, she could, at a pinch, always be able to raise a little cash on this prospect; besides, Alderman Smith, who had so generously taken upon himself to assist her to escape from prison and to fly to France, had given her sufficient ready money with which to start her last adventure. She had a French maid and an old servant, when she left the luxurious Hotel Dessin she went to good lodgings, then to a comfortable farmhouse outside the town.

A few months after her exile she wrote the following letter to Colonel Fulke-Greville.

"Common of St. Piere, 2 miles from Calais.

"Direct to me, chez Dessin, Sep^tr 21, (1814).

"Sir,—You know that my jointure of eightt hundred pounds a year has been now for a long time accumulating. If I was to die I should not have left that money a way, for the anuitants have no right to have it, nor can they claim it, for I was most dreadfully imposed on for my good nature, in being bail for a person whom I thought honourable. When I came a way I came with honor, as Mr. Alderman Smith can inform you, but mine own innocence keeps me up, and I despise all false publications and aspersions. I have given every thing up to pay just debts, but anuitants I never will. Now, sir, let me intreat you to send me a hundred pound, for I understand you have the money. I live very quiet in a farm house, and my health is now quite established. Let me, Sir, beg this favour to

"Your humble servant,

"E. Hamilton."

"P.S.—Sir Wm Scott writes me there is some hopes to my irresistible claims. Such are his words.

"The best meat here five pence a pound, 2 quarts of new milk 2 pence, fowls 13 pence a couple, ducks the same. We bought two fine turkys for four shillins, an excellent turbot for half-a-crown fresh from the sea, partridges five pence the couple, good Bordeux wine white and red for fiveteen pence the bottle, but there are some for ten sous halpeny. Lord Cathcart past thro 3 days ago. Horatia improves in person & education every day. She speaks french like a french girl, italian, german, english, &c."

The answer to this appeal was not satisfactory. Colonel Fulke-Greville would send no more money, till he knew exactly how things stood, and Emma was reduced to the usual expedient of pawning some pieces of plate and a few articles of jewellery that she had brought with her from England. Soon after the letter to Colonel Fulke-Greville was written Emma moved into rooms in Calais, the farmhouse affording but a bleak sojourn for the winter; her means were then straitened, but she was not galled nor even greatly inconvenienced by poverty.

Her circumstances were not those of dramatic, romantic privation, the garret, the hard pallet, the crust, the bowl of water; they were worse, of a drab and tedious respectability.

It was all very mean compared with the sumptuous splendours of Naples and Sicily, with the easy living of London, but it was very comfortable and even pretentious compared with the cottage at Hawarden. But her health failed from day to day, the winds swept over the sands and brought on discomforts that caused her to ease herself with opium; she had, some of her fellow country-people said, another consolation also; she had, they declared become a member of the Roman Catholic Church.

It was hardly a wonder if Emma, like so many who have sucked dry worldly delights, should have taken refuge with a Faith at once magnificent and kind; the priest is the natural consolation for the vacant minds of such women, as the drug is the natural consolation for their worn-out bodies.

Life had for some while been over for Emma, she had been merely existing in the dull exile, in the monotonous idleness of Calais that gradually eclipsed even her high animal spirits, that slowly extinguished the last faint hopes that had gilded her flight from England, and the winter of 1814, nine years after Trafalgar, saw the heavy woman going slowly through the cold alien streets, lying long in the furnished bedroom, where wind and sleet beat on the window-panes and the heaped-up fire could not warm her, nor the glasses of wine bring any sparkle into her sluggish blood.

Horatia went to and fro to school, a spirited, long-faced girl with an air of distinction, asking questions, wondering—"whose daughter am I?"

There were no more attitudes because there were no more audiences.

The last scenes in this gaudy drama were played quietly enough without spectators.

In the neat, decorous bed Emma drowsed, spread beneath the quilts, heavy in the pillows; no need now for shawls or roses, tambourines, wine or daggers, the parted lips, the upturned eyes; there was no one to see save the restless girl with her unanswered questions, the indifferent *bonne* a little curious, a little sorry, the cool French doctor who understood the case too well, and who waited for nature to draw the curtains across the last of the attitudes—not

Magdalene dying, lovely and weeping, in the Egyptian desert, as Emma had once shown her—but Amy Lyon in a respectable four-poster with a table of medicine-bottles at her side, a warming-pan at her feet, and on her face, no look of anguished penitence, but the mere apathy of boredom.

.   .   .   .   .

On January 20th, 1815, it was announced in the *Gazette de France* that—"Emma, widow of Sir William Hamilton," had died at Calais.

A few days later this item of news was copied into the *Morning Post*. A few people were interested; Colonel Greville wished to know if he might consider his estate free from the charge of £800 a year; and those to whom Emma had mortgaged her income were concerned about their prospects of repayment; Earl Nelson felt it his duty to repair to Calais. He found that Emma had left behind her a small sum of money, a few pawn-tickets, a modest wardrobe. Her death had not been dramatic, nor indeed very interesting, a stout woman with an inclination to dropsy had caught a chill that had settled on her liver and had died in a few days quietly enough; there had been nothing romantic about her funeral which had been decorous, dull, and attended by fifty people. Earl Nelson did his duty as one of the trustees of Horatia's little fortune; he took the girl back to England with him, together with such of Emma's trifling possessions as he had been able to get out of pawn. He did not feel himself obliged to do anything to mark Emma's last resting-place, nor would it have been to much purpose, if he had; for the cemetery was, before many years were over, turned into a timber-yard, and all traces of the lady's grave lost. There were romantic stories about a strange hand that had planted a wooden cross with "Emma Hamilton, England's Benefactress" on it, that another strange hand twice removed it; there was, after a while, a decent stone with a correct Latin inscription which became half-effaced by time, and then nothing.

Emma's wish that she might be laid in St. Paul's Cathedral beside Lord Nelson had no doubt a grotesque air, but the fulfilment of it would have pleased the hero better than all the monuments with which a gratified nation honoured his genius and his valour.

334

Emma Hamilton, however, did not need St. Paul's Cathedral to keep her name alive; her memory was as secure as that of her illustrious lover's, but through a means that it would have surprised both of them to know of; it mattered little what she had been or where she was buried. Emma, was, when all else was forgotten, for ever famous as the inspiration of the most seductive and popular of George Romney's paintings, where the glorification of English beauty will always gratify English eyes.

> "*O Love, what art thou, Love? a wicked thing?*
> *Making green misses spoil their work at school*
> *A melancholy man, cross gartering?*
> *Grave ripe faced wisdom made an April fool?*
> *A youngster tilting at a wedding ring?*
> *A sinner, sitting on a cutty-stool?*
> *A Ferdinand de Something in a hovel*
> *Helping Matilda Rose to write a novel?*

THE END

335

BIBLIOGRAPHY

A Modern History of England, G. R. Stirling Taylor. London, 1932.
Emma, Lady Hamilton, Walter Sichel. London, 1907.
Emma, Lady Hamilton, H. Gamlin. London, 1891.
Morrison Papers, British Museum.
National Dictionary Biography, Various headings.
Journal, 1799–1800, Mrs. St. George (afterwards Trench). Privately printed.
Horace Walpole. Travels.
Memoirs of the Life of Nelson, Dr. Pettigrew. London, 1849.
Nelson and the Neapolitan Jacobins, H. C. Gutheridge. Navy Records Society,
    London, 1903.
Robert Southey's Life of Lord Nelson, Annotated David Hannay.
Robert Southey's Life of Lord Nelson, Annotated M. Macmillan. 1903.
Life of Lord Nelson, The Old Sailor. 1838.
Life of Lord Nelson, Rev. James Stanier Clarke and John M'Arthur. 1809.
Life of Lord Nelson, Clennell Wilkinson.
Life of Horatio Lord Viscount Nelson, Harrison (written under the supervision
    of Lady Hamilton). 2 vols. 1806.
Robert Southey's Life of Nelson, Edited Geoffrey Callender. London, 1922.
Dispatches and Letters of Vice-Admiral Viscount Nelson, Sir Nicholas Harris
    Nicolas, G.C.M.C. 1845.
Memoirs of Lord Nelson, John Charnock. 1802.
Memoirs of Lord Nelson, Foster White. 1806.
Letters of Lord Nelson to Lady Hamilton. 1814.
History of the Mutiny at Spithead and the Nore, W. J. Neale. London, 1842.
Nelson at Naples, a Journal for June 10–30, 1799, F. P. Badham. London, 1900.
Autobiography, Cornelia Knight. 1861.
Lady Hamilton, J. C. Jeafferson. London, 1888.
Queen of Naples and Nelson, J. C. Jeafferson. 2 vols. 1889.
Saggio Storico sulla Rivoluzione Napoletana del 1799, Vincenzo Cuoco. 1799.
        Printed with :—
Rapporto al Cittadino Carnot, Francesco Lomanaco (Edited by Fausto Niolini).
    Bari, 1913.
Archives, Naples.
Carteggia di Maria Carolina, Edited Palembo, 1877.
Saggio Storica, etc., G. M. Arrigni. Napoli, 1809.
Storia d'Italia dal 1789 *all'*1814, Carlo Botta.
Monitore Napoletano, Newspaper. Issued in the year 1799.
Memoire Storiche, etc., Sacchinelli. Napoli, 1836.
L'Esame della storia del Reaume de Napoli. Carriatore, 1850 .
La Rivoluzione Napoletana del 1799, Benedetto Croce. Bari, 1912.
I Napoletani del 1799, G. Fortunato. 1877.
Napoli dal 1789 *al* 1796, L. Conforti. Naples, 1887.
Gabriel Manthoné, F. Masci. Casalbordino, 1900.
Napoli, R. Ficini. 1878.
*Correspondence inédite de Marie Caroline Reine de Naples et de Sicile, avec le Marquis
    de Gallo*, Edited by H. M. Weil and M. C. di Somma Arcello.
Discori critiche, P. Villari. 1905.
Francesi e Napoletani nel 1799, R. Polmarocchi. 1913.
Real Museo Borbonico, Stamperia Reale. Napoli, 1824.

J. N. Goethe, Voyage in Italy; var. ed.
Works of l'abbé Winckelmann on Herculaneum and Pompeii 1764-1784.
I Borboni di Napoli, A. Dumas. 10 tomes. Napoli, 1862.
Lady Hamilton et la Révolution de Naples, J. Turquan and J. D'Auriac. Paris, 1913.
Lady Hamilton, Fauchier Magnan. Paris, 1910.
Mémoires, Mme. de Boigne.
Mémoires, Mme. Vigée le Brun.
Marie Caroline, Reine de Naples, André Bonnefons. 1905.
Marie Caroline, M. A. Gagnière. Paris, 1886.
Storia di Napoli, 1734-1825, P. Colletta.
Mémoires, Madame de Lichtenau. Paris, 1808.
Mémoires, General Thiébault.
Horatio Nelson, Edinger and Neep. N. D.
Mémoires, General Macdonald. Paris, 1892.
Histoire de Nelson, E. D. Forgues. 1860.
Fabrizio Ruffo, Von Helfert.
Lord Nelson und der Herzog Franz Caracciolo, Robby Kossman. Hamburg, 1895.
Captain Footes Vindication of his Conduct.: 1807.
A Memoir of C. M. Young, J. C. Young. London, 1871.
Memoirs of Lord Malmesbury. 1845.

The above authorities contain all the material used in the foregoing sketch of Lady Hamilton.

The *Thompson* letters, published by Dr. Pettigrew, are of doubtful authenticity since the originals are not in existence. They bear in themselves, however, every mark of being genuine, and a few quotations from them have been used in *Patriotic Lady* since these do not in any way alter what is known of the facts from other sources. This question of the *Thompson* letters must be left to historians, as must the problems of Horatia Nelson's parentage and the precise nature of the friendship between Lady Hamilton and Maria Carolina; these matters have often been the subject of acute and learned controversy, and it was not thought necessary to dilate on them once more; those interested will find no difficulty in obtaining what information is available on these delicate matters, which must, from their very nature, remain always in doubt.

In this portrait of Emma Hamilton the usual explanations have been followed and on these points all controversial matter avoided. For the vexed question of the *Arethusa* letter, which may have been forged in the interests of Lady Hamilton, the reader is referred to the various excellent lives of Lord Nelson in existence.

Emma Hamilton has appeared so frequently in fiction that it is impossible to give here the names of the novels, romances, dramas and poems in which she has been used. The following list contains some little-known literary curiosities which introduce Emma in a guise unfamiliar to the English reader.

Luisa Sanfelice was for long a popular heroine with Italian romancers, and when her tale was related Emma Hamilton usually appeared as the villainess of the piece.

In 1852 there appeared on the Italian stage an historical drama entitled:
Emma Lyonna o i martiri di Napoli, by David Levi.

An elaborate romance on the same subject is:
Luigia Sanfelice, by Mastriani.

In 1882 one Richard Viss had a book published under this title: *Luigia Sanfelice*—and two years later the energetic pen of Alexandre Dumas had produced two volumes *Emma Lyonna* and *Sanfelice*, for which he had abundant material in the mass of original matter he had already incorporated in his history of the Bourbons in Naples.

One of Giuseppe Verdi's early operas has for its libretto and title *Luise Miller*.

NOTE

A coat of arms for Lady Hamilton was concocted by the College of Arms after she received the Cross of Malta, begged for her by Lord Nelson from Paul I. How even a lunatic Czar came to be concerned in this business of giving decorations to Lady Hamilton requires some explanation.

The power, virtually the existence, of the Knights of Malta, was shaken by the French Revolution and ended with the capitulation of Valletta 11–12th June, 1798, when the Grand Master Ferdinand Hompesch ceded the Islands and all the rights of the Order to General Bonaparte; the articles of surrender were signed on board *L'Orient*, and the Republican Flag (the Gallic Cock between two bundles of fasces) floated over Malta until the Mediterranean Fleet, under the command of Lord Nelson, retook it by blockade, April, 1800.

The Empress Catherine had entertained a great liking for the Order and had wished to establish a Russian Priory; in her son, Paul I, this inherited interest rose to a passion, and this despite the difference between the Latin Church and the Greek Rite. When "the standard of Liberty floated over the Forts of Malta" the last Grand Master, Hompesch, went in exile with a few faithful knights on board a French frigate; he died at Montpellier in 1805.

This was, in reality, the end of this famous Order, but a few knights, indignant at the surrender of Hompesch, went to Russia, where the Czar sheltered them; in return, in 1799 they issued a manifesto deposing Hompesch, and soon after elected Paul I to a position which really no longer existed. Paul, however, took this business so seriously that the British seizure of Malta and failure to restore it to the knights was one of the causes of his breaking with the allies.

INDEX

A

Abercorn, Marquis of, 68, 217
Abercrombie, Sir Ralph, 217
Abergele, 33
Aboukir Bay, 118, 123, 127, 129, 130, 131, 132, 142, 163, 251
Aboukir Harbour, 110
Abruzzi, 156
Acerra, 170
Acquaviva, Beatrice, 62
Acton, Sir John, 47, 54, 55, 75, 77, 78, 81, 85, 86, 88, 92, 101, 103, 126, 127, 138, 141, 156, 157, 160, 182, 183, 194, 201, 212, 213, 215, 218, 242, 246, 247, 267, 269, 270, 271
Addington, Mr., 291
Adelaide, Princess, 79
Adelphi, 13
Albano, 155
Alexandretta, 128
Alexandria, 109, 188
Algiers, Dey of, 149
Alquier, Baron, 131
Amelia, Princess, 76
American Colonies, 48
Ancona, 230, 258
Andrews, Miss, 187
Andrews, Rev. Mr., 116
Antigua, 116
Arcola, 265
Argyle, Duchess of, 57
Arlington Street, 278, 284
Ascoli, Duca di, 155
Augustus, Prince, Duke of Cumberland, 27, 93, 97, 98
Austerlitz, 321

B

Baffi, Pasquale, 183, 231, 269
Ball, Captain, 128, 193, 197, 200, 201
Baltic, 115
Banti, Signora, 65
Barham, 323
Barlow, Miss, 27, 302
Bassville, Hugo de, 86, 87
Bastia, 96

Beauharnais, Josephine, 146
Beckford, William, 69, 70, 99, 278, 279, 282, 283, 291, 313
Benevento, 247
Berry, Captain Edward, 124, 128, 130, 140
Berta, General, 157
Berthier, General, 103, 108, 132, 270
Bertie, Emily, 15, 16, 22
Billington, Mrs., 328
Black, Professor, 43, 45
Blackburn, Mrs., 42, 74
Blenheim, 302
Boigne, Madame de, 60
Bonaparte, General, 100, 107, 108, 109, 119, 124, 127, 128, 132, 146, 147, 149, 237, 250, 251, 255, 257, 303, 305, 306, 313, 321
Bond Street, 326
Botticelli, Sandro, 22
Boucher, François, 26
Boulogne, 296
Box Hill, 296
Brest, 186, 236
Bridewell, 8, 309
Brighton, 284, 290
Bristol, Lord, 98, 99
British Museum, 28
Bronte, 290, 295, 298, 304
Brueys, Admiral François Paul, 118, 119, 121, 122
Brutus, 172
Budd, Dr., 13
Burnham Thorpe, 114, 140, 144, 176, 226
Bush Inn, Staines, 296

C

Cadiz, 105, 306, 315
Cadogan, Mrs., 6, 7, 13, 15, 17, 18, 23, 28, 43, 59, 60, 64, 92, 126, 159, 167, 174, 228, 238, 249, 258, 263, 272, 285, 286, 297, 298, 303, 307, 328, 329
Calabria, 66, 168, 187, 190, 196
Calais, 330, 332, 334
Calvi, 96

341

343